The History and Future of Economics

Robert U. Ayres

The History and Future of Economics

 Springer

Robert U. Ayres
Economics and Political Science
Technology and Operations Management
INSEAD
Fontainebleau, France

ISBN 978-3-031-26207-4   ISBN 978-3-031-26208-1 (eBook)
https://doi.org/10.1007/978-3-031-26208-1

© The Editor(s) (if applicable) and The Author(s), under exclusive license to Springer Nature Switzerland AG 2023
This work is subject to copyright. All rights are solely and exclusively licensed by the Publisher, whether the whole or part of the material is concerned, specifically the rights of translation, reprinting, reuse of illustrations, recitation, broadcasting, reproduction on microfilms or in any other physical way, and transmission or information storage and retrieval, electronic adaptation, computer software, or by similar or dissimilar methodology now known or hereafter developed.
The use of general descriptive names, registered names, trademarks, service marks, etc. in this publication does not imply, even in the absence of a specific statement, that such names are exempt from the relevant protective laws and regulations and therefore free for general use.
The publisher, the authors, and the editors are safe to assume that the advice and information in this book are believed to be true and accurate at the date of publication. Neither the publisher nor the authors or the editors give a warranty, expressed or implied, with respect to the material contained herein or for any errors or omissions that may have been made. The publisher remains neutral with regard to jurisdictional claims in published maps and institutional affiliations.

This Springer imprint is published by the registered company Springer Nature Switzerland AG
The registered company address is: Gewerbestrasse 11, 6330 Cham, Switzerland

Acknowledgements

I need to confess that my single most important source of historical data about people and economics in recent years has been the many named and anonymous authors of Wikipedia. I think it is fair to conjecture that many of them have also used earlier sources, such as the academic tomes. If I could do so, I would regard Wikipedia as a "co-author" of this book. I have been careful to edit and rewrite, where necessary, to avoid actual plagiarism. I have tried to give credit for invention and innovation where it is due, and not where popular history assigns it.

The list of acknowledgments that follows is alphabetical because at this stage of my life—after working on this topic, on and off, for more than 50 years—it is very difficult to remember exactly what I have learned from each individual, some of whom I have disagreed with, and many of whom are now deceased (as indicated by an asterisk) or are otherwise inaccessible and cannot be interrogated.

Brad Allenby, Julian Allwood, Serge Antoine*, Kenneth Arrow*, Brian Arthur, Nick Ashford, Tom Astebro, Bob Aten*, Robert Axtell, Ed Ayres, Eugene Ayres*, Lesley Wentz Ayres*, Christian Azar, Jeroen van den Bergh, Eric Britton*, Paul Brockway, Harvey Brooks*, Peter Brown, Tom (and Sean) Casten, Cutler Cleveland, Joe and Vary Coates*, Bill Clark, James Cummings-Saxton*, Herman Daly*, Tiago Domingos, Rod Eggert, Nina Eisenmenger, Ike Ezekoya, Marina Fischer-Kowalski, Stefanos Fotiou, Paolo Frankl, Jeffrey Funk, Murray Gell-Mann*, Gael Girard, John Gowdy, Tom Graedel, Arnulf Grubler, Charles A. S. Hall, Bruce Hannon, Lu Hao,

Nassim Haramein*, Miriam Heller, Paul Horne, Rob Huffman*, Leen Hordijk, Bill Hornyak*, Herman Kahn*, Jean-Marc Jancovici, Erich Jansch*, Astrid Kander, Felix Kaufmann*, Ivy and Peg Kay*, Yoichi Kara, Michael Jefferson, Alan V. Kneese*, Reiner Kuemmel, Steve Keen, Ashok Khosla, Carey King, Paul Kleindorfer*, Michael Kumhof, Jean Laherrere, John (Skip) Laitner, Bob Lamson*, Tom Lee*, Michel Lepetit, Reid Lifset, Dietmar Lindenberg, Hal Linstone, Amory Lovins, Ralph (Skip) Luken, Leonard Lynn, Kataline Martinas, Andrea Masini, Richard McKenna*, Fran McMichael*, Dennis Meadows, David Meggysy, Gerhard Mensch, Steve Miller, John Molburg, Granger Morgan, Shunsuke Mori, Indira Nair, Neboysa Nakicenovic, Marc Narkus-Kramer, Michael Olenick, Robert Pastel*, Philippe Pichat, Laura Talens Piero, the Plant Family (Harry, Ethan, Isaac and Matthew), Paul Raskin, Van Kirk Reeves, Lee Remmers, Robert Repetto, Ron Ridker, Sam Rod*, Don Rogich*, Pradeep and Kalpana Rohatgi, Adam Rose, Tom Saaty*, Devendra Sahal*, Warren Sanderson, Manalur Sandilya, Ian Schindler, Friedrich (Bio) Schmidt-Bleek*, Uwe Schulte, Andre Serrenho, Stanislas Shmelev, Gerald Silverberg, Udo Simonis, Vaclav Smil, Robert Socolow, Marvin Sirbu, Lars Sjosted, Thomas Sterner, Wilbur Steger*, Martin Stern*, Joel Tarr, Ted Taylor*, Yuri Tchijov*, Valerie Thomas, John S. Toll, Richard Tredgold*, Antonio and Alicia Valero, Genevieve Verbrugge, Gara Villalba, Vlasios Voudouris, Ingo Walter, Benn Warr, Luk van Wassenhove, Ludo van der Heyden, David Wasdell, Ernst von Weizsaecker, Chihiro Watanabe, Roland Widgery*, Eric Williams, Phil Wyatt, Lan Xue, Ming Xu, Huseyin Yilmaz*, and Ehud Zuscovich*. I have forgotten quite a few, I'm sure, to all of whom I hereby apologize and blame encroaching old age.

I also wish to thank Anna McCavitt, Carole Tanguy, Muriel Larvaron, and Pat Wagner.

* **Deceased.**

Contents

1	From Pre-history to the Crusades	1
2	From the Crusades to the Renaissance	9
3	The Protestant Work Ethic and the Rise of Capitalism as Gods Work	19
4	The Enlightenment: From Leonardo to Galileo	31
5	The Rise of the East India Trading Companies	43
6	The "Glorious Revolution" and the BoE	57
7	Laissez-Faire and John Law's Premature Invention of "Futures"	73
8	**Classical Economics as Moral Philosophy**	87
	8.1 On Trade, Mercantilism and 'Laissez Faire'	87
	8.2 Adam Smith and the Invisible Hand	94
	8.3 Thomas Malthus and the Principle of Population	98
	8.4 David Ricardo and Value-Added	102
	8.5 Marx's Labor Theory of Value	108
	8.6 The Communist Manifesto	110
9	**Bentham and Utilitarianism**	113
	9.1 Precursors	113
	9.2 Utilitarianism	114

	9.3	Benthamites	118
	9.4	Say's Law of Markets: A View from an Entrepreneur	119
	9.5	Sismondi: Booms and Busts	121
	9.6	Dialectical Materialism and Academic Marxism	123
10	**The Rise of Physics: From Newton to Einstein**		**127**
	10.1	Background	127
	10.2	Variables	128
	10.3	Mathematics	133
	10.4	Crossing Disciplinary Boundaries	137
	10.5	The Steam Engine	139
	10.6	Falsification of Phlogiston	142
11	**Energetics**		**147**
	11.1	Heat as Energy	147
	11.2	The First and Second Laws of Thermodynamics	151
	11.3	Entropy and Statistical Mechanics	154
	11.4	Order and Disorder; Self Organization	158
12	**Evolutionary Theory and Genetics**		**161**
	12.1	The Age of the Earth	161
	12.2	The Idea of Species: Fossils and Extinction	163
	12.3	Darwin's Theory of Natural Selection	166
	12.4	Mendel's Theory of Inheritance	168
	12.5	The Tree of Life	170
	12.6	From Vitalism to Monism (Again)	172
13	**Entropy, Exergy, Information and Complexity**		**179**
	13.1	Background	179
	13.2	Complexity	180
	13.3	Sources of Exergy in the Cosmos	184
	13.4	The Standard Model of Physics	186
	13.5	Entropy and Information	189
14	**The "Marginal Revolution" in Economics**		**195**
	14.1	Mathematics in Economics	195
	14.2	The Theory of Utility	197
	14.3	Alfred Marshall and the Supply–Demand Diagram	200
	14.4	On the Causes of the Great Depression	203
	14.5	The Problem of Growth	209
	14.6	The Production Function and the Solow-Swan Model	214

	14.7 The Next Step: Adding a Third Variable to the C-D Function	217
	14.8 Evolutionary Game Theory	222
15	**Socialism and the Welfare State**	**231**
	15.1 Antecedents	231
	15.2 Political Marxism	236
	15.3 Utopian Socialism and Consumer Cooperatives	239
	15.4 Henry George	241
	15.5 Leo Tolstoy and Mahatma Gandhi	244
	15.6 Social Democracy as an Antidote to Marxism	251
	15.7 The Creation of the US Federal Reserve Bank	255
16	**Keynes v. Hayek and the Monetarists**	**259**
	16.1 The Great Divide from the Old World to the New	259
	16.2 From Woodrow Wilson to Adolph Hitler	261
	16.3 Unemployment and Financial Crises	272
	16.4 Unemployment and Wages, Short Run Versus Long Run	281
	16.5 Money Creation and Monetary Policy	283
	16.6 What Causes Recessions and Busts?	296
	16.7 The Other Side of Capitalism	301
	16.8 The End of the Gold Standard, Hayek and the Washington Consensus	306
	16.9 SVM, Buybacks and Inequality	314
	16.10 Positive Returns: Short Term Versus Long Term	320
17	**The Future of Economics and the Economics of the Future**	**325**
	17.1 The Population Problem	325
	17.2 The Problem of Resource Exhaustion	328
	17.3 Pollution as an Inevitable By-Product of Extraction and Industrial Production	334
	17.4 Energy Economics: The Price of Energy	338
	17.5 The Avalanche Model	339
	17.6 The Sources of Value	345
	17.7 The Circular Economy?	348

Appendix A: Bio-Geochemical Cycles 355

Appendix B: Climate Change: The Externality that Makes
Everything Else Irrelevant 375

Appendix C: The Rise and Fall of the Nuclear Dream 391

Appendix D: Capsule History 401

1

From Pre-history to the Crusades

Humans appear to be among the most sociable and territorial of all animals. The primary resource of primitive tribes, was territory in which to search for food. Land is the source of all biological and mineral resources. Since prehistory it has been "improved" by forest clearing, wild animal capture and breeding, agriculture, and irrigation. If the territory available to a tribe is inadequate (or is perceived to be inadequate) to support the population, leaders try to increase the territory under control by conquest. Throughout human history, the most effective leaders are remembered by their conquests. We make statues of "great" conquerors (usually on horseback) from Cyrus the Great to Alexander the Great, to Julius Cesar, to Attila the Hun, to Genghis Khan, to Tamerlane, Charlemagne, to Peter the Great, Napoleon Bonaparte, Frederick the Great, Catherine the Great… the names are familiar.

Conquest of land for agricultural colonization is now out of style. Adolf Hitler's stated goal of acquiring (by conquest) "Lebensraum" for German-Aryan colonists in Russia was a "pipe dream" from the start. Mr. Putin's dream of re-establishing the USSR seems is almost certainly another pipe dream. Conquest of territory, today, is accomplished by multi-national companies, by means of brands, not armies. Coca Cola and McDonalds are exemplars. (The continuing violence in the Middle East has its origins partly in competition for oil but mainly in Religious history.)

The concept of markets is so fundamental to economics that we are tempted to assume that no explanation is needed. We know a market when we see one. It is a congregation of buyers and sellers of goods and services. An important attribute of markets is that they provide an impersonal mechanism for nonviolent exchanges. Exchanges between individuals, in the absence of a market, are inherently unequal. One of the two will be stronger than the other, or needier than the other. Conflict is more likely than exchange. Thus the creation of markets was a crucial element in the decline of violence as policy.

In a hypothetical Hobbesian "state of nature, red in tooth and claw", where everyone is a competitor and a potential enemy, money and markets play no role. The existence of money and markets implies social structure. After defense, one of the primary roles of the central government and the ruler by "divine right" (that Hobbes advocated), must be to provide a marketplace his or her subjects to meet and exchange goods. A precondition of the existence of the market is *prevention* of violence, which also means—as a practical matter—protection of property and prevention of wealth acquisition by illegitimate means (theft, fraud, piracy, violence or threat of violence.)

Exchange, in turn, presupposes heterogeneity of economic output. If we are all self-sufficient creatures finding and consuming what we need to survive—as wild animals do—there would be no need to trade or exchange. But some of us till the soil and plant seeds, some hunt for deer in the forests, some collect birds eggs, some collect edible mushrooms, some catch fish, some weave fibers into threads, some weave cloth, some make clay pots, some smelt metal…Well, you get the idea.

Anthropologists think that money was originally invented as a unit of value for financing agricultural labor in Sumer: Labor was needed for plowing, planting, harvesting and probably for grinding. Loans and corresponding labor debts were recorded on clay tablets, back then in Sumer. But trade with distant markets required recognizable but portable forms of value, hence coins. The value of coins and paper money depends on trust in the stability of the issuer, usually a government, or an agency of the government (e.g. a bank).

Coins (money) were definitely a device for facilitating exchange transactions, and markets. The first copper coins we know of were first used in China in the eleventh century BCE). (Paper money came 2000 years later, also from China.) Money as portable exchangeable value—coinage—in the Middle East had a well recorded beginning: It was born in the city of Sardis, in the small Anatolian Kingdom of Lydia, during the 14 year reign of **King Croesus** (560–546 BCE).[1] The first proto-coins were minted from an alloy

---

[1] The legend of **king Midas** was about his pathological desire for gold, and its awful consequences; it was not about gold as money. Gold was not used for money, as coins, in China, India, Mesopotamia or Egypt, or in meso-America.

of gold and silver, called electrum, that was taken from the river that flowed through the town. The extraction technique was "panning" the silt in the river, to let the heavier metal particles accumulate at the bottom of the pan. The gold particles were the heaviest, so they could be gradually separated by successive pannings. (This technique is still employed in some remote areas of the world.)

The first proto-coins in Sardis were lumps of the alloy stamped with an image of a lion's head. Croesus' first innovation was to make the stamped lumps of electrum exactly the same weight and to assign them an equal value. This trick eliminated the need for merchants to weigh the proto-coins before agreeing to a transaction. All they needed to do was to count. The proto-coins became gold coins in the modern sense, between 640 and 630 BCE. Sardis's second innovation was the creation of a central market where all the merchants could gather and exchange their wares for coins. That market in Sardis became famous and famously attractive for visiting merchants with luxury items to sell. It was the model for all the Greek markets, called *agora*.

The combination of the two innovations was spectacularly successful for a few years. It made King Croesus—"as rich as Croesus"—and the merchant elite of Sardis very wealthy. It engendered conspicuous consumption in various forms (such as competitively fancier tombs). It enabled Lydia to conquer most of the nearby Greek cities of Anatolia, including Ephesus (which he rebuilt). His wealth engendered dreams of glory. He consulted the Greek oracle of Apollo and famously asked the oracle what would happen in case of war with Persia. The oracle cleverly replied that "*a mighty empire would fall*". So Croesus decided to go for it, in 547 BCE. Not surprisingly the Lydian proto-empire fell and disappeared from history. But Croesus' two innovations did not disappear.

What followed the invention of coinage in Lydia was the creation of a web of commerce among both the Greek-speaking cities and the Persians. It has been argued that the advent of coin-based markets—the agora—was the key to Athenian Democracy and commercial Greek civilization, followed by Rome. King Philip of Macedonia imitated Croesus' imperial ambitions, but prepared better. His son Alexander the Great (356–323 BCE (trained by Aristotle) conquered the known world in a decade, including Egypt, Babylon, Persia (and some of Mughal India) before reaching the limits of his administrative capability (and health). Greek was the language of markets. Yet the market trading links left by Alexander's successors created the information pathways for the spread of Christianity five centuries later.

Counting standardized coins, rather than weighing gold (or silver) in the marketplace of Sardis, in Lydia, led step-by-step to calculating, bookkeeping,

Fig. 1.1 The Croeseid, one of the earliest known coins. Classical Numismatic Group, Inc.—Wikimedia commons

arithmetic, geometry, mathematics, astronomy and even to science. But it also led to occasional bubbles, like the Dutch Tulip mania of 1636, and the rise and fall of the Mississippi Company followed by the South Sea Company of 1720.

Coinage was the beginning of monetization, and monetization was the beginning of Mediterranean civilization, which is the basis of our own western civilization. All exchangeable goods (and some services) were increasingly valued in terms of a common denominator: money as coins, and later just money as coin equivalents. Debt also was equated to money. In fact "debt bondage" was becoming an issue in market-oriented Greek—and later, Roman—society.

From being thought of as a 'sub stance' to being regarded as a mathematical artifact of a field to being just another way to express a symmetry" (Fig. 1.1).

Primitive markets must have existed as long as trade and as long as cities. Sumer, 3500 BCE, was the first urban civilization, as far as we know. Modern historians say that about 90% of its population already lived in walled cities. It is clear that money-equivalent loans, of some sort, were first used in Sumer for agricultural purposes. The residents of the city consumed agricultural products that had to be produced, and that the producers had to feed themselves, meaning that agricultural production at the time was already very efficient, and capable of yielding outputs significantly greater than aggregate inputs.

The situation of Sumer explains the broader need for trade and money. In David Graeber's words: "trade was crucial because while the river valley of ancient Mesopotamia was extraordinarily fertile and produced huge surpluses of grain and other foodstuffs, and supported enormous numbers of livestock, …it was almost completely lacking in anything else. Stone, wood, metal, even the silver used as money, all had to be imported "(Graeber, op cit. p. 64). Graeber's point being that the caravan trade had to be financed by loans (credit). Moreover, he argues that interest—call it rent—was invented, at that time, as a way for temple (government) functionaries to take their share of the of the trading profits. Much the same situation must have applied in ancient Egypt. The Phoenecian civilization was based entirely on inter-city trade around the Mediteranean Sea.

Trade was risky and loans for trade purposes had to reflect that reality. The Code of Hammurabi was written in Babylon, 1800 BCE. It formalized the laws dealing with credit. Loans were risky, and interest—the cost of risk taking by the lender—was part of every loan agreement. Hammurabi established the legal maximum interest rates that could be charged by lenders: 33.3% per year on loans of grain, and 20% per year on loans of silver. To be valid, loans had to be witnessed by a public official and recorded as a contract.

Solon of Athens (630–560 BCE) is reputed to have outlawed debt bondage and cancelled all outstanding debts. (This strategy to "start fresh" has been imitated many times, but the debtor's problems almost always recur.) Solon's most radical reform was to stop reserving public office for men of noble birth. This was arguable the first step toward Athenian democracy, and today's (almost) universal right to vote.

In the Roman Republic, 50 BCE, Marcus Cicero noted that his neighbor (Crassus) paid 11.5 million sesterces for bought 625 acres (250 hectares) of land. The weight of that much money in coins would have been about 11.5 tons (10 tonnes). It was done through credit and paper. Cicero wrote "*nomina facit, negotium conficit*" meaning "he uses credit to complete the purchase."

The "Dark Ages" in Europe 600 to 1000 CE followed the collapse of the Western Roman Empire, and economic activity slowed to a near-halt. The Church even banned the practice of charging interest on loans, calling it "usury", a sin. Usurers were called nasty names, ranging from "blood suckers" to "loan sharks". Needless to say it was very hard for Christian merchants to find lenders to borrow from. The exceptions (as lenders) were Jews, who were excluded by law and custom—perhaps deliberately—from every other profession. The Jewish lenders had to be quite tough about collateral. Shakespeare's Shylock in "The Merchant of Venice" demanded security for a non-payment in the form of "pounds of flesh". Rich people, especially unscrupulous aristocrats, were known to use Jews as surrogates for their own moneylending practices.

Usury is the practice of making unethical or immoral monetary loans that unfairly enrich the lender. In many historical societies charging of interest of any kind and was considered wrong, or was made illegal. The Catholic Church in medieval Europe, as well as the Reformed Churches, regarded the charging of interest (as well as charging a fee for the use of money) as sinful, though rents were allowed. Religious prohibitions on usury are predicated upon the belief that charging interest on a loan is a sin.

The invention of money, markets (and credit) was a human device for facilitating exchanges and, the "division of labor" thus made possible. More generally markets are a device for utilizing diversity and maximizing constructive competition, both among producers and consumers. The earliest markets back in pre-history may have happened by accident, but markets are so fundamental that they deserve serious attention as societal entities. Indeed, we need to introduce the topic of "market failures", meaning non-optimal outcomes of trading (and the other economic activities associated with trade).

Athenian democracy, followed by the Roman Republic, were arguably the first successful (for a while) societies where important decisions were based on debate among peers, not by decrees from an unelected warlord, king or emperor. But victory in a war with a neighboring country increased the wealth and resource-base of the victors (and the enslavement of the losers) but did not lead to the broadening of the citizenry and decision-making (voting) base. So the result of successive conquests by the Roman Republic was to narrow the power base (Roman citizens) and increase inequality. Imperial Rome was a large diverse territory ruled by a small fraction of the citizens of a single city.

The enforcers of Roman Law (and order) during the early years of the Republic, in Italy, were citizen-soldiers who served the Republic as needed and not for payment. But under the emperors, the enforcers were paid mercenaries. They had to be paid in money or land. Where did the money or land come from? The traditional means of paying con-career soldiers was to live off the countryside during campaigns, and after a victory, to let the soldiers loose in the conquered towns and cities to pay themselves by looting. Loot was portable wealth. Portable wealth was coins or garments or decorative objects that could be sold in a marketplace and exchanged for coins. One of the other ways in which conquering armies paid themselves was by capturing soldiers of the defeated army, or their families, and selling them in slave-markets. Rome was built and largely populated by slaves or ex-slaves. Roman Citizens—those descended from the early settlers—were a minority by Julius Caesars time.

But, as most of the good agricultural land in Italy was already occupied, soldiers in the permanent encampments in distant frontier countries had to be paid in coins of the realm. Gold and silver coins were recognizable as being valuable. Bits of paper or clay or anything else not inherently valuable, were too easily counterfeited, but gold and silver were not. Thus money and precious metals were increasingly the same thing: money was wealth and wealth was money, for much of human history.

Money (today) is a lot like phlogiston, a weightless substance that flows, except that it is not imaginary. But thanks in part to John Locke, most people in the 16th to eighteenth centuries associated money with coins issued by the Royal Mint, that were supposedly valued by their weight of silver or gold. John Locke famously argued in a parliamentary debate about the currency devaluation c. 1694: "A Pound Sterling means a pound of silver". Money gained recognition as a factor of production in the seventeenth century, when central banks were being created to serve the markets in the major cities of northern Europe, national currencies started being exchanged, and paper money (letters of credit or LOCs) were replacing coinage for long distance trade where it made no sense to carry money as bags of coins.

Despite this history, many economics textbooks—notably since {von Mises, 1951}—have tried to explain money by postulating a prior "barter economy" where money didn't exist. Ludwig Vin Mises, a theorist, postulated that money was "invented" to convert the imaginary barter-economy into a real economy. There is no evidence of an actual barter economy in human history. Well, there is one, the salt for gold trade in Africa (below).

The reality is that barter requires a "double coincidence" of a non-violent meeting between two persons, or possibly two tribes, each with a surplus of one commodity and a deficit in another, and that their surpluses and deficits exactly match {Graeber, 2011} Chap. 2. What did exist, in some places, was the use of portable, countable objects—such as cowrie shells, elephant tusks, cocoanuts or cattle—as measures of value (money equivalents) for accounting purposes, but that were rarely, if ever, physically exchanged. Having said that, there is some evidence that cowrie shells, in particular, were sometimes used as portable money in Africa and south Asia. There is also good evidence of a "market" on the headwaters of the Niger River in Mali, near Timbuktu (c. 1400 CE) where gold was exchanged for salt, but where the traders never actually met. Apparently, the gold/salt traders "bid" by leaving a fixed quantity of one commodity in a designated place and if the "price" was acceptable, it would be replaced overnight by an appropriate amount of the other commodity. See Fig. 1.2.

The salt for gold trade was discovered by Portuguese trader-explorers around 1500 CE, and was disrupted by them. But it was probably much older. A pure guess is that it began about the time when Timbuktu became a city. Timbuktu is located in the present day Republic of Mali at the edge of the Sahara desert. Timbuktu was founded by the Tuareg Imashagan or Kel Tamasheq in the eleventh century. The Kel Tamasheq roamed the desert during the rainy season in search of grazing lands for their herds and camels and settled in one location near the river, during the dry season (Fig. 1.3).

Fig. 1.2 Of Usury, from Brant's Stultifera Navis (ship of fools), 1494; woodcut attributed to Albrecht Dürer—Wikipedia

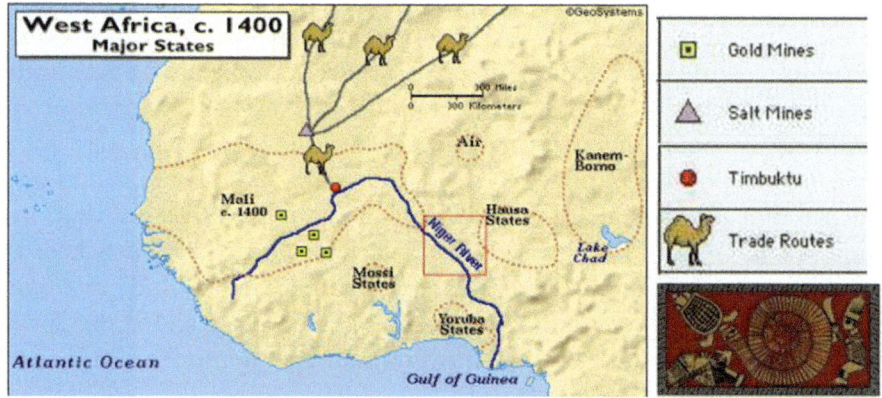

Fig. 1.3 Map of the gold-salt trade in Africa, c. 1500 CE https://www.thinglink.com/scene/503653900734169090

2

From the Crusades to the Renaissance

The crusades—basically a long-running war between Christianity and Islam—is not remembered with pride, by the descendants on either side.

In 1095, at the Council of Clermont, Pope Urban II proclaimed the First Crusade, to support the Byzantine emperor Alexios I against the Seljuk Turks. Having no army to command, he called for a pilgrimage to Jerusalem, relying on its participants to arm themselves. This call was met by an enthusiastic popular response. The first Crusaders were a melange of discontents with many motivations, including religious salvation, opportunities for fame and glory and hopes of loot.

Later crusades were generally more organized, some were led by a king (notably Richard "the Lion Heart"). All were motivated by papal indulgences. Initial successes established four Crusader States: the County of Edessa, The Principality of Antioch, the Kingdom of Jerusalem; and the County of Tripoli. The Crusader presence continued in some form until the fall of Acre in 1291. After this, there were no further crusades to recover the Holy Land, although violent skirmishes continued until much later, even after the conquest of Constantinople by the Ottoman Turks, in 1453.

During the thirteenth century the crusaders on a religious mission to capture or defend Jerusalem, fighting against the Saracens, included nobles with inherited estates (land) who felt a need to be sure of reclaiming their lands upon their return. Some of them—more over time entrusted the physical deeds to their properties in Europe, written on parchment or vellum, to one of the commanderies (fortresses) of the Knights of the Temple of Solomon (or "Templars").

The Templars undertook this security function. At first, it was simple Christian charity. But, in time, it became a service with costs, that had to be paid for. To avoid calling the fees "interest" (and risk a charge of usury, a sin), the Templars called it "rent". The Templars simultaneously offered an associated service, namely "Letters of Credit" (LOCs) allowing the traveling knights with property to borrow (in effect) against the deeds to their properties. By the beginning of the fourteenth century, the Templars mission had shifted largely away from guarding pilgrim's lives to protecting their property.

Moreover, the Templars found that they could make loans to others (such as sovereigns) secured by the value of the unclaimed properties they were guarding. In fact, they found that they could make more loans—in the form of paper letters of credit (LOCs)—than the value of the assets they actually had in hand as reserves. This "fractional reserve" lending practice ("leverage", in modern terms) was very profitable, because it was a great boost to trade. It was also extremely dangerous, as they discovered.

One unintended consequence of the Templar's lending activities was the sudden and catastrophic end of the Knights of the Temple of Solomon, themselves. This happened on Friday the 13th—still an unlucky day—in October the year 1307 CE when King Philip "le Bel" of France (who owed them money) decided not to pay. He mistakenly thought the Templars had a secret treasury full of gold. The King had the Templar leaders tortured for two years and finally burned at the stake. But no gold hoard was discovered.

After the Templar's disappearance, there was a financial service for travelers, such as traders, that needed to be filled. The gap was filled, after the Templars, by wealthy families in the well-defended northern Italian city-states, notably (but not only) Pisa, Florence, Genoa, Verona, Milan and Venice. The service they provided (loans and transferable credit) was needed to support burgeoning trade between Mediterranean and northern Europe, later with Asia and Africa, especially after the return of the Venetian traveler, Marco Polo, and his stories c. 1275. The early banks were family affairs (Bardi, Frescobaldi, Peruzzi, Accaluoli, Medici). Those family "super companies" were originally producers of olive oil, wine, lemons and (in the case of the Bardi) woolen cloth. Their banking business depended—as with the Templars—on trusting, and being trusted by, the borrowers, but the dealt with people of all nationalities and religions, and all social classes. When trust failed, as when King Edward of England defaulted, the Italian banks collapsed. This happened several times.

Nevertheless, the letters of credit (LOCs), originally guaranteed by the Templars, began to be traded among traveling merchants, in the fourteenth century in Italy and around the Mediterranean Sea. By the middle of the fourteenth century some successful merchant families in Italy evolved into banks. i.e. institutions that made loans (to suitably affluent clients) and received either interest on the money (called "rents" to avoid the accusation of usury), or other forms of return. One such form of return was shares in a new enterprise, such as a sugar plantation, an olive grove or a mine. LOCs became a form of money. Thence, their guarantors (who also physically protected the valuables of depositors) became banks, albeit under another name. LOCs were the first "paper money".

In 1310 international finance played a role in English political history. King Edward I and his son Edward II had borrowed £22,000 (a very large sum for a family bank) to finance his wars. The lenders were the Frescobaldi, Bardi and Peruzzi banks in Florence. This relationship financed Edward I's conquest of Wales, so Edward II wanted to conquer Scotland as well. He borrowed to finance his war against Robert The Bruce, of Scotland, which he lost in the battle of Bannockburn. There was no loot to reimburse the soldiers, and King Edward's Parliament did not want to tax themselves to pay for it. The default had a very bad effect on Italian bankers, as may be imagined. An even bigger financial collapse was the simultaneous failure of the three "super companies" of Florence, in 1344–45 due to another royal default (by Edward III of England), followed by an outbreak of the black death in 1348.

Yet banking thrived. In 1422 there were 72 "international banks" operating out of Florence alone {Weatherford, 1997 #5513} p.82. Things turned sour after that. This was partly due to internal Florentine power struggles, and partly due to the repudiation of war loans by Edward II of England. According to one source, Edward owed 900,000 gold florins (£135,000) to the Bardi and 600,000 florins (£90,000) to the Peruzzi, which he could not pay. (Peruzzi records suggest that King Edward did repay some of his loans in cash and some in wool.) But the overall effect of the losses on Florence was devastating.

The Medici family moved its HQ to Florence in 1397 CE, and engaged primarily in trade, especially wool cloth. They expanded to Venice in 1402. At their peak, in the 1450 s the Medici's had branch banks in Lyon, Geneva, Avignon, Bruges and London. The Medici's financed the Roman Curia and later intermarried with French royalty. Catherine de Medici (1519–89), married to Henry II of the Valois dynasty, was the "mother of three kings". Another Medici (Marie) was married to the next king, Henri the fourth (the first Bourbon), and later acted as regent to the young future King Louis XIII.

The Medici branch banks were financially independent of each other, in order to be protected from the failure of any one branch.

Other Florentine banking families included the Altoviti, Gondi, Pazzi, Salviati, Scali and Strozzi. As a matter of interest, there have been some great banking families, but virtually all of them were forced or induced—by elevation to the nobility—to lend money to kings or popes and all of them were ultimately destroyed by their royal debtors. The Medici bank was dominant in Florence in the fifteenth century, reaching its peak of power through its control (by Papal monopoly) of the alum mines of Tolfa.[1] It collapsed in 1494 when the Medici's were expelled from Florence.

The Fugger bank of Augsburg took over many of the Medicis' assets c. 1500 CE and their political power and influence. The Fuggers were closely affiliated with the House of Habsburg whose rise to world power they financed. Unlike the citizenry of their hometown and most other trading patricians of German free imperial cities, such as the Tuchers, they never converted to Lutheranism, as presented in the Augsburg Confession, but rather major family bank remained with the Roman Catholic Church and thus close to the Habsburg emperors.

It is commonplace to date the rise of science to the capture of Constantinople by the Ottoman Turks, in 1453, which triggered the Age of Exploration. A case could also be made to date the change to a year earlier, the birthdate of **Leonardo da Vinci** (1452–1519). Leonardo was one of the greatest geniuses of all time, not only as an scientist but also as an engineer, inventor, and the artist who painted "Mona Lisa", the most famous painting in the Louvre, if not world. Some credit must be given to the city of his birthplace, Florence, and its then-ruling family for creating the environment that allowed his genius (and others) to flower.

Leonardo da Vinci's interests ranged over many areas of science, including (alphabetically) acoustics, astronomy, botany, geology, hydrodynamics, optics and physiology, but human anatomy was his specialty. He was an empiricist to the core, long before Francis Bacon wrote *Novum Organum*, but he was not an experimentalist. He discovered by observation of dissected bodies (before William Harvey) that the circulation of the blood is controlled by the heart. His notebooks also noted that that the "humors"—blood, phlegm, yellow bile (choler), and black bile (melancholy)—that were thought to determine a person's physical and mental qualities by the relative proportions in which

---

[1] Alum (mineral aluminum sulfate) was used as a mordant (color fixing agent) in the textile dye business. Before the Ottomans came the only European source was in Anatolia. Another mine was discovered in Italy (Tolfa) about 1460 CE and its output was an asset of the Da Vinci bank.

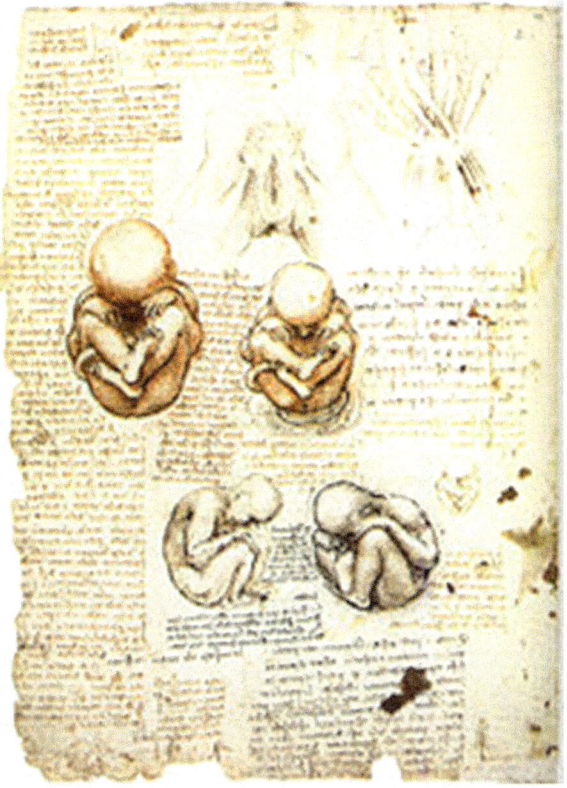

Fig. 2.1 Study of the human embryo, 1510–1513, royal collection—Windsor—Wikimedia

they were present could not be located in any of the body cavities that he investigated.

In short, Leonardo da Vinci initiated the overthrow of traditional medical anatomical assumptions although most of his insights and inventions were lost along with his notebooks (some of which have been rediscovered recently). He was the first to understand the impossibility of perpetual motion, though others sought it for centuries after. He invented scores of workable devices, famously including the helicopter, but only on paper because the materials and tools to make them were not available in his time (Figs. 2.1 and 2.2).

The second high Renaissance giant from Florence was **Michelangelo di Ludovico Simoni** (1475–1564) who designed and decorated the Sistine Chapel and much else in the Vatican, as well as the most famous nude male statue in the world ("*David*"). (His painting of The "*Creation of Adam*" on the ceiling of the Sistine chapel (1508–1512) helped to cement the power the

Fig. 2.2 This portrait attributed to Francesco Melzi, c. 1515–1518, is the only certain contemporary depiction of Leonardo—Wikipedia

Church of Rome, and to perpetuate the Biblical myth of The Creation, not to mention the dominant role of men over women. "*The Last Judgment*" by Michelangelo spans the whole altar wall of the Sistine Chapel. It depicts over 300 (mostly male nude) figures surrounding the central figure of Christ who chooses some to be saved while most are destined for Hell.

Dante Alighieri (1265–1321) wrote the "Divine Comedy" (1308–1320), which made it all seem very realistic His depictions of Hell, Purgatory and Heaven provided inspiration for the larger body of Western art and literature. The painting reproduced below conveys a flavor. He is often described as the "father" of the Italian language.

Dante's "Divine Comedy" and Michelangelo's "Last Judgment" might be regarded as the dark side of the Italian High Renaissance. At the time most of the people—even educated people—who read Dante's poem and saw Michelangelo's art believed that they were an accurate pre-vision of reality, conveyed from the mind if God by the artist in much the same way a TV camera transmits images today. Christians of all sorts believed fervently in life after death, either in Heaven, with Christ and the angels, or with Satan and his demons, in Hell (Figs. 2.3 and 2.4).

Fig. 2.3 Dante and Virgil in Hell painting by William-Adolphe Bouguereau (1850)—Wikimedia

Fig. 2.4 The creation of Adam on the Sistine Capel ceiling by Michelangelo—Wikipedia

Fig. 2.5 Portrait of Luca Pacioli attributed to Jacobo de Barbari, c. 1495—Wikimedia

The Italian banks gained an edge in the sixteenth century thanks to the invention (in 1494 CE) of double-entry bookkeeping by **Fra Luca Bartolomeo de Pacioli** (c. 1447–1517). He was an Italian mathematician, Franciscan friar, collaborator with Leonardo da Vinci, and an early contributor to the field now known as accounting. He is referred to as "The Father of Accounting and Bookkeeping" in Europe and he was the first person to publish a work on the double-entry system of book-keeping on the continent. He was also called **Luca di Borgo** after his birthplace, Borgo Sansepolcro, Tuscany (Fig. 2.5).

The key to this accounting invention is to record every transaction in two separate accounts, usually a "cash" account and an "asset" (credit) account. In this system a loan is recorded as a subtraction from the cash account and a corresponding addition to the credit account. The two accounts have to balance at all times. In fact, what accountants do to this day is called "balancing" and corporate financial statements are called "balance sheets". Keeping the two accounts physically separate (and maintained by different clerks) also constituted an effective protection against fraud.

How were the accounts themselves kept? We like to think that they were written on parchment and stored in a fireproof place. But we now know that virtually all the records of money payments to and from the government of England, from the 12th to the late eighteenth century, were kept on willow "tally sticks" that were kept in the Treasury. The tally stick for each transaction was split along the wood grain. The creditor's half was the "stock" and the debtor's half was the "foil". The end of that tally system, and the unfortunate destruction (by fire) of 600 years of financial records, is a sad story told by Felix Martin {Martin, 2014} pp. 16–19. Only a few of the tally sticks remain, as evidence of how it worked, once upon a time.

3

The Protestant Work Ethic and the Rise of Capitalism as Gods Work

In the fourteenth century, thanks to the failures of the Crusades and the demonstrated subsidiarity of Popes to Kings, the upper echelon of the Church-of-Rome was widely seen to have morphed into a gang of money-grubbers. The laity needed another moral guide. They found it in money-making. Whereas in the past, religious devotion often involved vows of celibacy and rejection of worldly affairs, the new form of devotion was to acquire tangible wealth and advertise it.

Markets facilitate the exchange of material products (goods) by providing an impersonal mechanism for determining relative values (prices). Price determination is an essential service, but it also has limits. We all know that money can't buy everything, especially happiness or love. As Oscar Wilde said (in the voice of a character in a play): "*The cynic knows the price of everything and the value of nothing*" (from "Lady Windermere's fan"). Of course that was part of a dialog written for amusement. But it carries a "sting in its tail", so to speak. Not everything of importance is exchanged or available in markets, and some things—environmental services, for example—are priceless.

Adam Smith and David Ricardo argued that ideal markets for exchangeable goods must be "free" from unnecessary regulation, yet hyper-competitive and efficient. But such perfect markets cannot exist without clear rules governing transactions and effective mechanisms for enforcement of the rules. In fact, the very existence of such an ideal market is doubtful.

It is easy to be misled by images of village marketplaces, as illustrated in children's stories and Christmas cards, where all transactions are personal, in cash, the goods (products of farms and artisan workshops) are portable and the community where everybody knows everybody else, is the only enforcer needed. The village pictured on the Christmas Card is peaceful because it is situated in a country not threatened by attack by barbarians (because the cavalry, or the navy, is keeping the barbarians away). The cavalry, and the navy work for a beneficent but invisible ruler who receives money from invisible sources—tariffs or a gold mine or a bit-coin mine—but not, please the Lord, by taxes collected by government agents physically knocking on their doors.

That picture was never realistic in Adam Smith's day, nor anywhere else, before or since. The village market in France or Italy or Morocco is attractive for tourists, but it cannot exist without a hinterland of farmers and factories and a system of laws and effective law enforcement. But in the vast majority of modern markets for portable goods, the village is a metaphor, not a model. In the metaphor, prices are arrived at by conversations—bargaining—between buyer and seller. The cost of regulation and enforcement remains largely invisible.

In reality, face-to-face bargaining is still applicable only for buying and selling of unique goods, such as works of art, and immobile goods (e.g. houses) where buyer and seller have roughly equal market power but the middle man—the broker—takes a share. (The government also takes a share from all transactions.) Rules are needed in these cases to define a valid and binding offer, an acceptance, a contract, a delivery, even a method of payment, as well as a penalty for breach of contract and an enforcement mechanism. Guarantees and warranties must be defined. Rules are also needed to deal with all the things that can (and do) go wrong in a transaction, ranging from departures from specifications and failures to perform as advertised, to 'acts of God' and deliberate fraud.

The reality of markets for non-unique portable goods is the chain-store (or, increasingly a web-site) where all goods have a "fixed price" determined by a mass-marketing enterprise that shares the value added gains with mass-producing enterprises on a more or less equal basis. But small-scale producers (such as farmers and artisans) lack the market power to share the gains from trade. The consequence of this inequity, over time, is that the big enterprises tend to get still bigger and claim a larger share of the gains from trade, and their owners get wealthier. Meanwhile, the non-unionized consumers, the non-unionized employees of the large enterprises, and the small local businesses receive a smaller and smaller share of the gains.

Demand and supply are two sides of the same coin: the buyer's willingness to pay constitutes "demand" while the seller's willingness to sell constitutes "supply". When a transaction occurs, they must be quantitatively equal, by definition (Menger 1871, 1994). Markets for mass-produced portable goods sold in shops and markets for stocks and shares of companies, are similar enough to be treated the same, in principle. But important details are different. For instance, the sellers may be "price makers" (large scale producers) having much greater market powers than the customers (clients).

Regulation is therefore needed to ensure that competition in markets is reasonably fair. To start with, this means that the rules are supposedly enforced by incorruptible "guardians", not by market participants. The primary requirement for regulation is to detect, eliminate and punish fraud, such as the sale of stolen goods, or fakes. After that, in most industrial countries, it also means limiting the role of debt, the use of leverage, and the so-called 'market power' of large players (lenders, borrowers, sellers or buyers). This is the main reason why anti-trust laws exist in most advanced economies, to minimize price-fixing and market sharing agreements by monopolies and cartels.

Evidently the markets in the real world never satisfy all of these conditions, resulting in so-called 'market failures'. Curiously the idea of market failures did not appear in theoretical economics until the twentieth century, and the idea that such failures could be quantitatively important—even critical—has only emerged in recent decades. In particular, public goods and environmental services are inherently troublesome from a regulatory point of view, because the underlying goods themselves cannot be, or are not, owned by any individual economic agent.

It is worth emphasizing that markets cannot be self-regulating, whatever capitalist ideologues may think. Markets are institutions where goods and services are for sale to the highest bidder, whereas law enforcement and justice must be provided by agents who are immune to commercial incentives. (We use the terms "*H. Economicus*" and "*H. Custodius*" in reference to traders, on the one hand and policemen (or women), health workers, teachers, preachers, judges and others who create and enforce the "rule of law", on the other hand.) Markets in the real world We assume, hereafter, that the markets discussed in this book (as in other economic texts) are imperfectly regulated by agents (belonging to *H. Sapiens*) who need to be trained and supervised to perform regulatory and enforcement functions honestly, without favor. In other words, the regulatory and enforcement system needs to be regulated itself. Free markets are an impossibility.

The greatest gap in economic theory is the role of energy (technically, exergy) and the laws of thermodynamics (physics), as applied to the direction of technological change. Without some understanding of thermodynamics, the crucial economic phenomena of today cannot be understood, or explained. Luckily, for our purposes, money flows in economics and information flows in society correspond to energy flows and exergy destruction.

Back to economics, meaning human activity behavior with respect to making, trading and utilization of material goods (things). The overlap with physics comes from the fact that making, trading and using complex objects (structures) things also involves energy transformations. In fact, as the first sentence of this sub-chapter states, every economic decision—to produce, exchange or purposefully utilize an economic object (product)—is also accompanied by an energy conversion (from exergy to anergy) and an increase in the entropy of the universe. According to standard neo-classical economics, physical actions and transformations are performed by "labor". In the eighteenth century practically all work on farms, and in households, was done by the muscles of relatively unskilled human workers or working animals (bullocks, horses). So, one could safely equate human (and animal) labor, in those distant days, with mechanical work.

Things have changed drastically. Now most work is done by machines; some machines are extensions of muscles, but some are not. Not all work is mechanical or even physical and not all physical work is done by that kind of machine. In increasing share is done by electronic machines that transmit and process data and store useful information. The word "useful" means only that we humans are the final users of all that information transmitted and processed by machines. It is intended for our use. Mostly it is just business and housekeeping data (records), entertainment (movies, games) or education. A very small fraction of information that circulates is devoted to the creation, transfer and storage of knowledge for future use. But that fraction is what creates new wealth. The stock of knowledge (and know-how) is what we mean by "human capital" in economics.

There is also another kind of capital that humans exploit but did not create, viz. natural capital. Natural capital is the stock of material resources, such as forests, fossil fuels and mineral ores that we extract from the Earth's crust, as well as the arable soil on which we grow crops, and the benign climate on which they depend. The biosphere, biodiversity and the ecosystems of the world are also underlying environmental assets. Those assets were not created by human activities. Those assets are now being degraded—and some are literally destroyed—by human activity in the name of capitalism and profit.

Martin Luther (1483–1546) was a theologian and scholar, and a professor at the University of Wittenberg. He protested against the corrupt practices by the Church of Rome, especially the sale of indulgences ("guarantees" of salvation) to lay Church-goers, not to mention the sale of Bishoprics and

Fig. 3.1 The door of the All Saint's Church in Wittenberg-Wikipedia

Cardinal's Hats to the scions of wealthy Italian merchant families (such as the Medicis). (The trade in indulgences had been established by Popes Julius II and Leo X to finance the construction of St. Peter's Basilica in Rome where Michelangelo was employed). On October 31, 1517 Luther's "95 theses"—all derived from scripture—were nailed to the door of the All Saints Church in Wittenberg. This action was an established invitation to debate. In fact, many thousands of copies of the "95 theses" soon were printed and sold (Fig. 3.1).

According to Luther, the salvation of the soul is a free gift from God, received through sincere repentance and authentic faith in Jesus Christ as the Messiah, without possible intercession of the Church. By holding the Bible as the only legitimate source of Christian authority, he denied papal authority. He was summoned on June 15, 1520 by Pope Leo X to retract, he refused and was excommunicated, on January 3, 1521, by the papal bull Decet romanum pontificem. Then the Holy Roman Emperor and King of Spain, Charles V, summoned Martin Luther before the Diet of Worms. A safe conduct was granted to let him go there without risk. Before the Diet of Worms, he refused to retract, declaring himself convinced by the testimony of Scripture and considering himself subject to the authority of the Bible and

Fig. 3.2 Portrait of Martin Luther by Lucas Cranach (1528)—Wikipedia

his conscience rather than that of the ecclesiastical hierarchy. The Diet of Worms, under pressure from Charles V, decided to ban Martin Luther and his followers from the Empire.

He was welcomed by his friend the Elector of Saxony Frederick III the Wise, at Wartburg Castle, where he lived and wrote his best-known works, including a translation of the Bible into German from the original texts In 1543, three years before his death, he published Des Juifs et de leurs mensonges, an antisemitic pamphlet of extreme violence, in which he advocated solutions later adopted by the Nazis, such as burning synagogues, demolishing the homes of Jews, destroying their writings, confiscating their money and killing rabbis who would teach Judaism (Fig. 3.2).

Jean Cauvin (John Calvin) (1509–1564) wrote another book that was, perhaps, an even greater agent of change. It was the "Belgic Confession" of 1561. Calvin said that God "delivers and preserves" from perdition "all whom he, in his eternal and unchangeable council, of mere goodness hath elected in Christ Jesus our Lord, without respect to their works" (Article XVI). (These words were actually written in 1559 by Guido de Brès a Dutch reformist who died a martyr to the faith in 1567.) Lutherans and Calvinists chose to believe that God selected those whom he will save and bring with him to Heaven before the world was created; it was the doctrine of "predestination". The Calvinists also believed that those not so destined for salvation would go to Hell.

The inability to influence one's own salvation (by good works) presented a problem for Calvin's followers. The prescribed solution was a circular argument: Calvinists had an absolute duty to believe that one was chosen for salvation. Doubt was evidence of insufficient faith and a sign of damnation. So, self-confidence took the place of priestly assurance of God's grace. Worldly success became evidence of being one of the "elect" who had been selected by the creator (God) before the creation. In the sixteenth century the Protestant Reformation changed people's attitudes toward visible wealth. By logical inference, lack of wealth must be proof of moral fault and destination for Hell. Those attitudes still survive in some circles in America.

The moral doctrines of Luther and Calvin played an important part in the economic development of northern Europe, the low countries—especially the Netherlands—Scotland, and later the English colonies in North America, especially in New England. They migrated to New England during the decades just before the English Civil War, between 1620 and 1638.

The "Puritans" (so called, because of their moral purity) adopted strict Lutheran-Calvinist religious practice, starting in the Plymouth Colony in 1620. The Massachusetts Bay colony followed in 1629. These were followed by the Saybrook Colony (1635), the Connecticut Colony (1636) and the New Haven Colony (1638). The Puritan immigrants formed tight-knit religious communities, with the explicit intention of becoming a nation of "saints", and "redeeming" corrupt Europe.

Luther's arguments led to polarization between feudal rulers in southern Europe, especially the Spanish, who were loyal to the Church of Rome (because they owned it) and feudal rulers in north Germany, who liked Luther's arguments and did not want to be ruled, either by a Holy Roman Emperor or by a Pope in the Vatican. That Polarization led to the 30 years' war (1618–1648) and that war resulted in a wave of Protestant refugees, including Huguenots from France, and Puritans from England, who moved into the Netherlands and north Germany.

The economic consequences of the rise of Protestantism were examined in an influential book "The Protestant Ethic and the Spirit of Capitalism" (Weber 1904–05). Max Weber wrote that the development of the "concept of the calling" gave to the modern entrepreneur a fabulously clear conscience, as well as industrious workers. Protestantism gave to the entrepreneurs the means to exploit their employees ruthlessly, as the price of their ascetic devotion to the prospect of eternal salvation. To illustrate his theory, Weber quoted the ethical writings of Benjamin Franklin (1706–1790), probably from "Poor Richard's Almanack" (1733):

> Remember, that time is money. He that can earn ten shillings a day by his labor, and goes abroad, or sits idle, one half of that day, though he spends but sixpence during his diversion or idleness, ought not to reckon that the only expense; he has really spent, or rather thrown away, five shillings besides. (…)

Remember, that money is the prolific, generating nature. Money can beget money, and its offspring can beget more, and so on. Five shillings turned is six, turned again is seven and three pence, and so on, till it becomes a hundred pounds. The more there is of it, the more it produces every turning, so that the profits rise quicker and quicker. He that kills a breeding-sow, destroys all her offspring to the thousandth generation. He that murders a crown, destroys all that it might have produced, even scores of pounds.

Max Weber noted that this is not a philosophy of mere greed. It is a statement laden with moral language. The Reformation profoundly affected the view of work, dignifying even the most mundane professions as adding to the common good –thanks to the "Invisible hand"—and thus blessed by God, as much as any "sacred" calling.

To emphasize the work ethic in Protestantism, relative to Roman Catholics, Max Weber noted a common problem that nascent industrialists faced when employing precapitalist laborers (e.g. Irish peasants or Inca or Zulu natives): Agricultural entrepreneurs may try to encourage workers to spend more time harvesting by offering a higher wage, expecting that laborers will see time spent working as more valuable (in monetary terms) and so engage it longer. However, in precapitalist societies where money was not the measure of everything, this often had the opposite result: laborers spent less time working if they could earn the same amount of money, while having more leisure.

But something in the air changed a lot between Martin Luther's impassioned attack on the corruption of the Church, and the day when Ben Franklin "disarmed the gods" in 1750, by flying a kite in a storm and proving that lightning is just an electric spark (Harari 2014). Already by Ben Franklin's time, the spiritual content of Calvinism had gone even though much of the cultural baggage survived. An historian in the twentieth century wrote that Calvinism was, "*a creed which transformed the acquisition of wealth from a drudgery or a temptation into a moral duty was the milk of lions. It was not that religion was expelled from practical life, but that religion itself gave it a foundation of granite. The good Christian was …the economic man*" (Tawney 1926).

René Descartes (1596–1650) was a mathematician, physicist and one of the founders of modern philosophy. His rationalism was exhibited from 1628 in "*Rules for the Direction of the Mind*", then in the "*Speech of the Method*" in 1637, a break from the scholasticism taught in the University. The "Method" speech opens with a proverbial remark "*Common sense is the most shared thing in the world*" to emphasize the importance of using a method that preserves us, as much as possible, from error. It is characterized by its simplicity and is inspired by the mathematical method, seeking to replace the Aristotelian syllogisms used in the Middle Ages since the thirteenth century. Like Galileo, he accepted the Copernican cosmological system; but, out of caution towards censorship, he "advanced masked", partially concealing his new ideas about man and the world in his metaphysical thoughts, ideas that revolutionized philosophy and theology.

Descartes' major books were *"Meditations on First Philosophy"* (1641) and *"Principles of Philosophy"* (1644) among several others. His name is associated with rationalism, Cartesian mathematics, analytic geometry, dualism, methodic doubt, anthropocentrism and conservation of momentum. As one critic has said *"Descartes scientific approach to seeing the world unquestionably represented a huge breakthrough, and this is doubly true for economists…Descartes ideas, of course, became absolutely key, if not determining, for the methodology of economic science"* (Sedlack 2011 #8355) p.171–172. We return to that point pater in this book.

He remains famous for the phrase *Cogito ergo sum"* ("I think, therefore I exist"), which seems very profound without being self-explanatory. It is regarded as the start of "modern subjectivity", focusing on the object of thought about the world, as it represents itself. In physics, he made a contribution to optics and is considered one of the founders of the idea of animal bodies as mechanisms. In mathematics, he was the originator of analytical geometry, as taught in every high school. It is not a criticism of his lifework to say that some of his theories were later challenged (animal-machine theory) or abandoned (theory of whirlpools or animal spirits).

Descarte's main contributions were, first, that he insisted on eliminating any dependence on myth, superstition and tradition, as well as on subjective feelings and emotions. In fact, he insisted on distinguishing very sharply between what we know for sure and what might be doubted ("methodic doubt"). Part of this involved doubting the information of the senses. Descartes did not believe in empiricism, as fervently as Leonardo of Francis Bacon. He relied on "pure reason". Immanuel Kant's later *"Critique of Pure Reason"* was aimed at resolving this impasse between Cartesian "rationalism" and the empiricism of his later critics (Kant 1781).

Second, rather than seeing the soul of man as suspended between good and evil, as the Catholic Church did, Descartes saw man as an entity combining (between?) matter and intellect. The phrase cogito ergo sum, or "I think, therefore I exist" expresses this notion. The theory of dual existence of mind and body is Descarte's signature. In *"Meditations on First Philosophy"*, he attempted to demonstrate the existence of God and the distinction between the human soul and the body. Descartes's dualism embraced the idea that mind and body are distinct but closely joined. Descartes explained, *"we can clearly perceive a substance apart from the mode which we say differs from it, whereas we cannot, conversely, understand the mode apart from the substance"*. He said that two substances are really distinct when each of them can exist apart from the other. Thus, he reasoned that God is distinct from humans, and the body and mind of a human are also distinct from one another. He argued that the great differences between body (an extended thing) and mind (an un-extended, immaterial thing) make the two ontologically distinct.

He argued that the existence of God was proven by the fact that, if God did not exist, it would be impossible to think of Him. This is an assumption (and obviously wrong). There is quite a lot more of prejudice and assumption in Descarte's works, masked as unshakeable fact. *"He struggled for objectivity (unity, or the unification of points of view) so he could rid the new philosophy (of science) of disputes, doubts, subjectivity, and the disunity of explanations that stem from it"* Sedlack p.181. Science didn't work out to be free of doubts and disputes, back then, or since then, as we all know today.

Third, Descartes saw physiological Man as a machine-like creature whose functions are derived from mechanical principles, as is the case for clocks, mills and even artificial fountains. Descartes dualism between the soul and the body was a break with Aristotelian tradition. For example, he radicalized his position by denying that animals are capable of thought, conceiving of the animal as a "machine», that is, a body entirely devoid of soul. This view was criticized, for example by Voltaire, Diderot and Rousseau.

Descartes' philosophy promoted mechanics and mechanism from their minor previous role in science, to a much greater and more fundamental role in philosophy—in fact, the highest rung of the ontological ladder. Yet, despite Descartes fame for *"cogito ergo sum"*, he gave thinking very little role in the process of discovery. For him that role was limited to the mathematical side of the process of discovery, leaving no room for emotion, intuition or chance.

The influence of René Descartes was great in the seventeenth century: the philosophers who succeeded him developed their own ideas in relation to his, either by extending it (Arnauld, Malebranche), or by opposing it (Locke, Hobbes, Pascal, Spinoza, Leibniz). Descartes rationalism was brought to England by his philosophical opponents, the empiricists: John Locke, David Hume, and the later advocates of utilitarianism, Jeremy Bentham and John Stuart Mill (Fig. 3.3).

Until the seventeenth century Christian theologians and most philosophers (like Descartes), believed in dualism, the doctrine that mind (or the religious concept of soul) existed independently of matter. The opposite doctrine,

Fig. 3.3 Portrait of René Descartes by Frans Hals—Wikimedia

monism, argues that there can be only one substance of the universe. This was explicitly argued openly, perhaps for the first time, by Giordano Bruno (1548–1600) in the 1580 s. (Bruno was burned at the stake for heresy in 1600, not for his ideas on astronomy, but for his denial that Moses and Jesus Christ performed miracles.) (Gatti, Hilary. *Giordano Bruno and Renaissance Science: Broken Lives and Organizational Power*. Cornell University Press, 2002, 1).

By the beginning of the seventeenth century Protestantism was well established in northern Europe, but the counter-reformation led by the Society of Jesus (Jesuits)—founded by Ignatius de Loyola in 1540—was tightening its hold south of the Alps. England, isolated from continental Europe by the Channel—an arm of the ocean—was the cockpit of the dispute. The Kings (and their allies) claimed that he had a 'Divine Right' to rule, to start wars (and to collect taxes) without Parliamentary approval. In the seventeenth century, In 1687 Isaac Newton showed that elliptical orbits could be derived from his laws of gravitation.

But whose God was lurking behind the scenes pulling the strings (so to speak)? Whose God was defining heresy and burning the heretics? Whose

God was organizing the motions of the stars? Whose God was in charge of the climate and the productivity of the land? Religion was no longer the private domain of anointed Priests and Bishops, to be discussed exclusively in Latin. By 1600 everybody (or at least every chapel) in England, had a Bible, printed in English, and many citizens demanded to be heard by the councils of government.

It was when the first treatises on economic theory were written by William Petty and others. The old admonition against usury (interest) was gone, too, although the prejudice against Jews remained. Thrift and hard work were already admirable for themselves. Making money from money, had become quite admirable. Benjamin Franklin's contemporary, the moral philosopher Adam Smith (1720–1790) in England, saw it exactly the same way, and wrote a best-selling book about how to get rich (Smith 1776 [2007]).

Today it is normal (albeit inaccurate) to see the economy as a circular flow system of money flows between producers (of goods) and consumers who are also workers—albeit with a reverse flow of material commodities and products. However, the circular flow was not a familiar idea in the seventeenth century. Most of the elite who ran the country believed that the total wealth of the world was finite, consistent with the Hobbesian view that everyone is an enemy, subject only to the sovereign, so international competition for resources—including piracy—was the key to survival.

One of the British East India Company (BEIC)'s directors, Thomas Mun (1571–1641), wrote a book "England's Treasure by Foreign Trade", subtitled "The Rule of Our Treasure". In brief, the rule was "to sell to strangers more yearly than we consume of them in value" (Mun 1664). The underlying idea of Mun's book—written to guide his son—and published post mortem, asserts that accumulating money (profits) is equivalent to increasing national wealth. It explains, in detail, all the ways this can be accomplished, both by reducing manufacturing and shipping costs and reducing English consumption of imported goods.

This was arguably the first formal statement of the economic idea behind mercantilism, the predominant British government economic policy of the next two hundred years. We come back to economics later.

4

The Enlightenment: From Leonardo to Galileo

In the years from 1550 to 1750 CE an important illusion was demolished, namely the embedded historic idea of geo-centrism, that the Earth is the center of the universe and that and that the sun, moon, planets and stars orbit around the Earth. The geocentric model was the predominant description of the cosmos in many ancient civilizations. It was accepted and taught by the wisest of the wise, including Aristotle in Classical Greece and Ptolemy in Roman Egypt.

This illusion was supported in prehistory by observation. At first sight, even from a mountain top, the Earth appears to be solid, flat and stationary. The ancient Jewish Babylonian uranography pictured a flat Earth with a dome-shaped, rigid canopy called the firmament placed over it. Ancient Greek, ancient Roman, and medieval philosophers gradually combined the geocentric model with a spherical Earth, in contrast to the older flat-Earth model implied in some mythology. Of course, the Portuguese explorers, including Christopher Columbus, had already discarded the flat-Earth idea before starting their voyages of exploration. The flat Earth idea was finally put to rest by Columbus' success in sailing west and finding land.

The established cosmological wisdom in 1540, from Ptolemy and Aristotle (despite Bishop Cusa) was still the pre-Copernican "geocentric" theory, that Earth is the center of the universe. True, Aristarchus of Samos (c. 310–c. 230 BCE) had developed a heliocentric model placing all of the then-known planets in their correct order around the Sun. The ancient Greeks believed that the motions of the planets were circular. The Sun appears to revolve around Earth once per day. The stars appeared, to Earthbound observers, to be fixed on a celestial sphere rotating once each day about an axis through the geographic poles of Earth. The Moon and the planets also have their own motions, but they also appear to revolve around Earth about once per day.

In 1620 two different lens grinders, both in the Netherlands town of Westerberg, kicked off a crucial role in technological evolution and mankind's view of himself and his place in the universe. A whole industry was born at that time, in that place, not only to make microscopes for physicians, and telescopes for astronomers (and astrologers), but mainly for spectacles to help—in some cases to enable—the Dutch citizens to read the Bibles and other books being produced by the busy printing presses in Amsterdam. Those spectacles along with books—became valuable exports for the Netherlands, which also made the low countries a valuable economic asset for the Dukes of Burgundy and Kings of neighboring France.

Nicolaus Copernicus (1473–1543) was a Renaissance polymath, active as a mathematician, astronomer, and economist.[1] He formulated a model of the universe that placed the Sun rather than Earth at its center. In all likelihood, Copernicus developed his model independently of Aristarchus of Samos, an ancient Greek astronomer who had formulated such a model some eighteen centuries earlier.

The geocentric model was still accepted by most philosophers in 1500, It was in 1543 that Copernicus challenged that theory (in a book written in Latin, of course). It was entitled "*De Revolutionibus Orbium Coelestium*" (On the revolutions of the celestial spheres) which argued that the Earth revolves around the sun, rather than the contrary. The Church authorities grumbled but God did not strike down the questioner. The Church did, by some accounts.

Giordano Bruno (1548–1600) was an Italian Dominican friar, philosopher, mathematician, cosmological theorist. He is known for his cosmological theories, which conceptually extended the Copernican model. He proposed that the stars were distant suns surrounded by their own planets, and he raised the possibility that these planets might foster life of their own, a cosmological position known as cosmic pluralism. He also insisted that the universe is infinite and could have no "center". Some later philosophers give him credit for being the first philosopher to espouse monism, the idea that the universe consists of a single substance, although it is hard to find any specific evidence of this in his writings. (Bruno was convicted and burned at the stake for his

---

[1] In 1517 he derived a quantity theory of money and in 1519 he formulated an economic principle that later came to be called Gresham's law.

Fig. 4.1 Astronomer Copernicus or conversations with God by Matejko—Wikimedia

heterodox views in 1600, but not for his ideas on astronomy, but for his denial that Moses and Jesus Christ performed miracles) (Fig. 4.1).

Tycho Brahe (1546–1601) was the observer par excellence, who improved the quality of astronomical data enormously. He criticized Copernican heliocentric theory and proposed his own hybrid geo-heliocentric scheme in which the moon and the sun orbit around the Earth, while the planets Mercury, Venus, Mars, Jupiter and Saturn revolve around the sun, and the whole solar systems is surrounded by a sphere of "fixed" (immutable) stars.

In 1572 Brahe observed for several months a "new star" (a supernova that is now known to be 7500 light years distant, but in our galaxy) and realized that it must have been quite far away because of the lack of "parallax". In other words, the point is that, if the "new" star was near the Earth, it would be seen in a different place in the sky as the Earth moves around the sun. But, being far away, it was always seen in the same place in the sky.

Johannes Kepler (1571–1630) followed Tycho Brahe with his quantitative "celestial physics". Kepler formulated (correctly) all three laws of planetary motion. He even calculated the ellipticity of the orbits. (He also provided astrological tables for powerful persons.) Johannes Kepler postulated that orbits were heliocentric and elliptical (Kepler's first law of planetary motion).

Francis Bacon (1561–1626) was an adopted son of a commoner, who thought he was a son of the Queen. Most of his life he was striving for preferment and promotion by Queen Elizabeth, and under King James he achieved both. His reputation as the father of scientific empiricism rests on one book, written in 1620, after the end of his political career. "*Novum*

Organum" ("A new tool for science") was influential among scholars, in particular Sir Thomas Browne, who in his *Encyclopedia "Pseudodoxia Epidemica" while* (1646–72) frequently cites the Baconian approach to scientific enquiries.

The Athenian Empedocles (494–434 BCE) formulated the classical theory that there were four elements: fire, air, earth and water, while love and strife were the "actors" responsible for motion, combination and separation. Of course meteoric iron, gold, copper (as nuggets), carbon (as charcoal), sulfur, tin (for bronze) and lead, zinc, mercury (smelted from sulfide ores) were all prehistoric. Fire was thus thought of as a substance and burning was seen as a process of decomposition which applied only to compounds.

Phlogiston was a theory to explain combustion, postulated in 1667 by alchemist **Johann Joachim Becher** (1635–1682) and later described, more formally, by Georg Ernst Stahl. William Cullen, the biographer of the Scottish Enlightenment, who knew everybody, considered Becher as a chemist of first importance and *Physica Subterranea* as the most considerable of Becher's writings. Phlogiston was supposed to be a weightless substance contained within combustible bodies and released during combustion, and absorbed by the air, which was assumed to be non-combustible. Thus explaining some observed facts. It was unable to explain weight increases, such as rusting and other examples of oxidation (that led to the discovery of oxygen.) It was disproved before the end of the eighteenth century following experiments by Antoine Lavoisier.

The first element discovered in modern times was phosphorus (from urine), in 1669. This was followed by cobalt (1735), nickel (1751), magnesium (1759), and hydrogen (by Cavendish) in 1766, followed by oxygen (1771), and nitrogen (1772) (Fig. 4.2).

Galileo di Vincenzo Bonaiuti de' Galilei (1564—1642) has been called the "father of modern science"—more deservingly than Francis Bacon—among other epithets. Galileo studied speed and velocity, gravity and free fall, the principle of relativity, inertia, projectile motion and also worked in applied science and technology, describing the properties of pendulums and "hydrostatic balances". He invented the thermoscope and various military compasses. He used the telescope for scientific observations of celestial objects. His contributions to observational astronomy include telescopic confirmation of the phases of Venus, observation of the four largest satellites of Jupiter, observation of Saturn's rings, and analysis of sunspots.

Galileo's championing of Copernican heliocentrism met with opposition from within the Catholic Church, led by the Jesuits, and from some astronomers. The matter was investigated by the Roman Inquisition in 1615,

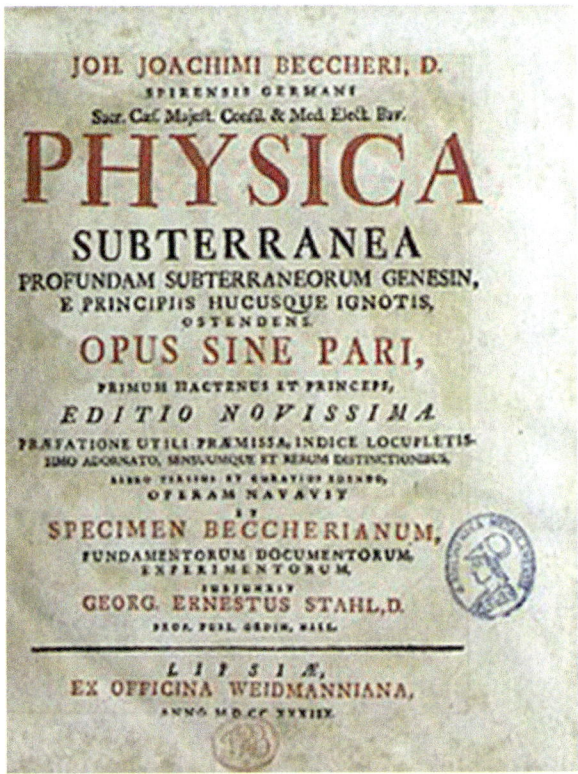

Fig. 4.2 Physica subterranea, 1738 edition—Wikipedia

which concluded that heliocentrism was "foolish, absurd, and heretical" since it contradicted Holy Scripture. Galileo was forced to recant and lived his later years under house arrest. (He was lucky to avoid Giordano Bruno's fate). He formulated the principle of relativity, namely that the laws of physics will be the same in any inertial system that is moving along a straight line.

The idea of inertia goes back in some respects to Aristotle, but Aristotle thought that a body would continue moving only as long as the "impressed force" continued. Leonardo da Vinci said much the same thing earlier (c. 1500). But neither Aristotle nor Leonardo had a clear understanding of friction as a force, especially air friction. Galileo (c. 1600) restated the inertial principle as follows: *that a moving body will continue its linear motion as long as the vector sum of forces, acting and resisting, equals zero.* This statement essentially corrected Aristotle and preceded Newton.

The idea of "simultaneity" has wider philosophical implications in the modern theory of relativity. Underlying all of this is the idea that there exists an absolute clock-time that will be the same everywhere in absolute space.

Fig. 4.3 Galileo showing the Doge of Venice how to use the telescope (fresco by Giuseppe Bertini)—Wikimedia

That idea was the one later challenged by Einstein, who imagined that every moving object has its own attached clock, keeping time independently of all others.

Galileo later defended his views in his "*Dialogue Concerning the Two Chief World Systems*" (1632), which appeared to attack Pope Urban VIII and thus alienated both the Pope and the Jesuits, who had both supported Galileo up until this point. He, like Giordano Bruno, was tried by the Inquisition, found "vehemently suspect of heresy", and forced to recant. All his books were banned or burned for a long time. He spent the last years of his life under house arrest. During this time, he wrote "*Two New Sciences*" (1638), primarily concerning kinematics and the strength of materials, summarizing work he had done around forty years earlier. Yet, According to Stephen Hawking, and Albert Einstein, the two most famous physicists of the twentieth century (by some tests), Galileo probably bears more of the responsibility for the birth of modern science than anybody else (Figs. 4.3 and 4.4).

Baruch (Benedict) Spinoza (1632–1677) was a Dutch optical lens grinder, by trade, with a Portuguese-Jewish background; he collaborated with Constantin and Christiaan Huygens on microscope and telescope lens designs. He was also one of the early biblical critics and thinkers about the self

4 The Enlightenment: From Leonardo to Galileo

Fig. 4.4 Portrait of Galileo in 1636 by Justus Sustermans—Wikipedia

and the universe. He was one of the first rationalists of seventeenth century philosophy; he was inspired by the ideas of René Descartes, but he was a free thinker. He had controversial ideas regarding the authenticity of the Hebrew Bible and the nature of the Divine. Jewish religious authorities issued a *herem* against him, causing him to be effectively expelled and shunned by Jewish society at age 23, including by his own family. His books were later added to the Catholic Church's Index of Forbidden Books. He was frequently called an "atheist" by contemporaries, although nowhere in his work does Spinoza argue against the existence of God. (*"Spinoza on God, Affects, and the Nature of Sorrow—Florida Philosophical Review". cah.ucf.edu. Retrieved* 29 October 2022.)

Spinoza had considerable influence on the thinking of John Locke, who spent 5 years in Amsterdam, from 1683 to 1688, before returning to England after the Glorious Revolution. Spinoza had died in 1677, but his friends and followers were still very active during Locke's visit. It was Locke who later wrote a book defending the idea of property, and its importance.

Fig. 4.5 Portrait of Baruch Spinoza, c. 1665, anonymous—Wikipedia

Spinoza's magnum opus, "Ethics", was published posthumously in the year of his death. The work opposed Descartes' philosophy of mind–body dualism and earned Spinoza recognition as one of Western philosophy's most important thinkers. Roger Scruton (2002) said, "*Spinoza wrote the last indisputable Latin masterpiece, and one in which the refined conceptions of medieval philosophy are finally turned against themselves and destroyed entirely*". Hegel said, "*The fact is that Spinoza is made a testing-point in modern philosophy, so that it may really be said: You are either a Spinozist or not a philosopher at all*" (Fig. 4.5).

The relation between natural and legal rights is fundamental to governance and political legitimacy. The topic was debated intensely in the latter years of the French Enlightenment. The term came from a 1762 book: "*The Social Contract* (French: *Du contrat social ou Principes du droit politique*), a 1762 book by **Jean-Jacques Rousseau** (1712–1778)."

The starting point for most modern theories of legitimacy is an examination of the human condition absent of any political order (termed the "state of nature" by Thomas Hobbes). In this condition, individuals' actions are bound only by their personal power and conscience. From this starting point, the argument focuses on the question: Why should rational individuals voluntarily consent to give up their natural freedom of choice to obtain the benefits of political order. The issue has arisen with renewed intensity in connection with the creation of the European Union after the second World War, and "Brexit", the recent departure of the United Kingdom.

Until the eighteenth century, "property" really meant land. Land ownership back then was tightly linked to the feudal prerogatives of monarchy, where all the land was owned by the king and the lands of the princes, dukes, counts and barons were "fiefs" held in fiefdom to the king. The *enclosure movement* was, effectively, a conversion of "common" (public) land into "private property." John Locke—an ardent opponent of the feudal notion of absolute monarchy—argued nevertheless that private property was a "natural right that pre-existed monarchy" (Locke 1960 [1698]). Adam Smith, on the contrary, viewed property as an "acquired right" (Smith, 1776 [2007] #4712).

Within a settled country there is competition among towns, and among organized groups, some seeking wealth, others seeking religious purity. The profit-seeking organizations compete for investments and for customers or clients, or they may cooperate by sharing markets (contrary to current "antitrust" laws in most capitalist countries). But other organizations (e.g., police, public health, education, communication), that provide services to the whole population, do not work well in a competitive profit-seeking environment.

The nature of reality—as matter (not "spirit")—had become an important topic (known as "materialism") for philosophers since the Greek "atomists". Discussion was encouraged by scientific discoveries of Copernicus, Galileo, Newton and others. René Descartes (1596–1650) was perhaps the first to see the human body as a kind of mechanism ("Discourse on Method"). In 1748, French doctor and philosopher La Mettrie introduced the first materialistic definition of the human soul in a book "L'Homme Machine".

Prominent seventeenth and eighteenth century theorists on the topic of natural rights versus social obligations include Hugo Grotius (1625), Thomas Hobbes (1651), Samuel von Pufendorf (1673), John Locke (1689), Jean-Jacques Rousseau (1762) and Immanuel Kant (1797). Each of these men approached the issue differently. Grotius insisted that individual humans have natural rights that must not be violated. Thomas Hobbes famously said that in a "state of nature", human life would be *"solitary, poor, nasty, brutish and short"*, meaning that without the rule of law everyone would have unlimited natural rights, including the "right to all things" including the freedom to plunder rape and murder. Hobbes foresaw an endless "war of all against all" (*bellum omnium contra omnes*). To avoid this, he said, free men contract with each other to establish political community (civil society) through an implicit social contract in which they all gain security in return for subjecting themselves to an absolute sovereign. The sovereign can be one man or an assembly of men. Though the sovereign's edicts may well be arbitrary and tyrannical, Hobbes saw absolute government as the only viable alternative to the terrifying anarchy of a state of nature.

Alternatively, Locke and Rousseau posited a trade-off: We gain civil rights in return for accepting the obligation to respect and defend the rights of others, within a framework of laws, giving up some freedoms in exchange for security. The central assertion that social contract theory approaches is that law and political order are not natural, but human creations. The social contract and the political order it creates are simply the means towards an end—the benefit of the individuals involved. They are legitimate only to the extent that they fulfil their part of the (unwritten) agreement. According to non-Hobbesian social contract theorists, when the government fails to secure their natural rights (Locke) or satisfy the best interests of society (called the "general will" by Rousseau), citizens can withdraw their obligation to obey or change the leadership through elections or other means.

The "other means" may include violence, when necessary (as exemplified later during the 1793 "reign of terror" in Paris.) Locke believed that natural rights were inalienable, whence the rule of God superseded government authority. Rousseau believed that democracy (majority-rule) was the best way to ensure welfare while maintaining individual freedom under the rule of law. The Lockean concept of the social contract was invoked in the United States Declaration of Independence. Social contract theories were largely eclipsed in the nineteenth century, after the French Revolution, in favor of other "isms", such as utilitarianism, Hegelianism and Marxism; they were revived in the twentieth century, notably in the form of a thought experiment by John Rawls.

Between 1780 and 1840 there was an intellectual revolution in philosophy, centered in Germany. It began with the publication of Immanuel Kant's "Critique of Pure Reason", which focused attention on the difference between a "thing in itself" that is inherently un-knowable (e.g., God, or the soul), versus the appearance (to the human observer of that thing (Kant, 1781). The perception of a thing depends upon human modes of receiving information, processing and organization of knowledge. They were also inspired by the industrial revolution in England and its "empiricist" philosophers (Hobbes, Locke, Hume, et al.) and the French Revolution.

But Kant's work led to a number of dualisms and contradictions that resulted in several decades of academic dispute among a group of philosophers, calling themselves "idealists" including Johann Fichte, Friedrich Jacobi,

Friedrich Schelling, Gotlob Ernst Schulze, and Jeorg Wilhelm Friedrich Hegel. The two major critiques of idealism were Pierre-Joseph Proudhon's "The Philosophy of Poverty", while Marx countered with "The Poverty of Philosophy". Proudhon was the first to call himself an anarchist, and was the author of many quotable quotes, including *"property is theft"*. Hegel had the greatest impact on later generations, especially on the ideas of Karl Marx and "Das Kapital" (Marx, 1867). Looking back, it was the idealists, especially Hegel, who first realized that knowledge has a social character and that the creation and spread of knowledge also moves society. It was mainly Hegel who conceived of political development as a dialectical process of social interaction or discourse, among groups.

5

The Rise of the East India Trading Companies

The "Age of Discovery", started after the capture of Constantinople by the Ottoman Turks in 1452, and the closing of the overland "Silk Road". Some overland trade from the far East was redirected to Aleppo and Damascus in Syria, but European explorers and merchants began to seek routes by sea and trading opportunities in distant countries, especially the Far East. Trading companies were created. One of the things that was already happening during the thirteenth century (see Chap. 2) was the weakening of the feudal system, where obligations between lower and higher layers of society were based on days of service owed by the lower to the higher rank.

During the thirteenth century CE that obligation was increasingly converted to monetary terms, i.e., payment of rent or a share of the annual crop (typically half) in lieu of cash rent. Ownership of land (inherited from the Norman Conquest, in the case of England and Scotland, or from other conquerors in other countries) morphed into the right to receive a money income from the land. Money, or the future prospect of it, gradually became a driver of long distance trade, by ship or caravan.

It was not a coincidence that the Protestant Reformation of the seventeenth century—and its work ethic—was soon followed by an explosive growth of long distance trading by wealth-seeking trading companies. The Spanish and Portuguese began it, even though they were not Protestants.

Christopher Columbus (a Genoese adventurer working for the King of Aragon) discovered the New World in 1492. On May 4, 1493, Pope Alexander VI issued the papal bull 'Inter caetera ' (Among other [works]), which granted to the Catholic Majesties of Ferdinand and Isabella of Spain all lands to the "west and south" of a pole-to-pole line 100 leagues west and south of any of the islands of the Azores or the Cape Verde islands. It established a dividing line between the Castilian and Portuguese spheres of power. (How the Pope divided the New World among Spain and the Rest of the World—SciHi BlogSciHi Blog).

After the Papal decree of Tordesillas (1494) Portugal focused on colonizing West Africa and Brazil. Portugal had pioneered the plantation system in the Atlantic islands of Madeira and São Tomé; they took that system to Brazil. Starting in the sixteenth century, sugarcane was grown on plantations called engenhos along the northeast coast (Brazil's Nordeste). At first, the settlers tried to enslave the native Brazilians to work the fields, but later they imported slaves from Africa. That industry, based on slave labor to produce sugar for Europe, became the base of Brazilian economy and society and the Spanish Caribbean islands of Puerto Rico, Santo Domingo and Cuba.

The Spanish focused on the Caribbean Islands and subsequently Mexico and South America. King Ferdinand of Aragon (1452–1516)—who was married to Queen Isabella of Castile from 1468 until she died in 1504—understood that the acquisition of gold was the only way to fund his ambitious scheme for colonizing the New World and, incidentally, spreading the Roman Catholic version of the word of God. King Ferdinando became strongly motivated to search for gold. On July 25, 1511, he unequivocally instructed his New World explorers not to colonize, but to *"get gold, humanely, if you can, but at all hazards, get gold"*. That objective was adopted by subsequent Spanish monarchs for the next three centuries. Two years later the "lNew World" was divided between Spain and Portugal by the papal decree.

The looting started on the Caribbean islands. One after the other, they were all visited by Spanish gold-seekers and cleaned out of their treasures of gold. The amount of gold that was extracted from those islands was considerable, amounting to just under 1 tonne each year from 1503 to 1530, say 25 metric tons in all. In 1518, a bold Conquistador, Hernan Cortes (who was wanted for mutiny by the Spanish governor of Cuba) landed an expeditionary force of 11 ships, with 13 horses and 500 men and several cannons on the mainland, where he encountered an advanced civilization (the Aztecs).

Cortes declared war on the Aztec king, Montezuma with the explicit purpose of seizing whatever gold he could find in the capital, Mexico. Gold was of little value to the Aztec's except as decoration. Thus, Montezuma surrendered his empire's treasures to the conquistadors without extraordinary resistance. However, the king's brother launched an attack on the Spaniards

5 The Rise of the East India Trading Companies

Fig. 5.1 Hernando Cortes, conqueror of Mexico—Wikipedia

and fierce hostilities ensued for a time between the Spaniards and the Aztecs. By 1521, the Aztec armies had been defeated and Mexico (which then included territory that is now California) with all its undiscovered gold and silver, became part of the Spanish Empire (and remained as part of that empire until the nineteenth century) (Fig. 5.1).

Far to the south of Mexico, in Peru, was the kingdom of the Incas. The Incas gold was partly from alluvial deposits of the streams of Peru and partly looted from the earlier Chimu civilization in 1470. It is also believed that the Incas mined gold in places such as the Curimayo valley, north-east of Cajamarca. Their hoarding stemmed from the fact that they worshipped the sun god, Inti, and the metal was inextricably linked with that deity. The Incas referred to gold as the "tears wept by the sun".

A Spanish contemporary described the gold wealth contained within the Temple of the Sun in the Inca capital of Cuzco: "*The interior of the temple was the most worthy of admiration. It was, literally, a mine of gold. On the western wall was emblazoned a representation of the deity, consisting of a human face looking forth from amidst innumerable rays of light, which emanated from it in every direction, in the same manner as the sun is often personified with us. The figure was engraved on a massive plate of gold of enormous dimensions, thickly powdered with emeralds and precious stones. It was so situated in front of the great eastern portal that the rays of the morning sun fell directly upon it at its rising, lighting up the whole apartment with an effulgence that seemed more than natural, and which was reflected back from the golden ornaments with which the walls and ceilings were everywhere encrusted."*

Unfortunately no human has ever seen that golden sight since that description was written.

Rumors of the immense stores of gold held by the Inca King Atahualpa, inevitably, reached the ears of the greedy Spanish. An expedition led by Francisco Pizarro set out in 1526 to see whether reports were true. Pizarro's discoveries in Peru exceeded his wildest expectations; gold abounded in the Inca cities, and their sun temples were decorated with golden ornaments of great beauty. The legend of El Dorado was based on the pre-Columbian Muisca, or chief, that covered himself in gold powder and jumped into Lake Titicaca (now in Bolivia) as a ritual to become crowned chief. The gold represented godliness to this ancient civilization that worshiped the deity or trinity of Chiminigagua (the supreme being). The mythical city of El Dorado has been sought ever since by many, notably Sir Walter Raleigh, since the Spanish conquistadors.

Motivated by their royal instruction to "get gold at all hazards", between 1531 and 1534, Pizarro declared war on the Incas. In due course, his men managed to capture King Atahualpa at Caxamalca. In an attempt to secure his release, King Atahualpa promised to completely fill his prison cell with gold ornaments. Although the ransom was paid (with some 6 tonnes of pure gold objects), Pizarro had the king killed anyhow. Unfortunately for posterity, the gold objects looted from the Incas were bulky, so the Spanish melted them into ingots and shipped almost all of the gold back to Spain in that more compact form.

A few years later, in 1536 to 1538 CE another Spanish conquistador, Gonzalo Jiménez de Quesada, discovered a third gold-hoarding civilization, namely the Muisca, who inhabited the central highlands of present-day Colombia's Eastern Range. Fortunately for those indigenous peoples, Quesada was less successful than Cortes and Pizarro in his campaign, as the bulk of the king's treasure had been hidden.

The Spanish were not content with the acquisition of the gold of Mexico and Peru. They were convinced that the dense jungles of Central and South America had more treasure that could be looted. Thus, the adventures of Cortes, Pizarro and Quesada are but three of the many episodes in South America's long, brutal and exploitative colonial history. It has been estimated that, between the year of discovery and 1800, the Spanish extracted between

145,000 and 165,000 tons of silver—mostly from the Potosi mine in what is now Bolivia. The Spanish and Portuguese together shipped between 2739 and 2846 tons of gold back to Europe between 1500 and 1800 CE (Weatherford, 1997 #5513) p. 100. Adam Smith, in 1776, estimated that the price of gold and silver (in Europe) declined by two thirds during the sixteenth century while other prices in Spain increased by 400% in the same century (between 1500 and 1600 AD).

In 1695 there was a significant gold discovery in Brazil, followed by a "gold rush" of prospectors and adventurers, similar to what happened in California (1849) and later in South Africa in the nineteenth century. The Portuguese imported between 400,000 and 500,000 African slaves for mining and plantations in Brazil. By 1725, half the population of Brazil was living Minas Gerais, the mining area of south-eastern Brazil. During the peak years of gold mining in Brazil (1741–1760) at least 320 tonnes of gold were extracted. Officially, 800 metric tons of gold were exported from Brazil to Portugal in the eighteenth century. Other gold circulated illegally, and still other gold remained in the colony to adorn churches and for other uses.

In the middle of the thirteenth century in Europe, "Merchant Adventurers" were merchants crossing the seas to trade. The term "adventurer" underlines the uncertainty and dangers of such a trip, at the time. To the extent that Dutch, Flemish, or English ships bypassed Jutland to reach the Baltic Sea, they were seen as intruders and competitors for the maritime trade of Northern Europe, controlled by the Hanseatic League. By the same token, the straits of Gibraltar marked the southern limit, until the defeat of the Spanish Armada in 1588.

In 1551, a limited company was set up by adventurous English merchants, with royal approval, to establish a trade route to China and India. The "Mystery and Company of Merchant Adventurers for the Discovery of Regions, Dominions, Islands, and Places Unknown" teamed up in 1553 with an exploration mission of three ships, one of which reached the White Sea. After contacts with Russia, the limited company was renamed the Muscovy Company. In 1554 obtained, from the English crown, the exclusive privilege of trade with Russia.

In 1577 **Francis Drake** (not yet knighted) set out on a solo expedition from England. Its announced purpose was to plunder the Spanish settlements in Central South America that were collecting gold and silver from the native civilizations. In his ship, the "Golden Hind"—appropriately named—he achieved this objective spectacularly. Two other ships, the Judith and the Tiger, sailed from Plymouth with Drake but sailed East instead of west. Those ships, were financed by **Thomas Gresham**, the Queen's merchant, and founder of the Royal Exchange in London. They sailed to Istanbul (formerly Constantinople) and returned in 1578 (Burgon, 1843 #8652). Others followed their piratical examples. Their loot helped to finance the defense of Elizabethan England.

Drake also sailed across the Pacific Ocean in 1579, and discovered the Moluccas, also known as the Spice Islands. There he met with Sultan Babullah. In return for linen, gold and silver, he acquired a cargo of exotic spices including cloves and Nutmeg, initially not knowing of their commercial value. Drake returned to England in 1580 and became a national hero; he was knighted in 1581. His investors received a return of some 5000 per cent. This started the policy of officially sanctioned piracy (privateering) that drove English foreign policy (focused on Spain) during the late sixteenth century. The Spanish put a huge price on his head, but he died of fever (dysentery, in 1596, not by violence.

The defeat of the Spanish Armada in 1588, was a boost to English sea-power and confidence. The captured Spanish and Portuguese ships with their valuable cargoes inspired Drake imitators to travel the globe in search of riches. In 1590, London merchants presented a petition to the Queen for permission to sail to the Indian Ocean. They asked for, and got, Letters of Marque, allowing them to attack other ships belonging to countries with which England was at war, in the name of the sovereign. They split the costs and the proceeds. It was a cheap way to get a navy. The idea was to deliver a decisive blow to the Spanish and Portuguese monopoly of Far Eastern Trade. Queen Elizabeth I granted her permission. On 10 April 1591 **James Lancaster** (1554–1618) in the Bonaventure with two other ships sailed from Torbay, around the Cape of Good Hope to the Indian Ocean on one of the earliest English overseas Indian expeditions. Having sailed around Cape Comorin to the Malay Peninsula, they preyed on Spanish and Portuguese ships there before returning to England in 1594.

The biggest capture, under a letter of marque, was the seizure near the Azores, of a large Portuguese carrack, the Madre de Deus by **Walter Raleigh** (1552–1618) and the Earl of Cumberland at the Battle of Flores on 13 August 1591. (It was a fleet action, part of the Anglo-Spanish war of 1585–1603) involving 22 English ships under Thomas Howard, and 55 Spanish ships under Alonso de Bazan. One of the English ships, the "Revenge" stayed behind and fought quite heroically to cover the retreat of the other 21, but that is another story.) When she was brought in to Dartmouth she was the largest vessel that had been seen in England and her cargo consisted of chests filled with jewels, pearls, gold, silver coins, ambergris, cloth, tapestries,

5 The Rise of the East India Trading Companies

Fig. 5.2 The Revenge in action at the Battle of Flores, 1591—Wikipedia

pepper, cloves, cinnamon, nutmeg, Boswellia (a tree that produces frankincense), red dye, cochineal and ebony. Equally valuable was the ship's rutter (mariner's handbook) containing vital information on the China, India, and Japan trades. These riches aroused the English to engage in this opulent form of capitalism (Fig. 5.2).

In 1596, three more English ships sailed east but all were lost at sea. On 22 September 1599, a group of merchants met and stated their intention "*to venture in the pretended voyage to the East Indies (the which it may please the Lord to prosper), and the sums that they will adventure*", committing £30,133 (over £4,000,000 in today's money). Two days later, "the Adventurers" reconvened and resolved to apply to the Queen for support of the project. Although their first attempt had not been completely successful, they nonetheless sought the Queen's unofficial approval to continue. They bought ships for their venture and increased their capital to £68,373. The Queen hesitated.

The Adventurers convened again a year later, on 31 December, 1600 and this time the Queen granted a Royal Charter to "*George, Earl of Cumberland, and 215 Knights, Aldermen, and Burgesses*" under the name Governor and Company of Merchants of London trading into the East Indies. For a period of fifteen years, the charter awarded the newly formed company a monopoly on English trade with all countries east of the Cape of Good Hope and west of the Straits of Magellan. Any traders in breach of the charter without a license from the company were liable to forfeiture of their ships and cargo (half of which went to the Crown and the other half to the company), as well as imprisonment at the "royal pleasure".

The governance of the company was in the hands of one governor and 24 directors or "committees", who made up the Court of Directors. They, in turn, reported to the Court of Proprietors, which appointed them. Ten committees reported to the Court of Directors. According to tradition, business was initially transacted at the Nags Head Inn, opposite St Botolph's church in Bishopsgate, before moving to India House in Leadenhall Street.

Sir James Lancaster commanded the first East India Company voyage in 1601 aboard the Red Dragon. After capturing a rich 1,200 ton Portuguese carrack in the Malacca Straits the trade from the booty enabled the voyagers to set up two "factories"—one at Bantam on Java and another in the Moluccas (Spice Islands) before leaving. They returned to England in 1603 to learn of Elizabeth's death. Lancaster was Knighted by the new King James I. By this time, the war with Spain had ended but the company had successfully and profitably breached the Spanish and Portuguese duopoly, with new horizons opened for the English.

In March 1604, Sir Henry Middleton commanded the second voyage. General William Keeling, a captain during the second voyage, led the third voyage aboard the Red Dragon from 1607 to 1610 along with the Hector under Captain William Hawkins and the Consent under Captain David Middleton.

Early in 1608 Alexander Sharpeigh was appointed captain of the company's Ascension, and general or commander of the fourth voyage. Thereafter two ships, Ascension and Union (captained by Richard Rowles) sailed from Woolwich on 14 March 1608. This expedition was lost at sea. The table below summarizes the investments during the years 1603–1616 (profits not shown). It is not clear how many different ships were employed (some, like Spacex, may have been recycled) but it will be noted that the value of goods sent on the outward bound ships during those years (12 voyages using 50 ships, 3 lost) was around £135,000 while the value of the bullion (gold and silver) exported during those years was about £228,000 (if my back of the envelope arithmetic is correct).

But in the sixteenth century the peoples of the "Spice Islands", Southeast Asia and China who produced the spices, tea, luxury fabrics, ceramics and other specialties wanted by the European aristocracy, had no interest in plebian European products like raw wool or woolen fabrics. They insisted in payment in metal: gold, silver, tin or copper, but especially silver or gold coins. That, in turn, motivated explorers and traders to search for those metals, especially gold. Preaching the Christian gospel to unbelievers, especially by the Jesuits, was another motivation for the Spanish; less for the English.

Walter Raleigh (1552–1618) was one of the most notable figures of the Elizabethan era. He was an adventurer to the core. In his late teens he spent some time in France taking part in the religious civil wars. In his 20s he took part in the suppression of rebellion in Ireland; he also participated in the siege of Smerwick. His exploits got royal attention. He rose rapidly in the favor of Queen Elizabeth and was knighted by her in 1585. He was granted a royal patent to explore Virginia, paving the way for future English settlements. In 1594, he came into possession of a Spanish account of a great golden city at the headwaters of the Caroní River. A year later, he explored what is now Guyana and eastern Venezuela in search of Lake Parime and Manoa, the legendary city once thought to be El Dorado. Once back in England, he published "The Discovery of Guiana" (1596), an account of his voyage that made exaggerated claims as to his discoveries. The book contributed to the gold fever but not the gold supply.

After Queen Elizabeth died in 1603, Raleigh was imprisoned in the Tower of London, this time for suspicion of being involved in the Main Plot against King James I (of which he was probably quite innocent). In 1616, he was released to lead a second expedition in search of El Dorado. During the expedition, men led by his top commander ransacked a Spanish outpost, resulting in many deaths, including civilians. This was a violation, both of the terms of his pardon and of the 1604 peace treaty with Spain. Raleigh returned to England and, to appease the Spanish, he was arrested, and beheaded, in 1618 at the age of 66 (Fig. 5.3).

The British East India Company (BEIC) and its Dutch counterpart Vereenigde Oostindische Compagnie, (VOC) were also the founder-leaders of the slave trade that provided African labor for the silver mines in Bolivia and Brazil, the sugar plantations of the Caribbean and the cotton and tobacco plantations in Georgia, the Carolinas, and Virginia.

English and Dutch trading companies began as importers of timber, tea, coffee, tobacco, pepper, spices, silk, calico and muslin, for which they paid in codfish, salmon, wool, copper, tin, lead, silver or gold. The first of the English trading companies was the Muscovy Company, chartered 1553. It was really the first multi-national company. The British East India Company (BEIC) was chartered in 1600. The Dutch East India Company (DEIC) followed in 1602, but grew a lot faster. Both were joint stock companies with private as well as public shareholders.

Fig. 5.3 Sir Walter Raleigh, 1588—Wikimedia

France wasn't far behind the English and Dutch. King Henry IV authorized the first Compagnie des Indes Orientales, in 1604, granting the firm a 15-year monopoly of the Indies trade. This was not a joint-stock corporation, and was funded by the Crown. The French Crown lost interest, temporarily, after Henry IV was assassinated in 1610. The Company was reformed by Cardinal Richelieu in 1642 and revived yet again by Jean Baptiste Colbert (1619–1683) in 1664. We'll return to the French case later in a different connection.

The initial capital of the revamped Compagnie des Indes Orientales was 15 million livres, divided into shares of 1000 livres apiece. Louis XIV funded the first 3 million livres of investment, against which losses in the first 10 years were to be charged. The initial stock offering quickly sold out, as courtiers of Louis XIV recognized that it was in their interests to support the King's overseas initiative. In 1664 the Compagnie des Indes Orientales was granted a 50-year monopoly on French trade in the Indian and Pacific Oceans, a region stretching from the Cape of Good Hope to the Straits of Magellan.

5 The Rise of the East India Trading Companies

The French monarch also granted the Company a concession in perpetuity for the island of Madagascar, as well as any other territories it could conquer.

The Company failed to found a successful colony on Madagascar, but was able to establish ports on the nearby islands of Bourbon and Île-de-France (today's Réunion and Mauritius). By 1719, it had established itself in India, but by then the firm was near bankruptcy. In the same year the Compagnie des Indes Orientales was combined, under the direction of John Law, with other French trading companies to form the Compagnie Perpétuelle des Indes. The reorganized corporation resumed its activities, mainly slave trading, but ceased operations in 1769.

These episodes explain several key aspects of European economics during those centuries, notably the need for gold and silver to finance wars in Europe, and trade with the Orient. By 1600 There was no primary source of gold in western Europe and only two significant sources of silver. The Spanish found significant amounts of previously mined gold in Mexico and Central America even more in the Inca territories (now Bolivia and Peru); they also found a very rich silver mine in Potosi (Boliva) discovered in 1545, that that was still productive into the nineteenth century. Portugal had primary sources of silver and gold on the West coast of Africa and in Brazil.

The Hapsburgs had a very productive silver mine in Kuttenberg, Bohemia from 1526 to 1546. The richest mine, at Kuttenberg was destroyed by a flood in 1546 (and was never reactivated). Their silver mine at Joachimsthal, leased to the Fugger bankers, produced 3 million ounces per year in the 1530s. ("Joachimsthalers" were coins from the mint, the origin of the word "dollar"). However, the Habsburgs also had silver mines in Schwaz, in the Tyrol, that allegedly employed 50,000 people in 1520. The British and Dutch had no domestic sources of either gold or silver, so they relied a lot on privateering.

William Paterson was a director of the BoE for several years, but after a disagreement with other directors, he relocated back to Edinburgh, where he conceived and led a Scottish colonization project, the Company of Scotland. Its objective was to colonize the Darien province in the Isthmus of Panama. The Scottish nobility and merchant class was in a mood for adventure. The Company of Scotland was backed by approximately 20% of all the money circulating in Scotland.

On July 14, 1698 five ships (Saint Andrew, Caledonia, Unicorn, Dolphin and Endeavour) departed from Leith, Scotland carrying about 1200 would-be colonists. Their orders were "to proceed to the Bay of Darien, and make the Isle called the Golden Island … some few leagues to the leeward of the mouth of the great River of Darien … and there make a settlement on the mainland". After calling at Madeira and the West Indies, the fleet made landfall off the coast of Darien on November 2. The settlers optimistically christened their new home "New Caledonia" (no connection with the French colony of the same name in the western Pacific). Paterson personally accompanied the first expedition to Panama in 1698. But things did not go well, for various reasons, including Spanish military opposition, tropical diseases for which they were unprepared (and had no resistance) and divided leadership. (Paterson was a persuasive idealist but not a leader of men.) In New Caledonia his wife and child died while he himself became seriously ill.

A year later, in 1699, a second Scottish expedition, with four ships (Rising Sun, Hamilton, Hope of Boroughstonness and Company's Hope) with a total crew of 1300 men. On November 30, 1699 they arrived safely at the port of Caledonia, but met greater resistance from Spanish forces. They were besieged, outnumbered and without external support. The landing attempt was abandoned in March 1700 after a siege by Spanish forces that had blockaded the harbor.

On March 28, 1700, they requested that the Spanish commander set conditions for surrender. Paterson was one of the few survivors who got back to Scotland (the rest went to Jamaica). Paterson). didn't give up on Darien. In 1701 he wrote "A Proposal to plant a Colony in Darién to protect the Indians against Spain, and to open the Trade of South America to all Nations" (1701). It was a broader version of the original Darién scheme intended to bring free trade to all of Central and South America. It was a bridge too far ahead of its time.

The failure of the Darien colony left the Scottish merchant class in financial difficulties. Furthermore, Scotland's nobles were almost bankrupted by the Darien fiasco. In fact, English financial incentives were a factor in persuading the Scots to support the 1707 Acts of Union. According to this argument, the Scottish establishment (landed aristocracy and mercantile elites) considered that their best chance of being part of a major economic power would be to share the benefits of England's international trade and the growth of the English overseas possessions, so its future would have to lie in unity with England (Fig. 5.4).

5 The Rise of the East India Trading Companies

Fig. 5.4 William Paterson from a wash drawing in the British Museum Innes, J. H. (John H.)—Wikipedia

6

The "Glorious Revolution" and the BoE

Thomas Hobbes (1588–1679) was born in the time that science itself was being born. His father was an Anglican cleric. He was educated in religious schools but also studied mathematics and physics at Malmsbury School, and even got the chance to attend a private school run by Robert Latimer. His scholastic records were impressive, so he continued his education at Magdalen Hall, closely connected to Hertford College, Oxford. Hobbes wasn't very interested in scholastic learning, so he moved to Puritan-friendly Cambridge where he graduated with academic honors in 1608. England was the first European country to discard rule by "divine (inherited) right" to rule of law.

After graduation, Hobbes was employed by the aristocratic Cavendish family, with which he was associated throughout his life. Hobbes became a companion to the younger William Cavendish, and they made a grand tour of Europe between 1610 and 1615. Thus began a lifelong connection with an important aristocratic family that was at the center of English royalist politics during the civil war and the Glorious Revolution thereafter. The son of William Cavendish, was a leading supporter of Charles I during the civil war. (Another Cavendish, Henry, was the discoverer of hydrogen).

In Venice, Hobbes made the acquaintance of Fulgenzio Micanzio, who introduced him to Paolo Sarpi, (1552–1623) a very influential Venetian scholar and statesman. Paolo Sarpi was a defender of the liberties of Republican Venice and a strong proponent of the separation of Church and state.

Sarpi's writings were critical of the Catholic Church and its Scholastic tradition. This probably inspired both Hobbes and (later) Edward Gibbon in their own debunking of priestcraft.)

After William Cavendish, then the Earl of Devonshire, died of the plague the Earl's widow dismissed him. At that point Hobbes moved back to Paris with another tutorial job and he remained in Paris, with occasional visits to Italy (where he met with Galileo Galilei and other scientists). In Paris he tutored various aristocratic boys, ending with Prince of Wales Charles II, until 1651. His first publication (c. 1636) was on law: "The Elements of Law, Natural and Politic".[1]

In the 1630s Thomas Hobbes was trying to defend the spendthrift English monarch (Charles I) against the rising tide of commerce and Parliamentary resistance to arbitrary taxation. King Charles lost that civil war, between the Protestant "roundheads" and the royalist "cavaliers" (and he lost his head as well) in 1642. Parliament was finally in charge.

His next book, more or less simultaneously, was "de Cive" (1642) about physics. Specifically, it was an argument that all matter is made of the same underlying "stuff", with different densities of it corresponding to different materials and geometry (shape and appearance) being just an abstract idealization of its properties. This was pure "monism", contradicting the dualism of Descartes and the established Christian Church. Finally, Hobbes spent several secluded years composing his magnum opus, "Leviathan, or the Matter, Form, and Power of a Common Wealth, Ecclesiastical and Civil" (1651). It had a title-page engraving (below) depicting a crowned giant overlooking a landscape, holding a sword and a crozier and made up of tiny human figures. The book had a major impact, thanks to its appearance at a time when the monarchy and the Republic were fighting for survival (Fig. 6.1).

Due to threats from the royalist expats, Hobbes appealed to the revolutionary English government under Cromwell for protection and returned to London in winter 1651. After his submission to the Council of State, he was allowed to subside into private life. He continued writing, both physics and philosophy. After the Restoration of the monarchy and the accession of King

---

[1] Charles Stuart II was the eldest surviving child of Charles I of England, Scotland and Ireland and Henrietta Maria of France. After Charles I's execution at Whitehall on 30 January 1649, at the climax of the English Civil War, the Parliament of Scotland proclaimed Charles II King on 5 February 1649. But England was a de facto republic led by Oliver Cromwell. Cromwell defeated Charles II at the Battle of Worcester on 3 September 1651, and ruled as a dictator for the next nine years. Charles II spent those years in exile. Cromwell's death in 1658 resulted in the formal restoration of the monarchy, and Charles II was invited to return to Britain. On 29 May 1660, his 30th birthday, he was received in London to public acclaim. After 1660, all legal documents stating a regnal year pretended that Cromwell had never existed.

Fig. 6.1 The Title page of Hobbes' Leviathan by Abraham Bosse—Wikimedia

Charles II. The young king, Hobbes' former pupil, now Charles II, remembered Hobbes teachings (mathematics) and called him to the court to grant him a pension of £100.

Charles II's first English parliament, under Edward Hyde, enacted the so-called Clarendon Code (1661–65), designed to cripple the power of the Nonconformists, or Dissenters and shore up the position of the re-established Church of England. King Charles acquiesced even and though he—like John Locke—favored a policy of religious tolerance.

But, In 1666, the House of Commons introduced a bill against atheism and profaneness. On 17 October 1666, the committee to which the bill was referred was "*empowered to receive information touching such books as tend to atheism, blasphemy and profaneness... in particular... the book of Mr. Hobbes* called the Leviathan." ("*House of Commons Journal Volume 8*". *British History Online*. Retrieved 14 January *2005*).

Hobbes was terrified at the prospect of being labelled a heretic (like Galileo, Giordano Bruno, and Christopher Marlowe, before him) and he proceeded to burn some of his compromising papers.

King Charles (II) protected his old tutor. The only practical consequence of that bill was that Hobbes could never thereafter safely publish anything in England on subjects relating to human conduct. The 1668 edition of his works was printed in Amsterdam. Other writings were not made public until after his death in 1679. In summary, Thomas Hobbes became famous because of his book, "Leviathan," which left a great mark on Western political philosophy. Hobbes was the champion of absolutism for the sovereign, but greatly contributed to many other subjects as well, including ethics, geometry, physics of gases, theology, and even political science.

King Charles attempted to introduce religious freedom for Catholics and Protestant dissenters with his 1672 Royal Declaration of Indulgence. But Parliament forced him to withdraw it.

In 1679 it was revealed that Charles's brother and heir presumptive, James, Duke of York, had become a Roman Catholic. This crisis led to the formation of pro-exclusion Whig and anti-exclusion Tory parties. Charles sided with the Tories. After the discovery of the Rye House Plot to murder both Charles and James in 1683, some Whig leaders were executed or forced into exile. Charles dissolved Parliament in 1681 and ruled alone until his death in 1685. He may have been received into the Catholic Church on his deathbed. Charles II is known as the *Merry Monarch*, thanks to the hedonism of his court. He acknowledged at least 12 illegitimate children by various mistresses, but left no legitimate children (Fig. 6.2).

William Petty (1623–1687) was born in Romsey. His father and grandfather were uneducated clothiers. He studied with the Jesuits in Caen, Normandy, as a boy, supporting himself by teaching English. After a year, he returned to England, with knowledge of Latin, Greek, French, mathematics, and astronomy. After a brief stint in the Navy, Petty left to study in Holland in 1643 (age 20), where he developed an interest in anatomy. Through an English professor in Amsterdam, he became the personal secretary to Hobbes allowing him contact with Descartes, Gassendi and Mersenne. In 1646, he returned to England and, after an attempt to market an invention, he studied medicine at Oxford and became a member of the Oxford Philosophical Club.

Petty became prominent serving Oliver Cromwell and the Commonwealth in Ireland, where he developed efficient methods to survey the land that was to be confiscated and given to Cromwell's soldiers. He was a charter member

Fig. 6.2 Thomas Hobbes. The Thinker—Wikipedia

of the Royal Society, and briefly a Member of Parliament. He is best remembered for his theories on economics and his methods of political arithmetic. He may have been the earliest to advocate the philosophy of "laissez-faire" in relation to government activity.

Two men crucially influenced Petty's economic theories, viz. Francis Bacon, and Thomas Hobbes, (for whom Petty acted as personal secretary during his time in Amsterdam). Bacon argued that mathematics and the senses must be the basis of all rational sciences. This passion for accuracy led Petty to declare that his form of science would only use measurable phenomena and would seek quantitative precision, rather than rely on comparatives or superlatives. He gave this approach a name, "political arithmetic". Petty was the first dedicated economic scientist, amidst the merchant-pamphleteers, such as Thomas Mun or Josiah Child, and philosopher-scientists occasionally dabbling in economics, such as John Locke.

From Hobbes, Petty learned that the rational requirements for "civil peace and material plenty". As Hobbes had focused on civil peace, Petty focused on the requirements for prosperity, before the subject was named political economy. Petty wrote three main works on economics, Treatise of Taxes and Contributions (written in 1662), *Verbum Sapienti* (1665) and *Quantulumcunque* Concerning Money (1682). These works, received significant attention in the 1690s, on major aspects of what later become economics.

Fig. 6.3 William Petty c. 1650—Wikipedia

He made early contributions on fiscal contributions (taxes), national wealth, the money supply and money circulation velocity, value, the interest rate, international trade and government investment.

William Petty developed the "quantity theory of money" (under another name); a core idea in modern economics. Petty calculated the money needed for all transactions in Ireland each year, the time it took for this money to circulate and an estimate of the amount of money needed to effectively keep interest rates under control. By doing so he was the first person to successfully link monetary policy in controlling interest rates.

Petty was knighted for his remarkable work, yet as an academician he was never truly appreciated. This is because he used quantitative data in everything he worked on, and he was the only person to use data of that kind in economics at that time. Many of his economic writings were collected by Charles Henry Hull and reprinted in 1899 (Fig. 6.3).

John Locke (1632–1704) was awarded a bachelor's degree from Oxford in February 1656 and a master's degree in June 1658. He also studied medicine and took a degree in that subject. In 1666, he met Anthony Ashley Cooper,

6 The "Glorious Revolution" and the BoE   63

Fig. 6.4 John Locke, portrait by Godffrey Kneller, National Portrait Gallery, London—Wikimedia

Lord Ashley, who had come to Oxford seeking treatment for a liver infection. Ashley was impressed with Locke and persuaded him to become part of his retinue. In 1667 he moved into Lord Ashley's home at Exeter House in London, as his personal physician. In London, Locke resumed his medical studies under the tutelage of Thomas Sydenham.

Locke's medical knowledge was put to the test when Ashley's chronic liver infection became life-threatening. He coordinated the advice of several physicians and was probably instrumental in persuading Ashley to undergo surgery (then life-threatening itself) to remove a cyst. (There were no local anesthetics, in those days, but opium was available.) Ashley survived the surgery and prospered, crediting Locke with saving his life. During this time, Locke also served as Secretary of the Board of Trade and Plantations and Secretary to the Lords Proprietors of the Carolina colony, which helped to shape his ideas on international trade and economics.

Ashley was a co-founder of the Whig movement, men who supported parliament in its continuing struggle with monarchists (now Tories), and he exerted great influence on Locke's political ideas. Locke became personally involved in politics when Ashley became Lord Chancellor in 1672 (Ashley was created 1st Earl of Shaftesbury in 1673). Following Shaftesbury's fall from favor in 1675, Locke spent some time travelling across France as a tutor and medical attendant to Caleb Banks. He returned to England in

1679 when Shaftesbury's political fortunes rebounded. briefly. Around this time, most likely at Shaftesbury's prompting, Locke composed the bulk of his "Two Treatises of Government". The work is now viewed as a more general argument against absolute monarchy (particularly the version espoused by Robert Filmer and Thomas Hobbes) and for individual consent as the basis of political legitimacy. Although Locke was associated with the Whigs, his ideas about natural (individual) rights and government are today considered quite revolutionary for that period in English history.

Locke fled to the Netherlands in 1683, because he was suspected of involvement in the Rye House Plot (an alleged Whig conspiracy to assassinate or mount an insurrection against Charles II of England because of his pro-Roman Catholic policies) of which Locke was probably innocent. During his five years in Holland, Locke chose his friends from among freethinking members of dissenting Protestant groups, such as Spinoza's confidants. (Baruch Spinoza had died in 1677.) Locke almost certainly met others in Amsterdam who spoke of the ideas of "that renegade Jew who… insisted on identifying himself through his religion of reason alone." Locke's strong empiricist views would have disinclined him to read metaphysical work such as Spinoza's "Ethics", but in other ways he was receptive to Spinoza's ideas. In particular, he adopted—and elaborated—the rational arguments for political and religious tolerance and "the necessity of the separation of church and state."

Locke returned to England in 1688. Most of his publications followed his return from exile. These included his "Essay Concerning Human Understanding", his "Two Treatises on Government" and "A Letter Concerning Toleration", all in quick succession. He exercised a moderating influence on political philosophy, by tempering Hobbesian absolutism while clearly separating the realms of Church and State. He had a strong influence on Voltaire who called him "le sage Locke" and on the "social contract" idea that inspired Alexander Hamilton, James Madison, Thomas Jefferson, and other Founding Fathers of the United States. Thomas Jefferson wrote about him thus: "Bacon, Locke and Newton… I consider them as the three greatest men that have ever lived, without any exception, and as having laid the foundation of those superstructures which have been raised in the Physical and Moral sciences."

Locke, wrote the classic rationale for religious tolerance: (1) that earthly judges, the state in particular, and human beings generally, cannot dependably evaluate the truth-claims of competing religious standpoints; (2) that even if they could, enforcing a single 'true religion' would not have the desired effect, because belief cannot be compelled by violence; and (3) that coercing religious uniformity will lead to more social disorder than allowing diversity.

(This is a lesson yet to be learned by the autocrats in power today.) Newly restored King Charles II supported Locke's arguments for toleration and tried to implement them.

Sadly, although he disapproved of slavery in general, Locke was an investor and beneficiary of the slave trading Royal Africa Company. In addition, while secretary to the Earl of Shaftesbury, Locke participated in drafting the Fundamental Constitutions of Carolina, which established a quasi-feudal aristocracy and gave Carolinian planters absolute power over their enslaved chattel property: the State constitution pledged that "every freeman of Carolina shall have absolute power and authority over his negro slaves". Locke also supported child labor. In his "Essay on the Poor Law," Locke lamented that "figures (below) The work had an immediate impact…" He suggested, therefore, that "working schools" be set up in each parish in England for poor children so that they will be "from infancy (three years old) inured to work." He went on to outline the economics of these schools, arguing that, "not only will they be profitable for the parish, but also that they will instill a good work ethic in the children".

Hobbes and Locke disagreed on several issues. For example, according to Locke, man (presumably including women) is by nature a social animal. Hobbes, however, thought otherwise. He didn't consider man to be a social animal; in fact, he didn't think that a human society could even exist independently, without an absolute ruler. In regard to the "state of nature", Locke believed that men are usually true to their word and fulfil their obligations. He used the American frontier and Soldania as his examples of individuals in the state of nature; they showed that peace and property rights could coexist harmoniously. Even though, in some places and times, violent conflicts could arise, they could mostly be resolved in a peaceful manner. Hobbes, on the other hand, made his stand on the state of nature perfectly clear in a brief statement; he said that there is no society that has no continual fear and danger of a violent death; in such a state, the life of man would be poor, brutal, short, and nasty.

Furthermore, the idea of the "social contract" is different in Locke and Hobbes' philosophies. Locke believed that we (the elite) have the right to life as well as the right to just and impartial protection of our property. Any violation of the social contract would one in a state of war with his fellow countrymen. Conversely, Hobbes believed that if you simply obey the monarch, you are safe. You will not violate the social contract because you do not have the right to rebel.

Monism, (nothing to do with money) was first asserted openly by Hobbes in his "De Cive" (1642), and elaborated by Spinoza. It was formally set

Fig. 6.5 David Hume, leading member of the Scottish enlightenment—Wikipedia

forth as a philosophy, in 1728, by Christian Wolff 1579–1674), in his book "Logic". Monism is the philosophical basis for a major developments in physics. We now recognize that there is one unique substance of the universe: its modern name is "energy".

David Hume (1711—1776) was another Scottish Enlightenment philosopher best known today for his highly influential system of philosophical empiricism, skepticism, and naturalism. Beginning with "A Treatise of Human Nature" (1739–40), Hume strove to create a naturalistic science of man that examined the psychological basis of human nature. Hume argued against the existence of innate ideas, positing that all human knowledge derives solely from experience. This places him with Francis Bacon, Thomas Hobbes, and George Berkeley as an Empiricist. David Hume was, by the way, a close personal friend of Adam Smith (Fig. 6.5).

The British empiricists were challenged in subsequent years by the German idealists (Kant, Fichte, and Hegel) who played an important role in setting the stage for the French philosophers of the Enlightenment, Voltaire and the French Revolution that followed.

King Charles II died in 1685. He was succeeded by his younger brother, James, Duke of York, who wanted to re-establish Roman Catholicism as the official religion of England. In this ambition he was supported by King Louis IV of France, but by very few of the "born to rule" class in England. From a well-born but not aristocratic family, John Churchill served first as a page at the court of the House of Stuart under James, Duke of York, through the 1670s and early 1680s. He earned military and political advancement through his personal courage and diplomatic skill. Churchill's role in defeating the Monmouth Rebellion in 1685 helped secure James II on the throne, briefly.

But John Churchill was also a key player in the military conspiracy that led to James being deposed during the Glorious Revolution. There was a period of confusion, resulting in a sort of *Coup d'Etat*, after which Parliament invited a Dutch king, William of Orange, (who was already related to the Stuarts by marriage) to be King of England. James Stuart quietly went into exile. William of Orange accepted the invitation. But he came with his own agenda and his own Dutch army. He wanted to liberate Spanish Netherlands and fight—along with the Germans—against the French King Louis IV. During William's reign (ending in 1702) the war was a stalemate. Actual fighting began with the death in November 1700 of Charles II of Spain, who had no son.

Although weakened by over a century of continuous conflict, in 1700 the Spanish Empire was still a global power. Its dominions included Spanish Netherlands, large parts of Italy, the Philippines, and much of the Americas. Charles's closest heirs were members of the Austrian Habsburgs or French Bourbons; acquisition of an undivided Spanish Empire by either threatened the European balance of power. Attempts by Louis XIV of France and William III of England to partition the empire in 1698 and 1700 were rejected by the Spanish.

Instead, Charles named Philip of Anjou, a grandson of Louis XIV, as his heir. Having accepted, Philip was proclaimed king of the Spanish Empire on 16 November 1700. The proclamation led to war, with France and Spain on one side and the Grand Alliance on the other. It was all about maintaining the separation of the Spanish and French thrones. It's outcome established that dynastic rights were secondary to maintaining the balance of power between different countries.

The English-Dutch-German alliance won an important battle in that war, notably at the famous Battle of Blenheim (1704), thanks to Marlborough's brilliant general-ship. (He was elevated to become the Duke of Marlborough as his reward for that victory). His leadership of the Allied armies fighting

Louis XIV from 1701 to 1710 consolidated Britain's emergence as a front-rank power, while his ability to maintain unity in the fractious coalition demonstrated his diplomatic skills.

But by 1694 the English Crown was broke, deeply in debt and unable to borrow more from its landowners and merchants. But the English Crown had been deeply in debt even before the war, and the war taxes—as usual—produced less revenue than the war costs. So, the government deficit got worse. Finally, the English Crown lost its creditworthiness and could find no domestic lenders. To find foreign lenders it needed to devalue the currency. By 1694, the financial situation of the English government had become really critical. Money was starting to become important.

The financial solution was proposed by a Scotsman named **William Paterson** (1658—1719. It was to create a private bank, to be called the Bank of England (BoE). This bank would receive the right to issue its own money in the name of the Sovereign, in exchange for promises of repayment from future revenues (government bonds). It worked, in retrospect, because British trade—notably the British East India Company (BEIC)—was increasing its business very rapidly.

After the death of Charles II in 1685 Paterson attempted to convince the English government under James II to undertake the Darién scheme to colonize Panama. When they refused, he tried again to persuade the governments of the Holy Roman Empire and the Dutch Republic to establish a colony in Panama, but failed in both cases. Paterson returned to London and made his fortune with the Merchant Taylors' Company, one of the great twelve livery companies of the City of London, (successors of the guilds). In 1694, he co-founded the Bank of England, described in his pamphlet A Brief Account of the Intended Bank of England, to act as the English government's banker. He proposed a loan of £1.2 m to the government; in return the subscribers would be incorporated as "The Governor and Company of the Bank of England" with banking privileges including the issue of notes. The Royal Charter was granted on 27 July 1694.

The BoE was not (yet) a National Bank, but it was an indirect way to make the parliamentary government responsible for the perceived value of privately issued currency. In return, the bank agreed to lend some of its newly created currency to the Crown, at a fixed rate of interest, for expenses. This "great settlement" occurred in 1694. The Bank of England (BoE) was created in that year, and it still exists, though it has since been nationalized (See 16.616.6). The Bank of England, (BoE) was a consortium of aristocratic English bankers, mostly Whigs, who joined forces to create a bank that loaned £1,200,000 to the King, at an annual interest of 8%. This primordial loan was, by definition, an asset of the bank. The Bank also received from the king the right to issue banknotes in his name, each of which was backed by a fraction of that asset. Others could also borrow from the bank, creating additional assets. What the BoE did was to "monetize" the asset (debt), by letting it be converted to money and spent.

But the problem of coinage had not yet been resolved. The silver shillings in circulation were then considerably under-weight, thanks to a variety of schemes to remove silver by clipping, filing or shearing, without making the coin unrecognizable. Something had to be done about the degraded coinage.

A former Treasury official named William Lowndes (1652–1724) was asked to make proposals. Lowndes proposal in 1695 was to reduce the weight of the silver in the new coins by 20%, thus extending the supply of silver It quickly turned out that the price of bullion in the money markets of Europe had risen so far that a deeper reduction in silver content was needed. The revised proposal was put to Parliament. All the practical "money-men" thought it was the right thing to do.

However, John Locke, chief theorist of the new constitutional government, was invited by Parliament to comment on the Lowndes proposal. Locke opposed Lowndes on the ground that money was wealth and wealth was money. He said: "Silver is the Instrument and Measure of Commerce in all the civilized and trading parts of the world….and the measure of commerce by its quantity, which is the Measure also of its intrinsic value". ….."a pound is a reference to a definite weight of silver". Locke was sarcastic about Loundes' "fanciful justification that there was some metaphysical plane on which a coin would retain its 'value' despite losing 20% of its weight" and many more words along those lines (Martin, 2014 #8304). Locke may not have been the first of the intrinsic value believers (sometimes known as 'gold-bugs') but he was by far the most influential, at least back then.

The bottom line is that John Locke got his way and won that day. Parliament proposed to collect all the light-weight silver coins in circulation, melt them down and reissue full-weight silver coins. A deadline was set. Citizens with under-weight silver coins were officially told to use them to pay taxes, or buy government bonds, to get credit for the face value of the coins they turned in. Otherwise they would receive only the partial value based on the actual silver content. Sadly, a lot of the citizens didn't get the message or didn't believe it. When the coins in circulation were collected, the face values added up to £4.5 million but the silver content was only worth £2.5 million in new full-weight coins (Martin 2014).

Fig. 6.6 The "Old Lady of Threadneedle Street" (BoE) founded 1694—Wikimedia Commons

A great many people complained. Predictably (but not predicted by Locke) all the new silver coins rapidly disappeared (Gresham's Law). This happened because the exchange value—what money can buy—of the silver in Antwerp or Amsterdam was even higher than the value of the full weight English coins. But, thanks to Locke, the government set a fixed price for gold and a fixed relationship between gold and silver. That was the origin of the "gold standard". More on that later (Fig. 6.6).

The "silver standard" later became the gold standard, and it caused an unnecessary demand for silver and gold that accumulated uselessly in the vaults of banks and (later) in Fort Knox. The world stayed on the gold standard—more or less—until President Nixon put an end to it in 1971. It is now understood that US money is backed by "faith and trust" in the government and not by actual gold or silver. We discuss the concept again in Chapter ???.

By the beginning of the seventeenth century Protestantism was well established in northern Europe, but Roman Catholic counter-revolution was tightening its hold south of the Alps. England, isolated from continental Europe by the Channel—an arm of the ocean—was the cockpit of the dispute. King James (and his allies) claimed that he had a 'Divine Right' to rule (and to collect taxes and fight wars without Parliamentary approval.

But whose God was lurking behind the scenes pulling the strings (so to speak)? Whose God was defining heresy and burning the heretics? Whose God was organizing the motions of the stars? Whose God was in charge of the climate and the productivity of the land? Religion was no longer the private domain of anointed Priests and Bishops, to be discussed exclusively in Latin. Everybody (or at least every chapel), had a Bible, printed in English, and many citizens demanded to be heard by the councils of government.

7

Laissez-Faire and John Law's Premature Invention of "Futures"

The term "laissez-faire" has been traced to a meeting that took place around 1681 between Louis XIV's Controller-General of Finances, **Jean-Baptiste Colbert**, a mercantilist, and a group of French merchants, including one M. Le Gendre. When Colbert asked how the French state could help promote commerce, Le Gendre replied simply: "Laissez-nous faire" ("leave it to us"). The anecdote on the Colbert–Le Gendre meeting appeared in a 1751 article in the Journal économique, written by French minister and champion of free trade René de Voyer, Marquis d'Argenson—also the first known appearance of the term in print. Argenson himself had used the phrase earlier (1736) in his own diaries, published later.

Vincent de Gournay, a French Physiocrat and intendant of commerce in the 1750s, popularized the term laissez-faire, adopted from François Quesnay's writings on China. Quesnay (1694–1774) joined the phrases laissez-faire and laissez-passer, laissez-faire being a translation of the Taoist Chinese term wu wei. Gournay also strongly backed the removal of restrictions on trade and the deregulation of industry in France. The Physiocrats popularized the phrase, and gave it a central place in their economic principles.

Today the diversity of products (and skills) available in the market-place is beyond counting. But in the eighteenth century there were a relatively small number of major categories of goods and services. Physiocracy (from the Greek for "government of nature") is an economic theory developed by a group of eighteenth century Age of Enlightenment French economists who believed that the wealth of nations derived solely from the value of terrestrial agriculture" (or "land development") and that agricultural products should therefore be highly priced. Physiocracy became one of the first well-developed theories of economics.

François Quesnay (1694–1774)—who was also the physician of the King Louis XV—and **Jacques Turgot** (1727–1781), Baron de l'Aulne, adopted Gournay's Laissez-Faire ideas. Quesnay persuaded the King of France (Louis XV) to give laissez-faire a try. On September 17, 1754 the King abolished all tolls and restraints on the sale and transport of grain. For more than a decade, the experiment appeared successful. But in 1768 the grain harvest was poor. The cost of bread rose so high that there was widespread starvation among the poor, in France, while merchants were exporting grain in order to maximize their profits. In 1770, the Comptroller-General of Finances Joseph Marie Terray revoked the royal edict that allowed free trade in grain.

Here below is a "systems view" of the French economy published in 1755 by Francois Quesnay (1694–1704). It distinguishes three activities: manufacturing (by artisans), farming (by farmers and farmhands) and merchanting (buying goods from artisans and farmers and selling them to consumers). It shows artisans as the source of manufactured goods and farmers as the source of agricultural goods. It shows two markets, one for manufactured goods and one for agricultural goods. It shows three "sinks" for manufactured goods, namely farmers, farmhands and merchants. It shows three "sinks" for agricultural goods sold in the market, apart from internal consumption, namely artisans, merchants and landlords. What this diagram omits is primary inputs to manufacturing or farming. The system also omits waste flows. The underlying assumption is that farming and manufacturing are both self-sufficient in material and energy terms (Figs. 7.1 and 7.2).

John Law (b. 21 April 1671–21 March 1729) was another adventurous Scot. He was born into a family of bankers and goldsmiths from Fife. On leaving the High School of Edinburgh, Law joined the family business at the age of 14 and studied the banking business until the age of 17, when his father died (in 1688). He subsequently left the family firm and travelled to London, where he gambled, and lost a lot of money. On 9 April 1694, he fought a duel over a woman in Bloomsbury Square, London. He killed his opponent, so he was arrested and charged with murder at the Old Bailey. He was found guilty (and sentenced to death) but his sentence was commuted to a fine. Law managed to escape to Amsterdam (c. 1695). For ten years he moved around Europe as a professional gambler and financial speculator.

In 1705 John Law (aged 33) returned to Scotland and involved himself in the debates leading up to the Treaty of Union (of England and Scotland) that

7 Laissez-Faire and John Law's Premature Invention ... 75

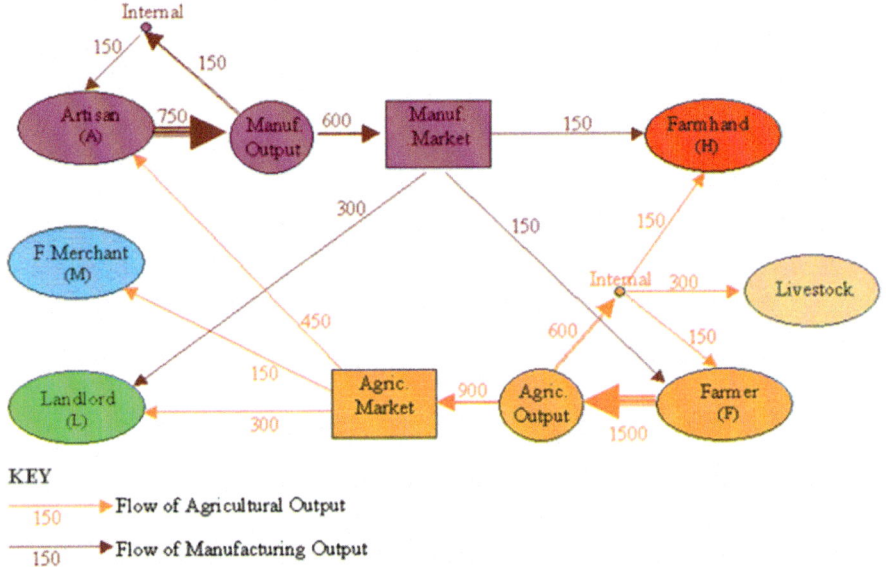

Fig. 7.1 Quesnay's economic table—Wikipedia

Fig. 7.2 François Quesnay, one of the leaders of the physiocratic school of thought—Wikipedia

created Great Britain, signed in 1707. He wrote a pamphlet entitled "Two Overtures Humbly Offered to His Grace John Duke of Argyll, Her Majesties High Commissioner, and the Right Honourable the Estates of Parliament" (1705). There he proposed a scheme for establishing a new national bank for Scotland, to create and increase instruments of credit and the issue of banknotes backed by land, gold, or silver.

Law's proposals for creating a national bank in Scotland were rejected, so he returned to Amsterdam where he gambled (privately but profitably) for several years and thought about financial economics. He also wrote "Money and trade considered, with a proposal for supplying the Nation with money", 1712.

In 1712 Antoine Crozat, Marquis du Chatel (1655–1738) was the most important French actor in the slave trade, and the richest man in France at the end of the reign of Louis XIV. He had amassed a fortune valued at twenty million pounds, a considerable sum for the time. The Kingdom of France had controlled the Louisiana territory from 1699, but Louis XIV, was no longer able to maintain Louisiana as a royal colony. He granted Crozat a 15 year monopoly on trade with French Louisiana, where "people of color" who had fled Santo Domingo, buccaneers and trappers lived. Crozat created the Louisiana Company to exploit this monopoly and make it profitable. From 1712 to 1717, Crozat was the majority owner and director of the company, in which was he invested 0.6 to 0.7 million pounds, mainly on fruitless searches for precious metals.

Meanwhile John Law had the idea of stimulating industry by replacing gold with paper credit. Then, increasing the supply of credit, and reducing the national debt by replacing it with shares in profitable future economic ventures. He originated ideas such as the scarcity theory of value and the real bills doctrine. He held that money creation stimulated an economy, paper money was preferable to metal, and dividend-paying shares as a superior form of money. The term "millionaire" was coined for beneficiaries of Law's scheme.

In 1714, Law moved to Paris and made his home in Place Louis-le-Grand, where he became a regular in high-stakes gambling parties attended by only the most affluent of Paris. His tall stature and elegant dress allowed Law to charm his way across Europe's financial hubs, from Amsterdam to Venice. At home, he hosted and entertained various Parisian notables. One of those was the Duke of Orleans.

The wars, especially the war of Spanish Succession, waged by Louis XIV had left the country completely wasted, both economically and financially.

The resultant shortage of precious metals led to a shortage of coins in circulation. That, in turn, limited the production of new coins. With the death of Louis XIV in 1715, seventeen months after Law's arrival, the Duke of Orleans finally presented John Law with the opportunity to display his ingenuity. John law set up the Banque Générale Privée ("General Private Bank"), in 1716 to issue paper money. It was one of only six such banks to have issued paper money back then, joining Sweden (the first, in 1668), England, the Netherlands, Venice, and Genoa.

On 1 May 1716, Law presented a modified version of his centralized bank plan to the private Banque Générale, to allow investors to supply one-fourth of an investment in currency (silver coins) and three fourths in defunct French government bonds. The second key feature of the proposal centered on the premise that this private bank was able to issue its own currency supposedly backed by gold. This enabled the currency to be redeemed by the weight of silver from the original deposit instead of the fluctuating value of the paper livre (which had been devaluing rapidly in relation to silver).

Law's very bold idea was to convert the enormous unpayable debt of the kingdom of France (defunct bonds) into implicit backing for shares of the Compagnie d'Occident (which soon became the Mississippi Company). It had a nominal capital of 100 million pounds, divided into 200,000 shares re-payable in those defunct French state bonds (that might be revalued). In 1719. The company conducted a modest settlement program by recruiting French settlers to locate in the Louisiana territory. Unemployed persons, convicts and prostitutes were also sent to the Louisiana Territory.

In 1717 Antoine Crozat gave up and sold the Mississippi Company to John Law's Banque Générale, though retaining some shares. On August 23, 1717 John Law, obtained the "retrocession" of the privileges of the Louisiana Company and the tobacco farm (another one of Crozat's worthless monopolies) to create the Law system. Control of trade with Louisiana and its 700 inhabitants was the only real asset of the Compagnie des Indes.

In December 1718 The Banque Générale Privée was "nationalized", at Law's request. Three-quarters of its capital consisted of government bills and government-accepted notes, effectively making it the nation's first central bank. Backed only partially by silver, it was a fractional reserve bank. From this new banking platform, Law was able to start to create the monopoly companies he envisioned by having France bankroll the endeavor with 100 million livres in the form of company stock. The subsequent founding of the Mississippi Company, later renamed the Occident Company and eventually part of the Company of the Indies, was financed in the same way as the Banque Générale.

In 1719, the French government allowed John Law to issue 50,000 new shares in the Mississippi Company at 500 livres with just 75 livres down and the rest due in seventeen additional monthly payments of 25 livres each. The share price rose to 1000 livres before the second instalment was even due, and ordinary citizens flocked to Paris to participate.

In 1719 Law refinanced the bankrupt French Indies companies. (His nephew, Jean Law de Lauriston, was later Governor-General of Pondicherry.) More or less simultaneously, Law became the architect of what would later be known as the Mississippi Bubble, an event that would begin with consolidating the trading companies of Louisiana into a single monopoly (The Mississippi Company), and ended with the collapse of the Banque Générale and subsequent devaluing of the Mississippi Company's shares.

In October 1719 Law's Company lent the French state 1.5 billion livres at 3% to pay off the national debt, a transaction funded by issuing a further 300,000 shares in the company. Between May and December 1719 the market price of a share rose from 500 to 10,000 livres and continued rising into early 1720, supported by Law's 4% dividend promise.

In the early months of 1720 John Law was appointed Controller General of Finances, directly under the regent, Duc Philippe d'Orléans, effectively giving him control over external and internal commerce. The rapid ascension of this new global monopoly led to massive speculation and stock prices ballooned to over sixty times their original value. As Controller General, Law instituted many beneficial reforms, some of which had lasting effect, while others were soon abolished. He tried to break up large land-holdings to benefit the peasants; he abolished internal road and canal tolls; he encouraged the building of new roads, the starting of new industries (even importing artisans but mostly by offering low-interest loans), and the revival of overseas commerce—and indeed industry increased by 60% in two years, and the number of French ships engaged in export exploded from 16 to 300.

Facing accelerating price inflation, Law sought to hold the Mississippi Company share price at 9000 livres in March 1720, and then on 21 May 1720 to engineer a controlled reduction in the value of both notes and the shares, a measure that was itself reversed six days later. Speculation gave way to panic as people flooded the market with future shares trading as high as 15,000 livres per share, while the shares themselves remained at 10,000 livres each.

By May 1720, prices fell to 4000 livres per share, a 73% decrease within a year. The rush to convert paper money to coins led to sporadic bank hours and riots. The company's shares were ultimately rendered worthless, and initially inflated speculation about their worth led to widespread financial stress, which saw Law dismissed at the end of 1720 from his sinecure as Controller General and his post as Chief Director of the Banque Générale. It was under the cover of night that John Law left Paris some seven months later, leaving all of his substantial property assets in France, including the Place Vendôme and at least 21 châteaux which he had purchased over his years in Paris, for the repayment of personal creditors.

Its chaotic rise and collapse has been compared to the seventeenth century tulip mania in Holland. The Mississippi bubble was followed not quite coincidentally by the South Sea bubble in England, which certainly borrowed some ideas from it. Law was a Scotsman to begin with, and he had made his first proposal for paying off the national debt in 1705 Edinburgh, just before the Treaty of unification in 1706 that united the Scottish, Welsh and English Kingdoms.

John Law's creation was a private bank that—after "nationalization"—became the Central Bank of France (1717). He financed it from the sale of shares in a speculative enterprise: namely the proposed economic development of the French territories in North America. This enterprise and the accompanying share sale, became known as the "Mississippi Bubble". By contrast, the shareholders of the Bank of England (BoE) were a small group of wealthy Whig grandees who subsequently controlled the British money supply and, indirectly, the government. Today the idea of financing future national economic growth by selling government-backed bonds to anyone who wants to buy, is standard practice. In John Law's day it was new.

In summary, John Law, a Scottish economist, came up with a very modern idea for paying off the national debt of France. His idea was to monetize financial "futures". He did this specifically by selling shares to the public in a newly created royal corporation. Its assets were a French government guaranteed trading monopoly in New France called The Mississippi Company. (The area was later acquired from France by the US government in the "Louisiana Purchase" of 1804.) The cash from the sale of those Mississippi Company shares was used to purchase defunct government bonds, thus "paying off the debt", as promised.

The idea was extremely popular and the market price of the shares rose rapidly to a peak. But like all bubbles, it collapsed when early investors started cashing in and the number of potential new investors declined. The Mississippi Company had no actual trading business when it was created, so there was no underlying money-making asset except the promise of big profits in the indefinite future. The collapse of the bubble was blamed on John Law, and he had to leave Paris (and France) or be lynched. But the asset was real

Fig. 7.3 Portrait of John Law by Alexis Simon Belle—Wikimedia

and valuable. The real problem was the absence of regulation on the trading of those shares, coupled with highly unrealistic expectations (Fig. 7.3).

The so-called South Sea Company (with a monopoly on English trade with the Spanish colonies of South America) was created in London, across the Channel, in the same year (1720). It was based on the same idea of paying off the government debt by exchanging bonds for shares. It was also a bubble, with a spectacular rise in the share price, followed by a spectacular fall. But the South Sea company did not fail completely, because it actually had a profitable maritime business (namely the slave trade). The South Sea Company survived into the nineteenth century.

French king Henry IV authorized the first Compagnie des Indes Orientales, in 1604, granting the firm a 15-year monopoly of the Indies trade. This was not a joint-stock corporation. The 15 year monopoly expired in 1619, just as the 30 Year's War was getting started and the French Government at the time was mainly concerned with staying out of that conflict. The *Compagnie des Indes Orientales* was reformed by Cardinal Richelieu in 1642, but still as an inactive arm of the state. It was revived yet again by Jean Baptiste Colbert (1619–1683) in 1664 with "Sun King" Louis XIV's support, and this time it was part of Louis XIV's foreign policy.

The initial capital (in 1664) of the revamped Compagnie des Indes Orientales was 15 million livres, divided into shares of 1000 livres apiece. Louis

XIV funded the first 3 million livres of investment, against which losses in the first 10 years were to be charged. The initial stock offering quickly sold out, as courtiers of Louis XIV recognized that it was in their interests to support the King's overseas initiative. In 1664 the Compagnie des Indes Orientales was granted a 50-year monopoly on French trade in the Indian and Pacific Oceans, a region stretching from the Cape of Good Hope to the Straits of Magellan. The French monarch also granted the Company a concession in perpetuity for the island of Madagascar, as well as any other territories it could conquer.

The Company failed to found a successful colony on Madagascar, but was able to establish ports on the nearby islands of Bourbon and Île-de-France (today's Réunion and Mauritius). By 1714, when the 50 year trading monopoly expired, it had established itself in India, but the firm was near bankruptcy. In the same year the Compagnie des Indes Orientales was combined, under the direction of John Law, with other French trading companies to form the Compagnie Perpétuelle des Indes. The reorganized corporation resumed its activities, in the midst of the chaos resulting from John Law's Mississippi ….It ceased operations in 1769.

By the middle of the eighteenth century, the British parliamentary government needed revenues to pay the interest it owed to the Bank of England. The need for gold as a monetary base for the pound sterling—strongly advocated by John Locke—was acute. This drove the second version of the so-called "mercantile" policy, under which England exported manufactured goods to its colonies only in exchange for payment in bullion (gold). In 1764 Parliament passed the Currency Act forbidding the American Colonies from printing their own money and requiring all taxes to be paid in gold or silver. (This was because of the continuous drain of silver to China and gold to India, to pay for tea and silk, as noted already).

As we know now, and should have been obvious then, the British protectionist mercantile policy combined with the Currency Act of 1764 was ruinous for the American colonies. It was especially hard on New England, which had no gold or silver mines, was prevented from domestic manufacturing of goods that were exported by the mother country, and had to compete in export markets (e.g. for whale oil or fish) with the mother country itself. The Townshend Acts (to tax the American Colonies in order to pay the cost of governors and judges) contributed to the conflict of interest. This foolish and self-destructive combination of policies was the primary underlying motivation for the Declaration of Independence and the American Revolution (Chapter 5.1–5.2). The American Revolution was followed in short order by the French Revolution, the Napoleonic era and the industrial revolution.

The first example of the circular view of economics that is commonplace today, is a diagram, by Richard Cantillon (1690 ?–1734), a French-Irish banker, who made a personal fortune by questionable financial practices. (He may have been murdered by one of his victims). An influential author of physiocracy, he spent most of his life in Paris, where he practiced as a banker. He left a theoretical work, "Essai sur la nature du commerce en général", which placed him among the great precursors of classical political economy along with Francois Quesnay (1694–1774) and the other physiocrats, He is now regarded as one of the most significant authors who mark the transition from mercantilism to classical economics.

His work (pub. 1830) was surprisingly sophisticated. It shows the economy as a circular flow system, with money and goods flowing in opposite directions. It introduces labor as an activity and "work" as the result of that activity. This is consistent with the thermodynamic definition of work, discussed later in this chapter. It also introduces "entrepreneurs" (capitalists) as a separate category of actors, also consistent with current ideas. In fact it distinguishes active capitalists who make decisions and take risks, from passive capitalists (e.g. landowners) who collect land-rents from farmers and convert commodities into "goods". (The latter conversion is unclear from the diagram). Since being "rediscovered" by Jevons (in 1881) Cantillon is now regarded as an important economic theorist, although he was forgotten for many years (Fig. 7.4).[1]

The picture above (Figure) suggests an equation. In words: Total economic output can be expressed in two ways, either as the sum total of monetary flows (expenditures) in exchange for goods (and services) received by all consumers or as the sum total of payments to the producers of those goods and services (wages, profits, rents).

This idea is easier to grasp if producers of goods (entrepreneurs and capitalists) are grouped on one side—say, the left—and consumers (workers) are grouped on the other side, the right. That way, we can also imagine that the monetary payments are divided into two categories, payments for work and payments for the services of capital stock (tools, buildings, animals, and land itself). Payments for work are classified as "wages" for "labor", while other payments include taxes to the government, interest on monetary debt,

---

[1] As a matter of interest, though irrelevant for this book, Cantillon worked with John Law, and helped to create the "Mississippi Bubble", which made him wealthy but also made him a lot of enemies. (There is even some suspicion that he may have been murdered by those enemies, or—even more interesting—possibly faked his own death to escape them.).

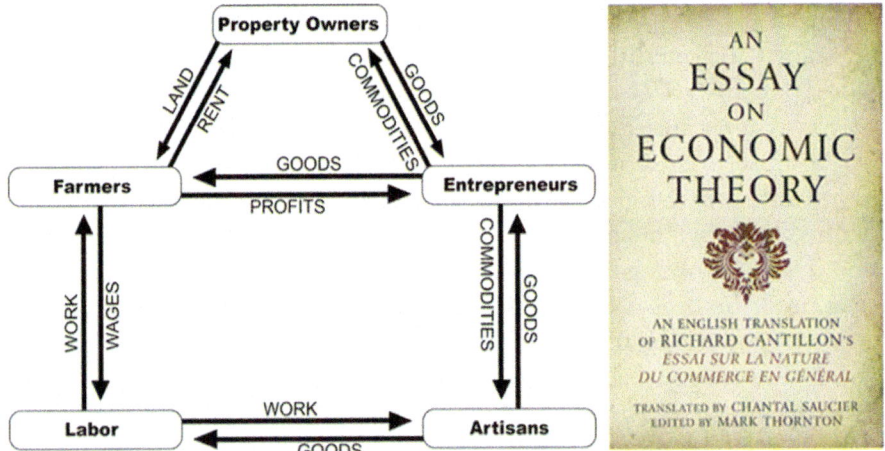

Fig. 7.4 Richard Cantillon's economic table—Wikipedia

rent (to landowners), royalties (to owners of other property) plus payments to repair or replace depreciated or obsolete capital. Anything left over after those unavoidable payments is "profit".

In Cantillon's lifetime property owners (landowners) were a different class of society entitled to receive rents for use of the land—by farmers—but otherwise contributing nothing to production. Government was an association of the property owners providing protection for the landowners and (later) for traders. Modern functions of government came gradually, as the middle class developed and the franchise—those entitled to vote—increased. By the mid-nineteenth century land had become only one, and a minor one, of the capital goods used to produce goods (and services). Marx regarded capital goods as the product of work done in the past. He regarded profits as economic surplus that should be owned, in common, by all workers.

During the Enlightenment, after Descartes, Newton, and Leibnitz, European thinkers began seeking "laws"—comparable to Newton's laws in physics—governing all aspects of life, including human interactions. They believed that a "natural law" exists and that it can and should be discovered. Hence, the failures of government systems are moral failures of those that implement the laws.

As noted previously, Thomas Hobbes postulated a "state of nature," before any government or laws, as a starting point to consider the question. In this time, life would be "war of all against all." Further, "In such condition, there is no place for industry; because the fruit thereof is uncertain… continual fear and danger of violent death, and the life of man solitary, poor, nasty, brutish, and short." One of Hobbes' school (so to speak) was Bernard

Mandeville (1670–1733). Mandeville was an Anglo-Dutch moral philosopher known for one little book "The Fable of The Bees: or, Private Vices, Publick Benefits" (1714). It consists of the satirical poem The Grumbling Hive: or, Knaves turn'd Honest, which was first published anonymously in 1705; a prose discussion of the poem, called "Remarks"; and an essay, An Enquiry into the Origin of Moral Virtue. In 1723, a second edition was published with two new essays.

In "The Grumbling Hive", Mandeville describes a bee community that thrives until the bees decide to live by honesty and virtue. As they abandon their desire for personal gain, the economy of their hive collapses, and they go on to live simple, "virtuous" lives in a hollow tree. Mandeville's implication—that private vices create social benefits—offended many enlightenment thinkers, who thought it scandalous. Mandeville's social theory and the thesis of the book, was that "contemporary society is an aggregation of self-interested individuals necessarily bound to one another not by shared civic commitments or a social contract (which came later) but, paradoxically, by negative feelings of envy, competition and mutual exploitation". Mandeville argued that society's overall wealth is the cumulative result of individual vices. Part of the problem was that, in his day, moral virtue was widely confused with Puritanism, or Quakerism, which were signified by rejection of decorative clothing, jewelry, games, dancing, singing (except religious hymns), drinking wine, or anything done for "fun". (One of the author's grandparents—Southern Baptists on one side and Quakers on the other side—were brought up like that.)

Mandeville's challenge to the popular idea of Christian virtue—in which only unselfish behavior is virtuous—caused a controversy that lasted through the eighteenth century and influenced thinkers in moral philosophy and economics. The Fable also influenced ideas about the division of labor and the free market (laissez-faire). The philosophy of "utilitarianism" (Bentham, Mill) was advanced by Mandeville's critics, to defending alternative views of virtue. His work especially influenced Scottish Enlightenment thinkers such as Francis Hutcheson, David Hume, and Adam Smith (Fig. 7.5).

The physiocrats made a significant contribution in their emphasis on productive work as the source of national wealth. This contrasted with earlier schools, in particular mercantilism, which often focused on the ruler's wealth, accumulation of gold, or the balance of trade. Whereas the mercantilist school of economics held that value in the products of society was created at the point of sale, by the seller exchanging his products for more money than the products had "previously" been worth, the physiocratic school of economics was the first to see labor as the sole source of value. However, for

Fig. 7.5 Mandeville's Fable of the Bees—Wikipedia

the physiocrats, only agricultural labor created this value in the products of society. For the physiocrats, all "industrial" and non-agricultural labor were "unproductive appendages" to agricultural labor.

In 1773, "An act to regulate the importation and exportation of corn" repealed Elizabethan controls on grain speculation; but also shut off exports and allowed imports when the price was above 48 shillings per quarter (thus compromising to allow for interests of producers and consumers alike). The issue however remained one of public debate (by figures such as Edmund Burke) into the 1790s; and amendments to the 1773 Act, favoring agricultural producers, were made in both 1791 and 1804.

Financial bubbles still happen from time to time (there was a big one in 1929) and new enterprises still raise money from investors on the basis of promises of future profits, long before those profits are realized. In fact this is the primary mechanism for new business creation in Silicon Valley, in the United States today.

8

Classical Economics as Moral Philosophy

8.1 On Trade, Mercantilism and 'Laissez Faire'

David Hume (1711–1776) was a Scottish Enlightenment philosopher, historian and essayist. He is best known today for his influential advocacy of philosophical empiricism, scepticism, and naturalism, along with Francis Bacon, Thomas Hobbes, John Locke, and George Berkeley. In A Treatise of Human Nature (1739–40), Hume strove to create a naturalistic science of man based on experience and psychology. Hume argued that inductive reasoning and belief in causality cannot be justified rationally; instead, they result from custom and mental habit. We never actually perceive that one event causes another but only experience the "constant conjunction" of events. He believed that to draw any causal inferences from past experience, it is necessary to assume that the future will resemble the past, an assumption that cannot be based on prior experience.

An opponent of Descartes and other philosophical rationalists, Hume held that passions rather than reason govern human behavior. He is famous for arguing that "Reason is, and ought only to be the slave of the passions." Hume held that ethics are based on emotion or sentiment rather than abstract moral principle. He sought naturalistic explanations of moral phenomena. He was the first philosopher to enunciate the "is–ought" problem, meaning that a statement of fact alone ("is") is not enough to imply a normative conclusion of what ought to happen.

Hume also denied that humans have an actual conception of the "self". He argued that we experience only a bundle of sensations, and that the "self" is nothing more than this bundle of causally-linked perceptions. Hume's theory of free will takes causal determinism as fully compatible with human freedom. His views on philosophy of religion, including his rejection of miracles and the argument from design for God's existence, were especially controversial for their time. Immanuel Kant credited Hume as the inspiration who had awakened him from his "dogmatic slumbers."

Regarding mercantilism, Hume believed that trade surpluses, by increasing the quantity of money in the territory, will caused a rise in wages and prices and thus decrease competitiveness. The reduced competitiveness will induce a trade deficit. (This was an early version of Hence, trade balances adjust naturally it is useless to continue demanding a surplus by legal or artificial means (the essence of mercantilism). Hence the mercantilist laws were unnecessary and counter-productive.

Adam Smith (1723–1790) continued the monetary critique of mercantilism begun by David Hume. He observed that, in England, *"the good natural effects of colonial trade, aided by several other causes, have largely overcome the bad effects of monopoly. These causes, it seems, are the freedom to export, frankly by law, almost all goods that are the product of domestic industry to almost all foreign countries, and the unlimited freedom to transport them from one place in our country to another, without being obliged to report to any public office, without having to undergo questions or examinations of any kind." Adam Smith's thesis on international trade is based on logic and reason, if not* a priori *evidence: it is prudent "never to try to do at home the thing that will cost less to buy than to do."*

The argument for free trade was also different for Smith. It was based on the notion of absolute advantage. If a first nation is better at producing a first good, while a second is better at producing a second good, then each of them has an interest in specializing in its preferred production and exchanging the fruits of its labor. David Ricardo elaborated that aspect of the theory of competition, as the theory of comparative advantage, half a century later.

In 1763, Charles Townshend—who had been introduced to Smith by David Hume—asked Smith to tutor his stepson, Henry Scott, the young Duke of Buccleuch. Smith resigned from his professorship in 1764 to take this extraordinary tutoring position. (As Scott's tutor he was paid roughly twice his former income as a professor). Smith and Scott first travelled to Toulouse, France, where they stayed for a year and a half. After touring the south of France, the group moved to Geneva, where Smith met with Voltaire and others of the enlightenment.

From Geneva, the Smith-Scott party moved to Paris. There, Smith met Benjamin Franklin, and discovered the Physiocratic school founded by

François Quesnay. Physiocrats were opposed to mercantilism, the dominating economic theory of the time, illustrated in their motto Laissez faire et laissez passer, le monde va de lui même! (Let do and let pass, the world goes on by itself!). There he also met Benjamin Franklin, whose influence led him to say that the American colonies were a nation, to be, that "would most likely become the greatest and most formidable ever in the world." This was before the Declaration of Independence. Like Franklin, Adam Smith met within the Lunar Society a generation of English and Scottish entrepreneurs whose inventions energized British society in the last quarter of the eighteenth century. Smith and Scott returned to London after their meetings with Quesnay and the physiocrats.

In 1776, after several years of dedication, Adam Smith published his treatise on political economy, the one for which he would make his fame, entitled "*Recherches sur la nature et les causes de la richesse des nations*" (often abbreviated to "Wealth of Nations". Although he was known during his lifetime for his works of philosophy, tradition has elevated him to the rank of founder of economic science. What is it in The Wealth of Nations that justifies such regard? Paradoxically, Adam Smith brought almost no new ideas to philosophy and economics in his book. Most of "his" ideas had already been set forth by moral philosophers and economists such as David Hume, John Locke, William Petty,. On trade, mercantilism and 'laissez faire'.

David Hume (1711–1776) was a Scottish Enlightenment philosopher, historian and essayist. He is best known today for his influential advocacy of philosophical empiricism, scepticism, and naturalism, along with Francis Bacon, Thomas Hobbes, John Locke, and George Berkeley. In A Treatise of Human Nature (1739–40), Hume strove to create a naturalistic science of man based on experience and psychology. Hume argued that inductive reasoning and belief in causality cannot be justified rationally; instead, they result from custom and mental habit. We never actually perceive that one event causes another but only experience the "constant conjunction" of events. He believed that to draw any causal inferences from past experience, it is necessary to assume that the future will resemble the past, an assumption that cannot be based on prior experience.

An opponent of Descartes and other philosophical rationalists, Hume held that passions rather than reason govern human behavior. He is famous for arguing that "Reason is, and ought only to be the slave of the passions." Hume held that ethics are based on emotion or sentiment rather than abstract moral principle. He sought naturalistic explanations of moral phenomena. He was the first philosopher to enunciate the "is–ought" problem, meaning that a statement of fact alone ("is") is not enough to imply a normative conclusion of what ought to happen.

Hume also denied that humans have an actual conception of the "self". He argued that we experience only a bundle of sensations, and that the "self" is nothing more than this bundle of causally-linked perceptions. Hume's theory of free will takes causal determinism as fully compatible with human freedom. His views on philosophy of religion, including his rejection of miracles and the argument from design for God's existence, were especially controversial for their time. Immanuel Kant credited Hume as the inspiration who had awakened him from his "dogmatic slumbers."

Regarding mercantilism, Hume believed that trade surpluses, by increasing the quantity of money in the territory, will caused a rise in wages and prices and thus decrease competitiveness. The reduced competitiveness will induce a trade deficit. (This was an early version of Hence, trade balances adjust naturally it is useless to continue demanding a surplus by legal or artificial means (the essence of mercantilism). Hence the mercantilist laws were unnecessary and counter-productive.

Adam Smith (1723–1790) continued a monetary critique of mercantilism begun by David Hume. He observed that, in England, "the good natural effects of colonial trade, aided by several other causes, have largely overcome the bad effects of monopoly. These causes, it seems, are the freedom to export, frankly by law, almost all goods that are the product of domestic industry to almost all foreign countries, and the unlimited freedom to transport them from one place in our country to another, without being obliged to report to any public office, without having to undergo questions or examinations of any kind." Adam Smith's thesis on international trade is based on logic and reason, if not a priori evidence: it is prudent "never to try to do at home the thing that will cost less to buy than to do."

The argument for free trade was also different for Smith. It was based on the notion of absolute advantage. If a first nation is better at producing a first good, while a second is better at producing a second good, then each of them has an interest in specializing in its preferred production and exchanging the fruits of its labor. David Ricardo elaborated that aspect of the theory of competition, as the theory of comparative advantage, half a century later.

In 1763, Charles Townshend—who had been introduced to Smith by David Hume—asked Smith to tutor his stepson, Henry Scott, the young Duke of Buccleuch. Smith resigned from his professorship in 1764 to take this extraordinary tutoring position. (As Scott's tutor he was paid roughly twice his former income as a professor). Smith and Scott first travelled to Toulouse, France, where they stayed for a year and a half. After touring the south of France, the group moved to Geneva, where Smith met with Voltaire and others of the enlightenment.

From Geneva, the Smith-Scott party moved to Paris. There, Smith met Benjamin Franklin, and discovered the Physiocratic school founded by François Quesnay. Physiocrats were opposed to mercantilism, the dominating economic theory of the time, illustrated in their motto Laissez faire et laissez passer, le monde va de lui même! (Let do and let pass, the world goes on by itself!). There he also met Benjamin Franklin, whose influence led him to say that the American colonies were a nation, to be, that "*would most likely become the greatest and most formidable ever in the world.*" This was before the Declaration of Independence. Like Franklin, Adam Smith met within the Lunar Society a generation of English and Scottish entrepreneurs whose inventions energized British society in the last quarter of the eighteenth century. Smith and Scott returned to London after their meetings with Quesnay and the physiocrats.

In 1776, after several years of dedication, Adam Smith published his treatise on political economy, the one for which he would make his fame, entitled "*Recherches sur la nature et les causes de la richesse des nations*" (often abbreviated to "Wealth of Nations". Although he was known during his lifetime for his works of philosophy, posterity has elevated him to the rank of founder of economic science. What is it in The Wealth of Nations that justifies such regard? Paradoxically, Adam Smith brought almost no new ideas to philosophy and economics in his book. Most of "his" ideas had already been set forth by moral philosophers and economists such as David Hume, John Locke, William Petty, and Richard Cantillon, not to mention the physiocrats, Quesnay and Turgot.

What gives Smith's work its real value is not its originality, but its synthesis of most of the relevant economic ideas of his time. Most of the authors who preceded him developed insights, but most were distinct from any coherent global system, and some were associated with other irrelevant economic conceptions. Smith corrected some of the errors of the authors who preceded him, he deepened their ideas and linked them together to weave a coherent theory of how things work.

Before Smith, economists had proposed two broad definitions of wealth. Smith takes up, in Book IV of The Wealth of Nations, a critique of the mercantilists, such as Thomas Mun. Many of the trading community defined wealth by the possession of precious metals and rare stones, because those things (like money) made it possible to finance wars. Precious metals (gold) and precious stones have a lasting value over time and are recognized everywhere. Those things constitute princely wealth, as Mun would see it. But for the physiocrats, agricultural production from land is the only source of wealth. All other activities are devoted only to adding value to this primary wealth.

For Smith, the wealth of the nation is the set of products that enhance the life of the entire nation, that is, of all classes and all their consumption. For him, gold and money therefore no longer constitute wealth, per se. Their utility is only as an intermediary of exchange. Adam Smith thus joins the vision of money proposed by Aristotle. For him, the origin of wealth is the work of men. He (following the physiocrats) thus laid the foundations of the doctrine of the labor theory of value, which was further developed in the following century by David Ricardo and after that by Karl Marx.

How is this wealth produced, and how can it be increased? Analyzing the economy of his time, Smith distinguished three major causes of the enrichment of the nation: the division of labor, the accumulation of capital, and the benefits of size (scale) of the market. The benefits of trade were to balance surpluses in one location with deficits in another location, thus increasing overall productivity and well-being.

On the producer side, natural resource inputs are inhomogeneous, variable in quantity (at a location) and variable in several dimension of quality. This means that output of any given product in a given place, is limited by the quantity and quality of the inputs required to make the product, in that location. Most locations have a surplus of some ingredients and deficits of others. As mentioned in another chapter, Mesopotamia was a place where agriculture was extremely efficient, and it produced far more grain (and livestock) than the local population needed to survive. But everything else, from stone to wood to metal (including the silver used for money, needed by the city of Babylon (or any other city) had to be imported. For another example, heavily forested tropical regions not near the sea could never support large populations because of the absence of salt. That absence, alone, necessitated trade with other regions.

In any complex production process it makes sense to use specialists, not for all workers to be 'jacks of all trades'. Special skills take time and practice to develop, and Adam Smith emphasized the importance of trade and specialization—"division of labor"—in his book. Human capabilities are also inhomogeneous: different people have different capabilities and skills, not to mention different needs and preferences. These differences are partly genetic, but mostly they are functions of age, gender, climate, education and income.

The division of labor meant dividing a task into individual elements, or repetitive motions. He recognized that Repeating the same motion many times is more efficient that performing a sequence of different motions.

This is because it eliminates waste motions. So, if each worker performs one motion many times, if the demand for a complex product is large enough, it is efficient to organize the production so each worker does only one thing, as efficiently as possible. The larger the market, for the product, the greater the degree of specialization is possible, as we all know today. What allows the division of labor is the existence of a market for labor-hours, not just for finished products of labor. This wasn't always possible, but as noted earlier (Chap. 3), it followed the spread of the Calvinist- Protestant "work ethic" in the sixteenth century. By Smith's time, labor had become a commodity, at least in some sectors of the economy.

Here is Smith's description of a pin factory: "*One man draws out the wire, another straights it, a third cuts it, a fourth points it, a fifth grinds it at the top for receiving the head; to make the head requires two or three distinct operations; to put it on, is a peculiar business, to whiten the pins is another; it is even a trade by itself to put them into the paper; and the important business of making a pin is, in this manner, divided into about eighteen distinct operations, which, in some manufactories, are all performed by distinct hands'. Smith (1827). ("Book I. Of the Causes of Improvement in the Productive Powers of Labour, and of the Order According to Which Its Produce Is Naturally Distributed among the Different Ranks of the People". An Inquiry into the Nature and Causes of the Wealth of Nations. University Press; Thomas Nelson and Peter Brown.)*

There was, in Smith's view: however, one serious downside to such an extreme division of labor, as exemplified by the pin factory. The problem is that it can have disastrous effects on the intellect of workers who are "dumbfounded by the repetition of gestures of ever greater simplicity". In this regard, Adam Smith anticipated one of the most effective later arguments against mechanization of production, as portrayed in Charlie Chaplin's famous movie"Modern Times" (Fig. 8.1). The "Tramp" works on an assembly line, where he suffers greatly due to the dehumanizing stress and pace of the repetitive work. He eventually suffers a nervous breakdown and runs amok, getting stuck within a machine and throwing the factory into chaos.

Jumping ahead, the division of labor was based on intuition and observation, at first. A hundred years after Adam Smith's description of the pin factory "Scientific Management", was advocated by Frederick Winslow Taylor (1856–1915) and adopted especially by Henry Ford in the period 1910–1920. Systematic time-and-motion studies were introduced during those years by Frank Bunker Gilbreth (1868–1924) and Lilian Moller Gilbreth (1878–1972). (Lillian Gilbreth, who bore twelve children, also wrote a best-seller called "Cheaper by the Dozen" in 1948). Their research was a core element of scientific management. But it was eventually phased out

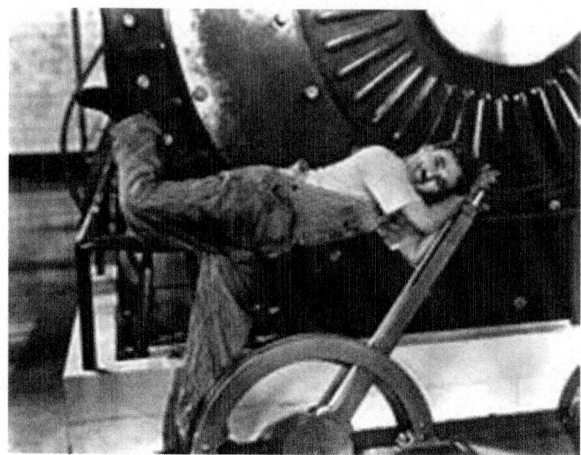

Fig. 8.1 Charlie Chaplin as a component of a great industrial machine, from Charlie Chaplin's 1936 movie "Modern Times"—Wikipedia

precisely due to strong opposition by labor organizations. The opposition was not primarily due to economic factors—Ford's workers were exceptionally well-paid—but to the psychological problem of "dehumanization" and "dumfounding", predicted by Adam Smith in the eighteenth century. A different pattern of factory work organization, based on small groups sharing a project and interacting with management, was developed mainly in Sweden.

Although scientific management as a distinct theory or school of thought was obsolete by the 1930s, most of its themes are still important parts of industrial engineering and management today. These include: analysis; synthesis; logic; rationality; empiricism; work ethic; efficiency and elimination of waste; standardization of best practices; disdain for tradition preserved merely for its own sake or to protect the social status of particular workers with particular skill sets; the transformation of craft production into mass production; and knowledge transfer between workers and from workers into tools, processes, and documentation.

8.2 Adam Smith and the Invisible Hand

Adam Smith (1723–1790) was the author of two important works: "Theory of Moral Sentiments" (1759) and "Wealth of Nations" (1776). He and his followers laid down the principles of economic liberalism. Most economists consider him "the father of political economy" though his work contained few original ideas some of which were demonstrably false.

In 1751, Smith was appointed professor at Glasgow University teaching logic courses, and in 1752, he was elected a member of the Philosophical Society of Edinburgh He worked as an academic for the next 13 years. He published "The Theory of Moral Sentiments" in 1759, embodying some of his Glasgow lectures. This work was concerned with how human morality depends on sympathy between agent and spectator, or the individual and other members of society. Smith defined "mutual sympathy" as the basis of moral sentiments. He based his explanation, not on a special "moral sense" as the Third Lord Shaftesbury and Hutcheson had done, nor on utility as Hume did, but on mutual sympathy, a term best captured in modern parlance by the twentieth century concept of empathy, the capacity to recognize feelings that are being experienced by another being.

Adam Smith is widely regarded as the father of classical economics, based on his thesis that the wealth of nations and of individuals is based on individual selfishness, plus the *"invisible hand of the market"*. Steven Leacock wrote a ditty:

Adam, Adam, Adam Smith,

Listen what I charge you with!

Didn't you say in the class one day

That selfishness was bound to pay?

Of all doctrines, that was the Pith, wasn't it, wasn't it, wasn't it Smith?"

(http://www.coursehero.com/file/11856485/3-Adam-Smith/).

Did he really that, or anything equivalent to that in longer words?

That thesis actually came from Mandeville's "Fable of the Bees", not from Adam Smith. On the other hand, Adam Smith's other book "The Theory of Moral Sentiments" began with the sentence *"How selfish soever Man may be supposed, there are evidently some principles in his nature, which interest him in the fortune of others, and render their happiness necessary to him, though he derives nothing from it except the pleasure of seeing it"*. Empathy is the name for that feeling. What Smith did believe is much more nuanced: that the motives of kindness and charity out of love to be strong enough to hold society together (Sedlacek 2011 #8355) p. 197. That is where, the economy as a system, comes into play.

The Theory of Moral Sentiments discusses the causes of the immediacy and universality of moral judgments. Smith asserts that the individual shares the feelings of others through a mechanism of sympathy. He evokes a hypothetical impartial spectator with whom the reader would always sympathize. The theses of this book were discussed widely, especially in Germany. After the publication of that book Smith began to give more attention to jurisprudence and economics in his lectures and less to his theories of morals. For example, Smith lectured that the cause of increase in national wealth is labor, rather than the nation's quantity of gold or silver, which is the basis for mercantilism, the economic theory that dominated Western European economic policies at the time.

Thanks to the laws of the market, Smith then describes an economic mechanism that must lead society towards increasing wealth. He praises saving money, as the manifestation of frugality, and the renunciation of immediate well-being in order for industry to survive and prosper. Smith saw in the accumulation of capital, that is, investment in machinery, the opportunity to increase productivity "tenfold" and to allow increased the division of labor (specialization of the workforce). In fairness, Smith also saw a downside to extreme division of labor, namely dehumanization.

For Adam Smith, and Thomas Malthus after him, the accumulation of machines implies a prior increase in demand for products and the need for labor, and therefore a rise in wages. This made sense when machines were plows or carts or crude substitutes or supplements for human workers. Smith also argued that the law of the market also governs demography. Rising wages allow the poor to support more children and thus eventually increase the available labor force, and the population. That causes wages to fall back to the subsistence and allows profit and therefore accumulation of capital to increase again. In the meantime, output has increased, while infant mortality has declined.

Smith speaks of a "living wage" that ensures the satisfaction of the physiological needs of the human being, as well as those of his offspring, which is necessary to provide the future workforce. Does this mean that living standards cannot rise? No, because capital accumulation always pulls wages up, so the very notion of the "subsistence minimum", evolves upwards. Because, as the population grows, capital accumulates, the division of labor deepens, production (and therefore wealth) per capita must increase.

There is an apparent conflict between the thesis of the *Wealth of Nations*, and that of the *Theory of Moral Sentiments*. The former postulates a moral explanation for the harmonious functioning of society, while the latter explains it by an economic mechanism based on individual self-interest, plus the workings of the "invisible hand". Of course, morality may be a partial explanation of the social tendency of humans to engage in economic exchanges, thus accounting for the creation of markets and market mechanisms in the first place.

As in the *Theory of Moral Sentiments*, Adam Smith wondered, in the *Wealth of Nations*, how a community can survives where each individual is primarily concerned with his or her selfish interest. He subsequently postulated forward a new and different amoral explanation from that proposed in his previous work: that actions of individuals are coordinated and made complementary by the market and the "invisible hand". Smith argued that the "laws" of the market, coupled with the selfish character of economic agents, lead to an unexpected result: social harmony.

How so? The confrontation of individual interests naturally leads to competition, and the latter leads individuals to produce what society needs. Indeed, high demand causes prices to soar, so it naturally leads profit-hungry producers to produce the desired good. The selfishness of individuals competing with each other is harmful, but the confrontation of egoisms leads to the general interest. If a producer tries to abuse his position and drives up prices, dozens of equally profit-hungry competitors will take the opportunity to conquer the market by selling cheaper. The "invisible hand" therefore directs the work towards the use most useful to society because it is also the one that is the most profitable. It correctly regulates prices, incomes and quantities produced.

In short, Adam Smith introduced the idea of a "self-regulating" market that the physiocrats had not suggested. Paradoxically, this mechanism, the paradigm of economic liberalism, is very restrictive for the individual entrepreneur, who is constrained both in his activity and his remuneration from it. The entrepreneur is not free to choose, very much, because failure to comply with market demands leads to ruin. In fact, "*the individual is led by an invisible hand to fulfil an end that is in no way in his intentions.*"

The idea that the economy can be regulated by amoral mechanisms was not new. Bernard de Mandeville had already pointed this out in his *Fable of the Bees*, where he explained how private vices, that is to say the consumption of wealth, turned out to be collective virtues, likely to stimulate economic activity. Adam Smith was not, however, the apostle of savage capitalism. The principle of the self-regulating market, as he described it, applied to the craft economy of his time. He was aware of the flaws, and he denounced the industrialists who, through agreements and monopolies, try to circumvent the law of the market for their own benefit.

In Adam Smith's view, in contrast to Reaganomics, it is not the State that threatens the market economy the most but rather the industrial lobbyists, and it is up to the sovereign authority to ensure compliance with the rules of the market. His version of liberalism advocates "*intentional perfection. of an unintentional sub-optimal order*". From a contemporary perspective, the thesis of optimal self-regulation of the market confuses two distinct ideas: the idea of unexpected consequences and that of the "natural course of things". It is important to distinguish "natural" in the sense of unintentional, with the "natural" in "natural course of things" which refers to an ideal.

8.3 Thomas Malthus and the Principle of Population

In the fifteenth century **Niccolo Machiavelli** (1469–1527) said: "*When every province of the world so teems with inhabitants that they can neither subsist where they are or remove themselves elsewhere ….the world will purge itself.*" (This was the basis of the plot of Dan Brown's thriller "Inferno".

Thomas Malthus (1766–1834), a cleric who dabbled in moral philosophy, publicized the subject because England in his day was suffering from deforestation, the after effects of enclosures and rapid growth of cities and slums. In his 1798 book "An Essay on the Principle of Population, as it affects the future improvement of society", that has been cited hundreds, if not thousands, of times in on-going debates about environmental issues and economic growth. The most) famous quote from that book is "*the power of population is indefinitely superior to the power of the earth to produce subsistence for man*".

Malthus elaborated Adam Smith's demographic thesis that an increase in a nation's food production temporarily improves the well-being of the population. But the improvement is temporary because it leads to population growth, which in turn restored the original per capita production level. In other words, based on historical examples, Malthus claimed that humans have an inherent propensity to utilize abundance for population growth rather than for increasing their standard of living. That view became known (to followers) as the "Malthusian trap" or the "Malthusian catastrophe".

Malthus was arguing from logic: that human demand is unlimited (infinite) whereas the planetary resources are finite. We now know that his worries were premature, if not altogether misplaced. Improvements in agriculture technology—irrigation, breeding, fertilizers and pesticides—have increased the productivity of land by a 100—fold, or more since Malthus' book was published. Of course, the industrial revolution is primarily responsible for this.

But the deeper Malthusian argument has recently revived in another form: the creation of new wants that didn't previously exist. Sedlacek traces it to the Epic of Gilgamesh p.86, in which Enkidu's satisfaction with basic needs was destroyed by the prostitute Shambat, who awakened in him new desires and estranged him from nature (Sedlacek 2011) p.218. Alfred Marshall wrote "*The uncivilized Man indeed has not many more than the wants of brute animal: but every step in his progress upwards increases the variety of his needs together with the variety in his methods of satisfying them*" (Marshall 1930) p.86. Frank Knight wrote "*It is human nature to be more dissatisfied the better of one is*" and his student, George Stigler wrote "*The chief thing which the common-sense individual wants is not satisfaction for the wants he had, but more and better wants*" (quoted by Sedlacek op cit.) What these economists are saying, is that the conventional economic wisdom—declining returns to scale—does not necessarily apply to personal wealth. This fact—assuming it is a fact—accounts for the number of recent books lamenting unsustainable global over-consumption (Daly 1991, 1989) and "Enough is Enough"(Dietz 2013).

Malthus criticized the "Poor Laws" for leading to inflation rather than improving the well-being of the poor. He supported taxes on grain imports (the Corn Laws). His views became influential and controversial across economic, political, social and scientific thought. Pioneers of evolutionary biology, notably Charles Darwin and Alfred Russel Wallace read Malthus monograph on population.

Malthus was skeptical of the popular view in eighteenth century Europe that saw society as improving and, in principle, as perfectible. He saw population growth as being inevitable whenever conditions improved, thereby precluding real progress towards a utopian society. He wrote: "*The power of population is indefinitely greater than the power in the earth to produce subsistence for man*". As an Anglican cleric, he saw this situation as divinely imposed to teach virtuous behavior. Malthus also wrote other quotable quotes, including that "*the increase of population is necessarily limited by the means of subsistence*"; "*population does invariably increase when the means of subsistence increase*"; and "*the superior power of population is repressed by moral restraint, vice and misery*".

Thomas Malthus was the first economist to worry about the availability of natural resources (agricultural land). He foresaw unlimited (exponential) growth of population, and consequently of demand confronting slow (at best) growth of the food supply. He pointed out that, as population approaches the limits of carrying capacity (for food crops), prices rise, real incomes fall, small businesses fail and poverty increases. As a consequence, death rates increase and birth rates decline, so population declines until the supply and demand for food is balanced again.

Moreover, any period of bad weather—drought or flood—can cause local or regional famines, resulting in civil unrest, civil wars and widespread destruction. (His gloomy analysis may have inspired Thomas Carlyle's characterization of economics as the 'dismal science'). Be that as it may, more recent studies by a variety of authors in recent decades, emphasizing this long-term concern, have been labelled "Malthusian". The best-known example of such a study is "Limits to Growth" (Meadows et al. 1972, 1992) (Fig. 8.2).

The Malthusian population growth (and decline) cycle has actually played out a number of times in human history, though the statistical evidence is recent. It has been collected and compiled in the last few years by social scientists and economic historians, especially Turchin and Nefedov in their book "Secular Cycles" (Turchin 2009). Turchin has introduced mathematical models of population cycles. He also argues that population peaks are often followed by periods of warfare, although the direction of causation is unclear. Causation may go from warfare to population decline as well as the converse.

This pattern is most evident in China, which has experienced a series of dynasties, separated by periods of anarchy, beginning four thousand years ago. Dynastic changes generally occurred because of uprisings triggered by food shortages The first unification with central authority came about in 221 BCE. At the peak of the Han dynasty (140–87 BCE) it's capital Xi'an had

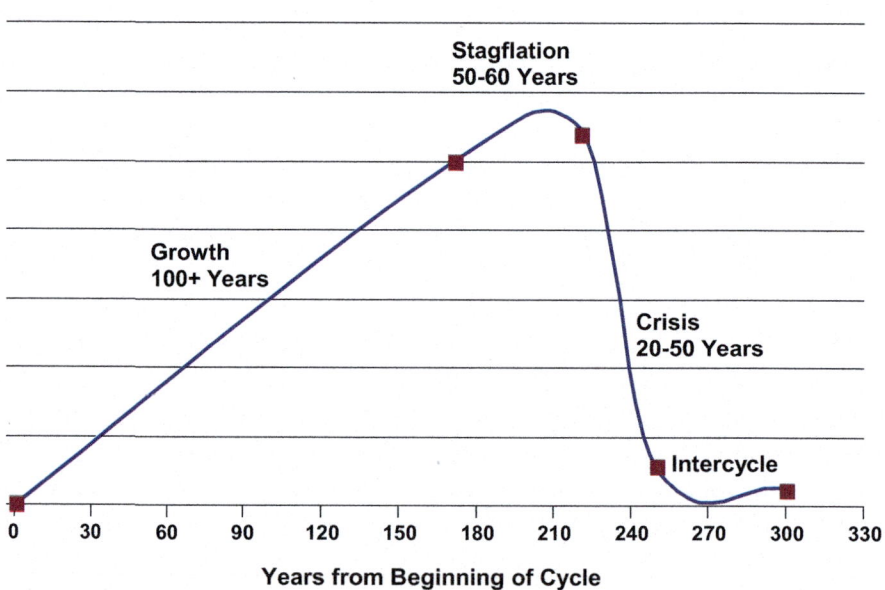

Fig. 8.2 The Malthusian : "secular" cycle—https://slatestarcodex.com/2019/08/12/book-review-secular-cycles/

a peak population estimated at 2 million, active trade with Europe (the silk road), a highly developed civil service and as much as 60 percent of global world product. But in and around 220 AD the Han dynasty broke up into three parts. (Dynastic changes did not occur on precise dates, because they usually involved military campaigns that lasted some time.) The provinces were gradually reunited from 265 to 618 AD under the Jin, Southern and Northern and Sui dynasties, reaching another period of peak prosperity and central government under the Tang dynasty (618–907 AD). But it all came apart again starting with a military revolt in 907 AD. The next three and a half centuries were violent and disunited, to say the least.

China was conquered and forcibly re-united by Kublai Khan in 1271 AD. It continued under centralized and relatively effective governments (Yuan and Ming dynasties) thereafter until 1600 AD. The population of China declined by 50 million (30%) between 1600 and 1644 when the Manchu invasions started. This series of crises corresponded to the "little ice age" in Europe (1550–1850), during which temperatures were, on average, 0.6 °C below norms, although there were major regional differences. In colder periods growing seasons were shorter, cultivated land declined, wheat prices rose dramatically and malnutrition was widespread (Parker and Smith 1997). The malnutrition has been confirmed by recent studies of skeletons. The nineteenth century saw a return to greater prosperity thanks to the industrial revolution, but the demographic contribution to prosperity is less clear because other factors were at work.

There were comparable periods of rising prices and falling populations in Europe. There was a period of rising prosperity in the thirteenth century followed by population decline (due to the "black plague") in the fourteenth century. There was another period of increasing prosperity in the sixteenth century, followed by decline, or equilibration (depending on the country) in the 17th. The 30 Years War in central Europe (1618–1648) sharply cut agricultural production, and Germany lost from 15 to 30% of its population due to famine and disease during those years. There were some extremely bad harvests in France (1693). There was another period of rising prosperity in the eighteenth century, ending with the Napoleonic wars. Harvests were poor in much of the world in 1815 ("the year without a summer"). That was caused by the massive eruption of the volcano Tomboro, in Indonesia. Some earlier famines may have had comparable environmental causes e.g. (Keys 1999) (Fig. 8.3).

It is clear from the historical evidence that the periods of prosperity alternated with periods of chaos, during which population pressure, food shortages and high prices played a large part. It is also clear that, during the

Fig. 8.3 Thomas Malthus, 1834—Wikimedia

chaotic periods, agricultural innovations of various kinds must have increased the carrying capacity of the land, if only because the population of China in the nineteenth century was far greater than it had been during earlier periods of famine. The historical pattern exemplifies Schumpeterian "creative destruction". We come back to this topic later (Chap. 18.3.)

8.4 David Ricardo and Value-Added

Since the early nineteenth century, when economic science was very young, the source of value has been a puzzle. Back to the beginning of the nineteenth century (but 50 years after Adam Smith) **David Ricardo** (1772–1823) worked to fix the issues he felt were most problematic with Adam Smith's Labor Theory of Value.

Both Smith and Ricardo worked with the assumption that land, labor, and capital were the three basic factors of production. However, Adam Smith focused on labor input as the determinant of value. Ricardo believed that, with production having 3 main factors, it was impossible for only one of them to determine value on its own. Ricardo illustrates his point by adapting Smith's deer-beaver fable that meat from beaver must be twice as expensive as meat from deer, because it takes twice as many hours to hunt down a beaver than a deer. Ricardo argued that even when labor is the only factor of production the hardships and tools of the workers will affect the relative value of the good. Countries also differ in production capabilities and in consumption patterns.

David Ricardo is remembered for his strong argument that countries should concentrate on making (and exporting) what they were most efficient at producing, while importing the rest. For England that meant selling textiles to Portugal and importing Portuguese wine. This argument was an unintended justification for England's mercantile policy at the time, which was to import raw materials from its colonies while selling manufactured goods to those colonies.

Between 1500 and 1750 most traders and some economic thinkers advocated Mercantilism, which aimed at earning bullion by running a trade surplus with other countries. Ricardo challenged the idea that the purpose of trade was merely to accumulate gold or silver. With "*comparative advantage*" Ricardo argued that industry specialization combined with free international trade always produces positive results. This theory expanded on the concept of absolute advantage. He advocated for industry specialization and free trade without mercantilist laws. Ricardo suggested that there is mutual national benefit from trade even if one country is more competitive in every area than its trading counterpart.

He said that a nation should concentrate resources only in industries where it has a comparative advantage, i.e. in those industries in which it has the greatest efficiency of production relative to its own alternative uses of resources, rather than industries where it holds a competitive edge compared to rival nations. Ricardo suggested that national industries which were, in fact, mildly profitable and marginally internationally competitive should be jettisoned in favor of the industries that made the best use of limited resources. He thought that subsequent economic growth due to better resource use would more than offset any short-run economic dislocation. (An argument for central planning?).

Ricardo attempted to prove theoretically that international trade is always beneficial. Like Adam Smith, Ricardo opposed protectionism for national economies, especially for agriculture. He believed that the British "Corn Laws"—imposing tariffs on agricultural imports—ensured that less-productive domestic land would be cultivated and rents would be driven up. Thus, profits would be directed toward landlords and away from the emerging industrial capitalists. Ricardo was concerned about the impact of technological change on workers in the short-term.

In 1821, he wrote that he had become "*convinced that the substitution of machinery for human labour, is often very injurious to the interests of the class of laborers,*" and that "*the opinion entertained by the labouring class, that the employment of machinery is frequently detrimental to their interests, is not founded on prejudice and error, but is conformable to the correct principles of political economy.*"

Ricardo contributed to the development of theories of rent, wages, and profits. He believed that the process of economic development, which increased land use and eventually led to the cultivation of poorer land, principally benefited landowners. He argued that any premium over "real social value", that is obtained due to ownership, constitutes value to an individual but is at best a monetary return to "society". The portion of such purely individual benefit, that accrues to scarce resources, Ricardo labelled "rent".

In his "Theory of Profit", Ricardo stated that as real wages increase, real profits decrease because the revenue from the sale of manufactured goods is split between profits and wages. He said in his Essay on Profits, "*Profits depend on high or low wages, wages on the price of necessaries, and the price of necessaries chiefly on the price of food*".

Ricardo's most famous work is his "Principles of Political Economy and Taxation" (1817). He advanced the labor theory of value as follows: "*The value of a commodity, or the quantity of any other commodity for which it will exchange, depends on the relative quantity of labor which is necessary for its production, and not on the greater or less compensation which is paid for that labor.*" The classical political economists found value to be created in production; since most of the cost of production, at the time, was labor from human muscles. This approach evolved into the Labor Theory of Value. Some economists looked for value in the market act of exchange. This became the Marginal Theory of Value. Both of these theories are currently under challenge by the post-Keynesians with their Sraffian Theory of Value which, like the labor theory of value, is based on production rather than exchange. Value theory is the major intersection between economics and moral philosophy.

Theories of value are at the heart of two of the major themes of economics: the distribution of wealth and income and the maintenance of microeconomic order (the marketplace). If we were all self-sufficient in our material lives there would be no problem of economic value. Each would produce and consume what he values. But most of what each of us produces is consumed by others and most of what each of us consumes is produced by others. So the *value* of what each of you produces, in terms of the conditions under which it can be exchanged for the things you consume (where money enters the picture) will determine the level of your material life.

The classical political economists, starting with Adam Smith, focused on the conditions of production in a two-class society where the upper class (to which they belonged) didn't work but consumed a lot. It was in the workshop or the factory, not the marketplace, that goods acquired value. The classical economists all adopted a subsistence theory of wages for workers (the lower class). They assumed that the cost of labor was equal to the value of the goods and services that a working-class family needed to survive. Obviously this applied only to the working class. Adam Smith had identified labor as the major factor responsible for the "natural price" of goods. But Smith's measure of labor itself varied from chapter to chapter. Sometimes it was the amount of labor needed to produce the product; sometimes it was the amount of labor that could be hired for an amount of money equal to the value of the product; sometimes it was the value of the goods and services that the worker could purchase with his wages.

Ricardo was much more rigorous than Smith. In the preface of *The Principles of Political Economy and Taxation* (1817), David Ricardo laid out the goal of his work: to develop a theory of value. He excluded goods such as "*rare statues and pictures, scarce books and coins, wines of a peculiar quality, which can be made only from grapes grown on a particular soil,*" since "*their value is wholly independent of the quantity of labour originally necessary to produce them, and varies with the varying wealth and inclinations of those who are desirous to possess them. These commodities, however, form a very small part of the mass of commodities daily exchanged in the market*".

This narrow theory of value was based on the goods and services that were typical products of competitive capitalism: "*In speaking, then, of commodities, of their exchangeable value, and of the laws which regulate their relative prices, we mean always such commodities only as can be increased in quantity by the exertion of human industry, and on the production of which competition operates without restraint*".

Ricardo was searching for an "invariable measure of value." This was an impossible goal. When the technology of production of a good or service changes, its value changes. Even gold and wheat, two candidates for such a measure (both rejected by Ricardo) will alter in value as the technology of production changes. The same is true for labor itself. If new farming and/or baking technology reduce the value of bread, then the value of labor must also fall since the worker's capacity to work can be "produced" at a lower cost.

Ricardo kept trying to find a measure of value which would not vary as the distribution of income changed, even though it would certainly vary with technological change. The best candidate for such a measure was labor. If profits rose and wages fell, or if profits fell and rents increased, it would still require the same amount of labor to weave a bolt of cloth or to build a ship. At least, so he thought.

Ricardo's theory of wages was similar to Smith's, but more impressed by Malthus' argument. He wrote: "*The natural price of labour...depends on the price of the food, necessaries, and conveniences required for the support of the labourer and his family. With a rise in the price of food and necessaries, the natural price of labour will rise; with the fall in their price, the natural price of labour will fall. ...*

It is when the market price of labour exceeds its natural price that the condition of the labourer is flourishing and happy, that he has it in his power to command a greater proportion of the necessaries and enjoyments of life, and therefore to rear a healthy and numerous family. When, however, by the encouragement which high wages give to the increase of population, the number of labourers is increased, wages again fall to their natural price, and indeed from a reaction sometimes fall below it.

When the market price of labour is below its natural price, the condition of the labourers is most wretched: then poverty deprives them of those comforts which custom renders absolute necessaries. It is only after their privations have reduced their number, or the demand for labour has increased, that the market price of labour will rise to its natural price, and that the labourer will have the moderate comforts which the natural rate of wages will afford".

Smith, Malthus and Ricardo were all wrong about the natural price of labor being based on subsistence, because their underlying assumptions about society, about technology and about human behavior were wrong. Profit occurs when a firm sells a good or service for more than it cost to produce. So we should be able to understand profit by understanding the prices of the goods and services the company sells and the prices of the inputs, including labor. However, economists needed a term that embodies the concept of the price that something would be if it were not for all these troublesome variations in demand, weather and so forth. A twentieth century economist might use "long-run equilibrium price" to express this concept. Other terms that have been used are natural price (Adam Smith), value-in-exchange, exchange value, exchangeable value and prices of production.

Today we mean value in terms of what other things the good could be exchanged for (value-in-exchange), not the inherent usefulness of the good in terms of meeting our needs or desires (value-in-use, or use value). Market price fluctuates, like the water level in the ocean. It goes up and down with the tides and the off-shore weather. Yet these movements will fluctuate around the level determined by the tides. The tides, then, are analogous to value, even though the actual price at any moment will be higher or lower than the value.

The starting point of neoclassical theories of value, is a capitalist economy in "long-run equilibrium", where all firms, workers and consumers have been able to adjust their output and/or their purchases to any and all changes in technology or tastes. Of course this equilibrium state has never existed in the real world. In that imaginary equilibrium, competition assures that the rate of profit will be the same in all industries, but capital will flow between industries, depending on their profitability. When there are no barriers to entry or exit, capital will flow from low profit industries to high profit industries. Output will increase in industries which are attracting new capital, just as output will decrease in industries from which capital is fleeing. Prices in both industries will adjust until the profit rates are in the same range.

Agricultural products presented a particular difficulty for economic theory. Smith's solution had been to make land rent one of the components of "natural price" and simply add it onto labor costs and profits to get value. Ricardo started by explaining how agriculture is different from manufacturing. When the demand for shovels increases, manufacturers can build more factories. He saw no reason that these new factories would not be as productive as the existing factories. That is, the amount of labor needed to produce a shovel will not change with demand for shovels. For them, the value of tools or other items of cost is the indirect.

But land varies greatly in productivity. It is usually the best land that is first drawn into agricultural production. Therefore, when the demand for wheat increases, the unit cost of production will increase. So will the land rent. Ricardo was satisfied with his theory: "*Happily, there is nothing in the laws of Value which remains for the present or any future writer to clear up; the theory of the subject is complete: the only difficulty to be overcome is that of so stating it as to solve by anticipation the chief perplexities which occur in applying it*".

But if there is a capitalist in the picture, who hires the workers and also provides the tools and the raw materials, the calculation is more complicated. For the capitalist, the workers will get a substance wage, paid for hours of work, and there will normally be profit, depending on the amount of capital invested and the length of time between investment and payment for the product. Whenever a product involves the use of land, there will be a third component included in its price: rent of the land, in money or as a share of the produce of the land.

In the eighteenth century, land was not a commodity and was practically never bought or sold. Ownership of land was what distinguished the upper class (aristocrats and gentle-folk) from the lower class (workers and peasants).

The workers and peasants paid rent to the upper class for the use of land to grow crops to provide for their own subsistence and to pay rent to the upper class to consume, by right. The real value of any commodity, than, was the sum of the labor cost and the profit (in the case of factory products) plus rent, in the case of agricultural products.

8.5 Marx's Labor Theory of Value

For the most part, Karl Marx worked within the framework of Adam Smith and David Ricardo's labor theory of value. The two most important differences were Marx's emphasis on fixed capital and his use of the labor theory of value to identify the *source* of profit. However, Marx used the labor theory of value to project capitalism's path in a way not anticipated by Ricardo: this aspect of Marx's thinking will be examined in Chap. 11.

That change reflected a change in attitudes. For Marx and his intellectual peers, land ownership was a fact of history, but not a natural right. The class structure of society had begun to crack, in Marx's day. It was seriously challenged in the United States of America, especially in the northern states, but in Europe the cracks were invisible to most people, including politicians, outside of academia. (A hundred years later, after the First World War, the class structure was still a factor in politics and economic life, but had become a target for reformers and a source of recruitment for revolutionaries.)

Like Ricardo, Marx started by adding up all of the direct and indirect labor used in production. So, in the imaginary equilibrium, where nothing changes, how can the capitalist make a profit? Only by being able to buy at least one of the inputs at a price below its market value. But he buys his machines and raw materials from other capitalists, who are able to sell them at their full value. So profit doesn't come from buying machines or raw materials at less than their market value. It must be that his profit comes from buying labor at less than its full value.

What is the value of labor? According to Adam Smith, and David Ricardo, The value of labor is itself the amount of labor it takes to produce the food and other necessities consumed by the worker and the worker's family (the subsistence theory of wages). Evidently labor, in aggregate, produces a Social Surplus—more than is necessary to simply sustain the working class at the level that society (the upper class) deems to be 'right' for workers. The surplus is, by definition, the profit.

Why doesn't the worker simply work on her own and keep the entire value of her output, rather than let the capitalist extract a large portion of it?

Because the *value* of any commodity is based on what Marx called the *socially necessary* amount of labor used to produce it. By virtue of law and institutions, the capitalist is able to appropriate the social surplus because the capitalist organizes the production and owns the machinery that allows the social surplus to be as large as it is.

Still, Marx was also unable to resolve Ricardo's difficulty with using labor as a standard of value. Even if Marx's version of the labor theory of value was useful at a macroeconic level, to explain the total profit that the economic system can generate, it still fails as a theory of natural price. Consider two industries, shirt-making, and petroleum refining. One uses a lot of direct labor and very little capital equipment. The other, uses lots of expensive capital equipment and very little human labor.

According to Marx's version of the labor theory of value, the natural price in each case would be equivalent to the total amount of labor used, per unit of output. The profit would be equal to the value of the direct labor minus the wages paid to those workers. The petroleum refinery would generate little profit, and since it required massive investment, the Profit Rate would be very small. The shirt-making firm would generate a lot of profit, and the profit rate would be very high.

This would violate one of the long-run equilibrium conditions, namely that the profit rate in long run equilibrium will be the same in every industry. This is one of the stylized facts of capitalism. Moreover, the differences in surplus value between the industries in the example above are not characteristic of real world differences in profit rates. (In the real world most capital-intensive industries are profitable because they are oligopolistic.)

Marx certainly recognized the problem. Unlike Ricardo, Marx was also investigating the effects of technological change on a capitalist economy. So differences across industries in labor or capital intensity (which Marx called the "organic composition of capital") could not be ignored. Labor values (the quantity of labor in a product), yield important insights into the nature of capitalism. This provides a framework for the investigation of the macroeconomic features of the economy—economic growth, the distribution of income and capitalism's crisis-prone nature. It was not so important that labor values were not the same as long-run equilibrium prices. To avoid confusion, Marx used the term *value* only when it was directly calculated by adding the hours of labor necessary for production. He used the term *prices of production* for the prices that would bring about a single rate of profit on invested capital. But it was important to Marx that labor-content bore some predictable relationship to the prices of products.

Certainly there is a rough relationship. In a capital-intensive industry such as petroleum refining, any price that will offer a normal return on investment will be much higher than the price calculated by the labor value of that industry's output. In a labor-intensive industry such as shirt-making, a normal return on investment will occur when the product price is below the labor value. One can envision an "average" industry, in terms of the mixture of labor and capital—in which labor value and natural price are the same.

Karl Marx focused on the exploitation of workers by "capitalists", i.e. those who hired the workers but did no "work"—in the physical sense—themselves. All of those pioneering economic scholars were groping in the dark. Smith and Ricardo noticed that machines can reduce the labor input, thus justifying lower prices and, thus, lower wages for the workers. Marx took this mechanism as the inherent motivation of the "class struggle" while neglecting its consequence for economic growth. What they both missed was two things: First, that human wants (or needs) keep changing as new products (like the automobile or the i-Phone) are invented and, second, that the work required for production of commodities (or widgets) is now mostly thermodynamic work from non-human sources.

Work done by humans is powered by food intake that is indirectly derived from the sun (via an agricultural crop). Work done by machines may be powered by burning wood (also indirectly from the sun) or by burning coal (from solar energy captured in the distant past) or by wind or flowing water. The amount of human labor is difficult to pin down because it depends on so many other factors. Moreover, the labor needed to produce commodities keeps declining because more and more of the work input for production—since start of the industrial revolution—is done by machines, not muscles.

8.6 The Communist Manifesto

In 1848, Marx and Engels co-authored "The Communist Manifesto" and other works. The slogan "To each according to his needs, from each according to his ability" was not in the Communist Manifesto. It was already common within the socialist movement. Louis Blanc first used it in 1839, in "The organization of work". Karl Marx made it popular later in his writing Critique of the Gotha program, published in 1875. The German original is *Jeder nach seinen Fähigkeiten, jedem nach seinen Bedürfnissen.*

There were ten "Planks" in the Communist Manifesto. Since then several of them have been advocated by Social Democrats and a few have actually been implemented by conservative governments. The following paragraphs list the most important of the original ten planks, along with contemporary libertarian commentary.

1. Abolition of private property and the application of all rents of land to public purposes. Libertarian Comment: Americans do this indirectly by devices such as the 14th Amendment of the U.S. Constitution (1868), and various zoning, school and property taxes. Also the Bureau of Land Management.
2. A heavy progressive or graduated income tax. Libertarian comment: This is a misapplication of the 16th Amendment of the U.S. Constitution, 1913, The Social Security Act of 1936.; Joint House Resolution 192 of 1933; and various State income taxes.
3. Abolition of all rights of inheritance. See Federal & State estate Tax (1916); or reformed Probate Laws, and limited inheritance via arbitrary inheritance tax statutes.
4. Confiscation of the property of all emigrants and rebels. See Public law 99–570 (1986); Executive order 11,490, Sections 1205, 2002 which gives private land to the Department of Urban Development; the IRS confiscation of property without due process. Forfeiture laws are used by DEA, IRS, ATF etc....).
5. Centralization of credit in the hands of the state, by means of a national bank with State capital and an exclusive monopoly. Comment: the Federal Reserve which is a privately-owned credit/debit system allowed by the Federal Reserve act of 1913. All local banks are members of the Fed system, and are regulated by the Federal Deposit Insurance Corporation (FDIC) another privately-owned corporation.
6. Centralization of the means of communications and transportation in the hands of the State. Comment: The Federal Communications Commission (FCC) and Department of Transportation (DOT) mandated through the ICC act of 1887, the Commissions Act of 1934, The Interstate Commerce Commission established in 1938, The Federal Aviation Administration, Federal Communications Commission, and Executive orders 11,490, 10,999, as well as State mandated driver's licenses and Department of Transportation regulations.
7. Extension of factories and instruments of production owned by the state, privatization of waste lands, and the improvement of the soil generally in accordance with a common plan. In modern America read "controlled" or "subsidized" rather than owned. See also the Department of Commerce and Labor, Department of Interior, the Environmental

Protection Agency, Bureau of Land Management, Bureau of Reclamation, Bureau of Mines, National Park Service, and DoD.
8. Equal liability of all to labor. Establishment of industrial armies, especially for agriculture.
9. Comment: We see it in the Social Security Administration and The Department of Labor. The National debt and inflation caused by government borrowing has caused the need for a two income family. Woman in the workplace since the 1920's, the 19th amendment of the U.S. Constitution, the Civil Rights Act of 1964, assorted Socialist Unions, affirmative action, the Federal Public Works Program and of course Executive order 11,000.
10. Combination of agriculture with manufacturing industries, gradual abolition of the distinction between town and country, by a more equitable distribution of population over the country.
11. Free education for all children in public schools. Abolition of children's factory labor. Schools tend to focus on producing workers with specialized skills, combining of education with industrial production.

The Communist Manifesto is now recognized, nevertheless, as one of the world's most influential political documents. The hope, (expressed by Marx and Engels was that the "intelligentsia" (i.e. the communist party) would naturally create a society that would allocate resources *"from each according to his ability, to each according to his need"*. As we know, this never happened when communists got power in the Soviet Union, in 1918–19, although (to be fair) the new regime was obsessed by the preliminary step of disfranchising the existing property owners.

9

Bentham and Utilitarianism

9.1 Precursors

The importance of happiness as an end for humans has long been recognized. Forms of hedonism were put forward by Aristippus and Epicurus; Aristotle argued that *eudaimonia* is the highest human good; and Augustine wrote that "*all men agree in desiring the last end, which is happiness*". Happiness was also explored in depth by Thomas Aquinas, in his *Summa Theologica*. Meanwhile, in medieval India, the eighth century Indian philosopher Śāntideva was one of the earliest proponents of utilitarianism, writing that we ought "to stop all the present and future pain and suffering of all sentient beings, and to bring about all present and future pleasure and happiness".

Different varieties of consequentialism also existed in the ancient and medieval world, like the state consequentialism of Mohism or the political philosophy of Niccolò Machiavelli. Mohist consequentialism advocated communitarian moral goods, including political stability, population growth, and wealth, but did not support the utilitarian notion of maximizing individual happiness.

Utilitarianism is a version of consequentialism i.e. that the consequences of any action are the only standard of right and wrong i.e. "the end justifies the means". In modern times the moral element has disappeared and concept of utility maximization in the sense of maximizing personal gains over losses has been adopted as a core aspect of economic theory. Utilitarianism is a family of normative ethical theories that prescribe actions that maximize happiness and well-being for all affected individuals. There are different varieties of utilitarianism, but the basic idea behind all of them is to maximize "utility", which is often defined in terms of well-being or related concepts.

Francis Hutcheson (1694–1746), an Irish philosopher (from Ulster), was the author of "A System of Moral Philosophy", that influenced both David Hume and Adam Smith. He introduced a key utilitarian phrase in an Inquiry into the original of "Our Ideas of Beauty and Virtue" (1725). In his words, when choosing the most moral action, the amount of virtue in a particular action is proportionate to the number of people such brings happiness to. In the same way, moral evil, or vice, is proportionate to the number of people made to suffer. The best action is the one that procures the greatest happiness of the greatest numbers—and the worst is the one that causes the most misery. In the first three editions of the book, Hutcheson included various mathematical algorithms "to compute the Morality of any Actions". In doing so, he pre-figured the hedonic calculus attributed to Bentham.

John Gay (1699–1745) offered systematic theory of utilitarian ethics In "Concerning the Fundamental Principle of Virtue or Morality" (1731), He argued that: "happiness, private happiness, is the proper or ultimate end of all our actions… each particular action may be said to have its proper and peculiar end…(but)…they still tend or ought to tend to something farther; Thus, the pursuit of happiness was given a theological basis as the will of God. Gay's theological utilitarianism was developed and popularized by William Paley. However decision rules and calculus of comparison remained vague.

9.2 Utilitarianism

Jeremy Bentham (1748–1832) is credited as the founder of utilitarianism. Bentham wrote many articles, but no single monograph covering the territory. His first book (1776) was *A fragment on government*. This was a criticism of some introductory passages relating to political theory in William Blackstone's Commentaries on the Laws of England. Bentham disagreed with Blackstone's defense of judge-made law, his defense of legal fictions, his theological formulation of the doctrine of mixed government, his appeal to a social contract and his use of the vocabulary of natural law.

In letters, speeches and articles Bentham described utility as "*that property in any object, whereby it tends to produce benefit, advantage, pleasure, good, or happiness…[or] to prevent the happening of mischief, pain, evil, or unhappiness to the party whose interest is considered*".

Bentham's main work "An Introduction to the Principles of Morals and Legislation" (1780) was published in 1789, partly translated into French, in 1802 and retranslated back into English by Hildreth as "The Theory of Legislation". Revisions were issued between 1838 and 1843. It opens with a statement of the principle of utility: "*Nature has placed mankind under the governance of two sovereign masters, pain and pleasure. It is for them alone to point out what we ought to do.… By the principle of utility is meant that principle which approves or disapproves of every action whatsoever according to the tendency it appears to have to augment or diminish the happiness of the party whose interest is in question: or, what is the same thing in other words to promote or to oppose that happiness. I say of every action whatsoever, and therefore not only of every action of a private individual, but of every measure of government…*".

Bentham's work focused on the principle of utility and how this view of morality ties into legislative practices. For him, good laws are those that produces the greatest amount of pleasure and the minimum o measure amount of pain and evil legislation produces pain without the pleasure. For quantification of the extent of pain or pleasure consequent to a decision, Bentham proposed measurable criteria of intensity, duration, certainty, proximity, productiveness, purity, and extent. By these criteria he tested the concept of punishment in terms of whether it creates more pleasure or more pain for a society.

In his hedonic "calculus of felicity", Bentham classified 12 pains and 14 pleasures, by which one might determine the "happiness factor" of any action. In general, Bentham did not favor the sacrifice of a few to the benefit of the many, although. Law professor Alan Dershowitz has quoted Bentham to argue that torture should may sometimes be permissible. Bentham says that the value of a pleasure or pain, considered by itself, can be measured according to its intensity, duration, certainty/uncertainty and propinquity/remoteness. In addition, it is necessary to consider "*the tendency of any act by which it is produced*" and, therefore, to take account of the act's *fecundity, or the chance it has of being followed by sensations of the same kind and its purity, or the chance it has of not being followed by sensations of the opposite kind. Finally, it is necessary to consider the extent, or the number of people affected by the action*".

Those words may seem excessively theoretical, but the issues obviously affect legislation, and the law. In "Principles of Morals and Legislation" Bentham distinguishes between evils of the first and second order. Those of the first order are the more immediate consequences; those of the **second** are when the indirect consequences spread through the community causing "alarm" and "danger". Today we would call them third party effects, or "externalities". Bentham says that It is not on account of the evil of the first order that it is necessary to characterize such actions as crimes, but on account of the evil of the second order.

Bentham considers, as an example, the physical desire of satisfying hunger. Suppose a vagabond, pressed by hunger, steals a loaf from a rich man's house, which perhaps saves him from starving. Can it be possible to compare the good which the thief acquires for himself, with the evil which the rich man suffers? (This is the story of Jean Valjean in "Les Misérables").

Bentham called for legislators to determine whether punishment—like torture—is more evil than the offense being punished. Instead of suppressing the evil acts, Bentham argues that certain unnecessary laws and punishments could ultimately lead to new and more dangerous vices than those being punished to begin with. He called upon legislators to measure the pleasures and pains associated with any legislation and to form laws that create the greatest good for the greatest number. He argued that an individual pursuing his or her own happiness cannot be necessarily declared "right", if such pursuits can lead to greater pain and less pleasure for a society as a whole. In his hedonic "calculus of felicity", Bentham classified 12 pains and 14 pleasures, by which one might determine the "happiness factor" of any action.

Law professor Alan Dershowitz has (mis?) quoted Bentham to argue that torture should may sometimes be permissible. However, in general, Bentham did not favor the sacrifice of a few to the benefit of the many. Kelly pointed out in "Utilitarianism and Distributive Justice: Jeremy Bentham and the Civil Law" (PhD thesis 2009) Bentham's theory of justice disallowed such an implication.

Bentham also attacked the Declaration of the Rights of Man decreed by the French Revolution, and the natural rights philosophy underlying it. In 1787 he wrote *Defence of Usury*. A series of thirteen "Letters" addressed to Adam Smith, arguing that restrictions on interest rates harm the ability to raise capital for innovation. He made the point that, If risky new ventures cannot be funded, economic growth is limited or prevented. Adam Smith did not make any changes in "Wealth of nations", but Bentham's arguments were increasingly accepted.

Bentham's opinions about monetary economics were completely different from those of David Ricardo; however, they had some similarities to those of Henry Thornton. He focused on monetary expansion as a means of helping to create full employment. He was also aware of the relevance of forced saving, propensity to consume, the saving-investment relationship, and other matters that form the content of modern income and employment analysis. His monetary view was close to the fundamental concepts employed in his model of utilitarian decision making. His work is considered to be an early precursor of modern welfare economics.

Elements of the two (naturalist and positivist) schools of international law were synthesized, especially, by German philosopher Christian Wolff (1679–1754) and Swiss jurist Emerich de Vattel (1714–67), both of whom sought a middle-ground approach in international law. Vattel's book was very influential in the discussions leading to the Declaration of Independence of the 13 colonies that became the United States of America, and the republican revolution of 1789–94 in France. It is interesting to note that Jeremy Bentham, best known as the "father of utilitarianism" wrote "A plan for an Universal and perpetual peace" in his "Principles of International Law" in 1786–89 (Bentham 1836–1843) (Fig. 9.1).

Fig. 9.1 Jeremy Bentham. Portrait by Henry William Pickersgill—Wikipedia

9.3 Benthamites

John Stuart Mill (1806–1873) was brought up as a Benthamite with the explicit intention that he would carry on the cause of utilitarianism. His "Utilitarianism" first appeared as a single book in 1863. Mill rejected a purely quantitative measurement of utility and says: "*It is quite compatible with the principle of utility to recognize the fact, that some kinds of pleasure are more desirable and more valuable than others. It would be absurd that while, in estimating all other things, quality is considered as well as quantity, the estimation of pleasures should be supposed to depend on quantity alone.*" (*Mill, John Stuart (1998). Crisp, Roger (ed.). Utilitarianism. Oxford University Press. p. 56.*)

The word utility is used to mean general well-being or happiness, and Mill's view is that utility is the consequence of a good action. Utility, within the context of utilitarianism, refers to people performing actions for social utility. With social utility, he means the well-being of many people. Mill's explanation of the concept in Utilitarianism, is that people really do desire happiness. Since each individual desires his or her personal happiness, it must follow that all of us desire the happiness of everyone, contributing to a larger social utility. Thus, an action that results in the greatest pleasure for the utility of society is the best action, or as Jeremy Bentham put it, as "the greatest happiness of the greatest number".

Mill not only viewed actions as a core part of utility, but as the directive rule of moral human conduct. The rule being that we should only be committing actions that provide pleasure to society. According to Mill, good actions result in pleasure, and define good character. Better put, the justification of character, and whether an action is good or not, is based on how the person contributes to the concept of social utility.

Critics accuse Mill of committing several fallacies: One was trying to deduce what people ought to do from what they in fact do (the naturalistic fallacy). Mill has been accused of equivocation: that if something is capable of being desired, it is desirable, i.e. that it ought to be desired. He is also accused of the "fallacy of composition": the fact that people desire their own happiness does not imply that the aggregate of all persons will desire the general happiness. This is arguably the main problem of Benthamite utilitarianism.

Henry Sidgwick (1838–1900) wrote a book "The Methods of Ethics (1874) that has been referred to as the culmination of classical utilitarianism. The main goal was to ground utilitarianism in common-sense morality and thereby dispense with the doubts, by his predecessors, that they are inconsistent with each other. For Sidgwick, ethics is about which actions are objectively right. Our knowledge of right and wrong arises from common-sense morality, not from a coherent principle at its core. Sidgwick tries to close the gap by formulating methods of ethics, i.e. rational procedures "for determining right conduct in any particular case".

Sidgwick identified three methods: "intuitionism", which involves self-evident moral principles to determine what ought to be done, and two forms of hedonism, in which rightness only depends on the pleasure and pain following from the action. He subdivides hedonism into egoistic hedonism, which only takes the agent's own well-being into account, and universal hedonism (i.e. utilitarianism), which is concerned with society's well-being.

The harmony between intuitionism and utilitarianism is a partial success in Sidgwick's overall project. But he sees full success as impossible since egoism, which he considers as equally rational, cannot be reconciled with utilitarianism unless religious assumptions are introduced. Such assumptions, for example, the existence of a personal God who rewards and punishes the agent in the afterlife, could reconcile egoism and utilitarianism. But without them, we have to admit a "dualism of practical reason" that constitutes a "fundamental contradiction" in our moral consciousness.

9.4 Say's Law of Markets: A View from an Entrepreneur

Jean-Baptiste Say (1767–1832) was a liberal French economist and businessman who argued in favor of competition, free trade and lifting restraints on business. He is best known for Say's law—also known as the law of markets—which he popularized. Scholars disagree on whether it was Say who first stated what is now called Say's law. Moreover, he was one of the first economists to study entrepreneurship and conceptualized entrepreneurs as organizers and leaders of the economy. Say was even rarer among economists for having started a successful manufacturing (cotton spinning) business himself, between academic appointments.

From 1794 to 1800, he edited a periodical, entitled *La Decade philosophique, litteraire, et politique*, in which he expounded the doctrines of Adam Smith. In 1803, he published his principal work, the *Traité d'économie politique ou simple exposition de la manière dont se forment, se distribuent et se composent les richesses*. For a while he was a tribune in Napoleon's government, but being unwilling to compromise his convictions in the interests of Napoleon, Say was removed from the office of tribune in 1804. He became an entrepreneur and established a spinning-mill at Auchy-lès-Hesdin in the Pas de Calais that employed some 400–500 people, mainly women and children.

In 1814, Say availed himself (to use his own words) of the relative liberty arising from the entrance of the allied powers into France after Waterloo to bring out a second edition of the work. The new French government sent him to study the economic condition of the United Kingdom. The results of his observations appeared in a tract, *De l'Angleterre et des Anglais*. A third edition of the *Traité* appeared in 1817.

The exact phrase *"supply creates its own demand"* was coined by John Maynard Keynes, who criticized it. Some economists, disputed his interpretation, claiming that Say's law can actually be summarized more accurately as *"production precedes consumption"* and that Say was claiming that in order to consume one must produce something of value so that one can trade this (either in the form of money or barter) in order to consume later.

Similar sentiments through different wordings appear in the work of John Stuart Mill (1848) and his father James Mill (1808). James Mill restated Say's law in 1808, writing that *"production of commodities creates, and is the one and universal cause which creates a market for the commodities produced"*.

In J-B Say's words, *"products are paid for with products"* (1803, p. 153) or *"a glut can take place only when there are too many means of production applied to one kind of product and not enough to another"* (1803, pp. 178–179). Explaining his point at length, he wrote the following: *"It is worthwhile to remark that a product is no sooner created than it, from that instant, affords a market for other products to the full extent of its own value. When the producer has put the finishing hand to his product, he is most anxious to sell it immediately, lest its value should diminish in his hands. Nor is he less anxious to dispose of the money he may get for it; for the value of money is also perishable. But the only way of getting rid of money is in the purchase of some product or other. Thus the mere circumstance of creation of one product immediately opens a vent for other products"*.

Say also wrote that it is not the abundance of money, but the abundance of other products in general that facilitates sales: *"Money performs but a momentary function in this double exchange; and when the transaction is finally closed, it will always be found, that one kind of commodity has been exchanged for another"*.

Say's law may also have been culled from Ecclesiastes 5:11—*"When goods increase, they are increased that eat them: and what good is there to the owners thereof, saving the beholding of them with their eyes?"* (KJV). Say's law has been considered by John Kenneth Galbraith as *"the most distinguished example of the stability of economic ide including when they are wrong"*. We should note, here, that his error—later emphasized by Keynes, was failure to notice the phenomenon of "leakage", i.e. that some of the income received by workers and consumers is not immediately spent on other goods in the market, but may be saved or otherwise removed from circulation. Thus it becomes the role of government to create demand if private consumption is inadequate.

In the Treatise, his main economic work, Say stated that any production process required effort, knowledge and the "application" of the entrepreneur. Entrepreneurs are intermediaries in the production process who combine productive agents such as land, capital and labor in order to meet the demand of consumers. As a result, they play a central role in the economy and fulfil a coordinating role. "When a workman carries on an enterprise on his own account, as the knife grinder in the streets, he is both workman and entrepreneur".

Say viewed entrepreneurial income primarily as wages that are paid in compensation for the skills and expert knowledge of entrepreneurs. He did so by making a distinction between the enterprise function and the supply-of-capital-function which allowed him to look at the earnings of the entrepreneur on the one hand and the remuneration of capital on the other hand. (This clearly differentiates his theory from that of Joseph Schumpeter, who described entrepreneurial rent as short-term profits that compensate for high risk (Schumpeterian rent).

Say also touched upon risk and uncertainty as well as innovation viz."*[In any enterprise activity] there is an abundance of obstacles to be surmounted, of anxieties to be repressed, of misfortunes to be repaired, and of expedients to be devised [...] [and] there is always a degree of risk attending such undertakings*". J.B. Say could have been a business school professor.

9.5 Sismondi: Booms and Busts

The first systematic exposition of economic crises, in opposition to the existing theory of perpetual economic equilibrium, was the 1819 *Nouveaux Principes d'économie Politique* by **Jean Charles Léonard de Sismondi** (1773–1842). Prior to that point classical economics had either denied the existence of business cycles, blamed them on external factors (notably war) or only studied long term trends. Sismondi found vindication in the Panic of 1825, which was the first unarguably international economic crisis, in peacetime. Sismondi and his contemporary Robert Owen both identified the cause of economic cycles as overproduction and underconsumption, caused by wealth inequality. They advocated government intervention and socialism, respectively, as the solution. This work did not generate interest among classical economists, though underconsumption theory developed as a heterodox branch in economics until being systematized by Keynes in the 1930s.

As an economist, Sismondi represented a humanitarian protest against the dominant orthodoxy of his time. In his 1803 book, "*De la richesse commerciale*" he followed Adam Smith. But in his later economic work, he argued that economic science studied the means of increasing wealth too much, and the use of wealth for producing happiness, too little. He also disagreed with other thinkers of his time (notably J. B. Say and David Ricardo).

Sismondi challenged the idea that economic equilibrium leading to full employment would be immediately and spontaneously achieved. He wrote, "*Let us beware of this dangerous theory of equilibrium which is supposed to be automatically established. A certain kind of equilibrium, it is true, is re-established in the long run, but it is after a frightful amount of suffering*". For the science of economics, his most important contribution was probably his discovery of economic cycles. He was not a socialist, but he protested against *laissez faire* and he invoked the state "*to regulate the progress of wealth*". In this respect he was a precursor of the German Historical school of economics.

Sismondi's theory of periodic crises was developed into a theory of alternating cycles by Charles Dunoyer. A similar theory, showing signs of influence by Sismondi, was developed by **Johann Karl Rodbertus** (1805–1875), a German economist and socialist and a leading member of the Linkes Zentrum (Centre-left) in the Prussian national assembly. He defended the labor theory of value as well as the inference from it, that interest or profit is equivalent to theft. He also believed that capitalist economies tend toward overproduction.

By 1837, he had formulated his social platform, and published his theory of value as three connected propositions. First, only those goods that result from labor may be thought to be economic goods; other goods, like sunlight, which do not result from labor are natural goods and consequently have nothing to do with economics. Second, an economic good is solely the product of the labor; any other view of it is to be left to physicists. No part of the value of grain, for example, is to be attributed to sunshine or soil. Third, economic goods are products of the labor that went into their composition and the labor that created the instruments that enabled that production. The value of grain, for example, is not to be found merely in the ploughman but also in the work of those who manufactured the plough. Sismondi's first proposition is wrong, of course, but it reflets widespread assumptions that are still implicit in economic models.

Mill called attention to a land-price speculation cycle in his "Principles of Political Economy" (Mill 1848). Henry George was strongly influenced by the recession of 1873. He identified land-price speculation around cities as the primary cause. The mechanism—with-holding land from development until the value has risen –followed by over-building with borrowed money, is described in his book (George 1879 [1946] #2004). Since then a variety of studies have identified an 18-year land price cycle (Harrison 1983, 2005}. Based on this research, Fred Harrison correctly (but retrospectively) predicted both the 2001 and 2008 financial crashes.

Periodic crises in capitalism formed the basis of the theory of Karl Marx, who claimed that these crises were increasing in severity and, on the basis of which, he predicted a communist revolution. In simple terms Marx's "*Das Kapital*" attributed cycles to a contest between over-production resulting in declining returns to scale (a standard assumption of most economic theory) and under-consumption due to falling wages, as producers cut costs in order to cut prices (Marx 1885,1894). Marx focuses more on the "contradictions" that lead to collapse than on the mechanisms that lead to recovery.

Theories of periodic crises are discussed later in Chap. 17.

9.6 Dialectical Materialism and Academic Marxism

During the nineteenth century, the rise of "Socialism" as an organized political movement is credited to **Karl Marx** (1818–1883) and **Friedrich Engels** (1829–1895), though Marx began as a Hegelian critic (of Proudhon, for example). Marx, in particular, was an economist of the first rank, although his "labor theory of value" failed to allow for either the role of natural capital or the important contribution of cooperation and risk-taking. He recognized the importance of natural capital, especially coal, as source of surplus value and capital accumulation. Yet, he over-valued the role of "labor", in the sense of human muscles, as this role was understood by the workers—the proletariat—who joined the movement named after him.

Karl Marx and Friedrich Engels borrowed the notion of Hegelian dialectics (without their "idealist" aspects) and developed "dialectical materialism", a methodology to explain societal change. Marxists, atheists to the core, argued that "society"—as a generality—is a misnomer, because it depends on the mode of production and has different meanings in different times and places. But Marxists did assume that, once the capitalists are gone, the educated elite could mold the old institutions to serve the new egalitarian society.

Marx and Engels together wrote "The Communist Manifesto" (originally Manifesto of the Communist Party). It was published, in 1848, just as the Revolutions of 1848 began to erupt, and undoubtedly helped to amplify that eruption. The eruption amplified the impact of the Manifesto, in turn. The Manifesto presents an analytical approach called "historical materialism" to the "class struggle" and the conflicts of capitalism and the capitalist mode of production, rather than a prediction of communism's potential for political influence.

There is no need to discuss in greater detail the historical materialism of Marx and Engels' or their rather naive economic theories, except to see its influence on later developments. The point is, they were children of their time, both of whom were prolific writer-journalists who happened to be in the right place at the right time to become famous. The adjunct "ism" could not easily be attached to the combination, so Marx, being the elder by two years, was treated as the senior. Marxism in the late nineteenth century and until the Russian Revolution of 1917 was a social phenomenon, not an economic theory. Their theory of class conflict followed by class consciousness, followed by the proletarian revolution, followed by the self-organization of a perfectly democratic society of people who worked for the community, without any profit motive, was supposedly based on a sophisticated Hegelian analysis called "dialectical materialism". It was very faulty in its assumptions, but very attractive to young idealists in the 1836–1848 period.

According to Marx, the capitalist does not buy the worker's 'labor' in a free market. If he did that there would be obvious theft, for the worker's wage is obviously smaller than the total value he adds to that of the raw materials in the course of the process of production. The worker is thus a victim of a social set-up which condemns him first to transform his productive capacity into a commodity, then to sell that commodity on a specific market (the labor market) characterized by institutional inequality, and finally to content himself with the market price he can get for that commodity, in that market, irrespective of whether the new value he creates during the process of production exceeds that market price (his wage) by a small amount, a large amount, or an enormous amount.

Karl Marx asserted that internal contradictions in capitalism arise from the need to compensate for falling rate of profit (taken for granted, not really explained or based on evidence) by cutting employees' wages and social benefits and pursuing military aggression. This contradiction was supposedly the cause of "class struggle" between the upper class minority who own the means of production (which Marx relabeled the "bourgeoisie") and the vast majority of the population who do the work, using their muscles (the "proletariat"). Starting with this premise Marxism asserted that capitalism necessarily exploits and oppresses the proletariat, therefore capitalism must inevitably lead to a proletarian revolution.

The major error of Marxism (as a social theory) was to assume that the proletarians of the world would recognize themselves as a group with common interests and then act together to overthrow the capitalist exploiters. The political slogan "Workers of the world, unite! You have nothing to lose but your chains!") was the rallying cry in the Communist Manifesto A variation of this phrase ("Workers of all lands, unite") is also inscribed on Marx's tombstone. The essence of the slogan is that members of the working classes throughout the world should cooperate to defeat capitalism and achieve victory in the class conflict. Marx and Engels thought that this socialist revolution was inevitable. The fact that spontaneous revolts did occur from time to time in Europe (notably in Paris (1789–94, 1830–32, 1848 and 1871) was misinterpreted by both the Marxists and by their opponents, as confirmation of the theory.

Despite its theoretical flaws, Marxism found many adherents—especially after 1848—and socialist—leaning political parties were created in Europe (especially in Germany and France). After 1848 they began to gain influence, as the right to vote was no longer limited to landowners, as had been the case before the French Revolution. The franchise had not yet become universal (women were still excluded) but most factory workers and small shop-keepers could vote in the second half of the nineteenth century, and they increasingly supported political parties that adopted (some) Marxist ideas, notably the ten planks in the Communist Manifesto (above).[1]

Having no property themselves, many voters liked the Communist Manifesto's call for abolition of private property and that all property should be owned "in common". Conservatives from the land-owning aristocracy that controlled the armed forces, the (disenfranchised) Church, and the new industrialists, still saw common interests. For all of them, socialism was a serious threat to their hold on power.

What happened in the 1880s in Germany was a strategy invented by Bismarck and the conservatives—and subsequently throughout the western world (except the United States)—was the creation and establishment of social democracy, beginning with national health insurance, accident and

---

[1] The fact that this equated ownership "in common" with ownership by the State, which meant (in effect) ownership by the small group of unelected leaders of the communist party running the system, was not obvious at first. The terrible flaw in that assumption only became evident when it was put into practice in Russia after the 1917 Bolshevik Revolution.

disability insurance and retirement pensions. Those programs gave the propertyless people of the "working class" a set of legal rights that gave them a stake in the system. That stake has grown over time (thanks to elections) and it has significant monetary value (and monetary cost). Did any scholar in 1890 see this coming? We know of none. Where is this trend going? The obvious answer is some version of the "Welfare State" and the universal basic income (UBI).

The first academic refutation of Marxist theory was "The Marxian Theory of Value. Das Kapital: a criticism" (1884), by Philip Wicksteed. It was followed by "The Jevonian criticism of Marx: a rejoinder" (in 1885) and the work of Böhm-Bawerk, "Zum Abschluss des Marxschen Systems" (1896). The Marxist responses were Rudolf Hilferding's Böhm-Bawerk's "Marx-Kritik" (1904) and "The Economic Theory of the Leisure Class" (1914) by Thorstein Veblen.

Karl Marx died before marginalism became the interpretation of economic value accepted by mainstream economics. His theory was based on the labor theory of value, which distinguishes between exchange value and use value. However the labor theory of value assumes that a certain amount of abstract human labor is needed to provide the work needed to produce every commodity. The exchange value is the price where supply and demand (in a given society and context), while use value is the market value of the work needed to produce it. These debates were common in the 1890s but died away as the distinction has largely proved barren.

10

The Rise of Physics: From Newton to Einstein

10.1 Background

The next four chapters are not obviously linked to economics, at first sight. But they are linked. Here we quote from a book, about the history of economics, entitled "*More Heat than Light*" (Mirowski 1989). At the beginning of the book the author says" *My first task is to convince the reader …that there is no way of understanding economics and social theory in the twentieth century without understanding 'energy' in some detail,.…and within a familiarity with the historical development of the energy concept. It will subsequently prove useful to see that the energy concept traced a trajectory from being thought of as a substance to being regarded as a mathematical artifact of a field to being just another way to express a symmetry* (p.11). We agree with this sentiment.

Mirowski goes on from there to accuse Joseph Schumpeter of offering a "*breathtakingly audacious misrepresentation of both the history of physics and the history of economics.*" (p.12). Mirowski's thesis, set forth in 450 densely-written pages, is that "*physics is the dog and economics is the tail throughout the whole history of economic thought*" (p.396). We have no intention of summarizing all of those pages, or interpreting them, except to say that it is all about the conservation (or not) of what we call "energy". It is also about "physics envy" in neoclassical economics. Discussions about the nature of energy have been diverted into arguments about the origin of the universe, the Big Bang, "black holes" and Einstein's General Theory of Relativity. Meanwhile, for the purposes of this book, energy is the substance of everything.

It is quite true that the concept of energy has changed quite a lot from the era of phlogiston. It is also true that conservation laws have a lot to do with symmetry. In fact, every symmetry in physics has a conservation law attached It is also true that energy can be thought of today as a state of the system—rather like temperature and pressure—and not a substance. Having said that, by way of warning, read on.

10.2 Variables

A number of physical concepts emerged from astronomical and philosophical thinking in the middle as ages, notably: force, velocity, acceleration, power, work, and momentum. The concept of heat, pressure and density as state variables came later). They were elucidated most clearly by **Isaac Newton** (1643–1727) in his *Philosophiæ Naturalis Principia Mathematica* (Mathematical Principles of Natural Philosophy) or just "Principia") published in 1687. By "work" we don't mean the kind of work people do to earn a living, while sitting at a desk. We mean "work" in the original sense of causing physical motion of a material object against inertia or a physical resistance, like plowing the soil, harvesting and grinding grain, or propelling a ship. Sources of power to do those things in the seventeenth century were human and animal muscles, flowing water or wind.

Newtonian physics (following Galileo) is not only attributable to **Isaac Newton** (1643–1727). In fact **Christiaan Huygens** (1629–1695) and **Gottfried Wilhelm Leibnitz** (1646–1716) were contemporaries and co-equal pioneers, albeit less famous. They all assumed that the state of the universe is defined by the positions and velocities of all the objects (masses) in it as determined by. Newton and Huygens both contributed to the science of optics, and Newton shares credit with Leibnitz for developing differential and integral calculus.

In "Principia", Newton formulated the laws of motion and universal gravitation that formed the dominant scientific viewpoint until it was superseded by quantum mechanics and the theory of relativity in the twentieth century. He wrote "Principia" to restate Galileo's inertial principle yet more precisely as his "first law of motion", along with two more laws.

Newton's three laws are as follows: (1) Inertia: every celestial body (such as a planet) remains in a state of rest or uniform motion In a straight line unless compelled to change by an external force. (2) The velocity of an object in motion changes when an external force is applied. Thus force is defined as a change in momentum. (3) For every action due to a force there is an equal and opposite reaction. (This rule has implications far beyond mechanics, or physics). There is some doubt as to whether Newton was actually the first to state the inverse square law for gravity. (It seems that Robert Hooke may have a legitimate claim on this discovery).

Newton used his mathematical description of gravity to derive Kepler's laws of planetary motion, to explain the tides, the trajectories of comets, the precession of the equinoxes and other phenomena, thus eradicating any doubt about the Solar System's heliocentricity. He demonstrated that the motion of objects on Earth and celestial bodies could be accounted for by the same principles. Newton's inference that the Earth is an oblate spheroid was later confirmed by the geodetic measurements of Maupertuis, La Condamine, and others. This persuaded most European scientists of the superiority of Newtonian mechanics over earlier systems.

In optics, Newton built the first practical reflecting telescope and developed a sophisticated theory of color based on the observation that a prism separates white light into the colors of the visible spectrum. His work on light was collected in his book "Opticks", published in 1704. He also formulated an empirical law of cooling, made the first theoretical calculation of the speed of sound, and introduced the notion of a "Newtonian fluid". In addition to his work on calculus, as a mathematician Newton contributed to the study of power series, generalized the binomial theorem to non-integer exponents, developed a method for approximating the roots of a function, and classified most of the cubic plane curves.

The physical ideas of mechanical power and work were explained by Isaac Newton when he was trying to explain the phenomenon of gravity. For this reason, the standard unit of force is named after him. A "newton" is now defined as the force needed to accelerate 1 kg by 1 m per second, every second. This happens to be the gravitational force accelerating an apple weighing 100 g as it falls from the tree. (According to legend, such an apple fell on Isaac Newton's head as he was lying in the grass, perhaps triggering some thoughts about gravity). This comment is not only intended as humor: we now know that thinking requires energy, and quite a lot of the energy we humans get from our food is consumed by our busy brains) (Fig. 10.1).

Christiaan Huygens (1629–1695) was 14 years older Isaac Newton and is properly regarded as one of the greatest scientists of all time. In 1655, Huygens began grinding lenses with his brother Constantijn to build telescopes for astronomical research. Huygens invented and patented the pendulum clock in 1657. It was by far the best time-keeping device available then and remained so until Harrison's chronometer a century later. He continued working on horology in a book *"Horologium Oscillatorium"*

Fig. 10.1 Portrait of Newton at 46 by Godfrey Kneller—Wikipedia

(1673), which happens to be one of the most important seventeenth century works in mechanics. Part from descriptions of clock designs, the book is mostly an analysis of pendulum motion and a theory of curves.

He was the first to identify the rings of Saturn as "*a thin, flat ring, nowhere touching, and inclined to the ecliptic,*" and he discovered the first of Saturn's moons, Titan, using a refracting telescope. In 1662 Huygens developed a telescope with two lenses, to diminished the amount of dispersion.

In 1659, as an outgrowth of his clockwork, Huygens derived the now standard formulae in classical mechanics for the centripetal force and centrifugal force in his work "*De vi Centrifuga*". Huygens correctly explained the laws of elastic collision, for the first time, in *De Motu Corporum ex Percussione* (published posthumously in 1703). He was the first to propose a wave theory of light, in "*Traité de la Lumière*" (1690). His wave theory of light was initially rejected by peers who in favored Newton's corpuscular theory. (This changed in 1821 when Augustin-Jean Fresnel adopted Huygens's theory to explain the propagation and diffraction of light in 1821. Today this principle is known as the Huygens–Fresnel principle).

In 1667 Jean-Baptiste Colbert, Controller of Finances for King Louis XIV, initiated a research project to develop new sources of power. He recruited Huygens to lead this effort, in Paris, and Huygens hired two assistants,

Gottfried Leibnitz and Denis Papin. In the course of this project, Huygens became interested in the mechanical "power of the vacuum" (i.e. air pressure), He had the idea of using gunpowder to produce a vacuum efficiently in a tube. In 1678 he outlined a gunpowder engine consisting of a vertical tube containing a piston. Gunpowder was inserted into the tube. It was lit, by a fuse, like a cannon. The expanding gasses would drive the piston up the tube until it reached a point near the top. Here, the piston uncovered holes in the tube that allowed the combustion products to escape. The weight of the piston and the vacuum formed by the cooling gases in the upper part of combustion drew the piston back into the tube.

Apparently, a single example of this engine was built in 1678 or '79 using a cannon barrel as the cylinder. Huygens presented a paper on this invention in 1680, A New Motive Power by Means of Gunpowder and Air. By 1682 a dram (1/16th of an ounce) of gunpowder, in a cylinder eight feet high and eighteen inches in diameter, could raise eight boys (or about 1100 pounds) into the air (See Figure below). I, but it was an impressive demonstration but commercialization was not feasible. Sealing the piston within the cylinder tightly proved to be a very difficult problem then and even now (Fig. 10.2).

Gottfried Wilhelm (von) Leibnitz (1646–1716) was, in 1673, a student-assistant to Huygens, in Paris. After 1677, he became a Privy Counsellor of Justice, to the House of Brunswick, in Hanover. He was a follower of Descartes and Spinoza. He served three consecutive rulers of the House of Brunswick as historian, political adviser, and as librarian of the ducal library. In his spare time—a great share of his time—he was an all-purpose mathematician, philosopher and political commentator.

Leibnitz differed from Newton in that he didn't believe in either absolute time or absolute space, which puts him closer to modern conceptions. (He also didn't believe in atoms). According to Newton's substantivalism, space and time are entities in their own right, existing independently of things. Leibniz's relationism, in contrast, describes space and time as systems of relations that exist between objects. The rise of general relativity and subsequent work in the history of physics has supported Leibniz's perspective. Indeed, Albert Einstein said, once, that he preferred Leibnitzian physics to Newtonian physics.

Leibnitz developed the ideas of differential and integral calculus, simultaneously and independently of Isaac Newton, as historians now believe, although he lost a demand for retraction of Newton's charge of intellectual theft. However, Leibniz's contributions to the development of calculus have had practical consequences for physical theory. Leibniz's biographers have identified seven fundamental logical-philosophical principles that he

Fig. 10.2 Portrait of Huygens by Caspar Netscher (1671) in Museum Boerhaave, Leiden—Wikimedia

invoked at one time or another during his career: (1) ***Identity/contradiction***. If a proposition is true, then its negation is false and vice versa. (2) ***Identity of indiscernibles***. Two distinct things cannot have all their properties in common. If every predicate possessed by X is also possessed by Y and vice versa, then entities X and Y are identical; to suppose two things indiscernible is to suppose the same thing under two names. This is often referred to as Leibniz's Law. It has attracted considerable controversy and criticism, especially from corpuscular philosophy and quantum mechanics. (3) ***Sufficient reason***. "*There must be a sufficient reason for anything to exist, for any event to occur, for any truth to obtain.*" (4) ***Pre-established harmony***. "[T]*he appropriate nature of each substance brings it about that what happens to one corresponds to what happens to all the others, without, however, their acting upon one another directly.*" (Discourse on Metaphysics, XIV) A dropped glass shatters because it "knows" it has hit the ground, and not because the impact with the ground "compels" the glass to break. (5) ***Law of Continuity***. *Natura non facit saltus* (literally, "Nature does not make jumps"). (6) ***Optimism***. "*God *assuredly always chooses the best."* (7) **Plenitude**. Leibniz believed that the "best of all possible worlds" would actualize every genuine possibility, and argued in Théodicée that this world will contain all possibilities, with our finite experience of eternity giving no reason to dispute nature's perfection. (This view was satirized by Voltaire).

Leibnitz's *vis viva* (Latin for "living force") was defined as mv^2, twice the modern formula for kinetic energy. He realized that the total energy would be conserved in certain mechanical systems, so he considered it an innate motive characteristic of matter. Some historians of science give Leibnitz credit for discovering the universal law of Least Action, and its consequence, the law of conservation of energy. This gave rise to another nationalistic dispute. Leibniz knew of the validity of conservation of momentum. In reality, both energy and momentum are separately conserved.[1]

By proposing that the earth has a molten core, Leibnitz anticipated modern geology. In embryology, he was a preformationist, but also proposed that organisms are the outcome of a combination of an infinite number of possible microstructures and of their powers. One of his principal works on this subject, Proctodaea, unpublished in his lifetime, has recently been published in English for the first time. He worked out a primal organismic theory. In medicine, he exhorted the physicians of his time—with some results— to ground their theories in detailed comparative observations and verified experiments, and to distinguish firmly scientific and metaphysical points of view.

Leibnitz was a prolific inventor of mechanical calculators. He added automatic multiplication and division to Pascal's calculator, he described a pinwheel calculator in 1685 and invented the Leibniz wheel, used later in the arithmometer, the first mass-produced mechanical calculator. He also refined the binary number system, which is the foundation of nearly all digital computers (Fig. 10.3).

10.3 Mathematics

The mathematics of Newton and Leibnitz was sufficient for calculating planetary orbits. However new problems inspired new approaches. One of the most important, in light of later developments in physics, was the calculus

---

[1] The stationary-action principle—also known as the principle of least action—is a variational principle that, when applied to the action of a mechanical system, yields the equations of motion for that system. The principle is used to derive Newtonian, Lagrangian and Hamiltonian equations of motion. It can also be extended beyond the bounds of mechanics.

Fig. 10.3 Gottfried Wilhelm Leibnitz—Wikipedia

of variations. Milestones were Newton's minimal resistance problem in 1687, followed by the brachistochrone curve problem raised by Johann Bernoulli (1696).

Leonhard Euler (1707–1783) first elaborated the subject, beginning in 1733. Lagrange was influenced by Euler's work to contribute significantly to the theory. After Euler saw the 1755 work of the 19-year-old Lagrange, Euler dropped his own partly geometric approach in favor of Lagrange's purely analytic approach and renamed the subject the *calculus of variations* in his 1756 lecture *Elementa Calculi Variationum*. Euler founded the studies of graph theory and topology and made pioneering advances in analytic number theory, complex analysis, and infinitesimal calculus. He introduced much of modern mathematical terminology and notation, including the notion of a mathematical function. He is also known for his work in mechanics, fluid dynamics, optics, astronomy and music theory.

His more than 850 publications are collected in 92 *quarto* volumes (including his Opera Omnia) more than anyone else in the field.

Euler is credited for popularizing the Greek letter π (lowercase pi) to denote Archimedes' constant (the ratio of a circle's circumference to its diameter), as well as first employing the term $f(x)$ to describe a function's y-axis, the letter i to express the imaginary unit $\sqrt{-1}$, and the Greek letter Σ (capital sigma) to express summations. He gave the current definition of the constant e, the base of the natural logarithm, now known as Euler's number. In the field of physics, Euler reformulated Newton's laws of physics into new laws in his two-volume work *Mechanica* to explain the motion of rigid bodies more easily. He also made substantial contributions to the study of elastic deformations of solid object (Fig. 10.4).

Joseph Louis de Lagrange (1736–1813) was a child prodigy, born in Sardinia, later moved to Berlin and finally to Paris. He was the founder of the calculus of variations, with Euler, and of the theory of quadratic forms,. We owe him a special case of the theorem to which we will give his name in group theory was a mathematician, mechanic and astronomer, naturalized French.

On July 23, 1754, barely eighteen years old, he sent a letter in Latin to Euler, setting out his work. A year later he obtained a curve known as the tautochrone and laid the foundations for variational calculus. Euler was so enthusiastic about this new method that he congratulated his young colleague on his work and proclaimed that, in his opinion, Lagrange's ideas represented

Fig. 10.4 Portrait of Leonhard Euler by Jacob Emanuel Handmann, 1753—Wikimedia

the pinnacle of perfection, generality and utility. From then on he treated the young man as intellectual equal. He made other contributions on continuous fractions, and the Lagrange differential equation.

By specifying the principle of least action, around 1756, he pioneered analytical mechanics. He invented the so-called Lagrangian function, to solve for equations of motion in a complex mechanical system. In 1788 he introduced so-called Lagrange multipliers, now standard tools for analysis. He also worked on the three-body problem in astronomy, one of his results being to identify gravitationally stable liberation points (known as Lagrange points) in 1772.

He co-developed the metric system of measures with Lavoisier during the Revolution. He was a founding member of the Bureau des longitudes (1795) with, among others, Laplace and Cassini. In fluid mechanics, he introduced the concept of velocity potential in 1781. He demonstrated that the velocity potential exists for any real fluid flow, for which the resultant forces are derived from a potential. In the same memoir of 1781, he introduced, in addition, two fundamental notions: the concept of the current function, for an incompressible fluid, and the calculation of the speed of a small wave in a shallow channel. In retrospect, this book marks a decisive step in the development of modern fluid mechanics. Lagrange also worked in the field of probability theory.

Robert Boyle (1627–1691) was one of the last alchemists (he believed in the transmutation of metals) and also one of the first physical chemists. He was an open follower of Francis Bacon's philosophy of skeptical experimentation and evidence gathering. He is known primarily for his discovery of "Boyle's Law", the inverse relationship between pressure and volume for a gas. He also did some work on the propagation of sound in air. He was one of the early members of the Royal Society of London (with Robert Hooke and Isaac Newton) and eventually became its president.

Chemistry as an earnest and respectable science is often said to date from 1661, when Robert Boyle of Oxford published *The Sceptical Chymist*—the first work to distinguish between chemists and alchemists—but it was a slow and often erratic transition. Into the eighteenth century scholars could feel oddly comfortable in both camps—like the German Johann Becher who postulated the phlogiston theory and thought that, with the right materials he could make himself invisible (Fig. 10.5).

Fig. 10.5 Robert Boyle—Wikimedia

10.4 Crossing Disciplinary Boundaries

Robert Hooke (1635–1703) was an English polymath active as a scientist and architect, who, using a microscope, was the first to visualize a microorganism. He an impoverished scientific inquirer in young adulthood, but working with **Christopher Wren**, he performed over half of the architectural surveys after London's great fire of 1666. He was an assistant to Robert Boyle, for several years. Hooke built the vacuum pumps used in Boyle's experiments on gas law, and himself conducted experiments. In 1673, Hooke built the earliest Gregorian telescope, and then he observed the rotations of the planets Mars and Jupiter. Hooke's 1665 book *Micrographia* spurred microscopic investigations.[2] Investigating in optics, specifically light refraction, he inferred a wave theory of light. And his is the first recorded hypothesis of heat expanding matter, air's composition by small particles at larger distances, and heat as energy.

In physics, he performed experiments confirming that gravity obeys an inverse square law. He was the first to postulate such a law governing planetary motion, too, a principle formalized by Isaac Newton in Newton's law of universal gravitation. Priority over this insight contributed to the rivalry

---

[2] Micrographia, or some physiological descriptions of minute bodies made by magnifying glasses, with observations and inquiries thereupon, Robert Hooke, 1665.

between Hooke and Newton, who did his best to diminish Hooke's mathematical legacy. Yet In geology and palaeontology, Hooke originated the theory of a terraqueous globe, disputed the literally Biblical view of the Earth's age, hypothesized the extinction of species, and argued that fossils atop hills and mountains had become elevated by geological processes. Thus observing microscopic fossils, Hooke presaged Darwin's theory of biological evolution. Hooke's pioneering work in land surveying and in mapmaking aided development of the first modern plan-form map, although his grid-system plan for London was rejected in favor of rebuilding along existing routes. Even so, Hooke's advice was key in devising for London a set of planning controls that remain influential. In recent times, he has been called "England's Leonardo".

Denis Papin (1647–1713) was a French physicist, mathematician and inventor. In 1671–1674 he was the assistant of Christiaan Huygens, then working in Paris. Some of his ideas concerning the uses of steam may have originated then. During 1675–79 Papin worked with Robert Boyle, in London. During this period, Papin invented the steam digester, a type of pressure cooker with a safety valve. He first addressed the Royal Society in 1679 on the subject of his steam digester.

After 1685, as a Huguenot, Denis Papin had to leave France, so in 1687, he took up an academic post in Marburg, Germany. In 1689, Papin built a model of a piston steam engine, the first of its kind. This was followed in 1690 by a model device for pumping or creating a water jet or fountain. That was the first attempt to use heat directly to perform physical work. Sometime during that period Papin was engaged to make such a fountain for the gardens of a German nobleman. The project ran into difficulties (a boiler exploded) and Papin's situation in Germany deteriorated.

In 1707 Papin was persuaded by Isaac Newton to work with **Thomas Savery** (1650–1715), who had previously patented—and built—a steam pump, based on atmospheric pressure. Savery's pump was marketed for purposes of pumping water from mines, but it was only operable at depths less than 30 feet (10 m) and had other disadvantages.

Denis Papin returned to London leaving his wife in Germany. Several of his papers were put before the Royal Society between 1707 and 1712 without acknowledgment or payment. He complained bitterly about this. Papin's ideas included a description of his 1690 atmospheric steam engine, similar to that built and er put into use in 1712 by Thomas Newcomen (1664–1729), probably the year of Papin's death in utter destitution.

Fig. 10.6 Thomas Savery's two valve steam pump—Wikiwand

10.5 The Steam Engine

Thomas Savery (1650–1715) was a military engineer promoted to the rank of captain in 1702. He made his first machines in his spare time. In 1698, Thomas Savery filed a patent on a steam-powered pump, that actually worked. That patent covered any use of fire to raise water. The patent had a life of 17 years, but that was later extended to 1733, by Parliament (possibly as a deliberate effort to freeze out Papin). The extensions also forced Thomas Newcomen (who had a better idea), to take Savery as an unwanted partner (Fig. 10.6).

Meanwhile, in 1705 while still teaching mathematics at the University of Marburg, Denis Papin developed a second steam engine with the help of Gottfried Leibniz. It was a cousin of the "fireplace invention" patented by Thomas Savery in 1698. Savery's pump was a kind of thermosyphon with no moving parts, except opening and closing of the taps. During one stroke the container would be filled with steam and the piston moved up. Then the steam was suddenly condensed by a water spray and a partial vacuum was created. Atmospheric pressure then pushed the piston back to its starting point. The details don't matter. But Papin proposed to use his piston design, which Newcomen later improved, rather than to rely totally on atmospheric pressure.

Thomas Newcomen (1664–1729) was an iron-monger who Newcomen added an important feature to the Savery "fireplace" pump. The new pump was built in 1712. It consisted of a large wooden beam balanced on central pivot. This enabled the up and down motions of the piston to alternate. Steam, produced in the boiler, was allowed into the cylinder pushing the piston up. A vacuum was then created suddenly (by a spray of cold water) condensing the steam. Atmospheric pressure above the piston then caused it to descend. This movement activated the pump, which then returned to its original position by its own weight. The steam was then injected again under the piston, driving the condensate through a drain pipe, and renewing the cycle.

Savery died in 1715. By 1733, when the Savery patent expired, about 125 Newcomen engines, operating under Savery's patent (extended by statute so that it did not expire until 1733), had been installed in most of the mining districts of Britain and on the Continent of Europe:

The Newcomen engine sold with minor changes for the next 75 years, spreading gradually to more areas of the UK and mainland Europe. Its mechanical details were significantly improved by John Smeaton, who built many large engines of this type in the early 1770s. By 1775 about 600 Newcomen engines had been built, though not all were still in service.

Newcomen's engine was gradually replaced after 1775 in areas where coal was expensive (especially in Cornwall) by an improved design, invented and patented by James Watt. In Watt's engine the steam was condensed in a separate condenser, saving much of the heat. The Watt patented steam engine, aided by better engineering techniques, including Wilkinson's boring machine, was much more fuel efficient. Watt subsequently made other improvements, including the double-acting engine, where both the up and down strokes were power strokes. These were especially suitable for textile mills, and many Watt engines were employed in those mills. many more Newcomen engines than Watt ones were built even during the period of Watt's patent (up to 1800), as they were cheaper and less complicated. Of over 2200 engines built in the eighteenth century, only about 450 were Watt engines (Fig. 10.7).

After 1800 high pressure steam engines, pioneered by Richard Trevithick, in Cornwall and Oliver Evans in Pennsylvania entered the picture. By 1820 their first application to railroads had begun. And a new industry was created.

Measurement of temperature improved dramatically in the first two decades of the eighteenth century. in the Dutch Republic, **Daniel Gabriel**

Fig. 10.7 James Watt. Portrait by Carl Frederik von Breda—Wikimedia

Fahrenheit made two revolutionary breakthroughs in the history of thermometry. He invented the mercury-in-glass thermometer (first widely used, accurate, practical thermometer) and the Fahrenheit scale (the first standardized temperature scale to be widely used). The Celsius scale was invented in 1742 by the Swedish astronomer and physicist **Anders Celsius**. The centigrade scale matches its zero with the temperature of the melting ice and 100 with the boiling temperature of the water under normal atmospheric pressure (1,013.25 hPa). It is slightly different from the Kelvin temperature scale. The Kelvin scale is zero at absolute zero, but temperature differences are the same in degrees Kelvin and degrees Centigrade (Celsius). This innovation was introduced by Lord Kelvin in the nineteenth century.

In practice, the measurement of temperature can be carried out by means of a mercury column thermometer. The thermometer is placed in a mixture of liquid water and ice and the height of mercury is marked, which indicates the zero level. Then the water is brought to a boil and the point 100 is marked. The interval between the two is finally divided into 100 graduations. Unlike electronic thermometers with fixed pressure conditions, the mercury thermometer does not get out of order, its zero and its height variations remain stable.

10.6 Falsification of Phlogiston

Joseph Black (1728–1799) was the dominant engineering pioneer of the second half of the eighteenth century. Like most eighteenth century experimentalists, Black's chemistry was based on five 'principles' of matter: Water, Salt, Earth, Fire and Metal. He added the principle of 'Air' when his experiments definitely confirmed the presence of carbon dioxide, which he called 'fixed air'. Black's research was guided by questions relating to how the 'principles' combined with each other in various different forms and mixtures. He used the term 'affinity' to describe the force that held such combinations together.

In about 1750, while still a student, Black developed the analytical balance based on a light-weight beam balanced on a wedge-shaped fulcrum. Each arm carried a pan on which the sample or standard weights was placed. It was far more accurate than any other balance of the time and became an important scientific instrument in most chemistry laboratories. Black discovered the element magnesium in 1755.

In 1761 Black noticed that the application of heat to ice at its melting point does not cause a rise in temperature of the ice/water mixture, but rather an increase in the amount of water in the mixture. Additionally, Black observed that the application of heat to boiling water does not result in a rise in temperature of a water/steam mixture, but rather an increase in the amount of steam. From these two observations, he concluded that the heat applied must have combined with the ice particles and boiling water and become latent. The theory of latent heat marks the beginning of thermodynamics. Black's theory of latent heat was one of his more-important scientific contributions, and one on which his scientific fame chiefly rests.

He also showed that different substances have different specific heats. Combined with the new methods of temperature measurement, it became possible to measure heat quantities and heat flows, for the first time. The theory ultimately proved important in the development of thermodynamics as a science.

Joseph Black also explored the properties of a gas produced in various reactions. He found that limestone (calcium carbonate) could be heated or treated with acids to yield a gas he called "fixed air." He observed that the fixed air was denser than air and did not support either flame or animal life. Black also found that when bubbled through an aqueous solution of lime (calcium hydroxide), it would precipitate calcium carbonate. He used this phenomenon to illustrate that carbon dioxide is produced by animal respiration and microbial fermentation (Fig. 10.8).

In 1756, **Mikhail Lomonosov** (1711–1765) tried to replicate Robert Boyle's experiment of 1673. He concluded that the commonly accepted phlogiston theory was false. Anticipating the discoveries of Antoine Lavoisier, he wrote in his diary: "*Today I made an experiment in hermetic glass vessels in order to determine whether the mass of metals increases from the action of pure heat. The experiments—of which I append the record in 13 pages—demonstrated that the famous Robert Boyle was deluded, for without access of air from outside, the mass of the burnt material remains the same*".. He concluded that the phlogiston theory was false. That is the Law of Mass Conservation in chemical reaction, which was well-known today as "*in a chemical reaction, the mass of reactants*

Fig. 10.8 Joseph Black, the engineer's engineer—Wikipedia

is equal to the mass of the products." Lomonosov, together with Lavoisier, is regarded as the one who discovered the law of mass conservation, viz. "*in a chemical reaction, the mass of reactants is equal to the mass of the products.*" Lomonosov, together with Lavoisier, is regarded as the discoverer of the law of mass conservation.

Antoine-Laurent de Lavoisier (1743–1794), was a French nobleman and chemist who was central to the eighteenth century chemical revolution and who had a large influence on both the history of chemistry and the history of biology. It is generally accepted that Lavoisier's great reputation in chemistry stem largely from his changing the science from a qualitative to a quantitative one. Lavoisier is most noted for his discovery of the role oxygen plays in combustion. He recognized and named oxygen itself (1778) and hydrogen (1783). He supported the "caloric theory" of opposed the "phlogiston" theory and wanted to substitute the "Caloric Theory". (**Joseph Priestley**, who actually discovered oxygen in 1774 (calling it "dephlogisticated air") defended the phlogiston theory and lost scientific credibility for doing so).

Antoine Lavoisier helped construct the metric system, wrote the first extensive list of elements, and helped to reform chemical nomenclature. He predicted the existence of silicon (1787). He discovered that, although matter may change its form or shape, its mass always remains the same, thus anticipating the first law of thermodynamics (conservation of energy). However, in terms of what followed, Lavoisier may be best remembered as the author of the rule that heat always flows from high temperatures to lower temperatures, and never in the reverse direction.

Anton Lavoisier prepared a list of 33 elements in 1789. His list included both heat and light as separate elements along with and several oxides. He was instrumental in replacing the "phlogiston theory" propounded in 1669 by the alchemist **Johann Becher**(1635–1682)). Lavoisier lost his head, literally, in the "reign of terror" in the French Revolution) (Fig. 10.9).

10 The Rise of Physics: From Newton to Einstein

Fig. 10.9 Portrait of Antoine Lavoisier and his wife by Jacques-Louis David—Wikimedia

11

Energetics

11.1 Heat as Energy

None of the early economists knew enough about physics to realize that muscular work by humans and horses, power from a water wheel or a windmill, heat from a fire and power from a steam engine, were all examples of a single process: performing physical "work", e.g. overcoming inertia. They did not understand that "doing work" required an invisible substance that was first recognized around 1850 as energy. (Later it was realized that not all of energy is capable of doing work. That part is now called *exergy* while the other part is called *anergy* (sorry, more terminology.) N.B. exergy is destroyed—used up—when work is done.

Energy, the sum of *exergy* and *anergy*, is "conserved", meaning that it is neither created nor destroyed. It was not until the 1860s and '70 s that physicists understood that mechanical, thermal and chemical energy—and later, nuclear energy—were all interchangeable. It was only in the twentieth century that all of this has come together in a coherent theory called thermodynamics.

The invention and development of the steam pump/engine by Papin, Savery, Newcomen and Watt changed the world of work. The Industrial Revolution was really all about learning to use heat from fire (by burning coal or coke from coal) to do other kinds of 'useful work' such as pumping water, spinning yarn, weaving cloth, making and forging iron for weapons and tools, or propelling a wheeled vehicle on a track. What was unclear at the time was the nature of heat itself.

Recognizing that heat and motion (of a mass) have something on common—they are both forms of energy—was an important insight in the eighteenth century, however obvious it seems today. Any device for converting heat into motion of a mass is called a "heat engine". A heat engine may be operated in reverse, to convert mechanical motion into a "heat pump", or refrigerator.

Indeed it is not too far off the mark to say that "science", as a distinct field of study, emerged from "philosophy" more or less coincidentally as the idea of "energy", as a kind of "universal substance"—distinct from mass—emerged from the confusion of related concepts of heat and physical motion. This emergence occurred as a series of physical discoveries, which were mostly quantified versions of what was previously known in principle.

The first such discovery was what now seems obvious, namely that frictional heat is equivalent to the heat from combustion. This discoverer of "the mechanical equivalent" of heat was **Benjamin Thompson** (1753–1814). He was an American "loyalist" army officer (one who had fought on the British side during the American Revolution) and who, after the American Revolutionary war, was making his living boring cannon barrels for the King of Bavaria, where he was anointed "Count Rumford". He was also a scholar in his spare time.

In 1798 Benjamin Thompson found time to publish an article entitled "An experimental inquiry concerning the source of the heat which is excited by friction" (Thompson 1798). This was actually quite a large step forward in understanding that energy is an intangible "substance" that can (and does) take many different interconvertible forms. In other words, Thompson's article established that heat energy can do work (i.e. by means of a steam engine) and that work also produces heat (e.g. by friction) as for instance, by boring cannons. So, the next question arose: is there a general law to explain both processes?

The answer to that question was provided by a French engineer (and genius) **Nicolas Sadi-Carnot** (1796–1832) in his book "*Reflections on the motive power of heat*" (1824). Carnot's work was entirely theoretical, which was amazing. It was based on the "caloric theory" of heat, by Antoine Lavoisier, but that fault did not matter.

Sadi-Carnot took the next step. He was the first to describe a heat engine as a cyclic scheme of successive compression, heating, expansion and cooling of an ideal working fluid (ignoring friction) operating between a hot reservoir and a cold reservoir. He also postulated that these heating, cooling, compression and expansion steps could all be adiabatic, meaning that no heat would

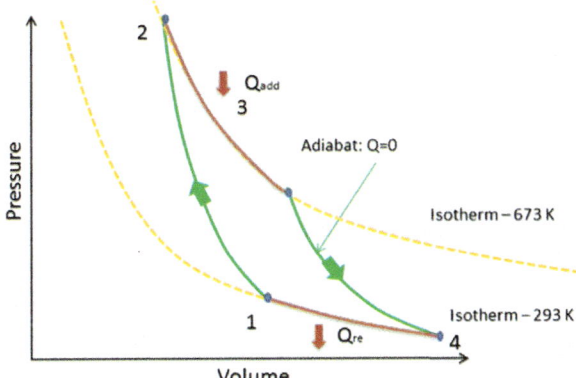

Fig. 11.1 An idealized Carnot cycle in pressure–volume space—Wikimedia

be gained or lost by the working fluid during compression or expansion (See Fig. 11.1).

For those readers who find this chart puzzling, the "working fluid" (undefined) is heated, and compressed, from point 1 to point 2 without gaining or losing heat. From point 2 to point 3 it expands at constant temperature (along an isotherm). From 3 to 4 it continues to expand while cooling. At maximum volume the compression begins again, along another isotherm (i.e. at constant temperature). The volume of the space enclosed by the curves represent the amount of work done during the cycle. This diagram (cycle) applies only to endothermic reactions, i.e. reactions that use heat to do work on the external environment. The case where the heat flows are reversed, taking heat from the environment, describes a refrigeration cycle, or "heat pump", as already mentioned.

Using this idealized conceptual scheme Carnot was able to prove two important things: (1) that the adiabatic version of that cycle (illustrated) is the most efficient possible, i.e. it maximizes the amount of work obtainable from a given amount of heat. It follows that no heat engine operating between two heat reservoirs at different temperatures can be more efficient than a Carnot cycle. Secondly, (2) he proved that the efficiency (of a Carnot cycle) is independent of the nature of the working fluid and depends only on the temperature difference between the hot and cold reservoirs. It was Carnot who, for the first time, clearly distinguished between reversible and irreversible processes in thermodynamics. Carnot's neglect of frictional losses does not detract at all from the importance of his insight.

Carnot assumed that heat (caloric) is neither created nor destroyed—i.e. is conserved –in the cycle, as Leibnitz had said earlier. In his case, the omission of frictional losses did not matter. His result, based on the further assumption (from Leibnitz) that perpetual motion is impossible, was that only temperature differences could account for the quantity of work done. This became known as "Carnot's theorem". Carnot is often given credit for inventing the second law of thermodynamics (before the first law was correctly formulated), but Carnot was still thinking in terms of Lavoisier's "caloric" theory, which was about to be discarded (Fig. 11.2).

The amount of work an engine can do depends on the power generated by the engine. Power is now measured in "watts" (or kilowatts, named after the Scots engineer who invented the condensing steam engine, a few years after the death of Sir Isaac Newton. Horsepower is often used to describe the power delivered by a machine. Horsepower (hp) is a familiar unit of power, e.g. for automobile engines. It is the power required to lift 550 pounds by one foot in one second. 1 hp is about 746 watts. Energy is measured in calories or joules or watt-hours. The standard unit is named for James Joule, who was one of the physicists who contributed notably to the modern theory of thermodynamics in the nineteenth century (discussed later). Energy consumed per unit time is the same as work done and the same as power output of a generator while power generated over time is exergy consumed and work performed.

Fig. 11.2 Nicolas Sadi-Carnot age 17 at the Ecole Polytechnique by Louis-Leopold Boilly, 1896—Wikipedia

11.2 The First and Second Laws of Thermodynamics

The German physician **Julius Robert Mayer** (1814–1878) is now credited with being the first to correctly articulate the mechanical equivalent of heat and the conservation of energy although energy was not yet well-defined. Moreover, Mayer's calculation, that the force ("Kraft") required to lift a kilogram 365 m would also raise the temperature of a liter (kg) of water by 10 °C, was not very accurate (it was 40% too high). In 1845 Mayer privately published a pamphlet "*Organic motion in its connection with nutrition*" which stated what we now call the first law of thermodynamics as "*A force (Kraft), once in existence cannot be annihilated.*" He confused force (Kraft) with energy. Because of this linguistic confusion, he did not receive immediate recognition.

Justus von Leibig (1803–1873), known today as the father of German industrial chemistry, bravely attempted to explain the heat produced in animal bodies in terms of chemical reactions and muscular work. However, Leibig took the experimental approach and could not prove his hypothesis about animal heat. But starting in the mid-1840s a number of scientists explored the implications of the mechanical equivalence of heat. **James Joule** (1818–1889), carried out a series of more accurate experiments and formulated the equivalence principle of work and heat more coherently than Robert Mayer had done. His results were published in the *Philosophical Magazine of the Royal Society*. That was the First Law of Thermodynamics. In 1847 **William Thomson** (1824–1907) –later he was anointed Lord Kelvin – introduced the absolute temperature (Kelvin) scale, using Carnot's theorem, and further elaborated the Carnot theory in another paper in 1849.

Another physician (as well as physicist) **Hermann Ludwig von Helmholz** (1821–1894)—later known for work in optics and acoustics—undertook a more general and mathematical follow-up to Leibig's work on animal heat. He published an influential paper in 1847 "Die Erhaltung der Kraft" or "On the conservation of force", still using the word Kraft instead of energy. This paper was really an argument against the so-called "vitalists" who still believed in the possibility of perpetual motion, which had already been rejected by Leonardo Da Vinci, and later by Leibnitz, on philosophical grounds. Helmholtz stated, in conclusion, that the sum total of all the energies of the universe, in whatever form, must remain a constant. His first published essay: "On the conservation of Energy" (*Über die Erhaltung der Kraft*, 1847), where he generalized the law of conservation of energy (already formulated by Robert-Mayer and James Joule) that also defines "potential energy". Later in his long life Helmholz devoted himself to integrating the concept of energy conservation with the principle of least action, as derived from the variational principles enunciated by Euler and Lagrange (Sect. 11.3).

Rudolf Clausius (1822–1888) rediscovered the work of Carnot and Mayer and took it one crucial step further. In 1850 he noted that Carnot's theorem can be derived from the conservation of energy (rather than conservation of caloric) together with the independent principle that heat always flows from higher to lower temperatures. That principle, nearly a law, had already discovered by **Antoine Lavoisier** (1743–1794). More precisely, Clausius showed that it is impossible for a self-acting cyclic heat engine, unaided by any external agency, to convey heat from a body at one temperature to a body at a higher temperature. In short, nature allows heat- to-work transitions only in one direction, from higher temperatures to lower temperatures.

In his most important paper published in 1854 Clausius focused on the two inverse transformations that occur in a heat engine, namely heat to mechanical work, while the heat itself experiences a drop in temperature, and mechanical work back to heat with a rising temperature. Clausius noted (as Carnot had pointed out previously) that not all the heat in the reservoir can be converted to work. The unavailable difference he termed "sensible heat", a term still used by thermodynamics experts and equipment designers. In that paper, he introduced the concept of "entropy" as a state function depending on temperature and pressure. He defined entropy as a differential, viz. $dS = dQ/T$ where dS is the change in entropy in a closed system where a quantity of heat dQ flows along a gradient from a higher to a lower temperature.

He also made use of Carnot's important distinction between reversible and irreversible processes, and noted that entropy never decreases but increases in all irreversible processes. This was the first formal statement of the famous second law of thermodynamics. We will have a little more to say about entropy, order and disorder later.

William Thomson (later Lord Kelvin) re-formulated the two laws of thermodynamics very carefully between 1851 and 1853. He attributed the first law to his collaborator, James Joule, and the second law to Carnot and Clausius. In his words: "*The whole theory of the motive power of heat is based on the following two propositions, due respectively to Joule and to Carnot and Clausius: Prop I (Joule)—When equal quantities of mechanical effect are produced by any means whatever from purely thermal sources, or lost in purely thermal effects, equal quantities of heat are put out of existence, or are generated. Prop II (Carnot and Clausius)—If an engine be such that, when it is worked backwards, the physical and mechanical agencies in every part of its motions are all* *reversed, it produces as much mechanical effect as can be produced by any thermodynamic engine, with the same temperatures of source and refrigerator, from a given quantity of heat*".

By "mechanical effect" he meant what we call mechanical work. In his last sentence he recognizes that operating an engine in reverse (as a refrigerator) will not reproduce as much heat as was needed to produce the work in the first place. In other words, there is a loss. This is the essence of the entropy law.

Thomson (Lord Kelvin) never used the term entropy (the word introduced by Clausius) but he was the first to introduce the idea of available energy or maximum work (now called "exergy") in 1855. Two other independent contributors to the idea of maximum work were G. Gouy who wrote "About available energy" (in French) (Gouy 1889) and Stodola who wrote about "the cyclic processes of the Gas Engine" (Stodola 1898). The distinction between energy as an indestructible substance and energy availability to do work, or "energy quality" gradually became clear in the late nineteenth century. Available energy and "essergy" were competing terms introduced later for this idea. The modern term, "exergy" was introduced by Rant in 1956. For more details, see also (Szargut 1988).

The terminology was further clarified by **William Macquorn Rankine** (1820–1872) (who got his name on the cycle of the steam engine, though he neither invented nor discovered it). In papers written during 1853–1855 Rankine defined energy as follows: "*Energy, or the capacity to effect changes, is the common characteristic of the various states of matter to which the several branches of physics relate: If, then, there be general laws respecting energy, such laws must be applicable mutatis mutandis to every branch of physics, and must express a body of principles to physical phenomena in general.*" Rankine also introduced the important distinction between actual or kinetic energy and potential energy.

Rankine proposed to found a new science of "energetics", which quickly found supporters eager to "*reduce a dualistic world consisting of matter and energy to a unified world consisting only of energy*" (Mirowski p. 54). A schoolteacher named George Helm wrote a book, published in 1887, that reiterated, in less academic language, Rankine's claim to have reduced all physics to energetics. That book was actively promoted by **Friedrich Wilhelm Ostwald**, the most authoritative physical chemist in Germany, in th elate nineteenth century (Nobel Prize, 2008).

Ostwald argued that the new science should be based on three primitive concepts and two fundamental principles. The two principles were (1) "*a perpetual motion of the first kind is impossible*" (i.e. energy can neither be created nor destroyed) and (2) *"perpetual motion of the second kind is impossible"*, meaning that energy cannot circulate endlessly among its various forms and manifestations (i.e. the second law). Ostwald championed the work of J. Willard Gibbs, in particular, though Gibbs did not associate himself with the energetics movement, but a number of German and French scientists did so.

Josiah Willard Gibbs' (1839–1903) was Ostwald's counterpart in the U.S. His work on thermodynamics was instrumental in transforming physical chemistry into a rigorous inductive science. It was Gibbs who introduced the now-familiar functions *enthalpy*, Helmholtz Free Energy and *Gibbs Free Energy*. Gibbs also invented vector calculus.

11.3 Entropy and Statistical Mechanics

Meanwhile, Gibbs. along with **James Clerk Maxwell** (1831–1879) and **Ludwig Boltzmann** (1844–1906), also integrated thermodynamics into "statistical mechanics" (a term that Gibbs coined),. Statistical mechanics is one of the pillars of modern physics. It describes how macroscopic observations (such as temperature and pressure) are related to microscopic parameters that fluctuate around an average. It connects thermodynamic quantities (such as heat capacity) to microscopic behavior, whereas, in classical thermodynamics, the only available option would be to measure and tabulate such quantities for various materials individually.

Gibbs, Maxwell and Boltzmann viewed nature as decaying irreversibly toward a final death of random disorder in accordance with the second law of thermodynamics. Boltzmann's greatest achievements were his contribution to the development of statistical mechanics, and the statistical explanation of the second law of thermodynamics. The three men explained the laws of thermodynamics as consequences of the statistical properties of ensembles of the possible states of a physical system composed of many particles.

In particular, Ludwig Boltzmann attempted to reduce the entropy law to a stochastic collision function, or law of probability, following from the random collisions of mechanical particles. Following Maxwell—best known for the mathematical equations of electromagnetism—Boltzmann modelled ideal gas molecules as tiny billiard balls colliding in a box, noting that with each collision nonequilibrium velocity distributions (groups of molecules moving at the same speed and in the same direction) would become increasingly disordered leading to a final state of macroscopic uniformity and maximum microscopic disorder—the state of maximum entropy—where macroscopic uniformity means absence of all field potentials or gradients.

In 1871 Maxwell asked an interesting question: whether intelligence could reverse the implications of Clausius' entropy. He postulated the existence of an intelligent being ("Maxwell's demon") that could "*follow every molecule in its course*". If this entity could open and close a trapdoor between two regions of space, part A and part B, this door-keeping entity could allow fast molecule to pass through the trapdoor, while not allowing the slower molecules to pass. The fast molecules would accumulate in one compartment, making it hotter, and the slow molecules would accumulate in the other compartment making it cooler. Of course maxwell's demon is impossible because it would need sensory data and muscles—hence useful energy (exergy)—to open and close the trap-door.

In 1872 Boltzmann stated his "H -theorem" that provided a statistical definition of entropy, viz.

$$S = K_B \log W$$

where S is the entropy, W is the number of possible microstates (or rearrangements) of the system (meaning the velocity distributions of the tiny billiard balls) and K_B is a physical constant interpreted as a measure of statistical disorder of a system. It is equal to 1.38065×10^{-23} J per degree on the Kelvin scale. (This equation is engraved on Boltzmann's tomb in Vienna, below.)

In short, the Boltzmann formula shows the relationship between entropy and the number of ways in which the atoms or molecules of a thermodynamic system can be re-arranged. He pointed out that the distribution of states becomes more predictable as the system approaches thermal equilibrium. The idea of atoms was relatively new idea at the time, though it was anticipated by Democritus in ancient Greece.[1]

Boltzmann's statistical theory correctly explained the observed relationship between the temperature, pressure and heat capacity of gases. Boltzmann took this fact (correctly) as evidence that gases did consist of "atoms". He committed suicide in 1906 (he was only 62 years old) because he was so discouraged by the negative reception of his atomic theory by some colleagues (notably **Ernst Mach**).

The (understandable) oversimplification of reality of Boltzmann's model left physical-chemistry reaction dynamics and phase changes unexplained.

---

[1] Joseph John (J.J.) Thomson (1856–1940). In 1897, Thomson showed that cathode rays were composed of previously unknown negatively charged particles (now called electrons), which he calculated must have bodies much smaller than atoms and a very large charge-to-mass ratio.

Gibbs completed the standard theory by introducing the notion of "chemical potential", to explain that particles tend to move from regions of high chemical potential to regions of low chemical potential. This provided the explanation of gas–liquid (condensation) and liquid solid (freezing) phase changes, as well as a number of other chemical phenomena such as reaction rates and equilibria.

Certainly Boltzmann's equilibrium- seeking, pessimistic view of the evolution of natural systems seems inconsistent with the evolutionary paradigm associated with Charles Darwin and Alfred Russell Wallace, i.e. of increasing complexity, specialization, and organization of biological systems through time (Chap. 13). The phenomenology of many natural systems shows that much of the world is inhabited by non-equilibrium coherent structures, ranging from convection cells to autocatalytic chemical reactions, to molecular reproduction, cellular reproduction and life itself. Living systems exhibit a march away from disorder and equilibrium, into highly organized structures that exist some distance from equilibrium.

We note that Boltzmann's billiard-ball model is not a very good model of real gases by modern standards. Real gases do not consist of tiny hard billiard-balls. They consist of molecules (or other particles) with different sizes and shapes and atomic compositions, due to different nuclear formulae. Real gases are consequently subject to short-range (Van der Waals) forces that are directional (not isotropic). This obviously affects the probability of various micro- and macro-states of the system.

This (understandable) oversimplification of reality on Boltzmann's part left some room for the explanation of gas -liquid (condensation) and liquid solid (freezing) phase changes, as well as a host of other chemical phenomena dependent on the idea of chemical potential. The final integration of statistical mechanics with thermodynamics and physical chemistry was carried out by **Josiah Willard Gibbs** (1839–1903), one of the most prolific scientists in history. Gibbs was able to fit friction, heat, pressure, motion and chemical reactions into a comprehensive picture of how the world works. (A mis-use of the word "work") (Fig. 11.3).

The "purpose" of the work being done by the expanding universe, or by our existence on this planet, can be quite variable, depending on whether there is a driving (human or divine) intention or not. But, in general, we now know that work done creates local order, either by separating components of a mixture, (purification) or by forming a shape or an image that reproduces itself and can grow. The second law of thermodynamics says that there is an upper limit to the potential for growth and reproduction. The cyclic conversion from work to heat and back to potential work can never be

Fig. 11.3 Boltzmann's tomb in the Zentralfriedhof, Vienna, with bust and entropy formula—Wikipedia

100% efficient. There is always a loss of potential work (exergy), even though the energy itself is not lost, it just becomes low temperature waste heat. That loss of exergy corresponds to an increase in global entropy, the ugly cousin.

So much for definitions. The point is that physicists late in the nineteenth century were still trying to grapple with a very difficult question, namely how to fit the mechanical, thermal and chemical aspects of energy into a pattern. The key point that needs to be made here is that Before 1905, physicists still believed (with Descartes) that matter and "life force" were distinct, like body and soul.

Science still couldn't provide a truly comprehensive theory even at the end of the nineteenth century, partly because other forms of energy were not yet included. In particular, chemical reactions and electro-magnetism were not yet well enough understood and nuclear energy wasn't understood at all. But chemistry was rapidly developing in the second half of the nineteenth century, especially thanks to the rapidly growing demand for synthetic dyes for the textile industry (Farbenindustrie in German), and parallel research in the chemistry of fertilizers and explosives.

11.4 Order and Disorder; Self Organization

Erwin Schrödinger (1887–1961), was one of the fathers of quantum mechanics (which we will not try to explain in this book) and also a Jewish refugee from Nazi Germany. He was living in Dublin, Ireland, during the war years. In a series of public lectures *"What is Life?"* (Schrödinger 1944), he attempted to draw together the fundamental processes of biology and the sciences of physics and chemistry. He noted that life is comprised of two fundamental processes; one "order from order" and the other "order from disorder".

Schrodinger observed that the gene generates order from order in a species: that is, the progeny inherit the traits of the parent. He predicted that something like DNA must exist to make this transmission possible. Over a decade later, in 1953, **James Watson** (b. 1928) and **Francis Crick** (1916–2004) discovered the mechanism intergenerational transmission of genetic information (traits), namely the double helix of DNA (Watson 1953, 1968). This discovery provided biology with a research agenda that has led to some of the most important scientific findings of the last fifty years.

However, Schrödinger's other equally important, but less understood, observation was his "order from disorder" premise. This was an effort to link biology with the fundamental theorems of thermodynamics. Schrödinger noted that living systems seem to defy the second law of thermodynamics. The second law insists that, within closed systems, the entropy of a system tends to be maximized. Living systems, however, are the antithesis of disorder. That is why so many scientists and philosophers until the end of the nineteenth century have believed in the existence of some version of "life force". They display multiple levels of highly complex order, created from disorder. For instance, plants are highly ordered structures of cells, which are synthesized from complex self-reproducing molecules, made of atoms, which are constructed from elementary particles (nucleons). How does this happen?

The theory of near-equilibrium thermodynamics, as it was developed in the nineteenth century by Carnot, Mayer, Helmholtz, Joule, Clausius, Rankine, Thomson (Lord Kelvin) and Gibbs. It has been subsequently extended and applied to all kinds of practical chemical engineering problems, and is a major part of the university engineering curriculum. This body of knowledge was revised and extended to regions for from equilibrium by

Ilya Prigogine (1917–2003), his student, **Gregoire Nicolis** (1939–2018), **Isabelle Stengers** (b. 1949) and other colleagues at the Free University in Brussels during the 1970s (Prigogine 1955,1971,1972,1976, 1984).

Prigogine's work introduced the fundamental concept of "self-organization" i.e. creating 'dissipative structures' characterized by maximum entropy production and driven by a source of free energy. This possibility arises from the non-linearity of the mass-balance rate equations for irreversible processes involving three or more simultaneous reactions far from equilibrium. The word equilibrium, as applied to a chemical reaction, means that it has reached a unique balance point. Two body rate equations are linear and the equations are soluble. But three-body (or more) rate equations are non-linear and much more complex. It turns out that with non-linear equations, multiple solutions are possible. Moreover, solutions are not necessarily unique. (For details see their monograph "Self-organization in non-equilibrium systems" (Nicolis and Prigogine 1977).

The first application of the new theory was to explain a peculiar phenomenon in chemistry, known as the trimolecular model, or "Brusselator", which is a chemical oscillator. Subsequently a number of other applications have emerged, first in biology, later in ecology and sociology. Self-organization can also enable the creation and preservation of order, either as material objects or as knowledge. Self-organization yields stable dissipative sub-systems that incorporate gradients, far from thermodynamic equilibrium (where gradients do not exist.) In Prigogine's words) a self-organized system is an "island of order and complexity"—embedded in a larger system, i.e. the planet, or the solar system.

Alfred James Lotka (1880–1949) is known today known mainly for the Lotka–Volterra equations used to explain the simple predator–prey relationship in ecology, Lotka was a bio-mathematician and a bio-statistician, who sought to apply the principles of the physical sciences to biological sciences as well. He is also known as the father of biophysics, for his book *Elements of Physical Biology* (1925), the first comprehensive book on biology. He is also known for his energetics perspective on biological evolution.

Lotka believed that natural selection is, at its root, a struggle among species for available energy; "Lotka's principle" postulates that organisms that survive and prosper are those that capture and use energy more efficiently than their competitors. Lotka extended his energetics framework to human society. In particular, he suggested that the shift in reliance from prehistoric forms of (mostly solar energy) to non-renewable sources from fossil fuels would pose unique and fundamental challenges to society. These theories made Lotka an important progenitor of biophysical economics and ecological economics.

Lotka proposed the theory that the Darwinian concept of natural selection could be quantified as a physical law. The law that he proposed was that the selective principle of evolution was one which favored the maximum useful energy flow transformation. The general systems ecologist Howard T. Odum later adopted Lotka's theory as a central guiding feature of his work in ecosystem ecology, renaming it the maximum power principle.

Eric Schneider and **James J. Kay** have extended the paradigm, based on Prigogine's work, that provides a thermodynamically consistent explanation of life, including the origin of life, biological growth, the development of ecosystems, and patterns of biological evolution observed in the fossil record (Schneider 1994, 1995). They illustrate this paradigm through a discussion of ecosystem development, arguing that as ecosystems grow and develop, they develop more complex structures with more energy flow, increase their cycling activity, develop greater diversity and generate more hierarchical levels, all to abet exergy dissipation. Species that survive in ecosystems are those that funnel exergy into their own production and reproduction and contribute to autocatalytic processes which increase the total dissipation of the ecosystem. In short, ecosystems develop in ways which systematically increase their ability to dissipate the incoming solar energy.

12

Evolutionary Theory and Genetics

12.1 The Age of the Earth

Before Darwin, all Christians believed that the creation of Adam occurred around 4004 BCE, or near that time. Those numbers came from calculations in 1640 by Dr. John Lightfoot, (1602–1675), an Anglican clergyman, rabbinical scholar, and Vice-Chancellor of the University of Cambridge who arrived at an estimate of 4004-OCT-23 BCE, at 9 AM.

A decade later the same date was found by Bishop **James Ussher**(1581–1656) based on the ages of famous pre-flood personages in the Bible to estimate the number of years between creation and the flood. In 1650 CE, he published his book "*Annales veteris testamenti, a prima mundi origine deducti*" ("Annals of the Old Testament, deduced from the first origins of the world.") There were many other such estimates, from many religions, mostly ranging between 6000 and 3500 BCE. (Isaac Newton and Johannes Kepler both made such calculations. Most of them equated the creation of Adam by God with the creation of the earth itself.

The stratification of the Earth into layers was noticed long ago. Yet these layers frequently contain fossils, i.e., the remains of unknown creatures no longer alive. This fact suggests a progression of organisms from layer to layer and, hence, a progression over time. **Nicolas Steensen** (1638–1686) in the seventeenth century was one of the first naturalists to appreciate this connection. He questioned explanations for tear production, the idea that fossils grew in the ground and explanations of rock formation. His investigations and his subsequent conclusions on fossils and rock formation have led scholars to consider him one of the founders of modern stratigraphy and modern geology. Steensen's work on shark teeth led him to the question of how any solid object could come to be found inside another solid object, such as a rock or a layer of rock.

The "solid bodies within solids" that attracted Steensen's interest included not only fossils, as we would define them today, but minerals, crystals, encrustations, veins, and even entire rock layers or strata. He published his geologic studies in *De solido intra solidum naturaliter contento dissertationis prodromus*, or Preliminary discourse to a dissertation on a solid body naturally contained within a solid in 1669. His contemporary Robert Hooke also argued that fossils were the remains of once-living organisms; so did Chinese polymath and early geologist Shen Kuo (1031–1095).

On stratigraphy, his words were:

The law of superposition: *"At the time when a given stratum was being formed, there was beneath it another substance which prevented the further descent of the comminuted matter and so at the time when the lowest stratum was being formed either another solid substance was beneath it, or if some fluid existed there, then it was not only of a different character from the upper fluid, but also heavier than the solid sediment of the upper fluid."*

The principle of original horizontality: *"At the time when one of the upper strata was being formed, the lower stratum had already gained the consistency of a solid."*

The principle of lateral continuity: "At the time when any given stratum was being formed it was either encompassed on its sides by another solid substance, or it covered the entire spherical surface of the earth. Hence it follows that in whatever place the bared sides of the strata are seen, either a continuation of the same strata must be sought, or another solid substance must be found which kept the matter of the strata from dispersion."

The principle of cross-cutting relationships: *"If a body or discontinuity cuts across a stratum, it must have formed after that stratum."*

These principles were applied and extended in 1772. Steensen's ideas still form the basis of stratigraphy and were key in the development of James Hutton's theory of infinitely repeating cycles of seabed deposition, uplifting, erosion, and submersion.

In 1856 Hermann von Helmholtz estimated the age of the earth to be 22 million years, the amount of time it would take for the Sun to condense down to its current diameter and brightness from the nebula of gas and dust from which it was born.

In 1862, William Thomson (Lord Kelvin) published calculations that fixed the age of Earth at between 20 and 400 million years. He assumed that Earth had formed as a completely molten object, and calculated time it would take for the near-surface temperature gradient to decrease to its present value. His calculations did not account for heat produced via radioactive decay (a then unknown process) or, more significantly, convection inside Earth, which allows the temperature in the upper mantle to maintain a high thermal gradient in the crust much longer. Kelvin's estimates of the age of the Sun were based on his estimates of its thermal output and a theory that the Sun obtains its energy from gravitational collapse.

Other scientists backed up Kelvin's figures. Charles Darwin's son, the astronomer George H. Darwin, proposed that Earth and Moon had broken apart in their early days when they were both molten. He calculated the amount of time it would have taken for tidal friction to give Earth its current 24-h day. His value of 56 million years added additional evidence that Thomson was on the right track. In 1895 John Perry challenged Kelvin's figure on the basis of his assumptions on thermal conductivity, and Oliver Heaviside entered the dialogue as a skeptic.

12.2 The Idea of Species: Fossils and Extinction

In 1751, **Pierre Louis Maupertuis** wrote of natural modifications occurring during reproduction and accumulating over many generations to produce new species. **Georges-Louis Leclerc, Comte de Buffon**, suggested that species could degenerate into different organisms, and Erasmus Darwin—grandfather of Charles—proposed that all warm-blooded animals could have descended from a single microorganism (or "filament"). Meanwhile Ray's ideas of benevolent design were developed by William Paley into the *Natural Theology or Evidences of the Existence and Attributes of the Deity* (1802), which proposed complex adaptations as evidence of divine design.

In the seventeenth century, the Aristotelian explanations of natural phenomena were still based on the assumption of fixed natural categories and divine cosmic order. The empirical Baconian approach was slowly taking root, but the biological sciences were the last bastion of the concept of fixed natural types. John Ray applied the term, "species", to plant and animal types, but he strictly identified each type of living thing as a species and proposed that each species could be defined by the features that perpetuated themselves generation after generation. The biological classification introduced by Carl Linnaeus in 1735 explicitly recognized the hierarchical nature of species relationships, but still viewed species as fixed according by divine plan.

In the 1790s, William Smith hypothesized that if two layers of rock at widely differing locations contained similar fossils, then it was very plausible that the layers were the same age. Smith's nephew and student, John Phillips, later calculated by such means that Earth was about 96 million years old. In 1779 the Comte du Buffon tried to obtain a value for the age of Earth using an experiment: He created a small globe that resembled Earth in composition and then measured its rate of cooling. This led him to estimate that Earth was about 75,000 years old. Other naturalists used these hypotheses to construct a history of Earth, though their timelines were inexact as they did not know how long it took to lay down stratigraphic layers. Geologists such as Charles Lyell, as well as Charles Darwin, had trouble accepting such a short age for the Earth. For biologists, even 100 million years seemed much too short to be plausible.

In 1739 Charles Le Moyne, Baron de Longueuil, conducting a body of French soldiers down the Ohio River, discovered huge thigh bones, large teeth for grinding and a tusk (for what?) in a swamp near what is now Cincinnati. He took them to New Orleans and had them shipped back to France, where they were presented to the King, who put them in his *cabinet du Roi* (private museum). Were they an elephant's bones and teeth? Buffon thought that they were from an elephant, a hippopotamus and a third unknown but larger species. We now know that they were all the bones of a mastodon, a different species. Buffon thus introduced the idea of species extinction (Kolbert, 2014). Other large specimens of unidentifiable bones were arriving in Paris.

The young new curator(?) of the Museum of natural History was **Jean-Leopold-Nicolas-Frederick Cuvier**. In April 1796 he gave a public lecture about the bones discovered in the Ohio River V. He had already identified four species of fossils and he was sure there would be others found. He wondered what sort of catastrophe could have wiped out all those species. By 1800 Cuvier's "fossil zoo" had grown to 23 species. The list grew rapidly thereafter. In 1812 he published a four volume compendium on fossil animals belonging to extinct species of quadrupeds. During the next two decades Cuvier was the most influential paleontologist in Europe, by far. Cuvier insisted that species were unrelated to each other and fixed, their similarities reflecting divine design for functional needs. He proposed that the extinct species, such as the mastodon, the mammoth and others, must have been wiped out by a great catastrophe, which he could not explain. But Cuvier had no explanation of how these different species came into existence in the first place.

Jean-Baptiste Pierre Antoine de Monet, chevalier de Lamarck (1744–1829), known simply as Lamarck was an early proponent of the idea that biological evolution occurred and proceeded in accordance with natural laws. After he published Flore Françoise (1778), he was appointed Chair of Botany at the Jardin des Plantes and was appointed to the Chair of Botany in 1788 and Chair of Zoology at the Muséum national d'Histoire naturelle in 1793. In 1801, he published Système des animaux sans vertèbres, a major work on the classification of invertebrates, a term he coined. In an 1802 publication, he was one of the first to use the term "biology" in its modern sense. He is remembered for a theory of inheritance of acquired characteristics, called Lamarckism (inaccurately named after him), also known as "soft inheritance", or "use/disuse theory", which he described in his 1809 Philosophie zoologique. Lamarck's contribution to evolutionary theory consisted of the first truly cohesive theory of biological evolution, in which an alchemical complexifying force drove organisms up a ladder of complexity, and a second environmental force adapted them to local environments through *use and disuse* of characteristics, differentiating them from other organisms. Lamarck envisaged spontaneous generation continually producing simple forms of life that developed greater complexity in parallel lineages with an inherent progressive tendency. He postulated that, on a local level, these lineages adapted to the environment by erosion and reforming continuously, and the rate of this change was roughly constant. Scientists have recently debated whether his theory laid the groundwork for the modern theory of transgenerational epigenetics.

James Hutton (1726–1797) was a Scottish geologist, who played a key role in establishing geology as a science. He insisted that the remote past of the physical world can be inferred from evidence in present-day rocks. Through his study of features in the landscape and coastlines of his native Scottish Lowlands, he concluded that geological features must have undergone continuing transformation over indefinitely long periods of time. From this he argued that the Earth could not be young. He was one of the earliest proponents of what in the 1830s became known as uniformitarianism, the theory that the Earth's crust is the outcome of continuing natural processes, like vulcanism, erosion and sedimentation.

Some reflections similar to those of Hutton were put forward in publications of contemporaries, such as the French naturalist **Georges-Louis Leclerc de Buffon**. But it is chiefly Hutton's pioneering work that established geology as a field. Hutton, had noticed that layers of sedimentary rock looked exactly like the sand and other small particles being laid down by modern oceans and lakes. Hutton found extensive evidence that rocks had been melting, recrystallizing, eroding, and getting redeposited again and again for a long time—maybe even forever.

In Hutton's and Lyell's day, however, most people believed that the Earth was young and had been created by powerful forces that were no longer operating by the time human civilization came along. For example, when they looked at layers of rock containing the fossils of marine animals, they believed these had all been deposited in a relatively short time after Noah's flood as described in the Book of Genesis. Volcanoes, they thought, must have grown all at once from gigantic eruptions—mega-disasters—that no humans or other advanced animals could have survived. This view, known as **catastrophism**, seemed to follow from religious texts. But also because the alternative implied time scales much longer than human history. For instance, if the Grand Canyon was formed by the same processes that cause small cracks in the walls of your church or castle, it must have taken millions of years. This was a very hard concept for humans in the early nineteenth century to accept.

Thinkers of the Scottish Enlightenment, like Hutton and Lyell, believed that people can understand their environment by studying the laws of nature and carefully observing the world. They also believed that since natural laws don't change, understanding the present helps us understand what happened in the past. Lyell, and Hutton before him, found extensive evidence that even the largest landforms had been shaped slowly over very long periods of time. This theory was given the name uniformitarianism by William Whewell, a reviewer of Lyell's most important book, *Principles of Geology*.

12.3 Darwin's Theory of Natural Selection

Charles Robert Darwin (1809b–1882) developed his theory of "natural selection" from 1838 onwards and was writing up his "big book" on the subject when **Alfred Russel Wallace** sent him a version of virtually the same theory in 1858. Their separate papers were presented together at an 1858 meeting of the Linnean Society of London. This theory was formulated by Darwin in terms of variegated populations. He used the expression "descent with modification" rather than "evolution", partly influenced by An Essay on the Principle of Population (1798) by **Thomas Robert Malthus** (Chap. 8). Darwin's theory differed from Lamarck's theory in one respect: it explained species evolution rather than evolutionary changes at the individual organism level. On the other hand, in Charles Darwin's theory of evolution, the process of random heritable variation with cumulative selection requires great durations of time, and Darwin himself stated that Lord Kelvin's estimates did not appear to provide enough of that.

The crucial break from Lyell's concept of constant typological classes or types in biology came with the theory of evolution through natural selection. In Darwin's day there were three observable facts about living organisms: (1) traits (attributes) vary among individuals in a population (2) different attributes confer different rates of survival and reproduction (differential fitness) and (3) fitness traits can be passed from generation to generation (heritability of fitness). Thus, in successive generations members of a population are more likely to be replaced by the offspring of parents with more favorable fitness attributes than otherwise.

Evolutionary biologist, **Ernst Mayr** (2004–2005), who is credited with originating the Biological Species Concept, wrote "I consider it necessary to dissect Darwin's conceptual framework of evolution into a number of major theories…I have partitioned Darwin's evolutionary paradigm into five theories…

1. Evolution as such. This is the theory that the world is not constant or recently created, nor perpetually recycling, but is steadily changing, and that organisms are transformed in time.
2. Common descent. This is the theory that every group of organisms descended from a common ancestor, and that all groups of organisms including animals, plants, and microorganisms, ultimately go back to a single origin of life on earth.
3. Multiplication of species. This theory explains the origin of the enormous organic diversity. It postulates that species multiply, either by splitting into daughter species or by "budding". That is, by the establishment of geographically isolated founder populations that evolve into new species.
4. Gradualism. According to this theory, evolutionary change takes place through the gradual change of populations and not by the sudden (saltational) production of new individuals that represent a new type.
5. Natural selection. According to this theory, evolutionary change comes about through the abundant production of genetic variation in every generation. The relatively few individuals who survive, owing to a particularly well-adapted combination of inheritable characteristics, give rise to the next generation.

(Mayr, 1991) Chap. 4.

Alfred Russel Wallace (1823–1913) is best known for independently conceiving the theory of evolution through natural selection; his paperwork on the subject was jointly published with some of Charles Darwin's writings in 1858. This prompted Darwin to publish On the Origin of Species.

Evolution by natural selection was first demonstrated by the observation that too many offspring are often produced than can possibly survive. This mismatch between birth-rates and survival is most extreme among primitive organisms, such as bacteria and insects. The question arises: What are the determinants of survivability? Is it strictly random or are there other factors in the selection?

Darwin and Wallace both realized that population growth would lead to a "struggle for existence" in which favorable variations would prevail as others perished. In each generation, many offspring fail to survive to an age of reproduction because of competition for limited resources. This could explain the diversity of plants and animals from a common ancestry through the working of natural laws in the same way for all types of organism.

At the end of 1859, Darwin's publication of his "abstract" of "On the Origin of Species" explained natural selection in detail—much of it derived from extensive observations during the voyage of the Beagle (1831–1836). This empirical support led to increasingly wide acceptance of Darwin's concepts of evolution at the expense of alternative theories. **Thomas Henry Huxley** (1825–1895) applied Darwin's ideas to humans, using palaeontology and comparative anatomy to provide strong evidence that humans and apes shared a common ancestry. Some religious traditionalists were disturbed by this, since it implied that humans did not have a special place in the universe.

12.4 Mendel's Theory of Inheritance

The exact mechanisms of reproductive heritability and the origin of new traits remained a mystery. Johannes (Darwin himself developed a provisional theory called "pangenesis" that was taken seriously for some years. **Johann (Gregor) Mendel** (1822–1884) was born and grew up on a farm in Moravia (now the Czech Republic). He became a monk in part because it enabled him to obtain an education without having to pay for it himself. Born Johann Mendel, he was given the name Gregor (Řehoř in Czech) when he joined the Order of Saint Augustine. He twice failed the oral examinations to become a certified high school teacher. Thereafter Mendel chose to study variation in plants in his monastery's two hectare experimental garden. After initial experiments with pea plants, Mendel settled on studying seven traits that seemed to be inherited independently of other traits: seed shape, flower color, seed coat tint, pod shape, unripe pod color, flower location, and plant height. He first focused on seed shape, which was either angular or round.

Between 1856 and 1863 Mendel cultivated and tested some 28,000 plants, mostly (*Pisum sativum*). This study showed that, when true-breeding different varieties were crossed to each other (e.g., tall plants fertilized by short plants), in the second generation, one in four pea plants had purebred recessive traits, two out of four were hybrids, and one out of four were purebred dominant. His experiments led him to make two generalizations: the Law of Segregation and the Law of Independent Assortment, which later came to be known as Mendel's Laws of Inheritance.

During Mendel's lifetime, most biologists held the idea that all characteristics were passed to the next generation through blending inheritance, in which the traits from each parent are averaged. Instances of this phenomenon are now explained by the action of multiple genes with quantitative effects. Charles Darwin tried unsuccessfully to explain inheritance through a theory of pangenesis. Mendel presented his paper, "Versuche über Pflanzenhybriden" ("Experiments on Plant Hybridization"), at two meetings of the Natural History Society of Brno in Moravia on 8 February and 8 March 1865. About forty scientists listened to Mendel's two ground-breaking lectures, but they failed to understand the implications of his work. Later, he also carried on a correspondence with Carl Nägeli, one of the leading biologists of the time, but Nägeli too failed to appreciate Mendel's discoveries.

When Mendel's paper was published in 1866 in Verhandlungen des naturforschenden Vereines in Brünn, it was seen as essentially about hybridization rather than inheritance. It had little impact, and was only cited about three times over the next thirty-five years. It is now considered a seminal work. Gregor Mendel showed that traits were inherited in a predictable manner through the independent assortment and segregation of elements (later known as "genes"). Mendel's laws of inheritance eventually supplanted most of Darwin's pangenesis theory. August Weismann made the important distinction between germ cells that give rise to gametes (such as sperm and egg cells) and the somatic cells of the body, demonstrating that heredity passes through the germ line only. Charles Darwin was not aware of Mendel's paper, and it is likely that, if he had been aware of it, genetic theory might have established itself much earlier.

It was not until the early twentieth century that the importance of Mendel's ideas was realized. By 1900, research aimed at finding a successful theory of discontinuous inheritance, rather than blending inheritance, led to independent duplication of Mendel's work by Hugo de Vries and Carl Correns. That led to the rediscovery of Mendel's writings and laws. Both acknowledged Mendel's priority. Erich von Tschermak was originally also credited with Mendel's rediscovery, but this is dubious because he did not understand Mendel's laws. All three men, each from a different country, published their rediscovery of Mendel's work within a two-month span in the spring of 1900.

There were other theories seeking to explain heredity. Mendel's results were quickly replicated, and genetic linkage quickly worked out. Biologists flocked to the theory; even though it was not yet applicable to many phenomena. Hugo de Vries connected Darwin's pangenesis theory to Weismann's germ/soma cell distinction and proposed that Darwin's pangenes were concentrated in the cell nucleus and when expressed they could move into the cytoplasm to change the cell's structure. De Vries was also one of the researchers who made Mendel's work well known, believing that Mendelian traits corresponded to the transfer of heritable variations along the germline. To explain how new variants originate, de Vries developed a mutation theory that led to a temporary rift between those who accepted Darwinian evolution and biometricians who allied with de Vries.

Most prominent of the competing approaches was the biometric school of Karl Pearson and W. F. R. Weldon, based on statistical studies of phenotype variation. The strongest support for Mendel's school came from William Bateson, who introduced the word "genetics", and much of the discipline's other terminology). This debate between the biometricians and the Mendelians was extremely vigorous in the first two decades of the twentieth century. Modern genetics shows that Mendelian heredity is in fact an inherently biological process, though not all genes of Mendel's experiments are yet understood. In the end, the two approaches were combined, especially by work conducted by R. A. Fisher as early as 1918. The combination, in the 1930s and 1940s, of Mendelian genetics with Darwin's theory of natural selection resulted in the modern synthesis of evolutionary biology.

12.5 The Tree of Life

All life on Earth shares a "last universal common ancestor" (LUCA) that lived approximately 3.5–3.8 billion years ago. The fossil record includes a progression from early biogenic graphite, to microbial mat fossils, to fossilized multicellular organisms. The "Tree of Life" (below) resulted from a sequence of branching events. Existing patterns of biodiversity have been shaped by repeated formations of new species (speciation), changes within species (anagenesis) and loss of species (extinction) throughout the evolutionary history of life on Earth. Morphological and biochemical traits are more similar among species that share a more recent common ancestor, and can be used to reconstruct trees, like the one below.

The intermediate steps between major families and genera are the still being filled in, especially the sequence following the separation between chimpanzees and human ancestors, starting with Australopithecus. Homo sapiens (us) share 98% of our genes with chimpanzees, yet the differences are colossal: human brains are roughly 4 times larger than the brains of chimps and other anatomical differences are quite significant.

The diversity of life—the "tree of life"—was hard to explain. It was finally explained (by Charles Darwin) as a process of selection among variations, on the basis of genetic advantage ("fitness"). Even so, the Mendelian laws of genetic inheritance were not understood until chromosome theory was established in the twentieth century (1915). Now we know (thanks to the discovery of radioactivity and the invention of radio-metrics) that all life on Earth shares a last universal common ancestor (LUCA) that lived approximately 3.5–3.8 billion years ago.

This evolutionary process has not led to increasing disorder, randomness, homogeneity or disappearance of species. It has given rise to biodiversity at every level of biological organization, including the levels of species, individual organisms and molecules. In a joint publication with Alfred Russel Wallace (1858), Darwin explained that the branching pattern of evolution resulted from a process that they called natural selection, in which the struggle for existence has a similar effect to the artificial selection involved in selective breeding of animals and plants.

Existing patterns of biodiversity have been shaped by repeated formations of new species (*speciation*), changes within species (*anagenesis*) and loss of species (*extinction*) throughout the evolutionary history of life on Earth. The evolutionary process of natural selection has also resulted in a vast increase in the complexity of the organisms, starting from the first cells and resulting in the human brain and our DNA. The activities of human brain have produced an even higher order of complexity of products, structures and organizations, all of which are activated indirectly by the flux of exergy from the sun, past or present.

How did all this happen by natural selection? It is the kind of question that anthropologists and geneticists still worry about today. There are still people who don't like the idea that humans are "descended from monkeys"; the truth is that we aren't descended from monkeys but we do have a common ancestor. There are still religious groups in the US committed to the idea of "special creation" of humans by God, and associated implications of that idea (Fig. 12.1).

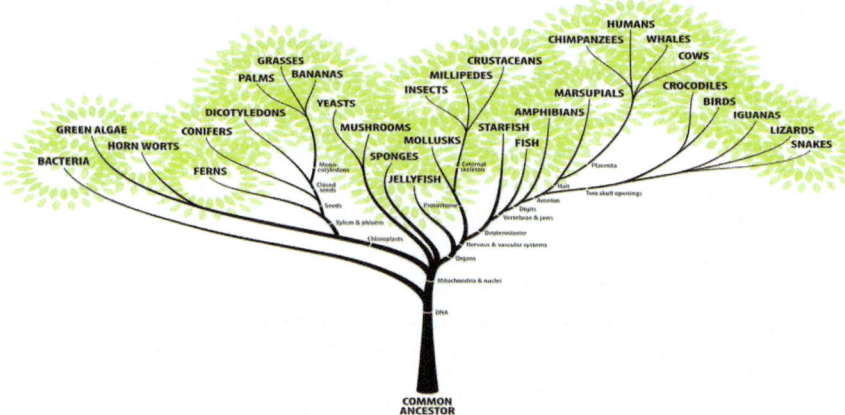

Fig. 12.1 The tree of life, as currently envisioned. https://assets.weforum.org/editor/58oflKwk6J9XthcBwG8kG2jN252m5y0wpdF3oZ1TtpU.jpg

Evolutionary biologists have continued to study various aspects of evolution by forming and testing hypotheses as well as constructing theories based on evidence from the field or laboratory and on data generated by the methods of mathematical and theoretical biology. Their discoveries have influenced not just the development of biology but numerous other scientific and industrial fields, including agriculture, medicine and computer science. According to modern radiological estimates, the total evolutionary history from the beginning of life to today has taken place since the last universal ancestor LUCA is not less than 3.5 to 3.8 billion years.

12.6 From Vitalism to Monism (Again)

Philosophers and scientists from Francis Bacon, René Descartes, Galileo Galilei, Isaac Newton and Gottfried Leibnitz developed the scientific method of rational empiricism. Like the established Church, of that time, they were dualists. They believed in the simultaneous but independent existence of mind (or spirit) and matter. But Baruch Spinoza, Thomas Hobbes, (and others) introduced the concept of *monism*—in opposition to the matter/spirit of Descartes (and all established religious authorities to this day). Monism is the fundamental idea that there is only one essential physical substance in the universe, from which everything else is composed. It didn't have a name in the seventeenth century, but now it does have a name: Energy. Today virtually all scientists are monists, without necessarily knowing the meaning of the word.

Vitalism had a long day in the nineteenth century sun. It starts from the dualist premise that living organisms are fundamentally different from non-living entities because they contain some non-physical element and are governed by different principles than are inanimate things. That element is often referred to as the "vital spark," "energy," or "élan vital," which some equate with the soul. In the eighteenth and nineteenth centuries biologists debated whether mechanics or physics would eventually explain the difference between life and non-life. Descartes voted for mechanics. Immanuel Kant and the idealists voted differently.

The notion that bodily functions are due to a vital principle existing in all living creatures has roots going back at least to ancient Egypt. Galen believed the lungs draw *pneuma* from the air, which the blood communicates throughout the body. The vitalists, such as **Georg Ernst Stahl**'s students—were supporters of the phlogiston theory of energy—active in the eighteenth century. The physician **Francis Xavier Bichat** of the Hotel Dieu was another. **Caspar Friedrich Wolff** (1733–1794), in his "*Theoria Generationis*" (1759) tried to explain the emergence of the organism by the actions of a *vis essentialis* (an organizing, formative force).

Carl Reichenbach (1788–1869) later developed the theory of Odic force, a form of life-energy that permeates living things. Vitalists argued that, whereas the chemical transformations undergone by non-living substances are reversible, so-called "organic" matter is permanently altered by chemical transformations (such as cooking).

Johann Friedrich Blumenbach (1752–1840) also was influential in establishing epigenesis in the life sciences with his 1781 publication of *Über den Bildungstrieb und das Zeugungsgeschäfte*. Blumenbach cut up freshwater *Hydra* and established that the removed parts would regenerate. He inferred the presence of a "formative drive" (*Bildungstrieb*) in living matter.

Jöns Jakob Berzelius (1779–1848), one of the early nineteenth century founders of modern chemistry, argued that compounds could be distinguished by whether they required any living organisms in their synthesis (organic compounds) or whether they did not (inorganic compounds). Vitalist chemists predicted that organic materials could not be synthesized from inorganic components. But in 1828, Friedrich Wöhler synthesized urea from inorganic components. That event did not end widespread belief in vitalism, but it undermined the chief argument of the believers.

Ernst Haeckel (1834–1919) was a German biologist, philosopher and free thinker. Haeckel was a physician, professor of comparative anatomy and one of the first scientists who understood psychology as a branch of physiology. He also participated in the introduction of certain notions of modern biology such as those of "branching" or "ecology". also referred to politics as applied biology. He promoted Charles Darwin's theory of natural selection in Germany. He developed a theory of his own on the origins of the human being.

Haeckel contributed much through his writings to the spread of the theory of evolution. He is considered a pioneer of eugenics, although he himself had no eugenic conception, because he expected, confident in the progress due to evolution, greater development and not a "degeneration". Philosophically, Haeckel professed a natural philosophy that conceived of a unity of God and the world ("monism" but not atheism).

Hæckel was not an atheist, but he rejected any intervention of a "creator" (hence his altercations with creationists). He came from a Christian home and considered that nature—up to inorganic crystals—was animated in some mysterious way. For him nature was a divine being ("Gaia"?) In this context, he spoke among others of "cellular memory" (*Zellgedächtnis*) and the "soul of crystals" (*Kristallseelen*).

Ernst Hæckel took part in 1904 in an international congress of free-thinkers, in Rome, that brought together nearly 2000 people. There, he was named "anti-pope" at a ceremonial luncheon. And at a demonstration that followed (on Campo Fiore in front of the memorial to Giordano Bruno) he tied a wreath of laurels on the monument. Haeckel was flattered: "Never before have so many honors been shown against me as at this international congress" (*Noch nie sind mir so viele persönliche Ehrungen erwiesen worden, wie auf diesem internationalen Kongreß*).

This provocation triggered a campaign of attacks from ecclesiastical circles. In particular, his scientific integrity was questioned, and he was described as a forger and a liar and called a "simian professor". Nevertheless, 46 recognized professors made amends for Haeckel, he was able to answer the accusations of falsification.

On January 11, 1906, the German Monist Union (Deutscher Monistenbund) was founded in Jena on his initiative. He was honorary president. He sketched a scientific basis for the Weltanschauung ideology of monism. His ideas were attractive to right-wing and national circles but also to liberal and left-wing circles. The monists around Haeckel at the time included Ferdinand Tönnies, Henry van de Velde, Alfred Hermann Fried, Otto Lehmann-Rußbüldt, Helene Stöcker, Magnus Hirschfeld and Carl von Ossietzky. Ernst Haeckel defended pacifist ideas.

He supported the pacifist movement of Bertha von Suttner (who had defended Darwin's theory of evolution). At the beginning of the First World War, however, Haeckel defended German participation in the war and expressed himself increasingly as a nationalist. Haeckel signed on October 2, 1914, the "Manifesto of the 93", which was also initialed by 92 other professors.

The monistic ethics described in "The Enigmas of the Universe", despite its revolutionary pretensions, did not go beyond the limits of ordinary bourgeois propriety. Haeckel nevertheless built on this ethic a utopia that would socially transpose the progress of science and technology.

Like other organizations of freethinkers, the German Monist Union was banned in 1933 by the Nazis. Nazi ideologues used excerpts from his writings as justification for their racist theories and social Darwinism, but at the same time they stated that essential elements of Haeckel's worldview were incompatible with National Socialism.

Wilhelm Ostwald (1853–1932) was a prolific physical chemist, credited with being one of the founders of the field of physical chemistry, with Jacobus Henricus van 't Hoff, Walther Nernst, and Svante Arrhenius. He invented the ammonia process for nitric acid production. He received the Nobel Prize in Chemistry in 1909 for his scientific contributions to the fields of catalysis, chemical equilibria and reaction velocities.

Ostwald's interest in unification through systematization led to his adaptation of the philosophy of Monism, first articulated by Spinoza and Locke in the seventeenth century. Initially, Monism was liberal, pacifist, and international, seeking in science a basis of values to support social and political reforms. Ostwald himself developed a system of ethics based on science, around the core idea that one should "not waste energy, but convert it into its most useful form."

Ostwald was a leader of the Monism movement in Germany, after Haeckel. He was the President of the German Monist Alliance from 1911–1915. Monists of that era believed that the process of natural selection ought to be organized and guided by society (eugenics) in order to reduce inequality and resulting suffering. Ostwald promoted eugenics by giving public speeches on the topic. He promoted eugenics and euthanasia as voluntary choices. Monist ideas may have indirectly facilitated acceptance of the later Social Darwinism of the National Socialists. Ostwald died before the Nazis adopted and enforced the use of eugenics and euthanasia as involuntary government policies, to support their racist ideology. Ostwald's Monism also influenced Carl G. Jung's identification of psychological types.

Louis Pasteur (1822–1895), performed several experiments, after his famous rebuttal of "spontaneous generation", that—in his view—supported vitalism. He argued that only the vitals spark could explain fermentation.

Rejecting the claims of Berzelius, Liebig, Traube and others that fermentation resulted from chemical agents or catalysts within cells, Pasteur insisted that fermentation was a "vital action". He was, arguably, the last respected vitalist (Fig. 12.2).

John Scott Haldane (1860–1936) adopted an anti-mechanist approach to biology and an idealist philosophy early on in his career. Haldane saw his work as a vindication of his belief that teleology was an essential concept in biology. His views became widely known with his first book Mechanism, life and personality in 1913. Haldane borrowed arguments from the vitalists to use against mechanism; however, he was not a vitalist. Haldane treated the organism as fundamental to biology: "*we perceive the organism as a self-regulating entity*", "*every effort to analyze it into components that can be reduced to a mechanical explanation violates this central experience*".

Haldane also insisted that a purely mechanist interpretation cannot account for the characteristics of life. Haldane wrote a number of books in which he attempted to show the invalidity of both vitalism and mechanist approaches to science. Haldane explained: "*We must find a different theoretical basis of biology, based on the observation that all the phenomena concerned*

Fig. 12.2 Louis Pasteur. Painting by Albert Edelfelt, 1885—Wikipedia

tend towards being so coordinated that they express what is normal for an adult organism."

Ernst Mayr (1904–2005) wrote: "*It would be ahistorical to ridicule vitalists. When one reads the writings of one of the leading vitalists like Driesch one is forced to agree with him that many of the basic problems of biology simply cannot be solved by a philosophy as that of Descartes, in which the organism is simply considered a machine…*" The logic of the critique of the vitalists was impeccable. No biologist alive today would want to be classified as a vitalist.

Vitalism (and dualism) lost scientific credibility, rather suddenly, a decade after Pasteur's death. The agent was a young Jewish physicist, named **Albert Einstein** (1879–1955), working for the Swiss Patent Office. The crucial event was the publication (1905) of Einstein's paper on the special theory of relativity. Here we skip over a lot of discussion on the meaning of relativity, and its link to cosmology and quantum mechanics, to emphasize one important implication of the paper: *mass is a form of energy*. A quantitative way of expressing this equivalence (and inter-convertibility) was expressed in the world's most famous equation. Here it is:

$$E = mc^2$$

where E is energy, m is mass and c is the velocity of light.

This famous formula was deduced by Einstein from a prior discovery by physicist **Max Karl Ernst Ludwig Planck** (1858–1947). Planck discovered that electromagnetic radiation consists of discrete "quanta"—now called photons—with definite frequencies. (Planck was awarded the Nobel Prize in Physics in 1918.) What Einstein's formula says is that mass and energy are inter-convertible, which implies that mass can be converted to energy (in the form of electromagnetic fields.)

We now know that very energetic photons (in high energy particle "colliders", like CERN) can also "split" momentarily into particle- antiparticle pairs that immediately recombine.[1] that fact led directly to the discovery of nuclear fission by German chemists **Otto Hahn** and **Fritz Strassmann** in 1938, and its theoretical explanation by **Lise Meitner** and **Otto Frisch**, made the development of the atomic bomb a theoretical possibility. As we now know, it was also a practical possibility.

There were fears, in 1939, especially among scientists who were refugees from Nazi Germany, that Germany might develop such a weapon first. Germany did have a nuclear program, under **Werner Heisenberg**, but it

---

[1] Dan Brown wrote a thriller about Illuminati's, based on the idea that anti-particles could be captured and collected, to form "anti-matter". That was also a pipe dream.

did not get beyond the preliminary stages, perhaps because Heisenberg was not enthusiastic about it. In August 1939, **Leo Szilard** and **Eugene Wigner** drafted a letter warning of the potential development of "*extremely powerful bombs of a new type*". It urged the United States to support the research of **Enrico Fermi et al.** on nuclear chain reactions. They persuaded Albert Einstein to sign the letter, and delivered it to President **Franklin D. Roosevelt**. The Manhattan Project was created under the US Army Corps of Engineers. Atomic bombs were developed and tested and two atomic bombs were dropped on Japanese cities in August 1945, ending the Second World War.

Most cosmologists today see the expanding universe as the outcome of an event that occurred 13.87 billion years ago, called the "Big Bang". That event can be interpreted as a colossal nuclear explosion, in which time started and mass was instantaneously converted to kinetic energy and radiation. We see the after-effects, as electromagnetic radiation and as shining stars, in galaxies and clusters, constantly getting farther apart, as the universe expands.

13

Entropy, Exergy, Information and Complexity

13.1 Background

The larger system is Planet Earth and the solar system—especially the sun—from which it draws useful energy (exergy) capable of doing physical work, for metabolic purposes. Self-organization enables such a dissipative subsystem not only to survive, but to grow and increase its internal order and complexity. Self-organization, in the form of stable structures, incorporating multiple gradients, exist far from thermodynamic equilibrium. They are crucial for the existence of life on Earth, and the future of Mankind, not to mention your pension fund. They are not consistent with the isolated world in equilibrium—meaning no gradients and nothing changing—that standard neoclassical economic theory assumes, thanks to its historical roots. We come back to this later.

The second law of thermodynamics says that every spontaneous materials transformation process (like combustion) is irreversible, but it can do useful (productive) work. Moreover, doing work can produce complex long-lived artifacts: it can create order out of disorder in a subsystem of the overall system. The Second Law of thermodynamics says that while the total energy in a closed system remains constant—energy is neither created nor destroyed—the usable fraction (we call it exergy) declines with every action n or transaction. And, while the usable fraction (exergy) declines, the overall level of disorder (entropy) increases.

What the Second Law, in its primitive form, does not say (but does not deny) is that an isolated system—such as the universe as a whole, or a solar system, or a planet—can also "self-organize" into separate stable subsystems, by dissipating exergy. It is possible to maintain an "island" of stability and increasing order (negative entropy) far from thermodynamic equilibrium. These subsystems can survive for a very long time, provided only that there is a continuous stream of exergy (fuel) from another part of the system, available to "feed" the exergy dissipation in the island of order.

This expansion and cooling have enabled the universe to do a lot of physical work. But as entropy has increased, so has local order and complexity. The expanding, cooling universe has created order and complexity (think of useful information) on every scale: galaxies, stars, planets, living organisms, the human brain, ecosystems, automobiles, rockets and smartphones, the Taj Mahal, the Mona Lisa, Beethoven's 9th symphony, and the Library of Congress (Hofstadter, 1980) (Ayres, 1994) (Hidalgo, 2015).

13.2 Complexity

Hierarchical information theory has emerged from efforts to reconcile genealogical evolution (increasing biodiversity) with ecological evolution (increasing organization and order. Yet these are inconsistent with the idea of information as negentropy. The reconciliation, proposed by Brooks and Wiley, is hierarchical information theory, in which there is a division between the domain of order and the domain of disorder, both measured in terms of information capacity. In this theory self-organizing systems are characterized by information capacity, where the total information capacity is the sum of order capacity and disorder capacity, both of which increase with time. But at low levels of the hierarchy disorder prevails, while at high levels order prevails.

The increase of complexity in our world has engendered a new science about complexity itself. **Stuart Kauffman** (b. 1939) is known for arguing that the complexity of biological systems and organisms might result as much from self-organization and far-from-equilibrium dynamics as from Darwinian natural selection. This thesis is discussed in his book *The Origin of Order* (Kauffman, 1993). Kauffmann has also led the self-organized emergence of collectively autocatalytic sets of polymers, specifically peptides, for the origin of molecular reproduction. This theory has recently found experimental support. The mechanism for spontaneous creation of auto-catalysis in chemicals is still mysterious, but we think it will be decrypted one day, soon. By mechanisms that we are just beginning to understand, in broad terms, evolution has created complexity on a grand scale. We humans are the culmination (so far) of that order-creation process. Will it continue? If so, in what direction?

Erwin Schrödinger (1887–1961), was one of the fathers of quantum mechanics (which we will not book) try to explain in this book. In his seminal book "*What is Life?*" (Schrödinger, 1944), he attempted to draw together the fundamental processes of biology and the sciences of physics and chemistry. He noted that life is comprised of two fundamental processes; one "order from order" and the other "order from disorder". He observed that the gene generates order from order in a species: that is, the progeny inherit the traits of the parent. He predicted that something like DNA must exist to make this transmission possible. Over a decade later, in 1953, **James Watson** (b. 1928) and **Francis Crick** (1916–2004) discovered the mechanism intergenerational transmission of genetic information (traits), namely the double helix of DNA (Watson, 1953) (Watson, 1968). This discovery provided biology with a research agenda that has led to some of the most important scientific findings of the last fifty years Fig. 13.1.

The double helix (DNA molecule) (actually a polymer) that carries information from generation to generation. The five nuclide bases are adenine, thymine, cytosine, guanine, uracil, all based on five or six elements H, C, N, O, S and P. The menstrual cycle of ovulation is perhaps the best illustration of life as a system of interactive bio-chemical cycles. It is a series of natural changes in hormone production and the structures of the uterus and ovaries of the female reproductive system. These changes make pregnancy possible, i.e., they enable the female to accommodate a fetus and enable it to grow large enough to survive outside the mother's body. It is a very complex process. The details don't matter here.

However, Schrödinger's other equally important, but less understood, observation was his "order from disorder" premise. This was an effort to link biology with the fundamental theorems of thermodynamics. Schrödinger noted that living systems seem to defy the second law of thermodynamics. The second law insists that, within closed systems, the entropy of a system should be maximized. Living systems, however, are the antithesis of such disorder. They display marvelous levels of order created from disorder. For instance, plants are highly ordered structures, which are synthesized from disordered atoms and molecules found in atmospheric gases and soils. How does this happen?

The theory of near-equilibrium thermodynamics, as it was developed in the nineteenth century by Carnot, Mayer, Helmholtz, Joule, Clausius, Rankine, Thomson (Lord Kelvin) and Gibbs was revised and extended to

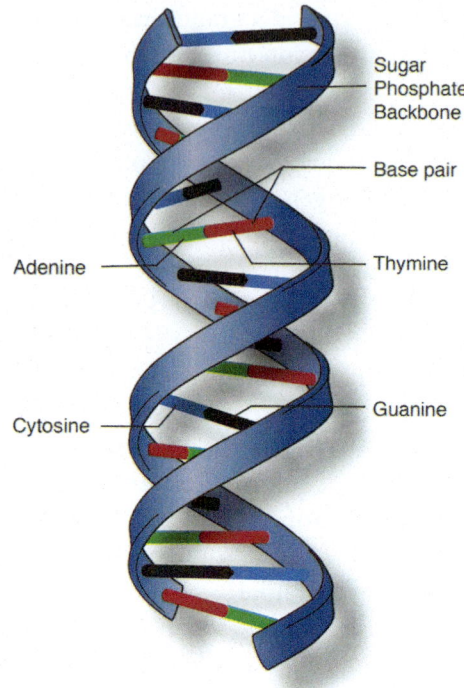

Fig. 13.1 The double helix (DNA) that carries genetic information from generation to generation—Wikipedia

regions for from equilibrium by **Ilya Romanovitch Prigogine (1917v–2003)** et al. at the Free University in Brussels during the 1970s (Prigogine, 1955) (Nicolis, 1971) (Nicolis, 1977) (Prigogine, 1984). Prigogine's work introduced the fundamental concept of "self-organization" i.e., creating 'dissipative structures' characterized by maximum entropy production and driven by a source of free energy far from thermodynamic equilibrium. The first application of their theory was to explain some peculiar phenomena in chemistry. Subsequently a number of other applications have emerged, first in biology, later in ecology and sociology. Self-organization can also enable the creation and preservation of order, either as material objects or as knowledge. Self-organization yields stable dissipative sub-systems that incorporate gradients, far from thermodynamic equilibrium (where gradients do not exist.) In Prigogine's words) a self-organized system is an "*island of order and complexity*"—embedded in a larger system, i.e., the planet, or the solar system.

E. D. Schneider and James J. Kay have also suggested a paradigm that provides for a thermodynamically consistent explanation of life, including the origin of life, biological growth, the development of ecosystems, and patterns of biological evolution observed in the fossil record (Schneider, 1994, 1995). They illustrate this paradigm through a discussion of ecosystem development, arguing that as ecosystems grow and develop, they develop more complex structures with more energy flow, increase their cycling activity, develop greater diversity and generate more hierarchical levels, all to abet exergy dissipation. Species that survive in ecosystems are those that funnel exergy into their own production and reproduction and contribute to autocatalytic processes which increase the total dissipation of the ecosystem. In short, ecosystems develop in ways which systematically increase their ability to dissipate the incoming solar energy.

The larger system is Planet Earth and the solar system—especially the sun—from which it draws useful energy (exergy) capable of doing physical work, for metabolic purposes. Self-organization enables such a sub-system not only to survive, but to grow and increase its internal order and complexity. Self-organization, in the form of stable structures, incorporating multiple gradients, existing far from thermodynamic equilibrium, are crucial for the existence of life on Earth, and the future of Mankind, not to mention your pension fund. They are not consistent with the isolated equilibrium world that standard neoclassical economic theory assumes, thanks to its historical roots.

To summarize: the first law of thermodynamics says that mass/energy is conserved in every transaction. It means that energy is neither created nor destroyed. This means that material transformations in the extraction and production processes, that our civilization depends on, unavoidably generate material residuals: garbage, sewage, trash, scrap, pollution) that remain in the environment. The residuals may be conveniently forgotten by the people who generated them (for a while) but they do not disappear.

The second law of thermodynamics says that every spontaneous materials transformation process (like combustion) is irreversible, but it can do useful (productive) work. Moreover, doing work can produce complex long-lived artifacts i.e., create order out of disorder in a subsystem of the overall system. The Second Law says that while the total energy in a closed system remains constant, the usable fraction (we call it exergy) declines with every action or transaction. And, while the usable fraction (exergy) declines, the overall level of disorder (entropy) increases.

What the Second Law, in its primitive form, does not say (but does not deny) is that an isolated system—such as the universe as a whole, or a solar system, or a planet—can "self-organize" into separate stable subsystems, far from equilibrium, by dissipating exergy. It is possible to maintain an "island" of stability and increasing order (negative entropy) far from thermodynamic equilibrium. These subsystems can survive for a very long time, provided only that there is a continuous stream of exergy (fuel) from another part of the system, available to "feed" the exergy dissipation in the island.

13.3 Sources of Exergy in the Cosmos

The sources of useful energy (exergy), available to us humans, that can drive the creation of complex organisms and structures (self-organization), on planet Earth, are thermonuclear processes that convert mass into exergy. The mass of the universe was created (according to current theory) by mysterious event a involving the "Higgs field" before the Big Bang. Ever since that event, billions of years ago, the universe has been losing mass by converting it into energy, in the form of photons.[1] Some of the photons arrive at the top of Earth's atmosphere, as sunlight. Some of the sunlight is converted immediately into carbohydrates (biomass) via the process of photosynthesis. Some is converted again into the kinetic energy of wind and flowing water. Others arrive later in the form of "fossil fuels, nuclear heat from radioactive decay in the Earth's core. All of these are "natural capital" and "gifts of nature". The fossil fuels are stores of chemical exergy from photosynthesis that occurred in the distant geological past, several hundred million years ago. This reservoir of fossil fuel is gradually being exhausted, although there is still enough left, as some witty journalist has noted, "to fry us all". The Earth's geological reservoir of radio-nuclides, and its store of useful chemical combinations—such as metallic sulfides—are other examples of natural capital in the form of exploitable mineral concentrations (ores) left over from the formation of the solar system.

The solar furnace in the sun that drives life on Earth, not to mention the winds and ocean currents, will run out of hydrogen fuel a few billion years in the future (Morris, 1980). (This will be followed by the "red giant" phase, as the sun starts burning its accumulated helium "ash"—and swallows up the inner planets. That will be followed by the "white dwarf" stage when the helium is also used up by making carbon: three helium atoms fuse to create one carbon atom, with a further small energy release. When fusion gradually slows down to a stop, several billions of years from now, the sun will

---

[1] The so-called Breit–Wheeler process represents the only known example of a process where energy (photons) is transformed into mass (positron–electron pairs); but even in this special experimental case, the resulting elementary particles cannot combine to form atomic structures having economic value. Dan Brown's novel "Angels and Demons" postulated such a process.

become a "black dwarf", meanwhile making heavier (than carbon) elements such as oxygen and silicon. But for the present, and the foreseeable future, what matters is that there is plenty of useful energy available for foreseeable human purposes, and that will be true for a very long time to come.

Since the "Big Bang" (BB) when it all began, as most physicists now believe (but I have dsoubt) the expansion of the universe has not just converted order into disorder. It has also created localized order of extraordinary complexity. Yes, the universe is like a heat engine: starting hot, it has expanded enormously—by hundreds of factors of ten (orders of magnitude) since the hypothetical Big Bang—and it has cooled by a comparable amount, notwithstanding the trillions of very hot stars still cooling out there and new ones are being created.

The expanding and cooling of the universe are seen as evidence of the irreversibility and unidirectionality of all processes with the possible exception of the Big Bang itself. This uni-directionality is expressed by the second law of thermodynamics—the entropy law. The Big Bang has killed vitalism and dualism, and established monism, in the sense that we now can say, as Spinoza once did, that the stuff of the universe is energy and energy is everything, including mass. There is nothing else.

The sources of useful energy (exergy) that can drive self-organization available to us humans, on Earth, are sunlight, fossil fuels, nuclear heat from radioactive decay in the Earth's core, biomass, wind, and flowing water. All of these are "natural capital" and "gifts of nature". The fossil fuels are stores of chemical exergy from photosynthesis that occurred in the distant geological past, several hundred million years ago. This reservoir is gradually being exhausted, although there is still enough left, as some witty journalist has noted, "to fry us all". The Earth's geological reservoir of radio-nuclides, and its store of useful chemical combinations—such as metallic sulfides—are other examples of natural capital in the form of exploitable mineral ores.

The solar furnace that drives the hydrological cycle—which drives both winds and ocean currents—will run out of hydrogen fuel a few billion years in the future (Morris, 1980). (This will be followed by the "red giant" phase, as the sun starts burning its accumulated helium "ash"—and swallows up the inner planets. That will be followed by the "white dwarf" stage when the helium is also used up creating carbon, oxygen and iron. When fusion gradually slows down to a stop, scores or hundreds of billions of years from now, the sun will become a "black dwarf", according to current cosmological theory. But for the present, and the foreseeable future, what matters is that there is plenty of useful energy available for foreseeable human purposes, and that will be true for a very long time to come.

13.4 The Standard Model of Physics

The complexity creation process has been accompanied by differentiation. Differentiation is another word for "symmetry-breaking". It occurs on every scale, from the micro to the colossal, as temperatures fall. For instance, physicists now think there are two kinds of particles, **bosons** (massless force carriers) and **fermion**s with mass. The standard theory of physics now assumes 6 species of quarks, 6 species of leptons, 4 species of gauge bosons plus one scalar boson known as the Higgs particle.

We didn't take the physics course that explained this diagram, so we merely note that most of these particles have very short lives, measured in tiny fractions of tiny fractions of seconds, and they exist only at extremely high temperatures. Most of them don't exist most of the time. The last one (The Higgs) existed—and was observed—only for a very tiny fraction of a second in the high energy particle accelerator at the European Research Center (CERN) in France, in June 2012. But the scheme in Fig. 11.3 is sort of symmetrical. Nature seems to like symmetry. Or perhaps it is we who like it and try to see it everywhere.

At reasonably low temperatures—by which we mean temperatures that might exist on the surface of a star—there are only three elementary particles, most of the time. They are *electrons*, with a negative charge, *protons* (with a positive charge) and *neutrons* (with no charge). Isn't it interesting that the universe as a whole is also neutral (as far as we can tell)? There are exactly enough electrons to mate with all the protons. Or we could say it the other way around: there are exactly enough protons in the universe to marry all the electrons. The married couple of one proton and one electron is a hydrogen atom. There is no surplus of either gender (charge). That suggests a broken symmetry, does it not? Maybe there was an earlier time when there were only neutrons. OK, that is a pointless speculation.

At a later time the universe consisted of hydrogen atoms. When the positively charged nucleus in a hydrogen atom encounters a free neutron, the proton and the neutron can join hands (so to speak), emitting photons in the process. The result is heavy hydrogen nucleus or atom. Two of those combine to form a helium nucleus or a helium atom. The visible mass of the universe, just after the Big Bang, was about 75% hydrogen and 25% helium (100% of the total mass), with no other elements. But today the hydrogen–helium share of mass is down to 98% and the other 2% consists of 90 heavier-than-helium, long-lived species of atoms, combined into tens of thousands of species of molecules and probably billions of species of living organisms, not to mention super-organisms. That is complexity. Figure 13.2 shows the periodic table of elements arranged in rows and columns, by atomic number (the number of protons in the nucleus). Hen.

All the boxes for atomic numbers above 92 (uranium) have been named for physicists, but they are empty in the sense that no elements with that atomic number has yet been found on Earth. This is because there was so little of those heavy elements in the first place, and the element would be extremely unstable, meaning a very short half-life (i.e., likely to split into elements with smaller nuclei spontaneously) (Fig. 13.3).

The next question you might ask is this: Why is the distribution of elements by size so uneven? Part of the answer is that, in the centers of small stars, the temperature is around 10 million degrees K and hydrogen atoms keep merging to form helium until the hydrogen is used up. Near the end of that stage the star expands and becomes a "red giant". The star then shrinks to the size of the Earth and becomes a "white dwarf. In the white dwarf, more fusion occurs spontaneously. Three helium atoms combine to form carbon,

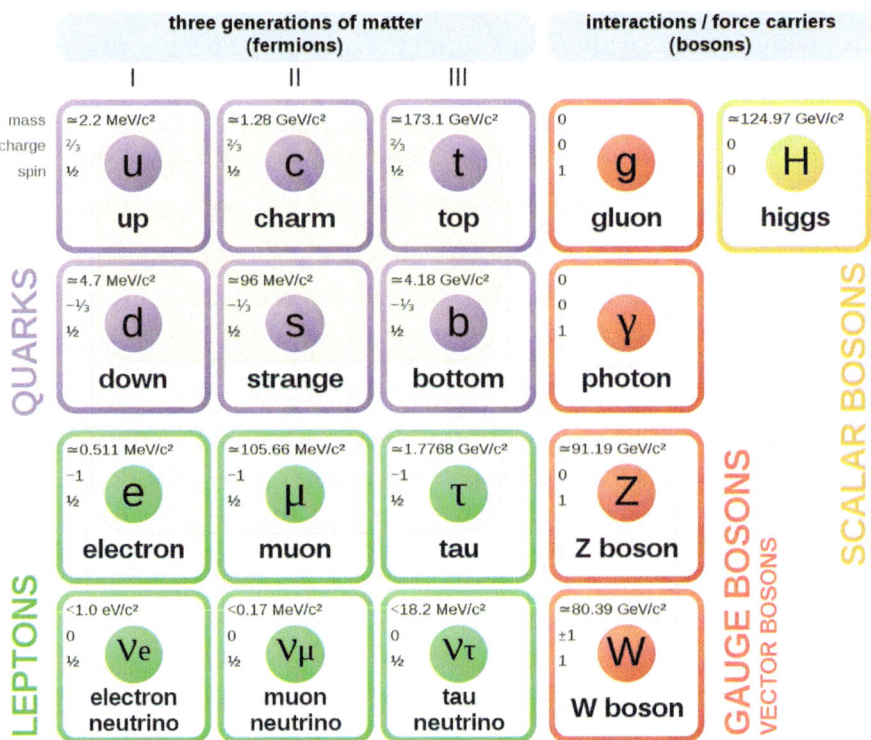

Fig. 13.2 The So-called standard model of elementary particles—Wikipedia

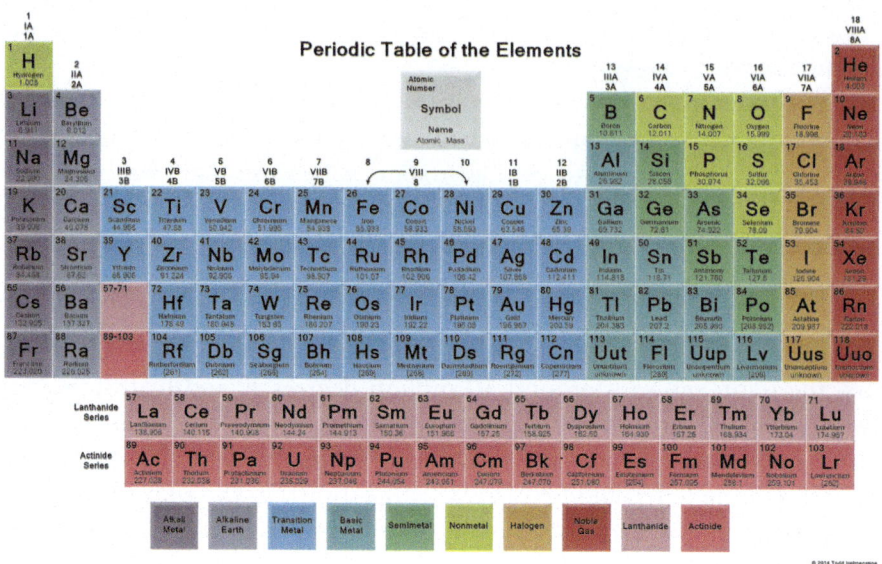

Fig. 13.3 The periodic table—Wikipedia

plus photons, as the white dwarf shrinks. Carbon and helium fuse to form oxygen. The sequence stops there unless the star is very large, more than 8 solar masses. In the latter case, it continues, step by step through neon, silicon and iron. Iron is the most stable of all the atoms. Over 99% of all stars behave like this.

The creation of elements heavier than iron occurs only in supernovae. In those very large stars all of the heavier elements are created, first in the "crust" on the surface, and later in the interior, as the star explodes. This nucleosynthesis process accounts for the creation of all the other elements. Elements with atomic numbers greater than carbon (atomic weight = 12) and less than iron (a.w.56) are made in the white dwarves. But heavier elements, from cobalt (a.w. = 57) to uranium (a.w. = 238) were entirely created by the explosions (called "*supernovae*") of very large stars when they run out of fuel. At that point gravitational collapse begins, the radiation pressure falls and the temperature rises, partly due to intense neutrino bombardment. The ultra-high pressures and temperatures cause fusions that create all the heavy elements in the periodic table. That still doesn't explain the uneven mass distribution. (We were hoping you wouldn't notice.) We can't explain it, and we aren't aware of any theory that explains it convincingly, but it probably doesn't matter for the purpose of this book.

13.5 Entropy and Information

How does an entropic theory of information fit into economic theory? To be honest, we find it hard to explain, but some thoughts may be worth recording here. Now it is time to call up the ghosts of Boltzmann and Shannon. Boltzmann thought that the second law of thermodynamics ("entropy law") is a law of "disorder". What he meant was that if there are a large number N of molecules in a box, there must be an even larger number of possible arrangements of them. Each of those possible arrangements is "infinitely improbable". But the box of gas molecules, as a whole, has a characteristic probabilistic state S, depending on temperature, pressure and density. The equation for entropy, on Boltzmann's tombstone, is provided by statistical mechanics, viz.

$$S = k_B \log W$$

where S is the entropy, and W is the number of possible microstates (or rearrangements) of the system. (W does depend on other variables, such as pressure, temperature and density.) The Boltzmann constant $k_B = 1.38 \times 10^{-23}$ in Joules per degree Kelvin). Although Boltzmann first linked entropy and probability in 1877, the value of k_B was actually calculated for the first time in 1900–1901 **by Max Planck** (1858–1947) from his law of black-body radiation. Planck calculated $k_B = 1.346 \times 10^{-23}$ J/K, which is about 2.5% lower than today's correct figure. (Planck introduced the notation in the same work as his eponymous uncertainty constant h which appears in many equations of quantum mechanics.)

Fifty years later, more or less, the exact same mathematical formula was discovered at Bell Telephone Laboratories (BTL) by a completely different route: It came from an analysis of the probabilities a sequence of symbols—e.g., letters of the alphabet in a message—where the inherent probabilities of the letters are known. The discoverer was **Claude Shannon** (1916 -2001), who is now regarded as the father of modern information theory and one of the fathers of artificial intelligence. (The photo below was taken during an experiment to teach a mechanical "mouse" to find and learn its way through a labyrinth.) Shannon was advised to call it "entropy" by John von Neumann, who allegedly said that nobody would challenge this definition because nobody knows what entropy means.

The idea that the second law of thermodynamics or "entropy law" is a law of disorder (or that dynamically ordered states are "infinitely improbable") is due to Boltzmann's view of the second law of thermodynamics. Fifty years later the exact same mathematical formula was discovered at Bell Telephone

Laboratories (BTL) by a completely different route, with a different interpretation as the information content of a sequence of symbols—e.g., letters of the alphabet in a message, where the inherent probabilities of the letters are known. The discoverer was **Claude Shannon** (1916—2001), the father of modern information theory and one of the fathers of artificial intelligence. The photo below was taken during an experiment to teach a mechanical "mouse" to find and learn its way through a labyrinth (Fig. 13.4).

Let us start again, at the beginning: consider the ways in which an organism receives information from its environment. Humans have five senses, viz. vision (eyes), sound (ears), pressure or heat on the skin (touch), odor (nose) and taste (tongue). The five senses are restricted to animals, though not all animals have all five. The logic of natural selection suggests that the senses are needed for locomotion, predation or defense against predators.

We all know that dogs, and other predatory animals depend, far more than we humans, on the olfactory sense (smell). A significant part of a dog's brain is devoted to identifying smells, which are actually complex chemical molecules. Dogs recognize people by smell, more than by sight. Predators probably developed that sense especially for hunting purposes. The senses of taste and smell are probably for protection against eating poisonous foods. Plants do not have sensory organs.

The last several million years of human evolution took place in and among trees, where vision and hearing were more important for survival, than smell.

Fig. 13.4 Claude Shannon and his electromechanical mouse Theseus—Wikipedia

Vision is even more important for birds, which have little or no need for smell and little need for touch, but use sound for communication, using language, as we do. The sense of touch (pressure on the skin) is ancient. It probably evolved to assist animals to locate themselves in hiding places (e.g., by touching with whiskers), to avoid discomfort, to find food or to perform sexual (reproductive) functions.

Much of the modern human brain especially the cerebral cortex, is devoted to sensory information processing, information storage (memory), decision-making and "thinking". The other (older) part of the brain is for controlling autonomic sensory bodily functions. The autonomic functions are programmed in the DNA, and respond to relatively simple signals, such as light/dark, heat/cold, thirst, hunger, alarm, and so on.

Having said all that, the next question is this: How have humans amplified or otherwise extended the primitive signal detection and information processing capacity of the natural brain, eyes, ears, skin, lungs and voice-box. Here, the obvious starting point was voice communication within the tribe, perhaps amplified by drums, whistles or horns.

The transmission of signals over a distance for the purpose of communication with strangers began with the use of smoke signals and drums in many places. In AD 26–37 the Roman Emperor Tiberius ruled the empire from the island of Capri by signaling with metal mirrors to reflect the sun. Ships on Ferdinand Magellan's voyage (1520 AD) conveyed signal to each other by firing cannon and raising flags. In the 1790s the first fixed semaphore systems emerged in Europe. However it was not until the 1830s that electrical telecommunication systems (the telegraph) started to appear.

Writing was a supplement for human memory. It is now known thanks to recent archeological discoveries that writing (of inscriptions on turtle shells or bones) was practiced in China long ago (1400–1200 BCE) and by the Olmecs of meso-America as early as 600 BCE. The Mesopotamian cuneiform script was invented in Sumer (c. 3200 BCE) and can be traced without any discontinuity from a prehistoric antecedent to the present-day alphabet. Phonetic signs were introduced to transcribe the name of individuals, when writing started emulating spoken language. Writing was invented several times in different places. It evolved differently from each. There were 4 phases: ideography, logography, syllabaries, and the alphabet. The alphabet, with two dozen letters, each standing for a single sound of voice, was the 4th phase. Chanting, singing and music followed, also beginning thousands of years ago. Printing, starting in China, was the big breakthrough for memory storage. Movable type mechanized it.

Modern telecommunications began with the telegraph in 1837 and was swiftly followed by the voice telephone (by wire), the radio telephone and the radio broadcast, TV, the electronic computer, and the Internet. There is no need to comment on the underlying technology, except to say that today the transmission of messages is almost entirely based on use of the electromagnetic spectrum. Moreover, while telecommunications technology was once transmitted over copper wires, and later via microwaves, using satellites, the global system in use today is mainly based on laser beams transmitted through glass fibers. The messages themselves are converted from analog to digital form to enable processing by digital computer technology. Those messages, passing through optical (glass) fibers, carry information in binary code, at maximum rate at minimum cost and minimum exergy consumption.

Today a large volume of messages are sent and received by machines. However, human users require modems that convert analog messages to digital form, and conversely. Received digital messages are finally converted to analog and conveyed to the human brain through the eyes and ears. From modem to modem we have defined a "channel" of communication. It is the visual signals that convey most of the information. We can usually follow a movie without hearing the sound track—in fact all the early movies were silent—but not in the reverse case.

OK, so now in 2022 we humans have a huge global communications system, with modems and "channels" between them. Of course we want to maximize the system's performance. To do so we need a way to measure the message substance that is passing back and forth between modems. Of course, by this time you know that we are going to call it "information". We also need to determine the value—hence the price—of that information. What we can do is to estimate expenditure on information, in monetary units, or as a fraction of income, or perhaps as a fraction of productive time.

Information is commonly used in three ways: in the semantic sense (as data), in the pragmatic sense of "knowledge" or "know-how", and in a formal technical sense as the resolution of doubt or uncertainty. Shannon was thinking about the latter definition It must be emphasized that knowledge is an inherently anthropocentric concept, information (data) can be meaningless. Information in the third (Shannonian) sense of the word is the probability of selecting a given state or outcome from the universe of physically possible states. The more physically possible states there are, the more information is embodied in a given selection (or set of selections).

Using the standard notation for entropy S, we postulate that the two kinds of entropy are really identical, except for the sign, as has been argued by several physicists. One of them, **Leon Nicolas Brillouin** (1889–1969) calculated the thermodynamic equivalent of 1 bit of Shannonian information to be $k_B \ln 2 = 9.52 \times 10^{-34}$ J/K. In words, a "bit" of information corresponds to a very small flow of energy (exergy) or a very small change of temperature or both.

Myron Tribus and **Edward McIrvine** have actually estimated the very small absolute amounts of energy (exergy) required to process and deliver useful information in familiar communication and information-processing activities {Tribus, 1971}. For example, a television broadcast in 1970 required about 6 J of energy to deliver 300,000 bits (0.3 megabits) of information—as pixels—to the TV screen, through x wires. But that pixel information had an available energy (exergy) equivalent of only 1.3×10^{-15} J. (The exergy consumed by the light emitted by the TV screen itself, during a broadcast, is many orders of magnitude greater.)

The 6 J of energy-content in the information conveyed by the TV broadcast in 1970 was just "noise", in relation to other sources of waste heat lost to the environment. Today, thanks to the Internet, information flows (and corresponding exergy losses) are many factors of ten larger. Hence the exergy consumed by information transmission per se is much greater today, but the pixel information is delivered to the screen far more efficiently (via optical fibers).

The physical identification of information as "negentropy" suggests the possibility that stores of information embodied in structures and organizations can be regarded, in some sense, as reserves or storehouses of useful negative entropy (knowledge). These structures can be utilized to increase the ability of dissipative open systems to capture both negative entropy and materials from the environment and thus to grow and evolve.

Three related notions are suggested by the identification of information stocks with negative entropy. First, a dissipative structure far from equilibrium may itself capture and store negative entropy from in environment for future use, in the form of more complex organizations or structures. Second, evolutionary level can be defined, tentatively, as the ability of a living system to capture and store negative entropy (in genetic structures or brains). And third, intelligence can be defined as the ability to learn or modify the external environment. The vertical scale in the diagram below, from **Carl Sagan** (1934–1996), is supposed to be the number of bits of information per nucleotide pair in the DNA and the horizontal scale is the total information embodied in the DNA of the species (Fig. 13.5).

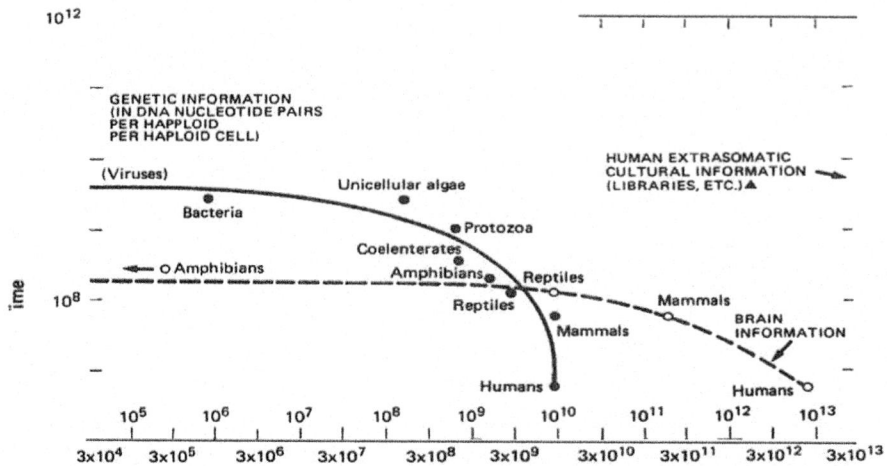

Fig. 13.5 Genetic Information vs Brain Information. *Source* Reproduced with Permission from Sagan 1977

OK, the Sagan graph above is interesting but strictly irrelevant. What we need to go further is a way of incorporating information (in the "know how" sense) into a production function. That topic is discussed in the next Sect. (16.7).

14

The "Marginal Revolution" in Economics

14.1 Mathematics in Economics

Mark Blaug, probabl5y the most widely read economic historian of the twentieth century, as identified a shift, in economic theorizing, between a focus on economic quantities at a point i5n time, and focus on marginal rates of change over time. This shift became possible as economic time series data became available, and variables could be regarded as functions of time. The retrospective virtue of this shift is that it enables the use of calculus, differentiation, integration, statistical analysis and Lagrangian variational methods, all of which required smoothly changing functional relationships. To be fair, this was not really possible earlier, because the data was too imprecise and incomplete.

Antoine Augustin Cournot (1801–1877) was a French philosopher and mathematician who contributed to theories on monopolies and duopolies are still famous. In 1838 his book "Researches on the Mathematical Principles of the Theory of Wealth" was published. Cournot was apparently the first to introduce functions and probability into economic analysis. He derived the first formula for the rule of supply and demand as a function of price and was also the first to draw supply and demand curves on a graph (see Fig. 14.1). different income levels for a 'representative consumer'. This figure, or something like it, is in every economics textbook.

The intersection of supply and demand curves for commodities or products (as a function of quantity) defined an equilibrium price where supply matches demand. The neoclassical argument is this: for a consumer with a

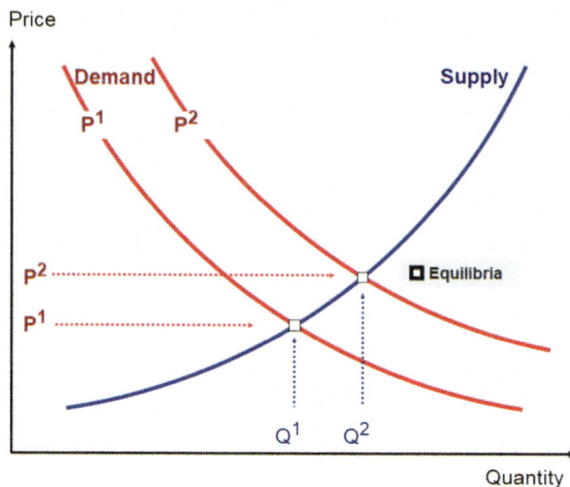

Fig. 14.1 Textbook version of supply and demand—Wikipedia

fixed income, the lower the price of a desirable good or service (say, cotton cloth) the more of it she will want, i.e., the greater the demand for it. This relationship is expressed by means of a "demand curve", for a "representative agent" that declines monotonically from upper left to lower right. The slope of that curve is called the price elasticity of demand. The different demand curves of actual consumers represent different preferences. But the supply of each commodity and the demand for it, depends upon the supply of and demand for other commodities in the system. Is there a set of prices allowing a general equilibrium where all commodities are produced and consumed without any surplus or deficit?

Questions rarely discussed include: what if the supply curve for a given commodity (blue) is not rising? What if it is also declining, from upper left to lower right? (That is not only possible, for aggregates, but likely.) Evidently the two demand curves for a given entity might never meet, or they might meet more than once. If they never meet, that consumer will not buy that good or service at any price. But the other case, where the curves cross more than once, suggests multiple equilibria, at different output levels (and prices). In any case, the "representative consumer" makes very little sense in the real world of heterogeneous agents, where income distribution depends on relative prices.

The two demand curves in the figure represent different goods or services, or they could correspond to difference groups of consumers with different incomes. Both interpretations have been used.

14.2 The Theory of Utility

Marie-Esprit-Léon Walras (1834–1910) was a French mathematical economist who formulated the marginal theory of value in equations. Walras came to be regarded as one of the three pioneers of the marginalist revolution, but he worked independently and was not acquainted with either of them. (The others were William Stanley Jevons and Carl Menger).

For Walras, exchanges only take place after a "tâtonnement" (French for "trial and error"), guided by an auctioneer. He recognized that certain conditions have to be met for each exchange, in equilibrium. The first condition is that the stock of the good owned by the buyer, after the exchange, increases by exactly the same amount as the stock owned by the seller decreases as a result of the exchange. The second condition is almost the same, except that it applies to the two stocks of money: the buyer's stock of money (or his bank account) decreases by the same amount as the seller's stock of money increases. Each of these conditions is an equation. In equilibrium the total stock of the good does not change and the total stock of money does not change. (The sum of the changes in each variable is zero.) Although Walras set out the framework for thinking about the existence of equilibrium clearly and precisely. His attempt to demonstrate existence by counting the number of equations and variables was slightly flawed: it is easy to see that not all pairs of equations in two variables have solutions.

In 1874 and 1877 Walras published *Éléments d'économie politique pure*. The notion of general equilibrium was very quickly adopted by later economists such as Vilfredo Pareto, Knut Wicksell or Gustav Cassel. John Hicks and Paul Samuelson used the Walrasian contribution in their elaboration of the neoclassical synthesis. A more rigorous version of the argument was developed independently by Lionel McKenzie and separately by Kenneth Arrow and Gérard Debreu in the 1950s {McKenzie, 1954} {Arrow, 1954}.

According to Schumpeter: "*Walras is … greatest of all economists. His system of economic equilibrium, uniting, as it does, the quality of 'revolutionary' creativeness with the quality of classic synthesis, is the only work by an economist that will stand comparison with the achievements of theoretical physics.*"{Schumpeter, 1943}. It was the general equilibrium obtained from a single hypothesis, rarity, that led Joseph Schumpeter to give him that accolade.

William Stanley Jevons (1835–1882) was an English economist and logician, and one of the first to recognize the importance of natural resources. Jevons broke off his studies of the natural sciences in London in 1854 to work as an assayer in Sydney, Returning to the UK in 1859, he published *General Mathematical Theory of Political Economy* in 1862, outlining the marginal utility theory of value. For Jevons, the utility or value to a consumer of an additional unit of a product is inversely related to the number of units of that product he already owns, at least beyond some critical quantity.

Jevons received public recognition for his work on *The Coal Question* (1865), in which he called attention to the gradual exhaustion of Britain's coal supplies and also put forth the view that increases in energy production efficiency leads to more, not less, consumption. This is known today as the Jevons paradox. Due to this work, Jevons is regarded today as the first economist of some standing to develop an 'ecological' perspective on the economy.

Irving Fisher described Jevons's book *A General Mathematical Theory of Political Economy* (1862) as the start of the mathematical method in economics. It made the case that economics as a science concerned with quantities is necessarily mathematical. In so doing, it expounded upon the "final" (marginal) utility theory of value. Jevons' work, along with similar discoveries made by Carl Menger in Vienna (1871) and by Léon Walras in Switzerland (1874), marked the opening of a new period in the history of economic thought. Jevons's contribution to the marginal revolution in economics in the late nineteenth century established his reputation as a leading political economist and logician of the time.

The most important of his works on logic and scientific methods is his *Principles of Science* (1874), as well as *The Theory of Political Economy* (1871) and *The State in Relation to Labour* (1882). He was also an inventor. Among his inventions was the "logic piano", a crude mechanical computer.

Jevons arrived quite early in his career at the doctrines that constituted his most characteristic and original contributions to economics and logic. The theory of utility, which became the keynote of his general theory of political economy, was practically formulated in a letter written in 1860; and the germ of his logical principles of the substitution of similars may be found in the view which he propounded in another letter written in 1861, that *"philosophy would be found to consist solely in pointing out the likeness of things."*

Jevons the theory of utility says that the degree of utility of a commodity is some continuous mathematical function of the quantity of the commodity available. The implied doctrine, that economics is essentially a mathematical science, took more definite form in a paper on "A General Mathematical

Theory of Political Economy", published four years later in the *Journal of the Statistical Society*. In 1871, Jevons set forth his doctrines in a fully developed form in his *Theory of Political Economy*. Only later did he encounter the prior works of Antoine Augustin Cournot and H. H. Gossen.

The theory of utility was simultaneously being independently developed, on somewhat similar lines, by Carl Menger in Austria and Léon Walras in Switzerland. The Neoclassical Revolution, which would reshape economics, had been started. Jevons did not explicitly distinguish between the concepts of ordinal and cardinal utility. (Cardinal utility allows the relative magnitude of utilities to be discussed, while ordinal utility only implies that goods can be compared and ranked according to which good provided the most utility.) Although Jevons predated the debate about ordinality or cardinality of utility, his mathematics required the use of cardinal utility functions (Fig. 14.2).

It was not as a theorist but as a writer on practical economic questions, that Jevons first received general recognition. *A Serious Fall in the Value of Gold* (1863) and *The Coal Question* (1865) placed him in the front rank as a writer on applied economics and statistics; and he would be remembered as one of the leading economists of the nineteenth century even had his *Theory of Political Economy* never been written.

In *The Coal Question*, Jevons covered a breadth of concepts on energy depletion that have recently been revisited by writers covering the subject of peak oil. For example, Jevons explained that improving energy efficiency typically reduced energy costs and thereby increased rather than decreased energy use, an effect now known as the Jevons paradox. *The Coal Question* remains a paradigmatic study of resource depletion theory. Jevons's son, H. Stanley Jevons, published an 800-page follow-up study in 1915 in which the

Fig. 14.2 Portrait of Jevons published in the *Popular Science Monthly* in 1877—Wikisource

difficulties of estimating recoverable reserves of a theoretically finite resource are discussed in detail.

In 1875, Jevons read a paper *On the influence of the sun-spot period upon the price of corn* at a meeting of the *British Association for the Advancement of Science*. This captured the attention of the media and led to the coining of the word "sunspottery" for claims of links between various cyclic events and sun-spots. In a later work, "Commercial Crises and Sun-Spots", Jevons analyzed business cycles, proposing that crises in the economy might not be random events, but might be based on discernible prior causes. To clarify the concept, he presented a statistical study relating business cycles with sunspots. His reasoning was that sunspots affected the weather, which, in turn, affected crops. Crop changes could then be expected to cause economic changes. Subsequent studies have found sunspots (solar flares) do have an effect on climate, though neither immediate nor strong. That sunny weather has a small but significant positive impact on stock returns is probably due to its impact on traders' moods.

14.3 Alfred Marshall and the Supply–Demand Diagram

Alfred Marshall (1842–1924) was a minor theorist but primarily a teacher and integrator of existing knowledge. He tried to improve the mathematical rigor of economics and transform it into a more scientific profession. In the 1870s he wrote a few tracts on international trade and the problems of protectionism. In 1879, some of these works were compiled into a work entitled *The Theory of Foreign Trade: The Pure Theory of Domestic Values*. In the same year (1879) he published *The Economics of Industry* with his wife Mary Paley. He perfected his *Economics of Industry* while at Bristol, and published it more widely in England as an economic curriculum. Upon the death of William Jevons in 1882, Marshall became the leading British economist of the scientific school of his time.

At Cambridge he labored to create a new tripos for economics, a goal achieved only in 1903. Until that time, economics was taught under the Historical and Moral Sciences Triposes. Those failed to provide Marshall the kind of energetic and specialised students he sought.

Marshall began his chief economic work, the *Principles of Economics*, in 1881. He spent much of the next decade at work on the treatise. His plan for the work gradually extended to a two-volume compilation on the whole of economic thought. The first volume was published in 1890. The second volume, which was to address foreign trade, money, trade fluctuations, taxation, and collectivism, was never published.

Principles of Economics established his worldwide reputation. It appeared in eight editions, starting at 750 pages and growing to 870 pages. It decisively shaped the teaching of economics in English-speaking countries. Its main contribution was a masterful analysis of the issues of elasticity, consumer surplus, increasing and diminishing returns, short and long terms, and marginal utility. Some of the ideas were original with Marshall; others were improved versions of the ideas by W. S. Jevons and others.

In a broader sense Alfred Marshall hoped to reconcile the classical and modern theories of value. John Stuart Mill had examined the relationship between the value of commodities and their production costs, on the theory that value depends on the effort expended in manufacture. Jevons and the Marginal Utility theorists had elaborated a theory of value based on the idea of maximising utility, holding that value depends on demand.

Marshall's work combined these approaches, but he focused more on costs. He noted that, in the short run, supply cannot be changed and market value depends mainly on demand. In an intermediate time period, production can be expanded using existing facilities, such as buildings and machinery. But, since these do not require renewal within this intermediate period, their costs (called fixed, overhead, or supplementary costs) have little influence on the sale price of the product. Marshall pointed out that it is the prime or variable costs, which constantly recur, that influence the sale price most in this period.

In a still longer period, machines and buildings wear out and have to be replaced, so that the sale price of the product must be high enough to cover such replacement costs. This classification of costs into *fixed and variable* and the emphasis given to the element of time probably represent one of Marshall's chief contributions to economic theory. He was committed to partial equilibrium models over general equilibrium on the grounds that the inherently dynamical nature of economics made the former more practically useful (Fig. 14.3).

Much of the success of Marshall's teaching and *Principles* book derived from his effective use of diagrams, which were soon emulated by other teachers worldwide.

Alfred Marshall was the first to develop the standard supply and demand graph. It was borrowed from Cournot, but forgotten. Marshall made it into a teaching tool. He used it to demonstrate a number of fundamentals including the supply and demand curves, market equilibrium, the relationship between quantity and price in regards to supply and demand, the law of marginal utility, the law of diminishing returns, and the ideas of consumer

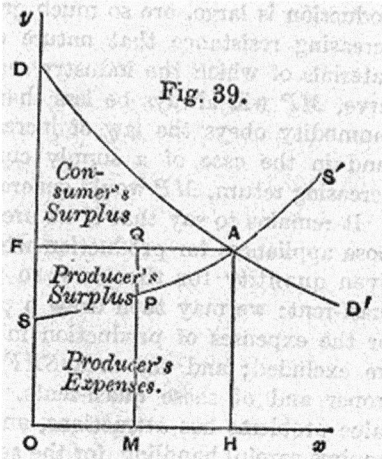

Fig. 14.3 Alfred Marshall's supply and demand graph. https://www.econlib.org/library/Marshall/marP.html?chapter_num=64#book-reader

and producer surpluses. This model is now used by economists in various forms using different variables to demonstrate several other economic principles. Marshall's model allowed a visual representation of complex economic fundamentals where before all the ideas and theories were only capable of being explained using words.

Marshall is considered to be one of the most influential economists of his time, largely shaping mainstream economic thought for the next fifty years. His economics was advertised as extensions and refinements of the work of Adam Smith, Thomas Malthus and John Stuart Mill, he extended economics in another way. It's classical focus was on the market economy, in isolation from the context, instead Alfred Marshall explained it as a study of human behavior.

Marshall used Jevons utility theory, but not as a theory of value. He used it mainly to explain demand curves and the principle of substitution. Marshall's scissors analysis—which combined demand and supply, that is, utility and cost of production, as if in the two blades of a pair of scissors—effectively removed the theory of value from the center of analysis and replaced it with the theory of price. While the term "value" continued to be used, for most people it was a synonym for "price". Prices no longer were thought to gravitate toward some ultimate and absolute basis of price; prices were existential, between the relationship of demand and supply.

Marshall's influence on codifying economic thought is undeniable. He popularised the use of supply and demand functions as tools of price determination. The idea that consumers attempt to adjust consumption until marginal utility equals the price was one of his contributions. The price elasticity of demand was presented by Marshall as an extension of this idea. Economic welfare, divided into producer surplus and consumer surplus, was a contribution of Marshall, and indeed, the two are sometimes described eponymously as 'Marshallian surplus.' He used this idea of surplus to rigorously analyse the effect of taxes and price shifts on market welfare. Marshall also identified quasi-rents.

Another contribution that Marshall made was differentiating concepts of internal and external economies of scale. Thus, when costs of input factors of production go down, it is a positive externality for all the other firms in the market place, outside the control of any of the them.

The doctrines of marginalism and the Marginal Revolution are sometimes interpreted as a response to the rise of socialist theories of the exploitation of labor, especially Marxism. There was another 'external' cause, namely its successful explanation of the Long Depression of the 1870s and the resurgence of class conflict in Europe after the peaceful 1848–1870 period. Marginalism offered a theory of perfect free markets that performed optimal resource allocation of resources, while allowing economists to blame any departures from optimality on the interference of workers' coalitions (unions) or governments.

14.4 On the Causes of the Great Depression

The Treaty of Versailles, which usts ended the war in Europe in 1918, was designed (by the victors) to punish and permanently disarm Germany. It was extremely vengeful, partly because of the gross asymmetry of the war damage. German armies had caused enormous physical damage in France and the Low countries. But Germany itself was physically undamaged. The French and Belgians, especially, demanded financial reparations, as did the Russians. However, the reparations demanded (in gold) were unpayable, since Germany did not have a large gold source or reserve.

John Maynard Keynes, the English economist who began his public career (so to speak) by resigning from his position in the British Treasury—where he was a member of the British delegation to the Versailles conference in 1919—and denouncing the Treaty that resulted. Towards the end of the conference, Keynes came up with a plan that, he argued, would not only help Germany and other impoverished central European powers but also be good for the world economy as a whole. It involved the radical writing down of war debts. That would have had the beneficial effect of increasing international trade, but at the same time left over two thirds of the total cost of European reconstruction to be paid by the United States.

Prime Minister David Lloyd George agreed it might be acceptable to the British electorate. However, the US was then the largest creditor. Wilson (and most Americans) believed that their country had already made excessive sacrifices to defend the Allies in a war in which America had no stake. Hence, the result of the conference was a treaty which disgusted Keynes both on moral and economic grounds and led to his resignation from the Treasury.

Keynes's analysis appeared in his highly influential book, "*The Economic Consequences of the Peace*", published in 1919. In addition to economic analysis, the book appealed to the reader's sense of compassion: He wrote "*I cannot leave this subject as though its just treatment wholly depended either on our pledges or on economic facts. The policy of reducing Germany to servitude for a generation, of degrading the lives of millions of human beings, and of depriving a whole nation of happiness should be abhorrent and detestable,—abhorrent and detestable, even if it was possible, even if it enriched ourselves, even if it did not sow the decay of the whole civilized life of Europe.*"

The book included striking imagery such as "*year by year Germany must be kept impoverished and her children starved and crippled*" along with bold predictions which were later justified by events: "*If we aim deliberately at the impoverishment of Central Europe, vengeance, I dare predict, will not limp. Nothing can then delay for very long that final war between the forces of Reaction and the despairing convulsions of Revolution, before which the horrors of the late German war will fade into nothing.*" Keynes's predictions of disaster were borne out when the German economy suffered the hyperinflation of 1922–3, and again by the collapse of the Weimar Republic and the outbreak of the Second World War.

The "Great Depression" was a severe worldwide economic depression that took place mostly during the 1930s, beginning in the United States. The timing of the Great Depression varied around the world; in most countries, it started in 1929 and lasted until the late 1930s. It started in the United States after a major fall in stock prices—now remembered as "The Crash"—that began around September 4, 1929. The Dow Jones Industrial Average dropped from 381 in September to 198 by October 24 (which was remembered as "Black Tuesday"). But optimism persisted for some time. The stock market turned upward again in early 1930, with the Dow returning to 294 (pre-depression levels) in April 1930, before steadily declining for years, to a low of 41 in 1932.

Between 1929 and 1932, worldwide gross domestic product (GDP) fell by an estimated 15%. (By comparison, worldwide GDP fell by less than 1% from 2008 to 2009 during the "Great Recession"). Some economies—notably Nazi Germany—started to recover by the mid-1930s. However, in many countries, the US among them, the negative effects continued until the beginning of World War II.

Personal income, tax revenue, profits and prices dropped, while international trade fell by more than 50%. Unemployment in the U.S. rose to 23% at its peak and in some countries rose as high as 33%. Cities around the world were hit hard, especially those dependent on heavy industry. Construction was virtually halted in many countries. Farming communities and rural areas suffered as crop prices fell by about 60%. Facing plummeting demand with few alternative sources of jobs, areas dependent on extraction (primary sector) industries such as mining and logging were hit hardest.

Many economic historians consider the catalyst of the Great Depression to be the sudden devastating collapse of U.S. stock market prices, starting on October 24, 1929. However, a catalyst is not a cause. In retrospect, some economists attribute the depression to perverse policies by the Federal Reserve Bank, which raised interest rates instead of cutting them. Some economists see the stock crash itself as a symptom of deeper problems, rather than a direct cause, of the Great Depression. Looking back from 2020 it is pretty clear that the "crash" was the end of a real estate investment Bubble that started in about 1924 and was driven by "leverage": borrowing based on the market value of corporations that existed only on paper {Galbraith, 1954}.

The causes of the great depression have been the subject of thousands of academic articles and a series of leveraged a series of hundreds of books by scores of authors. The best known of them, in retrospect, was probably John Kenneth Galbraith (1908—2006). In his last book Galbraith quoted parts of President Coolidge's last address to congress, on Dec. 4 1928. Coolidge said *"No Congress of the United States ever assembled, on surveying the state of the Union, has met with a more pleasing prospect than that which appears at the present time. In the domestic field there is tranquility and contentment....and the highest record of years of prosperity"* {Galbraith, 1994} pp. 58–59.

Of course, Coolidge was talking to the rich, the well-endowed and the comfortable, not the great majority of the US population. Industrial workers were paid as little as possible (except by Henry Ford) and had no union protection. Minorities, especially descendants of slaves, were still living in the South as sharecroppers, in conditions not much different (except in name) from slavery. As Galbraith said much later *"The feudal structure remained. Women and children were unprotected from the crudest of exploitation"* (op cit).

The most memorable picture of the era is the photo of a 32-year old mother of seven children, one of the destitute migrant workers known as "Okies".

The Okies were victims of an environmental disaster that occurred in 1934, again in 1936 and a third time in 1939–40. The Okies were people who moved to California as "pea-pickers" to escape the "dust bowl", a consequence of mechanized deep plowing of the virgin topsoil of the Great Plains during the previous decade. This plowing had displaced the native, deep-rooted grasses that normally trapped soil and moisture even during periods of drought and high winds.

The rapid mechanization of farm equipment, especially small gasoline tractors, and widespread use of the combine harvester induced farmers to convert arid grassland (much of which received no more than 10 inches (~250 mm) of precipitation per year) to cultivated cropland for wheat and soya beans. During the drought of the 1930s, the unanchored soil turned to dust. The prevailing winds blew the dust away in huge clouds that sometimes blackened the sky hundreds of miles away. The causes of the dust bowl were finally understood and changes were introduced by the newly created Soil Conservation Service and the Department of Agriculture, agencies that libertarians would like to eliminate (Fig. 14.4).

During the Great Depression of the 1930s, Keynes challenged the core neoclassical economics doctrine on unemployment, known as "Say's Law", which said that the income generated by past production and sale of goods is the source of spending that creates demand to purchase current production. The standard neoclassical theory in 1930 held that free markets woul of years of prosperity, in the short to medium term, automatically provide full employment, as long as workers were flexible in their …wage demands. Keynes disagreed. He argued that such flexibility was both unrealistic and ineffective. He said that aggregate demand (total spending in the economy) determined the overall level of economic activity, and that inadequate aggregate demand could lead to prolonged periods of high unemployment, and that labor costs and wages were rigid ("sticky") downwards, which means the economy will not automatically rebound to full employment. The error in the neoclassical theory, as now generally understood, was that it neglected the phenomenon of "leakage".

In economics, a leakage is a diversion from a circular flow of funds. For example, in the Keynesian depiction of circular flow of income and expenditure, leakages are the non-consumption uses of income, including saving, taxes, and imports. In Keynes' model, leakages must be compensated by injections of spending from outside the flow at the equilibrium aggregate output. Savings, taxes, and imports are "leaked" out of the main flow, reducing the

Fig. 14.4 "Migrant Mother" (1936) by Dorothea Lange featuring Florence Owens Thompson—Wikipedia

money available in the rest of the economy. Private savings against a "rainy day" is one kind of leakage. What seems prudent at the individual or family level, can be bad for the economy as a whole. Buying imported goods is another kind of leakage; transferring money earned in one country to another country is a third.

The concept of "multiplier" was first developed by Richard F. Kahn in his article "The relation of home investment to unemployment" In the economic journal of June 1931. Kahn introduced the employment multiplier while Keynes borrowed the idea and formulated the investment multiplier. Keynes advocated the use of fiscal and monetary policies to mitigate the adverse effects of economic recessions and depressions. He detailed these ideas in his magnum opus, *The General Theory of Employment, Interest and Money*, published in late 1936. By the late 1930s, leading Western economies had begun adopting Keynes's policy recommendations. Almost all capitalist governments had done so by the end of the two decades following WW I.

Keynes was very critical of the British government's austerity measures advocated by mainstream neoclassical economists worried about inflation, during the Great Depression. He believed that budget deficits during recessions were a good thing and a natural product of an economic slump. He wrote, "*For Government borrowing of one kind or another is nature's remedy, so to speak, for preventing business losses from being, in so severe a slump as the present one, so great as to bring production altogether to a standstill.*"

In 1933, Keynes published *The Means to Prosperity*, which contained specific policy recommendations for tackling unemployment in a global recession, chiefly counter-cyclical public spending. Similar policies were adopted by Sweden and Germany, but Sweden was too insignificant and small to command much attention, and Keynes was deliberately silent about the successful efforts of Nazi Germany to recover by re-arming. He was dismayed by Hitler's imperialist ambitions and its treatment of Jews. Apart from Great Britain, Keynes's attention was primarily focused on the United States. In 1931, he received considerable support for his views on counter-cyclical public spending in Chicago, then America's foremost center for alternative economic views. However, orthodox economic opinion remained generally hostile until just before the outbreak of WW II in 1939.

Keynes's *magnum opus*, "The General Theory of Employment, Interest and Money" was published in 1936. The work served as a theoretical justification for Keynes' https://en.wikipedia.org/wiki/Economic_interventionism interventionist policies. In addition, Keynes introduced the world to a new interpretation of taxation: since the legal tender is now defined by the state, inflation becomes "*taxation by currency depreciation*". This hidden tax implied (a) that the standard of value should be governed by a deliberate decision process; and (b) that it was possible to maintain a middle course between deflation and inflation. The General Theory challenged the earlier neoclassical economic theory that, without government interference, the market would naturally establish a full employment equilibrium. Under this theory, still popular among business leaders, the lack of full employment was the fault of the government.

Keynes believed the classical theory was based on a "special case" that applied only to the particular conditions of post-Napoleonic nineteenth century, the twentieth century being the more general case. Classical economists had believed in Say's law, which, simply put, states that "supply creates its demand", and that in a free market workers would always be willing—having no choice in the matter—to lower their wages to a level where employers could profitably offer them jobs.

An innovation from Keynes was the concept of "price stickiness"—the recognition that, in reality, unionized workers often refuse to lower their wage demands even in cases where a classical economist might argue that it is rational for them to do so. Aggregate demand, which equals total un-hoarded income in a society, is defined by the sum of consumption and investment. In a state of unemployment and unused production capacity, one can enhance employment and total income *only* by *first* increasing expenditures for either consumption or investment. Without government intervention to increase expenditure, an economy can remain trapped in a low-employment equilibrium. The demonstration of this possibility has been described as the revolutionary formal achievement of the work. In such cases, it is incumbent on the state, not the market, to save the economy by creating demand from the public sector.

The *General Theory* advocated activist economic policy by government to stimulate demand in times of high unemployment, for example by spending on public works. "*Let us be up and doing, using our idle resources* (with coordinated international Keynesian policies, an international monetary system that did not pit the interests of countries against one another, and a high degree of freedom of trade), then this system of managed capitalism could promote peace rather than conflict between countries.

In the late 1930s and 1940s, John Hicks, Franco Modigliani, and Paul Samuelson, among others, attempted to interpret and formalize Keynes's writings in terms of formal mathematical models. In what had become known as the neoclassical synthesis, they combined Keynesian analysis with 18.3. for the next 40 years.

14.5 The Problem of Growth

The most important change in perspective is that machines can reduce the labor input, thus justifying lower prices and, thus, lower wages for the workers. Marx took this mechanism to be the inherent motivation of the "class struggle" while neglecting its consequence for economic growth. In *Das Kapital*, he rejected the explanation of long-term market values in terms of supply and demand. The Marxists and the marginalists spent a lot of time arguing over these distinctions.

What they both missed was two things: human wants (or needs) keep changing as new products (like the automobile or TV or the i-Phone) are invented and that the work required for production of commodities (or gadgets) is mostly thermodynamic work from non-human sources. Work done by human muscles or brains is powered by food intake that is indirectly derived from the sun (via an agricultural product). Work done by machines may be powered by burning wood (also indirectly from the sun) or by burning coal (from solar energy captured in the distant past.) The amount of human labor needed to produce commodities keeps declining because more and more of the work input for production, since start of the industrial revolution, is from machines, not muscles.

The question of causation: whether the natural growth rate is driven by exogenous technological change, or whether technology itself responds to changing consumer demand, lies at the heart of the debate between neoclassical economists and Keynesian/post-Keynesian economists. The latter group argues that growth is primarily demand-driven because the size of the labor force as well as labor productivity (due to technology) both respond to demand. This does not mean that there are no constraints on supply, but they claim that demand constraints (such as inflation and balance of payments difficulties) tend to arise before supply constraints are ever reached.

Roy Harrod, in a seminal paper {Harrod, 1948}, developed a model, subsequently refined by Evsey Domar {Domar, 1957}, that tried to explain an economy's growth rate in terms of the level of saving and of the productivity of capital, treating capital supply as a given. Neoclassical critics found weaknesses in the Harrod–Domar model, in particular, the lack of a mechanism to bring the "warranted" growth rate in line with the "natural" (full employment) growth rate. This started an academic dialogue that went on for over two decades. The neoclassical side was represented by Paul Samuelson, Robert Solow, and Franco Modigliani, all at MIT, in Cambridge, Massachusetts, USA, while the Keynesian and Post-Keynesian sides were represented by Nicholas Kaldor, Joan Robinson, Luigi Pasinetti, Piero Sraffa, and Richard Kahn, mostly at the University of Cambridge in England. This gave rise to the so-called "Cambridge capital controversy."

Both camps generally treated the "natural" (full employment) rate of growth as a given. The focus of the debate was on the mechanisms by which the warranted growth rate might be made to converge on the "natural rate", giving a long-run, equilibrium growth-path. The MIT side focused on adjustments to the capital/output ratio through capital-labor substitution, if capital and labor were growing at different rates. The English Cambridge side concentrated on adjustments to the saving ratio through changes in the distribution of income between wages and profits, on the assumption that the propensity to save out of profits is higher than out of wages.

This debate eventually led to the Solow–Swan economic growth model, that was developed separately and independently by Robert Solow at MIT

{Solow, 1956} and by Trevor Swan in the UK {Swan, 1956}. Solow and Swan both proposed to explain long-run economic growth as a function of aggregate capital accumulation; labor force growth (or population growth) and exogenous increases in productivity, commonly referred to as "technological progress". The model assumes an aggregate production function, usually specified to be of Cobb–Douglas type.

Much of the considerable emotion behind the debate arose because the technical criticisms of marginal productivity theory were connected to wider arguments with ideological implications. The famous neoclassical economist **John Bates Clark** (1847–1938) saw the equilibrium rate of profit (which helps to determine the income of the owners of capital goods) as a market price determined by technology and the relative proportions in which the "factors of production" are employed. Just as wages are the reward for the labor that workers do, profits are supposed to be the reward for risk-taking and the productive contributions of capital: thus, the normal operations of the system under (hypothetical) competitive conditions produce profits for the investor-owners of capital.

Responding to the "*indictment that hangs over society*" that it involves "*exploiting labor*"s Clark wrote (in 1899): "*It is the purpose of this work to show that the distribution of the income of society is controlled by a natural law, and that this law, if it worked without friction, would give to every agent of production the amount of wealth which that agent creates. However wages may be adjusted by bargains freely made between individual men (i.e., without labor unions and other "market imperfections"), the rates of pay that result from such transactions tend, it is here claimed, to equal that part of the product of industry which is traceable to the labor itself; and however interest (i.e., profit) may be adjusted by similarly free bargaining, it naturally tends to equal the fractional product that is separately traceable to capital.*" {Clark, 1899}.

Clark saw profits as rewards for saving, i.e., abstinence from current consumption, leading to the creation of the capital goods. (Later, John Maynard Keynes and his school argued that saving is "leakage", that does not automatically lead to investment in tangible capital goods.) Thus, in Clark's view, profit income is a reward for those who value future income highly and are thus willing to sacrifice current enjoyment—and to take risks—for greater enjoyment in the future. But Keynes pointed out that things don't always work out that way, and the fact that they don't explains a lot.

Despite the religious origins of the Protestant Ethic (Chap. 3), however, modern neoclassical theory does not say that capital's or labor's share of the national income is "deserved" in some moral or normative sense. However, in the real world the distribution of income has never been a consequence of free bargaining between capital owners and labor, in Clark's sense of the word. (In fact Clark, himself, was more concerned by collectivism among workers (labor unions) than he was about trusts and cartels—greatly favored by J. P. Morgan et al.—that are combinations to restrain trade.)

We note that the huge wealth and income inequity existing today is a consequence of an important market failure, i.e., the fact that wealth can be—and is—used routinely to "buy votes" in our representative democracy. That fact, in turn, has resulted in laws that tilt the powers of government to favor the capitalists and allow the rich to get richer, without limit {Stiglitz, 2012} {Ayres, 2020}.

This competition of interpretations yielded a core proposition in textbook neoclassical economics: that the income earned by each "factor of production" (i.e., labor and "capital") is equal to its marginal product. Thus, with perfect product and input markets, the wage (of labor), divided by the price of the product, is assumed to be equal to the marginal physical product of labor. By the same argument, the rate of profit (not to be confused with the rate of interest on borrowed funds) is supposed to equal the marginal physical product of capital. This proposition is only true if the economy is in equilibrium; it is one of the definitions of equilibrium.

A second core proposition is that a change in the price of a factor of production will lead to a change in the use of that factor. For instance, an increase in the rate of profit (associated with falling wages) will lead to more of that factor (labor) being used in production. The law of diminishing marginal returns implies that greater use of either input will imply a lower marginal product, all else being equal. In the 1920 Piero Sraffa contributed to the understanding of why marginal returns on capital decrease or increase in different cases: returns decrease as the quality of an important input (e.g., soil for agriculture) decreases thanks to exhaustion, while returns may increase if scale of production permits greater capital intensively, cutting costs.

Piero Sraffa and Joan Robinson, whose work set off the Cambridge controversy, pointed out that there was an inherent measurement problem in applying this model of income distribution to capital. Capitalist income is defined as the rate of profit multiplied by the amount of capital. But the measurement of the "amount of capital" involves aggregating incomparable physical object—e.g., hammers, wheelbarrows, and lasers. Just as one cannot add heterogeneous "apples and oranges," we cannot simply add up physical simple units of "capital." As Robinson argued, there is no such thing as "leets," an inherent element of each capital good that can be added up independent of the prices of those goods.

Neoclassical economists assumed that there was no real problem here. They said: just add up the money value of all these different capital items to get an aggregate amount of capital (while correcting for inflation). But Sraffa pointed out that the price or market value of the capital equipment (as a whole) is determined partly by the rate of profit achieved. But neoclassical theory tells us that this rate of profit is itself supposed to be determined by the amount of capital in use. There is circularity in the argument. A falling profit rate has a direct effect on the amount of capital employed; it does not simply cause greater employment.

Sraffa suggested an aggregation technique (stemming in part from Marxian economics) by which a measure of the amount of capital could be produced: by reducing all machines to a sum of dated labor from different years. A machine produced in the year 2000 can then be treated as the labor and commodity inputs used to produce it in 1999 (multiplied by the rate of profit); and the commodity inputs in 1999 can be further reduced to the labor inputs that made them in 1998 plus the commodity inputs (multiplied by the rate of profit again); and so on until the non-labor component was reduced to a negligible (but non-zero) amount. Then you could add up the dated labor value of a truck to the dated labor value of a laser.

However, Sraffa then pointed out that this measuring technique still involved the rate of profit, as the amount of capital depends on the rate of profit. This reverses the direction of causality that neoclassical economics assumed between the rate of profit and the amount of capital. Further, Sraffa showed that a change in the rate of profit would change the measured amount of capital, and in nonlinear ways: an increase in the rate of profit might initially increase the perceived value of the truck more than the laser, but then reverse the effect at still higher rates of profit. This analysis offers a serious challenge to the neoclassical vision of prices as indices of scarcity and the simple neoclassical version of the principle of substitution.

The aggregation problem arises in another way that does not involve the Classical pricing equations. A decrease in the rate of return on capital (corresponding to a rise in the wage rate) causes a change in the distribution of income, the nature of the various capital goods demanded, and thus a change in their prices. This causes a change in the value of capital equipment (as discussed above). So, again, the rate of return on capital is not independent of the quantity of capital, as assumed in the neoclassical model of growth and distribution. Causation goes both ways, from quantity of capital to rate of return and back from rate of return to quantity employed.

14.6 The Production Function and the Solow-Swan Model

Philip Wicksteed (1844–1927) introduced the concept of Production Function. Wicksteed's production function (1894) was related to a specific product. It had a number of inputs because he explicitly rejected the possibility of grouping inputs into larger sets (for all the reasons that led to the Cambridge Controversy in the 1950s). Thus each input had to be measurable as a physical flow.

His essay on the "Co-ordination of the Laws of Distribution" sought to prove mathematically that a distributive system which rewarded factory owners (and workers) in proportion to their "marginal productivity" would exhaust the total product produced. This result became known as the "cost-share theorem" {Wicksteed, 1894}. But it was in his 1910 "The Common Sense of Political Economy "(1910) that most clearly presented Wicksteed's economic system. The 1932 work by Lionel Robbins, "An Essay on the Nature and Significance of Economic Science", picked up and developed his ideas.

A production function hereafter can be thought of as a model to explain output (GDP) consisting of a function of two (or three) independent variables. The traditional two-variable scheme involves only capital stock—or capital services—(K) and labor supply (L). The two variables are supposed to be substitutable.

In 1928, **Charles Cobb** (1870–1949), a mathematician, and **Paul Douglas** (1892–1976), an economist (and later a US Senator from Illinois) published the article "A Theory of Production". It modified Wicksteed's concept of production function by a double aggregation: first, the function concerned the whole of American manufacturing output: it became macroeconomic; second, it retained only those two generic aggregate inputs: capital and labor. That selection has given rise to a long-standing debate about productivity and the role of technology.

Based on statistics on U.S. manufacturing output between 1899 and 1922, Cobb and Douglas developed indices (set at 100 for the year 1899) for employment, installed capital stock and output. Using this data, they did a statistical fit (regress) and obtained the following equation for GDP (Y):

$$Y = AY(t) K^{1/4} L^{3/4}$$

where A is a constant or a function of time, K is the capital index and L is the employment (labor) index. Wicksteed's function can be rewritten in a more general form,

$$Y = AY K^\alpha L^\beta$$

where the sum of the exponents is unity ($\alpha + \beta = 1$). That is the Lagrange condition for constant returns to scale, meaning that the size (scale) of the country or other production unit doesn't affect the relative importance (weight) of the factors K and L in the national accounts. A third multiplicative factor, with another exponent, can be added by keeping the sum of exponents equal to unity.

Partial derivatives of ln Y with respect to K and L, respectively, are equal to the exponents. According to Wicksteed's "cost-share theorem", they can be interpreted as the relative shares of these factors in total output. If the sum of these exponents is equal to unity the whole output is thus accounted for. This is what Wicksteed proposed, and what Cobb and Douglas postulated in their article.

Most neoclassical economists assume that both individual firms (or sectors), and the entire economy, depend to a large extent on the simple doubly-aggregated production function model of economic growth, known the Cobb–Douglas model {Cobb, 1928}. The Solow-Swan growth model, introduced in 1956, treated technological progress as an exogenous factor, meaning not caused by the economic system itself. They did that mainly for mathematical simplicity {Solow, 1956}{Swan, 1956}. The model postulates that economic growth arises from increasing inputs of just two "factors of production", viz. labor supply L and capital stock K. We have a suggestion to modify that model.

Yet the usual measure of labor L in economic models is employed man-hours (from the Bureau of Labor Statistics). This is unsatisfactory, both because that measure ignores a great deal of unpaid home and farm labor by women and children (and others) and because, in reality, physical work then (1955) and even more so by now (2022) is mostly done by machines, driven by energy (exergy) from flowing water, wind, or heat (from combustion) engines.[1] The graphical form of the two-factor Cobb–Douglas function of K and L is shown in Fig. 14.5: we show it because it is quite pretty.

---

[1] The combustion engines were driven, at first, by steam produced in an external boiler and later (after 1885 or so) by the expanding gases from combustion in an internal combustion engine (ICE). Those hot gases exert force against a piston or a turbine wheel. The combustion products are emitted into the atmosphere.

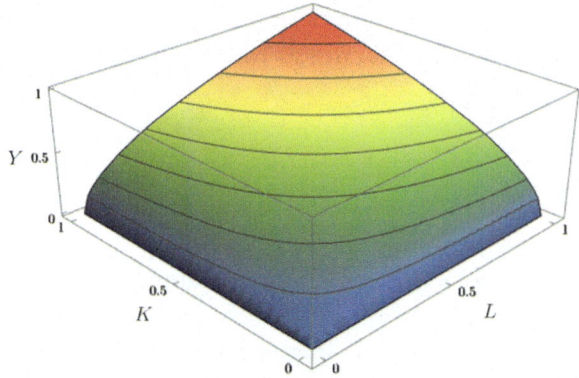

Fig. 14.5 Graph of the Cobb–Douglas function—Wikimedia

But Solow showed in 1957 that historical US GDP growth was not explained by increased supply of labor or capital inputs. Most of the GDP growth—the "Solow residual"—was unexplained (Fig. 14.6). Moreover, the two variable production function was problematic for other reasons. For one thing, K and L are not perfect substitutes for each other, as they should be. Another problem is that the standard form of the C-D function just didn't fit with the fact that energy costs were only 5% or less of total inputs, while labor costs were much too great as a growth driver. Energy was missing.

Since Schumpeter's PhD thesis in 1912 (if not earlier), technological change, independent of the labor input or the capital stock, has been increasingly recognized as the primary driver of economic growth. It follows that

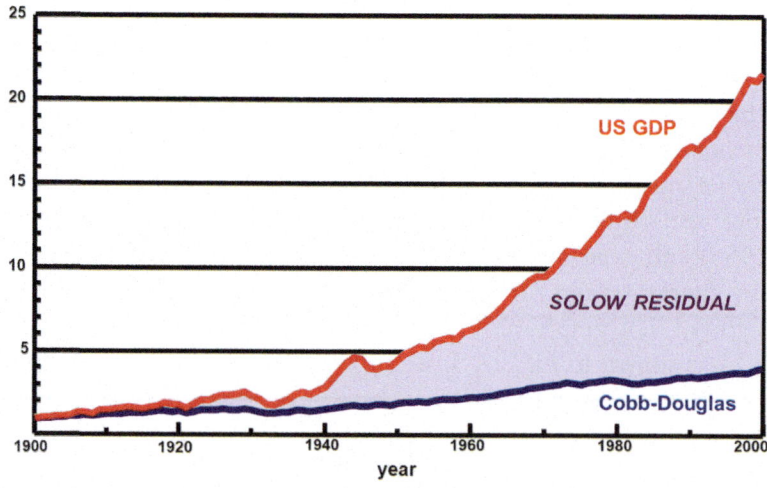

Fig. 14.6 The Solow Residual, 1900–2000, not explained by the C-D function

the term A(t) in the C-D function above must be a measure of technology change over time. It is hard to believe that technological change occurs "on its own", without economic drivers. This empirical reality makes technological innovation and diffusion a new and serious subject for economic research on "endogenous growth" theory. That theory still remains far from resolution, primarily because the creation of radical new technologies is unpredictable and occurs—by definition—far from economic equilibrium.

The three-factor scheme involves energy or natural resource use—call it X for the moment. The factors of production (K, L, X) are regarded as *independent* variables. The assumption is that some combination of these variables can explain changes in a fourth dependent variable, namely the groworkss domestic product (Y) over a long period of time. We also assume (in common with most economists) that the production function exhibits constant returns to scale. Mathematically this implies that it is linear and homogeneous, of degree one (the Euler condition), which implies that the individual variables are subject to declining returns. That assumption is also questionable, given the importance of networks with positive returns {Arthur, 1994}.

14.7 The Next Step: Adding a Third Variable to the C-D Function

In the 1980s (probably due to increasing concerns about the rise of OPEC and the possibilities of oil scarcity) the idea emerged (from the oilpatch?) of incorporating "energy" in some form into the production function. There is reason to believe that the human economic system is the latest evolutionary example of a "super-cyclic" system driven by exergy dissipation. It generates information, as well as increasingly complex physical and informational structures. Meanwhile human economic activity has engendered other material cycles—or proto-cycles. These include the "industrial metals (chromium, copper, lead, manganese, nickel, tin and zinc that are mined and refined on a large scale, and later discarded or recovered and re-used on a significant scale. The "precious metals" (gold, silver and the platinum group) are kept in circulation—or in storage—because their properties are economically valuable. In addition, there are several "electronic metals", including gallium, germanium, indium, lithium, neodymium, selenium, tantalum and zirconium, that may become economically viable candidates for recovery from waste and recycling in the near future {Ayres, 2013, 2014}.

That dominance of labor as the key "factor of production" was accepted in the eighteenth century. It has become axiomatic that all wealth is actually created by human labor, plus capital services from previous human labor. This paradigm is still widely accepted, today despite the fact that most work converting "raw materials into useful products is done by machines driven by exogenous power sources. Since 1895 the "production function"—especially the mathematical form introduced by Charle Cobb and Paul Douglas in 1928 – has been widely adopted by the economics profession (despite serious criticism). It was central to the growth model introduced by Robert Solow {Solow, 1956, 1957}. The model is simple

$$Y = A(t)K^{\alpha}L^{\beta}$$

where Y is output (GDP), $A(t)$ is a function of time, K^{α} is the marginal productivity of capital, L^{β} is the marginal productivity of labor, and $\alpha + \beta = 1$. The latter condition is means that there are no returns to scale (i.e. big is not more productive than small).

The core of the problem is expressed in a 2008 letter to me from Robert Solow, about a paper I sent to him for comment {Ayres, 2005}. I quote only a few lines: "*I have a lot of sympathy with the impulse that lies behind the paper: to understand and estimate the limitations on growth arising from the (possibly) increasing real cost of a ubiquitous factor of production like energy... It seems to me that the right and direct way to go at this is to recognize that energy (or "useful work") is an intermediate good, and to treat it as such explicitly.*" Solow goes on to suggest a multi-equation scheme treating L_i and energy E_i as independent variables, and treating energy E_i for the ith sector as a sectoral product, depending on inputs from other sectors, including the annual flow R of "natural resources". A possible interpretation of this argument is that R is the energy (exergy) input to economic activity and that L and K are actually intermediates.

If this conjecture is correct, the output Y over time for a country should be explained almost entirely by the flux of energy (exergy) from the sources summarized above (Sect. 14.2) captured and "consumed" by the economic system. There is some contribution, of course, from capital services, where capital goods are products of exergy flows in the past. In other words, the "Solow residual", meaning the fraction of historical economic growth not explained by increasing capital stock or labor supply, should be explained quite well by energy (exergy) consumption {Ayres, 2021}.

It turns out that a more general form of production function can be derived from a different mathematical condition, namely "path independence" or "twice differentiability". (Take our word for it, they are equivalent).

This condition of twice differentiability takes the form of a pair of differential equations that can be solved explicitly. (We will get to that a little later.) **Reiner Kümmel** (b. 1938?) proposed a Linear Exponential (LINEX) production function that satisfies these conditions {Kümmel, 1980}. Moreover, Kümmel et al., showed that by adding a third variable E (for total energy) and imposing another simple condition, the range of allowable substitution between pairs of variables can be limited. Perfect substitutability was no longer necessary with a third variable.

What if we re-interpret human labor L as brainwork and coordination, excluding muscle work (which was what human labor was, back in the days of Adam Smith). Suppose we introduce a new variable, "useful work" by machines? Kümmel, et al., did this in the 1980s by introducing the so-called linear-exponential LINEX production function. The parameters a and b can be functions of time, and should be related to boundary conditions. The three variable model was tested by Ayres and Warr,

Ayres and Warr altered the equation slightly by inserting useful work U (in exergy terms) in place of total energy E.

$$Y = AU \exp a(t)\left(2 - \left(\frac{L+U}{K}\right)\right) + a(t)b(t)\left(\frac{L}{U} - 1\right)$$

where A is a function of time, L is "brainwork" or information and U is "machine work". Where is information H? The temptation is to include information H with machine work, since computers are machines.

As it happens, when three factors are used it turns out that the output elasticity of exergy (or work) calculated from historical econometric data, is much larger than the cost of (payments to) exergy {Ayres, 2009} Chap. 6.

In this graph, the C-D curve was calculated assuming L = 0,70, K = 0.26 and E = 0.04, adding up to 1.00. The 0.04 for energy means that payments for energy were a very small fraction of total payments in the economic system for the years of the graph. Energy inputs were hidden in other categories.

In other words, it looks like exergy is currently underpriced—too cheap— whereas human labor is overpriced, based on current measures (man-hours of paid employment). That means energy (exergy) is really more productive, in GDP terms, than its current market price suggests. That implies, in turn, that the optimum (profit-maximizing) consumption, of energy (work) in the economy would be larger than recent average energy (work) consumption.

Can this possibly be true? Main-stream economists doubt it. They could point out (correctly) that there is plenty of empirical, if anecdotal, evidence that firms use too much—not too little—commercial energy. They can save money by using commercial energy more efficiently. The evidence from many empirical studies says that firms neither minimize costs nor maximize profits even when there are obvious opportunities to do so {UNIDO, 2011}. Firms consistently neglect cost-saving investments in energy conservation, with very high returns, in favor of investments in share buy-backs, developing new markets, new products or in capacity expansion. Governments and consumers behave in roughly the same way, preferring to spend money on current consumption goods or services rather than investment in future cost savings. The fundamental reasons for this behavior, which is inconsistent with the standard axiom of profit maximization and SVI, is that energy (exergy) is currently too cheap to be worth saving, relative to other factors of production. This implication deserves much more attention than it has received from economic theorists.

So what is the contrary evidence that firms should use more exergy and less labor? The answer, in broad general terms, is simple: It usually pays to automate, i.e., to replace human workers by machines wherever possible. Machines keep getting cheaper and smarter and workers (in the industrialized economies) keep getting more expensive but not necessarily stronger or smarter. So businesses continue to replace human workers by machines.

The same tendency can be seen in consumer behavior. It is exemplified by the strong demand for home appliances that reduce household manual labor, from washing machines and dryers to electric mixers, knife grinders, vacuum cleaners, hedge clippers, leaf blowers and lawn mowers. The two variable C-D function, with capital K and labor L, measured in terms of expenditures in the National Accounts, won't do the job, for a number of technical and other reasons. That model assumes that the economy has one sector, and that capital and labor are substitutable.

The history of light touches virtually every technology today. But when the sun wasn't shining, the only practical source of light for human purposes was flame from a fire, either stationary in a or as a torch. Early lighting fuels consisted of olive oil, beeswax, fish oil, whale oil, sesame oil, nut oil, and similar substances. These were the most commonly used fuels for light (in lamps) until the late eighteenth century.

The phrase "seeing the light", in one form or another, usually in the sense of uncovering a truth, is ubiquitous. Another version is "turning night into day" and I always think of what it was like to be a law student (like Abraham Lincoln), studying for the bar by candlelight because he had to earn a living while the sun was shining.

In 1994, Yale economics professor William Nordhaus wrote a paper for the Cowles Foundation about the historic pricing of artificial light across the eons. For him it was a way to normalize the buying power of a worker's wage throughout history(something Smith and Ricardo tried but failed to do. In his paper "*Do Real-Output and Real-Wage Measures Capture Reality? The History of Lighting Suggests Not* " Nordhaus pointed out that the history of lighting has been remarkably uneven {Nordhaus, 1994}. Nordhaus's point was that historical progress in lighting technology was extraordinarily uneven, being very slow for thousands of years and then very fast, especially after town gas and electricity became available. Before 1800 or so, people spent a high proportion of their available income on lighting, whereas by 1900 the fraction was already quite low and today it is close to zero. Yet expenditure for light, as a fraction of GDP, is also declining, but far from zero, because demand for illumination has increased so much (Table 14.1).

Table 14.1 Price of lighting for different lighting technologies

Device	Stage of technology	Approximate date	Price(cents per 1000 lm-hours)
Open fire	Wood	From earliest time	
Neolithic lamp	Animal or vegetable fat	38,000–9,000 BC	
Babylonian lamp	Sesame oil	1750 BC	
Candles	Tallow	1800	40,293
	Sperm oil	1800	91,575
	Tallow	1830	18,315
	Sperm oil	1830	42,124
Lamp	Whale oil	1815–45	29,886
	Silliman's experiment: Sperm oil	1855	160,256
	Other oils	1855	59,441
Town gas	Early lamp	1827	52,524
	Silliman's experiment	1855	29,777
	Early lamp	1875–85	5.035
	Welsbach mantle	1885–95	1.573
	Welsbach mantle	1916	0.346
Kerosene lamp	Sillimans' experiment	1855	4.036
	nineteenth century	1875–85	3.479
	Coleman Lantern	1933	10.323
Electric lamp	Edison carbon lamp	1883	9.228
	Filament lamp	1900–1990	2.692–0.60
	Compact fluorescent bulb	1992	0.124

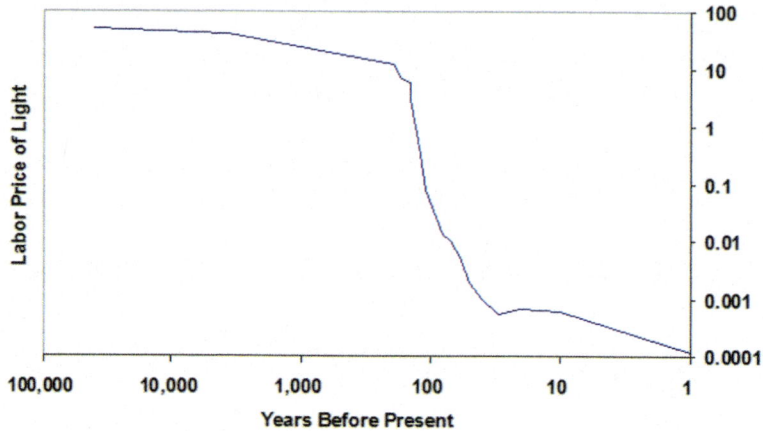

A fascinating table of historic light prices:

When Nordhaus wrote his paper (1994), the state of the art of illumination was compact fluorescent lights. Today it is LEDs. Moreover, the single most important step towards decarbonization of the economy, to date, is probably the substitution of LED lighting for incandescent and fluorescent lighting ("Waitz's law"). That substitution is allowing the existing power generating system to accommodate the increased demand for electric vehicles that would otherwise threaten to overload it. Increasing demand for food from large high-tech "greenhouses" (to replace grain from distant farmlands, such as Russia and the Ukraine) will also increase future demand for LED illumination (Fig. 14.7).

The next graph (attributed to Waitz) shows the declining cost of LEDs (green) along with the increasing power output available from commercial LED products. The substitution of LEDs for other kinds of illumination had reached the 50% level a few years ago. It must be approaching 100% now, except for a few applications requiring very high power (Fig. 14.8).

I have argued, in several papers and a book, that exergy, as a measure of physical work, should be the sole "factor of production". Yet something seemed to be missing.

14.8 Evolutionary Game Theory

In reality, evolution is a contest between survival strategies. The survival strategies of plants and animals have been characterized—a bit too crudely—as Neo-Darwinism. But the survival strategies of humans are more complex. They are increasingly being understood in terms of the theory of games. We think the best simple characterization of human history is in terms of

14 The "Marginal Revolution" in Economics

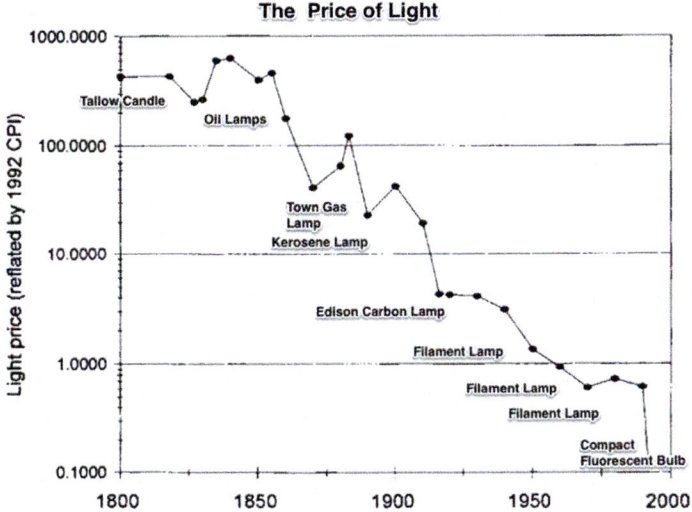

Fig. 14.7 The price of light in terms of 1992 consumer Prices (CPI)

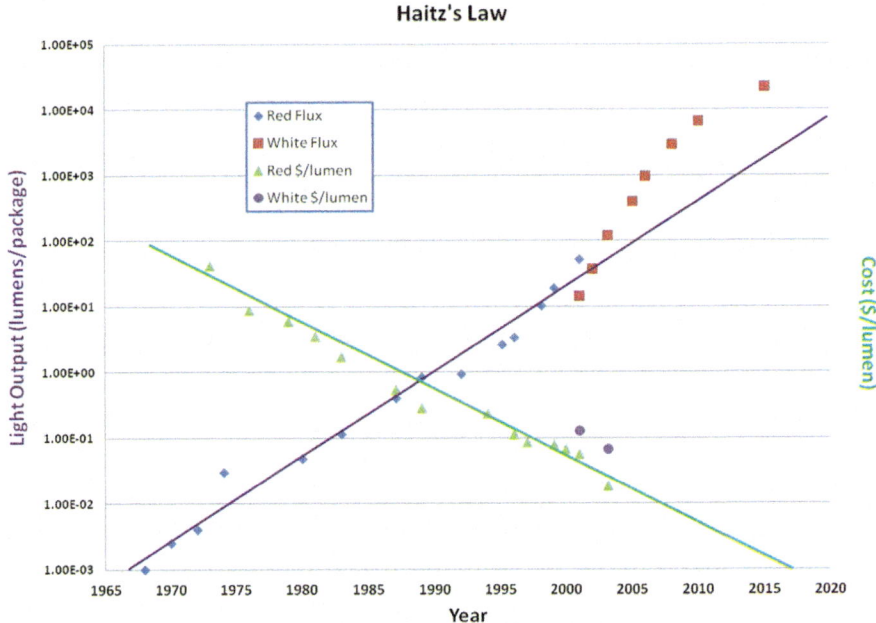

Fig. 14.8 Diagram of Haitz's Law: cost versus flux

the competition between strategies of competition versus strategies involving cooperation.

Game theory began in 1928 when the mathematician **John von Neumann** (1903–1957) wrote a paper about two-person "zero-sum" games (i.e., games such that winnings by one player are balanced exactly by the losses of the other). Poker is a multi-player zero-sum game. In 1944 von Neumann and Oskar Morgenstern—inspired by the global contest then underway—wrote a book entitled "*The Theory of Games and Economic Behavior*" that put game strategy into the economic language of utility maximization and probability theory. The book attempted to create a generic mathematical methodology to determine optimal strategies in competitions between adversaries. A contest involves players, all of whom have a choice of moves, possibly subject to rules. Games can be a single round or repetitive, cooperative, or not.

A game is *cooperative* if the players are able to form binding commitments externally enforced (e.g., through contract law or international law). Chess is a cooperative game). Rules govern the outcome for the moves taken by the players, in cooperative games and outcomes produce payoffs for the players, expressed as decision trees or in a payoff matrix. Classical theory requires the players to make rational (utility maximizing) choices. Cooperative game theory focuses on predicting which coalitions will form, the joint actions that groups take, and the resulting collective payoffs.

A game is *non-cooperative* if players cannot form alliances or if all agreements need to be self-enforcing (e.g., through credible threats. Von Neumann's work was extended by **John Forbes Nash**, in 1950 -1953 {Nash 1950, 1951,1953}. Nash showed that there can be equilibrium outcomes of non-cooperative games without a single "winner", when each player takes into account the strategies of other players. Non-cooperative game theory also looks at how bargaining procedures will affect the distribution of payoffs within coalitions. The world needs a Nash equilibrium to settle several issues, right now.

Evolutionary game theory (EGT) is the application of game theory to evolving populations in biology. It originated when **John Maynard Smith** (1920–2004) and **George R. Price** formalized contests as strategies, and identified mathematical criteria that can be used to predict the results of competing survival strategies {Maynard-Smith, 1973}. Evolutionary game theory focuses on the dynamics of competition among strategies and the frequency of the competing strategies in the population.

Evolutionary game theory tries to explain Darwinian evolution, mathematically. It covers competition (the game), natural selection (replicator dynamics), and heredity. Evolutionary game theory has created models that contribute to the understanding of group selection, sexual selection, altruism, parental care, co-evolution, and ecological dynamics. Many counter-intuitive situations in these areas have been explained mathematically by the use of these models.

The common way to study the evolutionary dynamics in game theory is through replicator equations. These equations show the growth rate of the fraction of the organisms using a certain strategy. They equate the growth rate to the difference between the average payoff of that strategy and the average payoff of the population as a whole. Continuous replicator equations assume infinite populations, continuous time, complete mixing and that strategies breed true. The "attractors" (stable fixed points) of the equations are regarded as evolutionary stable states. A strategy that can survive all "mutant" strategies is considered stable, in the evolutionary sense. In the case of animals, survival strategies are strongly influenced by genetic factors.

Evolutionary games are mathematical objects with different rules, payoffs, and mathematical characteristics. Each "game" represents different environmental problems that organisms have to confront, and the strategies they might adopt to survive and reproduce. Evolutionary games are commonly given evocative names and "cover stories" that describe the general situation of a particular game. Representative games include "hawk-dove", "war of attrition", "stag hunt", "producer-scrounger", "tragedy of the commons", and "prisoner's dilemma". Strategies for these games also have names, ranging from search, hide, disguise, serve, defect, stalemate, and retaliate. The various strategies compete under the particular game's rules, and the mathematics are used to determine the outcomes (Fig. 14.9).

The simulation process starts with a population (Pn) that exhibit variation of characteristics among competing individuals. The game tests the strategies of the individuals under the specified rules. These rules produce different payoffs, in units of fitness (the production rate of offspring). The contesting individuals meet in pairwise contests with others, given a distribution of the genetic characteristics of the population. The mix of strategies in the population affect the payoff results by altering the odds that any individual may meet others in contests with various strategies.

The contest outcome is in the form of a *payoff matrix*. Each fraction of the population then undergoes replication or culling determined by the *replicator dynamics process*. This overall process then produces a *new generation* P(n + 1). Each surviving individual has a new fitness level determined by the game result. The new generation then takes the place of the previous one and the cycle repeats. The population mix may, or may not, converge to an

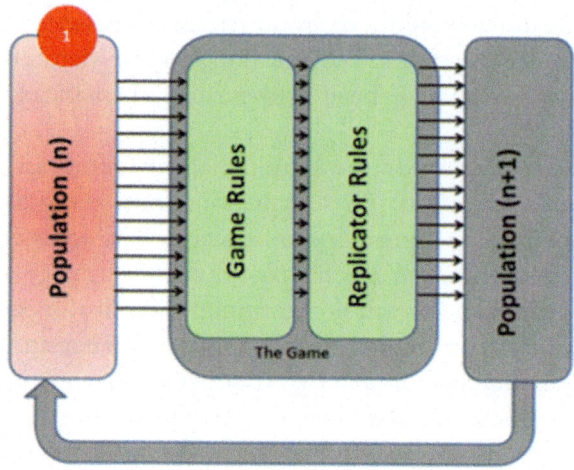

Fig. 14.9 EGT meta-model with three component—*population*, *game*, and *replicator dynamics*. Wikipedia

evolutionarily stable state, i.e., a state that cannot be defeated by any mutant strategy.

Evolutionary game theory has helped to explain the existence of altruistic behavior in Darwinian evolution. More important, it bears on the core socio-economic problem of our time: inequality. This is absolutely inconsistent with the "equality of opportunity" we profess to believe and advocate. Game theory explains why the rich get richer. Yet *"A rising tide lifts all ships"* is the slogan of politicians. So the question is: Does the tide really rise for all? If not, why not?

The standard answer, by classical economists and political conservatives, is that the most important key to economic growth is re-investment of profits, from trade or production. The re-investment can be in capital stock, or in new products and new markets. Government regulation is widely regarded as a "headwind" whereas "animal spirits" and competition (based on greed) are the "tailwinds" that keep the game of wealth creation going. Innovation is supposed to be a driver of investment behavior. True, competition is a powerful spur to innovation, whereas cooperation is not an effective incentive to innovate. But, extreme inequality, being inconsistent with equality of opportunity, is also a headwind.

Since 1982, thanks to a change in the rules of the US securities and exchange commission (SEC) encouraged by self-interested players in financial games, a new way to invest profits was invented: the "buyback".

Without cooperation we would, indeed, have Hobbes hypothetical "*state of nature… red of tooth and claw.*" In that world, the competition never ends until the final confrontation, when the winner takes all and becomes a dictator (Gilgamesh, Caesar Napoleon, Hitler, Putin) or an absolute monarch: *L'Etat c'est moi*" (Louis XIV). Unconstrained individualism— Hobbes' "state of nature"—leads eventually to unrestrained domination by a few oligarchs or only one. Of course, Hobbes' defense of a strong king was an argument based on false assumptions about the "state of nature". In reality, the actual state of nature was a hunter-gatherer society that certainly depended on cooperation and may, actually have been quite egalitarian.

Pure unconstrained capitalism is essentially a zero-sum game. It is "zero-sum" because the game is about money accumulation (monetary wealth) and the amount of money on the table, during any given round of bets, is fixed by the amount of gold in reserve, or by the Central Bank. Gains by winners as the game progresses are matched by losses by other players. As the game goes on—under conventional rules—there is a systematic transfer of wealth from the losers to the winners. This happens because, in the real (economic) game, the winners have significant advantages that improve their chances in every bet.

The most important of those advantages is the law of compound interest: those with money in the bank earning interest, or in long term investments, get richer automatically, as long as the economy itself grows. How could anybody with a few dollars to invest in nineteenth century America in the fail to make money? "*To he who hath, it shall be given*" says the Bible (Matthew 13:1), reflecting reality. Apart from making money from their own, or access to (other people's) money, the rich can afford better education, better sources of information, more and better contacts, better lawyers, better financial advisors, better credit ratings, and so forth.

The transfer of wealth, from losers to winners—given a fixed pool to start with—means that, as time goes on, there is less and less opportunity for the rest of the players. In the real economy more and more people are "out of the game" in the sense of having no economic surplus with which to"bet" i.e., to save, invest, or speculate. The fraction of the US population that is now "*out of the game*", in this sense, is about 60% {Dalio, 2019}. The "winners" not only capture the wealth that is at risk and "up for grabs", they also keep reducing the opportunity for others to compete—to play the game—as they become richer. Less opportunity means less hope. The game ends when one player finally captures all of the wealth that is "on the table. In the real world, things don't usually get quite that far without a violent revolution led by those who have nothing more to lose, having been deprived of opportunity, or never had any.

The only way to keep the "game" going—to avoid riots in the streets and a *coup d'état* of some sort—is to do one of two things. Either keep adding money to the "pot" by creating new wealth, or redistribute the existing wealth from the winners. The creation of new wealth is usually by discovery, invention or innovation. It is largely outside the domain of central government, though government activity in several domains, especially biotech, aviation and space programs, has been critical. Government support for scientific research in general, and R&D in certain fields, such as health care, also creates wealth.

Given a rising cost curve as shown in Fig. 14.1 only to make a point, it follows that the rational producer's desire to maximize his income and the consumer's desire to maximize her utility will drive the price of a given basket of commodities toward the equilibrium point. Neo-classical economic textbooks assume that the curve applicable to a "representative consumer" shopping for a representative basket of commodities will also apply to an aggregate of consumers, such as an industry or a country.

However, the "representative agent" is a lazy convenience for textbooks but a very misleading representation of reality. In 1976 Robert Lucas insisted that a valid macroeconomic model had to be based on the microeconomic theory of individual utility maximizing consumers and profit maximizing firms. {Lucas, 1976}. However, this proposition has been falsified by several mathematical economists, starting with Hyman Minsky {Minsky, 1982} and amplified by Steve Keen {Keen, 2011} {Keen, 2017}.

In brief, the fault of the Lucas thesis is that standard microeconomic theory assumes that relative prices can change without affecting individual consumers fixed incomes. But that is not true for aggregates, where price changes can radically alter income distribution. For instance, increasing gasoline prices hurts tourism and encourages increasing use of public transport and games. And vice versa. This fact, in turn, invalidates the simple supply–demand equilibrium assumption that is implied by the diagram at the beginning of this chapter.

To the creators of economic science, their subject is concerned with relationships between entities involved in "value creation" (by undefined means), trade and markets. The problem of production was neglected in the early days. Economic models were (and are) very narrowly focused. This was (is) partly to find simple "models" that have some apparent resemblance to reality. However, simplification can leave out crucial factors. Those missing factors account for externalities, and the difference between micro-economics and macro-economics. Microeconomics is about pairwise exchanges between buyers and sellers in perfect markets: a closed system. Macroeconomics tries to take into account social effects, third party effects, money creation and other factors that micro-economics neglects.

Neo-classical economics today (2022) makes several other hidden but fallacious assumptions. One is the assumption underlying all optimization models that all economic decision-makers base their choices by maximization of self-interest. This is how "*Homo economicus*" behaves, but not how real people behave. Another fallacy is the widespread assumption that social systems are equilibrium-seeking (viz. the popularity of "general equilibrium" models). A third—and crucial—gap is the lack of market prices for third-party environmental and social benefits—and costs—that are neglected by current theories. We need (but lack) a monetary cost of environmental degradation (from decreasing biodiversity, deforestation, rising sea level and climate warming to natural resource exhaustion) as a function of human activity (in exergy terms).

15

Socialism and the Welfare State

15.1 Antecedents

Georg Wilhelm Friedrich Hegel (1770–1831) was one of the most influential German philosophers of the early nineteenth century. Hegel's principal achievement, seen in retrospect, was the development of a distinctive re-articulation of idealism, sometimes termed absolute idealism. For Hegel the classical mind–body or matter-spirit dualism of Descartes, or sykof the Catholic Church, for instance, was a contradiction that could be overcome by logic (dialectics). In contrast to Immanuel Kant, who believe that the subject imposes rational a priori pure concepts of understanding upon the sense-data of intuitions, Hegel believed that the pure concepts are grounded in reality itself. Discussions like that were popular in German universities at the time.

Pierre-Joseph Proudhon (1809–1865). A precursor of anarchism, he was the only revolutionary theorist of the nineteenth century to come from the working class. He was the first to claim to be an anarchist. In 1840, a supporter of anarchy, understood in its positive sense: "*Freedom is anarchy, because it does not admit the government of the will, but only the authority of the law, that is, of necessity*". Proudhon was a printer who taught himself Latin in order to better print books in the language. He wrote more than sixty books. His best-known quotation is that "*property is theft!*" contained in his first major work "*What Is Property? Or, an Inquiry into the principle of Right and Government*" (Qu'est-ce que la propriété? Recherche sur le principe du droit et du gouvernement), published in 1840. In the same work, he used the expression "scientific socialism", when he writes: "*The sovereignty of the* *will yields to the sovereignty of reason, and will eventually be annihilated in a scientific socialism*".

The book attracted the attention of the French authorities, as well as of Karl Marx who started a correspondence with the author. They met in Paris while Marx was exiled there. Their friendship finally ended when Marx responded to Proudhon's *The System of Economic Contradictions, or The Philosophy of Poverty* with the provocatively titled *The Poverty of Philosophy*. The dispute led to the split between the anarchist and Marxist wings of the International Working Men's Association.

Proudhon favored workers' councils and associations or cooperatives as well as individual worker/peasant possession vs private ownership or nationalization by the state. He considered social revolution to be achievable in a peaceful manner. In *The Confessions of a Revolutionary*, Proudhon asserted that "*Anarchy is Order Without Power*", the phrase which much later inspired the anarchist circled-A symbol, one of the most common graffiti on city walls. Proudhon unsuccessfully tried to create a national bank, to be funded by an income tax on capitalists and shareholders. Similar in some respects to a credit union, it would have given interest-free loans. After the death of his follower Mikhail Bakunin, Proudhon's libertarian socialism diverged into individualist anarchism, collectivist anarchism,

The rise of proto-socialism as a political philosophy may have originated with the Jacobins, in France. They, believed that all human beings should be regarded as equally worthy of respect. They rejected rank differentiation in clothing, for instance. And before the revolution of 1789–1793, they also respected private property. In retrospect, it is clear that the "winners" of the French Revolution were the bourgeoisie and the entrepreneurs (both French words). But the exigencies of the "reign of terror" probably confused popular opposition to aristocracy with opposition to the ownership of wealth, meaning land. This seems to have morphed into a contest between the bourgeoisie and the proletarians (another French word). Marx saw that as a "class struggle".

In Chap. 16 we have discussed one gaping (until recently) hole and several smaller holes in macroeconomic theory. The big one was the lack of a coherent macroeconomic theory to explain the periodic "busts". According to traditional neoclassical economic theory ("Say's Law") unemployment results from a "glut". The economic system self-corrects as employers cut costs until the glut disappears and growth can resume.

John Maynard Keynes spent a lifetime pointing out the flaw in this argument: the problem of "leakage" (unspent savings and financial diversions that don't create demand). Hicks modified the Keynes theory, to make it tastier, but the longer the Keynesians were in power, the easier it was to forget the need for deficit management. The anti-tax budget balancers finally had their day. It ended badly, as usual, but some lessons may have been learned. Macroeconomics is not derivable from microeconomics. Rationality doesn't work. Irrationality must be taken into account. The central bank matters a lot. Leverage needs to be kept under control. Fisher's Paradox is important; in a deflationary deleveraging environment "*The more the debtors pay, the more they owe*". The point is that just as credit is inflationary, paying debts is deflationary. The money, credit, debt system needs to be managed positively. Public debt is manageable by the central bank. Private debt is still problematic, but not out of control.

Banks are the modern counterparts of the land owners (both urban and rural) in the 19th and earlier centuries: they get paid for renting capital land in the past, money today. As noted above, banks, unlike ordinary citizens, have the right to create credit i.e. to make risky loans. Moreover, they can lend other people's money in amounts considerably greater than their equity (financial reserve). In other words, banks have a "fractional reserve", meaning the equity (reserve) is only a fraction of the total amount of loans outstanding. They are betting their depositors money on the proposition that not all depositors will try to withdraw their deposits at the same time. When that does happen the bank goes bust and the depositors lose everything. That happened a number of times in the nineteenth century and again in 1907 and 1932. It has not happened since WW II, because some learning has taken place.

In 1963 Milton Friedman and Anna Schwartz wrote an influential book, *A Monetary History of the United States, 1867–1960*, and argued "inflation is always and everywhere a monetary phenomenon". Milton Friedman, who was among the generation of economists to accept Keynesian economics and then criticise Keynes's theory of fighting economic downturns using fiscal policy (government spending).

Monetarist theory asserts that variations in the money supply have major influences on national output in the short run and on price levels (the Phillips curve) over longer periods. Monetarists assert that the objectives of monetary policy are best met by targeting the growth rate of the money supply rather than by engaging in discretionary monetary policy by raising and lowering the interest rate paid to banks, by the Fed for their mandatory deposits. That interest rate is determined, by the independent Federal Reserve Bank, without political interference. It drives all of the other interest rates (and government bond dividends) in the economic system. Monetarism is commonly associated with supply-side economics, Reaganomics and so-called neoliberalism.

Milton Friedman (1912–2006) was an American economist and statistician who received the 1976 Nobel Memorial Prize in Economic Sciences for his research n consumption analysis, monetary history and theory and the complexity of stabilization policy. With George Stigler and others, Friedman was among the intellectual leaders of the Chicago school of economics, a neoclassical school of economic thought that rejected Keynesianism in favor of monetarism until the mid-1970s. Though he opposed the existence of the Federal Reserve Bank, Friedman advocated—given its existence—that the central bank should adopt a long-run money supply policy commensurate with the growth in productivity and demand for goods. Young professors and academics who were recruited or mentored by Friedman at Chicago went on to become leaders in the profession, including Gary Becker, Robert Fogel, Thomas Sowell and Robert Lucas Jr.

Friedman's challenges to what he later called "naive Keynesian theory" began with his interpretation of consumption, which tracks how consumers spend. He introduced a theory which would later become part of the mainstream, namely the theory of "consumption smoothing." Friedman theorized that there exists a "natural" rate of unemployment and argued that unemployment below this rate would cause inflation to accelerate. He argued that the Phillips curve was in the long run vertical at the "natural rate" (see graph) and he predicted what would come to be known as stagflation. Friedman argued that a steady, small expansion of the money supply was the preferred policy, as compared to rapid, and unexpected changes. His ideas concerning monetary policy, taxation, privatization and deregulation influenced government policies, especially during the 1980s. His monetary theory did influence the Federal Reserve's monetary policy in response to the global financial crisis of 2007–2008.

Economists no longer use the Phillips curve in its original form because it was shown to be too simplistic. This can be seen in a cursory analysis of US inflation and unemployment data from 1953–1992. There is no single curve that will fit the data, but there are three rough aggregations—1955–1971, 1974–1984, and 1985–1992—each of which shows a general, downwards slope, but at three very different levels with the shifts occurring abruptly. The data for 1953–1954 and 1972–1973 do not group easily, and a more formal analysis posits up to five groups/curves over the period.

Aided by the prestige gained from his successful forecast and explanation of stagflation, Friedman led increasingly successful criticisms against the Keynesian consensus, convincing not only academics and politicians but also much of the general public with his radio and television broadcasts. The academic credibility of Keynesian economics was further undermined by criticism from other monetarists trained in the Chicago School, by the Lucas critique and by criticisms from Hayek's Austrian School. So successful were these criticisms that by 1980 Robert Lucas claimed economists would often take offence if described as Keynesians.

After retiring from the University of Chicago in 1977, and becoming Emeritus professor in economics in 1983, Friedman was an advisor to Republican President Ronald Reagan and Conservative British Prime Minister Margaret Thatcher. His political philosophy extolled the virtues of a free market economic system with minimal government intervention in social matters. He once stated that his role in eliminating conscription in the United States was his proudest achievement.

In his 1962 book *Capitalism and Freedom*, Friedman advocated policies such as a volunteer military, freely floating exchange rates, abolition of medical licenses, a negative income tax and school vouchers and opposition to the war on drugs and support for drug liberalization policies. His support for school choice led him to found the Friedman Foundation for Educational Choice, later renamed "EdChoice". Several of Friedman's policy proposals recall the ideas of Henry George; the negative income tax is a version of George's social dividend.

However, monetarism had been tried and failed outright in Margaret Thatcher's government. The US Federal Reserve Bank officially discarded monetarism, after which Keynesian principles made a partial comeback in policy making. Not all academics accepted the anti-Keynes arguments. Hyman Minsky argued that Keynesian economics had been debased by excessive mixing with neoclassical ideas from the 1950s, and that it was unfortunate that this branch of economics had even continued to be called "Keynesian". Writing in *The American Prospect*, Robert Kuttner argued it was not Keynesian activism that caused the economic problems of the 1970s but the breakdown of the Bretton Woods system of capital controls. That breakdown allowed capital flight from regulated economies into unregulated economies—an example of Gresham's law (where weak currencies undermine strong currencies). Keynes loyalists pointed out that the main cause of the rising tide of inflation in the US in the 1970s was due to the Republican refusal to raise taxes to finance the Vietnam War, which was contrary to Keynesian advice.

A more typical response in academia was to accept some elements of the criticisms while refining Keynesian economic theories to defend them against arguments that would invalidate the whole Keynesian framework. The resulting body of work became known as "New Keynesian" economics. In 1992 Alan Blinder wrote about a "Keynesian Restoration", as work based on Keynes's ideas had to some extent become fashionable once again in academia, though the mainstream was somewhat polluted by monetarism. In the world of policy making, "free market" influences broadly sympathetic to monetarism and skeptical of managing interest rates by committee, have remained very strong. This is especially true at the top level in Washington-based institutions like the World Bank, the IMF and the US Treasury, and in prominent opinion-forming media such as the *Financial Times* and *The Economist*.

15.2 Political Marxism

Marx's political theories were seriously faulty in certain respects. The main faults (in retrospect) were: (1) He thought that production could, and should, be planned by the State to maximize the use-value of output. (2) He thought there was no need to reward innovation and risk-taking in a planned economy because those attributes are present in every person. (3) He thought that State ownership in a democratic society would automatically assure a fair distribution of the products of the economy, each worker to be rewarded according to his work contribution and his need. Finally, (4) he thought that socialism was a transition to communism, and that it must incorporate vestiges of capitalism, thus sharpening the contradictions and triggering periodic crises. He was wrong on all of those beliefs, except the crisis mechanism. He was pretty much right about degradation of nature and exploitation of workers.

All three of Marx's basic assumptions about how State ownership would work turned out to be false, which is why his fourth assumption also turned out to be wrong. Thus, political socialism failed when it got power. Was this due to a flaw in the socialist idea? We think it was mostly due to the underestimation of the importance of technological change and their blind faith in the assumption of (some) intellectuals that resources can be allocated better by central planners than by free markets.

The idea that industrial workers and miners might self-organize into "unions" for common benefit emerged in the early eighteenth century. Mines and ships were among the earliest. The first proto-union—to provide mutual insurance against sickness, old age and death—was the "keelmen" (lightermen) in Newcastle, England. This happened in 1699. The idea took off (so to speak) in the nineteenth century, partly due to the spread of primary education, and partly due to the growth of large enterprises with many workers.

In Fig. 15.1, the proletariat, at the bottom of the societal pyramid "works for all and feeds all" in the Marxist view. Curiously, this caricature is almost exactly the opposite of Ayn Rand's view of Atlas, the mythical giant (entrepreneurial genius) who carries the whole Earth on his shoulders and creates all the wealth.

Looking back, the political triumph of Marxism in Russia, in 1917, was almost a freak. The circumstances were that Russia was exhausted. The Tsar and his family were out of power (and were later executed by the Bolsheviks to foreclose any possible royalist revival). Moderate socialists (Mensheviks) took over when the Tsar resigned, but they were unable to agree on policy, even though virtually everybody wanted to stop fighting and sign a peace treaty with Germany. The difficulty for the Mensheviks was that the Western allies (Britain and France) wanted Russia to stay in the war, and there were factions in the Russian government wanting to maintain good relations with those countries after the war.

Meanwhile the Germans also wanted Russia out of the war, so as to be able to concentrate its forces in the Western Front. Germany saw the Bolsheviks, who were refugees in Switzerland at the time, as the way to break the deadlock in Moscow. The Germans facilitated Lenin's return to Russia with his inner circle, in a secret train, and the gamble paid off. The Treaty of Brest-Litovsk was signed and Germany was free to move its armies from the Eastern Front to France. That move, in turn, probably persuaded the United States to enter the war.

The triumph of the extremist Bolsheviks over the moderate Mensheviks had other consequences. The Bolsheviks believed in central planning and state ownership of "the means of production". But when mines and factories were actually nationalized in Russia, after 1917, the owners (including Ayn Rand's Jewish family) were expelled or impoverished. For the first twenty years, the workers in those nationalized factories were probably better off than they had been under the Czar's rule. But, under Stalin's rule—with central planning—the State under-invested in the nationalized industries and failed to encourage, or reward, innovation. As time passed they competed less and less effectively with privately owned industries elsewhere that did invest and innovate.

Fig. 15.1 Pyramid of capitalist system from 1911 industrial worker magazine. https://www.researchgate.net/profile/Julia-Elyachar-2/publication/275445017/figure/fig1/AS:461775440224256@1487107252428/The-Pyramid-of-Capitalism-as-Class-Struggle-in-1911-image-courtesy-of-Walter-P-Reuther.png

15.3 Utopian Socialism and Consumer Cooperatives

The other branch of socialism—called "utopian" for some reason, perhaps because it did not envision class conflict—was envisaged by Christian reformers like Robert Owen, Charles Fourier, J.P. Godin, and (in the twentieth century, by Adriano Olivetti) has recognizable religious antecedents. It is fundamentally based on the *antithesis* of "greed is good". It assumes that greed is immoral, by definition. (Roman Catholic doctrine forbade lending money at interest, calling it *usury*, a sin). It assumes that a society based on cooperation can exist and that it matters. Utopian socialism was based on the idea of sharing and reciprocity, associated with teachings of Jesus Christ (as well as Confucius, Buddha and others). The utopians, too, have been disappointed. It is clear enough from the results of a number of idealistic social experiments in the past that the elimination of greed in commerce was a vain hope.

The most effective British reformer of the early nineteenth century was **Robert Owen** (1771–1858) a Welshman who had managed cotton mills in the Manchester area. In 1799 he visited the New Lanark Mill in Scotland in 1799, fell in love with (and married) the proprietor's daughter, Carolyn Dale. He then bought the mill with partners from Manchester. When he bought it, the workers were mostly uneducated paupers from work-houses or prisons. They were paid (like workers in other mills) in tokens usable only in the mill's "truck" store where prices were set high to give the owners another source of profit. Owen changed that practice in New Lanark, and created the first of the "consumer cooperative" stores that are now widespread. He also was the first to propose the 8 h day in 1810, although it was not approved by his partners and not implemented nationally until much later.

In 1813 Owen had to buy out his partners, who wanted to continue the "standard" industrial practices on the usual grounds ("our competitors do it, so we have to do it in order to compete"). Luckily he persuaded Jeremy Bentham (whom he greatly admired) and one of the Quaker merchants, William Allen to invest, on the basis of a fixed return on their capital of £5000 each. After that he had more freedom to innovate. His innovations included education for the workers and their children, and worker housing. He gradually converted New Lanark into an industrial and social success story that attracted wider attention.

In 1813 he wrote a book, entitled "*A New View of Society*" (Owen 1813 [1946]). (It was followed by several other books in later years, developing his utopian themes.) In 1817 he joined the fledgling socialist party and co-wrote a report to the committee on the Poor Law, in the Houses of Parliament. His influence led to two failed utopian experiments during 1825–1827 at Orbiston, Scotland, and "New Harmony", Indiana (1824). (The Orbiston failure was partly due to problems beyond his control.) But in later years he tried again with a more carefully planned utopian enterprise called "New Moral World" which was started but sadly never actually built. It would have been a small town surrounding a factory. (A drawing of the design is shown in Fig. 15.2). Later Owen helped to get the first *Truck Acts* passed by Parliament (1831 et seq.) Today Robert Owen is known and revered as the founder of the cooperative movement and of "utopian socialism."

Robert Owen was a rarity, but not quite unique. In 1844 a "Society for the Improvement of the Conditions of the Laboring Class" opened its first model housing estates in England. This was neither a corporation (in the modern sense) nor a partnership, but rather an eleemosynary organization.

The first successful co-operative was the Rochdale Society of Equitable Pioneers, established in England in 1844. This became the basis for the development and growth of the modern cooperative movement. As the mechanization of the Industrial Revolution forced more skilled workers into poverty, these tradesmen decided to band together to open their own store selling food items they could not otherwise afford.

With lessons from prior failed attempts at co-operation in mind, they designed the now-famous Rochdale Principles, and over a period of four

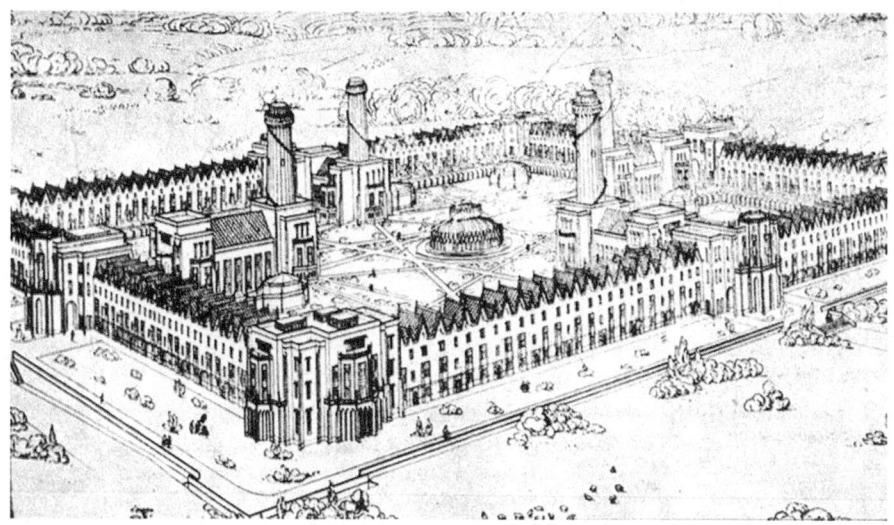

Fig. 15.2 Drawing of the plan for "New Moral World", by Robert Owen—wikivisually.com

months they struggled to pool one pound sterling per person for a total of 28 pounds of capital. On December 21, 1844, they opened their store with a very meagre selection of butter, sugar, flour, oatmeal and a few candles. Within three months, they expanded their selection to include tea and tobacco, and they were soon known for providing high quality, unadulterated goods.

The Co-operative Group formed gradually over 140 years from the merger of many independent retail societies, and their wholesale societies and federations. In 1863, twenty years after the Rochdale Pioneers opened their co-operative, the North of England Co-operative Society was launched by 300 individual co-ops across Yorkshire and Lancashire. By 1872, it had become known as the Co-operative Wholesale Society (CWS). Through the twentieth century, smaller societies merged with CWS, such as the Scottish Co-operative Wholesale Society (1973) and the South Suburban Co-operative Society (1984).

15.4 Henry George

The most widely read book on economics in history (with the possible exception of "Wealth of Nations" by Adam Smith) was a book by a self-taught political economist named **Henry George** (1839–1897). His formal education ended at age 14. He made his living as a journalist and later became a politician. Yet, his magnum opus, entitled "Progress and Poverty" is taken very seriously by economists, and justifiably so (George 1879 [1946]). The substance of that book is his argument that the increase of economic value (rent) of land, attributable to (location, should be shared by society. He argued that urban locations gain in value because of overall economic activity. In "*Progress and Poverty*" he wrote: "*We must make land common property.*" He argued that, by taxing land values, society could "*recapture the value of its common inheritance*", raise wages, improve land use, and eliminate the need for taxes on productive activity. George believed this tax would remove existing incentives toward land speculation and encourage development, as landlords would not profit by holding valuable sites vacant, nor suffer tax penalties for any buildings constructed on their land.

In Henry George's time, this scheme became known as the "single-tax" movement and sometimes associated with movements for land nationalization (especially in Ireland). However, *Progress and Poverty* did not advocate land nationalization. He said: "*I do not propose either to purchase or to confiscate private property in land. The first would be unjust; the second, needless. Let the individuals who now hold it still retain, if they want to, possession of what they are pleased to call their land. Let them continue to call it their land. Let them buy and sell, and bequeath and devise it. We may safely leave them the shell, if we take the kernel. It is not necessary to confiscate land; it is only necessary to confiscate rent."*

The book sold 3 million copies in English, in the first years after publication, 6 million copies in thirteen languages, by 1936, and many more since then. It is justifiably included as one of the ten all-time economics classics.

Henry George was a reformer in many areas apart from his signature land tax policy, including intellectual property law, free trade (versus tariffs), woman's suffrage, the secret ballot, and currency reform.

For instance, he noted that most debt was (is) not issued for the purpose of creating capital for industrial development (as Alexander Hamilton had earlier proposed) but instead as an obligation against rental flows from existing "economic privilege" (i.e. land ownership). He the use of "debt free" (sovereign money) currency, such as the greenback, which governments would spend into circulation to help finance public spending. He opposed the use of metallic currency, such as gold or silver, and "fiat money" created by private commercial banks. In effect he advocated the current (post 1971) system, although he did not specifically call for a national bank.

He argued that the state should not sponsor creditors (usually banks) in the form of sheriffs, constables, courts, and prisons to enforce collection of such "illegitimate" debt obligations. In ancient times debtors became debt slaves, or went to prison. Thanks to his agitation, bankruptcy law in the United States is less onerous for debtors than in most other countries, and debtors prisons were outlawed by the. Much of the supply of credit in developed economies is created to purchase land (and claims on future land rents) rather than to finance "bricks and mortar". (Michael Hudson (Chap. 16) has estimated that about 80% of credit finances real estate purchases.)

Henry George acknowledged that this policy would limit the banking system but he argued that it would actually be an economic boon, since the financial sector, in its existing form, is mostly devoted to augmenting rent extraction, as opposed to productive investment. *"The curse of credit is that it expands when there is a tendency to speculation, and sharply contracts just when most needed to assure confidence and prevent industrial waste."* George even said that a "debt jubilee" could remove the accumulation of burdensome obligations without reducing aggregate wealth. Henry George was active in advocating the elimination of debtors prisons in the United States.

Henry George argued that businesses relying on exclusive right-of-way over land had to be "natural" "monopolies". Examples include utilities (water, electricity, sewage), information (telecommunications), goods, and persons moving from one location to another (travellers). He wanted all systems of transport along "public ways" (roads) to be managed as public utilities and provided free of charge or at marginal cost. On roads, he would have allowed competition between private transport service providers. But wherever competition was not realistic, he advocated complete municipalization (e.g. of railroads). He argued that "right of way" should be provided without cost to users, because investments in beneficial public goods always tend to increase land values by more than the total cost of those investments. He used the example of urban buildings that provide free vertical transit, paid out of the increased value that residents derive from the elevators.

Henry George proposed to abolish all intellectual property privilege (copyrights and patents), because his classical definition of "land" included "*all natural forces and opportunities.*" In his view, owning a monopoly over specific arrangements and interactions of materials, governed by the forces of nature, allowed title-holders to extract royalty-rents from producers, in a way similar to owners of ordinary land titles. George later supported limited copyright, on the ground that temporary property over a unique arrangement of words or colors did not inhibit others from making other works of art. He did not see mechanical designs (e.g. of guns), for example, as works of art. He argued that customers could choose not to buy a specific new product, but they "cannot choose to lack a place upon which to stand", so benefits gained for inventors would tend to eventually be captured by owners and financers of a location monopoly. He did not see a need to provide financial returns for risk-taking innovators.

Henry George was a free-trader, along with Adam Smith, David Ricardo and the corn law advocates in England, hurting land-owners and benefitting consumers. He opposed tariffs, on principle, although they which were (at the time) both the major method of protectionist trade policy and an important source of federal revenue before the federal income tax was introduced. He argued that tariffs kept food and commodity prices high for consumers, while failing to produce any corresponding increase in overall wages. He also asserted that tariffs protected monopolistic companies from competition, thus augmenting their power. (This set him against the industrialists of New England, who wanted protection from foreign competition.)

Free trade became a major issue in federal politics in his lifetime. His book *Protection or Free Trade* was the first book to be read entirely into the Congressional Record. (This was done by five Democratic congressmen.) In 1997, Spencer MacCallum wrote that Henry George was "*undeniably the greatest writer and orator on free trade who ever lived.*" In 2009, Tyler Cowen wrote that George's 1886 book *Protection or Free Trade* "*remains perhaps the best-argued tract on free trade to this day.*" Milton Friedman said it was the most rhetorically brilliant work ever written on trade. Friedman paraphrased one of Henry George's arguments in favor of free trade: "*It's a very interesting thing that in times of war, we blockade our enemies in order to prevent them from getting goods from us. In time of peace we do to ourselves by tariffs what we do to our enemy in time of war.*"

Henry George's most radical idea was what called a "citizen's dividend" to be paid for by a land value tax. He made this proposal first, in an April 1885 speech to a labor audience in Burlington, Iowa entitled "The Crime of Poverty" and later in an interview with former U.S. House Representative David Dudley Field II. That interview was published in the July 1885 edition of the *North American Review*. He proposed to create a pension and disability system, and an unconditional basic income from surplus land rents. It would be distributed to residents "*as a right*" instead of as charity. This idea—not yet implemented—is now called Universal Basic Income (UBI).

Henry George was one of the earliest and most prominent advocates for adoption of the secret ballot in the United States, as a basic condition of free elections.

Henry George was also an early and vocal advocate for women's political rights. He argued for extending suffrage to women and even suggested filling one house of Congress entirely with women: "*If we must have two houses of Congress, then by all means let us fill one with women and the other with men*" (Fig. 15.3).

15.5 Leo Tolstoy and Mahatma Gandhi

Count **Lev Nikolayevich Tolstoy** (1828–1910), usually referred to in English as **Leo Tolstoy**, was a Russian writer and one of the greatest authors of all time. Tolstoy's notable works include the novels *War and Peace* (1869) and *Anna Karenina* (1878), both regarded as pinnacles of realist fiction.

In the 1870s, Tolstoy experienced a profound moral crisis, followed by what he regarded as an equally profound spiritual awakening, as outlined in his non-fiction work *A Confession* (1882). His literal interpretation of the ethical teachings of Jesus, based on the Sermon on the Mount, caused him to become a fervent Christian anarchist and pacifist. His ideas on nonviolent resistance, expressed in such works as *The Kingdom of God Is Within You* (1894), had a profound impact on such pivotal twentieth century figures

Fig. 15.3 Henry George—Wikipedia

as Mahatma Gandhi and Martin Luther King Jr. He also became a dedicated advocate of the economic philosophy of Henry George, which he incorporated into his writing, particularly *Resurrection* (1899) (Fig. 15.4).

Mohandas Karamchand Gandhi (1869–1948), also known as **Gandhi**, was an Indian lawyer, anti-colonial nationalist and political ethicist. He employed nonviolent resistance to lead the successful campaign for "swaraj" meaning self-rule, and India's independence from British rule. Gandhi, later inspired movements for civil rights and freedom across the world. The honorific **Mahātmā** (Sanskrit: "great-souled", "venerable"), was first applied to him in 1914 in South Africa.

Born and raised in a Hindu family in coastal Gujarat, Gandhi trained in the law at the Inner Temple, London, and was called to the bar at age 22 in June 1891. After two uncertain years in India, where he was unable to start a successful law practice, he moved to South Africa in 1893 to represent an Indian merchant in a lawsuit. He went on to live in South Africa for 21 years. It was in South Africa that Gandhi raised a family and first employed nonviolent resistance in a campaign for civil rights. In 1915, aged 45, he returned to his home country, India and soon set about organising peasants, farmers, and urban laborers to protest against excessive land-tax and discrimination. One thing led to another.

Assuming leadership of the Indian National Congress in 1921, Gandhi led nationwide campaigns for easing poverty, expanding women's rights, building religious and ethnic amity, ending untouchability, and, above all, achieving

Fig. 15.4 Tolstoy on 23 May, 1908 at Yasnaya Polyana—Wikimedia

swaraj or self-rule. Gandhi used **fasting** as a political device, often threatening suicide unless demands were met. Congress publicised the fasts as a political action that generated widespread sympathy. In response, the government tried to manipulate news coverage to minimise his challenge to the Raj. He fasted in 1932 to protest the voting scheme for separate political representation for Dalits; Gandhi did not want them segregated. The British government stopped the London press from showing photographs of his emaciated body, because it would elicit sympathy.

Gandhi adopted the *dhoti* woven with hand-spun yarn as a mark of identification with India's rural poor. He began to live in a self-sufficient residential community, to eat simple food, and undertake long fasts as a means of both introspection and political protest. Bringing anti-colonial nationalism to the common Indians, Gandhi led them in challenging the British-imposed salt tax with the 400 km (250 mi) Dandi Salt March in 1930 and in calling for the British to quit India in 1942. He was imprisoned other times and for many years in both South Africa and India.

Gandhi strongly favored the emancipation of women, and urged "*the women to fight for their own self-development.*" He opposed *purdah*, child marriage, dowry and *sati*. *He insisted that a* wife is not a slave of the husband, but his comrade, better half, colleague and friend. At various occasions,

Gandhi credited his orthodox Hindu mother, and his wife, for first lessons in *satyagraha*. He used the legends of Hindu goddess Sita to expound women's innate strength, autonomy and "lioness in spirit". To Gandhi, the women of India were an important part of t" (Buy Indian), and his goal of decolonising the Indian economy.

Even though Gandhi often and publicly expressed his belief in the "equality of the sexes", his vision was nuanced. He wanted a society of gender difference and complementarity between the sexes. Women, to Gandhi, should be educated to be better in the domestic realm and educate the next generation. (His views on women's rights were less liberal and more similar to puritan-Victorian expectations of women, than some other Hindu leaders.)

Gandhi spoke out against untouchability early in his life. Before 1932, he and his associates used the word *antyaja* for untouchables. In a major speech on untouchability at Nagpur in 1920, Gandhi called it a great evil in Hindu society but observed that it was not unique to Hinduism, having deeper roots, and stated that Europeans in South Africa treated "all of us, Hindus and Muslims, as untouchables; we may not reside in their midst, nor enjoy the rights which they do". Calling the doctrine of untouchability intolerable, he asserted that the practice could be eradicated, that Hinduism was flexible enough to allow eradication, and that a concerted effort was needed to persuade people of the wrong and to urge them to eradicate it.

Gandhi considered untouchability to be wrong and evil, but he believed that caste or class is based on neither inequality nor inferiority. Gandhi believed that individuals should freely intermarry whomever they wish, but that no one should expect everyone to be his friend: every individual, regardless of background, has a right to choose whom he will welcome into his home, whom he will befriend, and whom he will spend time with. In 1932, Gandhi began a new campaign to improve the lives of the untouchables, whom he began to call *harijans*, "the children of god".

Gandhi rejected the colonial Western education system on the grounds that it led to disdain for manual work, while creating an elite administrative bureaucracy. Gandhi favored an education system with far greater emphasis on learning skills in practical and useful work, one that included physical, mental and spiritual studies. His methodology sought to treat all professions equal and pay everyone the same. This led him to create a university in Ahmedabad, Gujarat Vidyapith.

Gandhi called his ideas *Nai Talim* (literally, 'new education'). He believed that the Western style education violated and destroyed the indigenous cultures. A different basic education model, he believed, would lead to better self-awareness, prepare people to treat all work equally respectable and valued, and lead to a society with less social diseases.

Nai Talim evolved out of his experiences at the Tolstoy Farm in South Africa, and Gandhi attempted to formulate the new system at the Sevagram ashram after 1937. Nehru's vision of an industrialised, centrally planned economy after 1947 was inconsistent with Gandhi's village-oriented approach. Gandhi believed that military force is unnecessary, because any aggressor can be overthrown by the method of non-violent non-co-operation. While the military is unnecessary in a nation organised under *swaraj* principle, Gandhi added that a police force is necessary given human nature. However, the state would limit the use of weapons by the police to the minimum, aiming for their use as a restraining force.

According to Gandhi, a non-violent state is like an "ordered anarchy". In a society of mostly non-violent individuals, those who are violent will sooner or later accept discipline or leave the community, stated Gandhi. He emphasised a society where individuals believed more in learning about their duties and responsibilities, not demanded rights and privileges. On returning from South Africa, when Gandhi received a letter asking for his participation in writing a world charter for human rights, he responded saying, "*in my experience, it is far more important to have a charter for human duties.*"

Swaraj to Gandhi did not mean transferring colonial era British power brokering system, favors-driven, bureaucratic, class exploitative structure and mindset into Indian hands. He warned such a transfer would still be English rule, just without the Englishman. "This is not the Swaraj I want", said Gandhi. Gandhi saw democracy as more than a system of government; it meant promoting both individuality and the self-discipline of the community. Democracy meant settling disputes in a nonviolent manner; it required freedom of thought and expression. For Gandhi, democracy was a way of life.

Gandhi believed in the *sarvodaya* economic model, which literally means "*welfare, upliftment of all*". This was very different from the socialist model championed by Nehru—India's first prime minister. To both, according to Bhatt, removing poverty and unemployment were the objective, but the Gandhian economic and development approach preferred adapting technology and infrastructure to suit the local situation, in contrast to Nehru's large scale, socialised state owned enterprises.

To Gandhi, the utilitarian economic philosophy that aims at "greatest good for the greatest number" was fundamentally flawed, and his alternative proposal *sarvodaya* set its aim at the "greatest good for all". He believed that the best economic system not only cared to lift the "poor, less skilled, of impoverished background" but also empowered to lift the "rich, highly skilled, of capital means and landlords". Violence against any human being, born poor or rich, is wrong, believed Gandhi. He stated that the mandate theory of majoritarian democracy should not be pushed to absurd extremes, individual freedoms should never be denied, and no person should ever be made a social or economic slave to the "resolutions of majorities".

Gandhi challenged Nehru and the modernisers in the late 1930s who called for rapid industrialisation on the Soviet model; Gandhi denounced that as dehumanising and contrary to the needs of the villages where the great majority of the people lived. It was Nehru's vision, not Gandhi's, that was eventually adopted by the Indian State. Gandhi called for ending poverty through improved agriculture and small-scale cottage rural industries.

Gandhi disagreed with Marx's view that economic forces are best understood as "antagonistic class interests". He argued that no man can degrade or brutalise the other without degrading and brutalising himself and that sustainable economic growth comes from service, not from exploitation. Further, believed Gandhi, in a free nation, victims exist only when they co-operate with their oppressor, and an economic and political system that offered increasing alternatives gave power of choice to the poorest man.

While disagreeing with Nehru about the socialist economic model, Gandhi criticized capitalism driven by endless wants and a materialistic view of man. Capitalism, he believed, created a materialist system at the cost of other human needs, such as spirituality and social relationships. To Gandhi, both communism and capitalism are wrong, in part because both adopted a materialistic view of man, and because the former deified the state with unlimited power of violence, while the latter deified capital. He believed that a better economic system is one which does not impoverish one's culture and spiritual pursuits.

Gandhi's vision of an independent India based on religious pluralism was challenged in the early 1940s by a Muslim nationalism, led by Mohammad Ali Jinnah which demanded a separate homeland for Muslims within British India. In August 1947, Britain granted independence, but contrary to Gandhi's advice, the British Indian Empire was partitioned into two dominions, a Hindu-majority India and a Muslim-majority Pakistan. As many displaced Hindus, Muslims, and Sikhs made their way to their new lands, religious violence broke out, especially in the Punjab and Bengal. Abstaining from the official celebration of independence, Gandhi visited the affected areas, attempting with little success, to alleviate distress.

In the months following, he undertook several hunger strikes to stop the religious violence. The last of these, begun in Delhi on 12 January 1948 when he was 78 years old, also had the indirect goal of pressuring India to pay out some cash assets owed to Pakistan. Although the Government of India relented, as did the religious rioters, the belief that Gandhi had been too resolute in his defence of both Pakistan and Indian Muslims, especially those besieged in Delhi, spread among some Hindus in India. Among these was Nathuram Godse, a militant Hindu nationalist who assassinated Gandhi by firing three bullets into the chest at an inter-faith prayer meeting in Delhi on 30 January 1948.

Gandhi's death was mourned around the world. Field Marshal Jan Smuts, former prime minister of South Africa, and once Gandhi's adversary, said, *"Gandhi was one of the great men of my time and my acquaintance with him over a period of more than 30 years has only deepened my high respect for him however much we differed in our views and methods. A prince among men has passed away and we grieve with India in her irreparable loss."*

The British prime minister Clement Attlee said in a radio address to the nation on the night of January 30, 1948: *"Everyone will have learnt with profound horror of the brutal murder of Mr Gandhi and I know that I am expressing the views of the British people in offering to his fellow-countrymen our deep sympathy in the loss of their greatest citizen. Mahatma Gandhi, as he was known in India, was one of the outstanding figures in the world today, ... For a quarter of a century this one man has been the major factor in every consideration of the Indian problem..."*.

Leo Amery, the British secretary of state during the war said, *"No one contributed more to the particular way in which the charter of British rule in India has ended than Mahatma Gandhi himself. His death comes at the close of a great chapter in world history. In the mind of India, at least, he will always be identified with the opening of the new chapter which, however troubled at the outset, we should all hope, will develop in peace, concord and prosperity for India."*

Lord Pethick-Lawrence, the British secretary of state in 1948 said: *"What was the secret of his power over the hearts and minds of men and women? In my opinion it was the fact that he voluntarily stripped himself of every vestige of the privilege that he could have enjoyed on account of his birth, means, personality and intellectual pre-eminence and took on himself the status and infirmities of the ordinary man. When he was in South Africa as a young man and opposed the treatment of his fellow-countrymen in that land, he courted for himself the humiliation of the humblest Indian that he might in his own person face the punishment meted out for disobedience. When he called for non-cooperation with the British in India he himself disobeyed the law and insisted that he must be among the first to go to prison. ... He never claimed to be any other than an ordinary man. He acknowledged his liability to error and admitted that he had frequently-learnt by his mistakes. He was the universal brother, lover and friend of poor, weak, erring, suffering humanity."*

Albert Einstein wrote: "*He died as the victim of his own principles, the principle of non-violence. He died because in time of disorder and general irritation in his country, he refused armed protection for himself. It was his unshakable belief that the use of force is an evil in itself, that therefore it must be avoided by those who are striving for supreme justice to his belief. With his belief in his heart and mind, he has led a great nation on to its liberation. He has demonstrated that a powerful human following can be assembled not only through the cunning game of the usual political manoeuvres and trickery but through the cogent example of a morally superior conduct of life. The admiration for Mahatma Gandhi in all countries of the world rests on that recognition.*"

The New York Times in its editorial wrote: "*It is Gandhi the saint who will be remembered, not only on the plains and in the hills of India, but all over the world. He strove for perfection as other men strive for power and possessions. He pitied those to whom wrong was done: the East Indian laborers in South Africa, the untouchable 'Children of God' of the lowest caste of India, but he schooled himself not to hate the wrongdoer. The power of his benignity grew stronger as his potential influence ebbed. He tried in the mood of the New Testament to love his enemies. Now he belongs to the ages.*"

Muhammad Ali Jinnah, Governor general and founder of Pakistan, said, on the day of Gandhi's assassination "*I am shocked to learn of the most dastardly attack on the life of Mr. Gandhi, resulting in his death. Whatever our political differences, he was one of the greatest men produced by the Hindu community, and a leader who commanded their universal confidence and respect. I wish to express my deep sorrow, and sincerely sympathize with the great Hindu community and his family in their bereavement at this momentous, historical and critical juncture so soon after the birth of freedom for Hindustan and Pakistan. The loss of dominion of India is irreparable, and it will be very difficult to fill the vacuum created by the passing way of such a great man at this moment.*"

15.6 Social Democracy as an Antidote to Marxism

The 1880s were a period when Germany started on its long road towards the welfare state as it is today. Several political parties were working on social legislation, but it was Otto von Bismarck who moved this program into government. The program of the Social Democrats included all of the programs that Bismarck eventually implemented, but they also included programs designed to pre-empt the more radical programs championed by Karl Marx and Friedrich Engels. Bismarck's idea was to implement the minimum functions of the Social Democratic programs without any of their overtly socialistic or redistributional aspects.

Bismarck opened debate on his program on 17 November 1881 in the Imperial Message to the Reichstag, using the term "practical Christianity" to describe it. Bismarck's scheme was designed to increase the productivity of German workers and secondarily on supporting the government. His insurance program included health insurance, accident insurance (workman's compensation), disability insurance and an old-age retirement pension. None of them had existed previously to any great extent.

Despite his impeccable right-wing credentials, Bismarck would be called a socialist for introducing these programs, as would President Roosevelt 70 years later. In his own speech to the Reichstag during the 1881 debates, Bismarck would reply: "Call it socialism or whatever you like. It is the same to me." Based on Bismarck's message, the Reichstag filed three bills designed to deal with the concept of accident insurance and one for health insurance, although other bills were passed after Bismarck left office. Retirement pensions and disability insurance were placed on the back burner for the time being.

Bismarck worked closely with large industry—the Krupps and Thyssens and their ilk—with the primary aim of stimulating German economic growth by giving workers greater security. A secondary concern was trumping the Socialists, who had no actual welfare proposals of their own but who opposed Bismarck's proposals on principle. They were waiting for capitalism to self-destruct. Bismarck especially listened to Hermann Wagener and Theodor Lohmann, advisers who persuaded him to give workers a corporate status in the legal and political structures of the new German state. In March 1884, Bismarck declared:

> The real grievance of the worker is the insecurity of his existence; he is not sure that he will always have work, he is not sure that he will always be healthy, and he foresees that he will one day be old and unfit to work. If he falls into poverty, even if only through a prolonged illness, he is then completely helpless, left to his own devices, and society does not currently recognize any real obligation towards him beyond the usual help for the poor, even if he has been working all the time ever so faithfully and diligently. The usual help for the poor, however, leaves a lot to be desired, especially in large cities, where it is very much worse than in the country.

Bismarck's idea was to implement welfare programs that were acceptable to conservatives without any "socialistic" aspects such as higher taxes or (God Forbid) property redistribution. He was dubious about laws protecting workers at the workplace, such as safe working conditions, limitation of work hours, and the regulation of women's and child labor. He believed that such regulation would force workers and employers to reduce work and production and thus harm the economy.

Based on Bismarck's message, the Reichstag filed three bills to deal with the concepts of accident and sickness insurance. The subjects of retirement pensions and disability insurance were placed on the "back-burner" for the time being. The social legislation implemented by Bismarck in Germany in the 1880s played a key role in the sharp, rapid decline of German emigration to America. Young men considering emigration looked, not only at the gap between higher hourly "direct wages" in the United States compared to Germany, but also at the differential in "indirect wages" (social benefits) which favored staying in Germany. Many young men moved into German industrial cities, as Bismarck's insurance system partly offset low wage rates in Germany. This reduced the German emigration rate.

Sickness Insurance Law of 1883

The first successful bill, passed in 1883, was the Sickness Insurance Bill. Bismarck considered the program, established to provide sickness insurance for German industrial laborers, the least important and the least politically troublesome. The health service was established on a local basis, with the cost divided between employers and the employed. The employers contributed one third, and the workers contributed two-thirds. The minimum payments for medical treatment and sick pay for up to 13 weeks were legally fixed.

The individual local health bureaus were administered by a committee elected by the members of each bureau. This move had the unintended effect of establishing a majority representation for the workers, on account of their large financial contribution. This worked to the advantage of the Social Democrats who, through heavy worker membership, achieved their first small foothold in public administration.

Accident Insurance Law of 1884

Bismarck's government had to submit three draft bills before it could get one passed by the Reichstag in 1884. Bismarck had originally proposed that the federal government pay a portion of the accident insurance contribution. He wanted to demonstrate the willingness of the German government to reduce the hardship experienced by the German workers so as to wean them away from supporting the various left-wing parties, most importantly the Social Democrats.

The National Liberals took this program to be an expression of "State Socialism", which they opposed for ideological reasons. The Centre Party was afraid of the expansion of federal power at the expense of "states' rights". (Germany was a federation of 39 states, after the Congress of Vienna in 1816. Today, since the Weimar Republic, it is a federation of 16 states, or Länder).

As a result, the only way the insurance program could be passed at all was for the entire cost to be underwritten by the employers. To facilitate this, Bismarck arranged for the administration of this program to be placed in the hands of Der Arbeitgeberverband in den beruflichen Korporationen (the Organization of Employers in Occupational Corporations). This organization established central and bureaucratic insurance offices on the federal or the state level to actually administer the program. Its benefits 'kicked in' to replace the sickness insurance program after the 14th week of disability. It paid for medical treatment and a pension of up to two-thirds of earned wages if the worker were fully disabled. This program worked so well that it was expanded, in 1886, to include agricultural workers.

Old Age and Disability Insurance Law of 1889

The old age pension program, equally financed by employers and workers, was designed to provide a pension annuity for workers who reached the age of 70. Unlike the accident and sickness insurance programs, this program covered all categories of workers (industrial, agrarian, artisans and servants) from the start. Also, unlike the other two programs, the principle that the national government should contribute a portion of the underwriting cost, with the other two portions prorated accordingly, was accepted without question. The disability insurance program was intended to be used by those permanently disabled. This time, the state or province supervised the programs directly.

The law also set up stricter regulations to ensure greater workplace safety. It banned work on Sundays, introduced a maximum working day of eleven hours for women and ten hours for workers under 16 years of age. It also prohibited night work by children and banned those under the age of 13 from working in industry. It also encouraged the establishment of worker's committees, in factories, to address disputes. Industrial tribunals were set up to settle disputes between employees and employers.

After Bismarck left office in 1890, Social Democrats introduced further legislation to regulate working time and conditions and to protect more vulnerable workers (women and children). They also introduced a system to allow redress for employer abuse. The social insurance based program introduced by Bismarck was adopted throughout most of the world, except the United State of America, in the aftermath of World War I. The US finally got "social security" (the pension part) in the 1930s, but the health insurance part—"Obamacare"—is still being opposed by most manifesto Republican politicians.

15.7 The Creation of the US Federal Reserve Bank

The panic of 1907 threatened several New York banks with failure, an outcome avoided through loans arranged by JPMorgan. Morgan succeeded in restoring confidence to the New York banking community, but the panic revealed structural weaknesses in the U.S. financial system, such that a private banker (Morgan) could dictate the terms of a bank's survival. In other parts of the country, clearing houses briefly issued their own money notes to carry on business.

In response, Congress created the National Monetary Commission to investigate options for providing currency and credit in future panics. This was sponsored and headed by Senator Nelson Aldrich. He was an unapologetic right-wing Republican supporter of big business—the bigger the better—and opponent of any sort of regulation. (His daughter married a Rockefeller). A proponent of Progressive Era themes of Efficiency and scientific expertise, he led a team of experts to study the European national banks. After his trip, he came to believe that Britain, Germany and France had superior central banking systems. He worked with several key bankers and economists, including Paul Warburg, Abram Andrew, Frank A. Vanderlip, and Henry Davison, to design a plan for an American central bank. After issuing a series of 30 reports, this commission drew up the Aldrich Plan, in 1911, forming the basis for a proposed centralized Federal Reserve system, to be controlled by the banks themselves, not the government, on the European model (Fig. 15.5).

Fig. 15.5 Reformers hated and feared Senator Aldrich for killing reforms disliked by big business. 1906 Puck cartoon—Wikiwand

In 1913 newly elected President Woodrow Wilson signed into law the Federal Reserve Act patterned in some ways after Aldrich's vision, but differing in a number of crucial fundamentals. The main difference was decentralization into 12 self-financing regional banks. The one in New York branch was (and still is) by far the largest but it is only one of twelve. The other Federal Reserve Districts are Atlanta. Boston, Chicago, Cleveland, Dallas, Kansas City, Minneapolis, Philadelphia, Richmond, San Francisco and St. Louis. Some of the regional banks also possess branches, with the whole system being headquartered at the Eccles Building in Washington, D.C.

The regional banks are jointly responsible for implementing the monetary policy set forth by an entity called the Federal Open Market Committee, that meets periodically. The result was the Federal Reserve System. It was established, initially, to provide liquidity (loans), to commercial banks, when needed to prevent collapses triggered by other bank failures, such as the one that killed the Knickerbocker Bank in 1907. The Federal Reserve Banks opened for business in November 1914.

The Federal Reserve Banks created in 1914 are neither the earliest nor the latest of the institutions that the United States government has created to provide functions of a central bank. Prior institutions have included the

First (1791–1811) and Second (1818–1824) National Banks of the United States, the Independent Treasury (1846–1920) and the National Banking System (1863–1935). Several policy questions have arisen with respect to these institutions. They include the degree of influence by private interests, the balancing of regional economic concerns, the prevention of financial panics, and the type of reserves used to back the currency.

There are few heroes in this story, but Senator **Carter Glass** (1858–1946) deserves mention. He was elected to Congress in 1902, and was re-elected nine times, until becoming Secretary of the Treasury for President Wilson. He only served one year in that job until being appointed to a vacant Senatorial seat, in 1920, which he held until his death in 1946. He was, throughout his career, a "Jeffersonian Democrat" and (in President Roosevelt's words "an unreconstructed Rebel") meaning that his sympathies were Southern and anti-Hamiltonian to the core.

Senator Glass was a very important participant in the financial restructuring associated with President Franklin Roosevelt's "New Deal". As noted he was a social conservative but he left a large fingerprint on legislation He disagreed with much of the "New Deal" and especially opposed "unconstitutional" federal interference in private affairs. He fought for a balanced budget in 1936 (which turned out to be a bad mistake). On civil and voting rights he was a reactionary. Truman wrote in a letter to Mrs. Glass after her husband's death that "to the end he glorified in the title of "Unreconstructed Rebel".

Some give him credit for inventing the existing Federal Reserve System of the United States of America, which was a world-changing event (though barely noticed at the time). Glass himself credited and Woodrow Wilson. In any case they worked closely together on the legislation. After the stock market crash in 1929 he fought for reform legislation. He was the name author of the Glass-Steagall Act of 1932, The Banking Act of 1933, the Reconstruction Finance Act of 1933, the Securities and Exchange Act and the Banking Act of 1935. He opposed the creation of the Federal Deposit Insurance Corporation (FDIC) (Fig. 15.6).

Fig. 15.6 Senator Carter Glass—Wikipedia

16

Keynes v. Hayek and the Monetarists

16.1 The Great Divide from the Old World to the New

Was it an awakening or more like catching a cold? Wars before the Great Divide were fought by armies of anonymous foot-soldiers from the lower class led by generals who had their pictures painted or their statues created riding horses and carrying swords and flags. They rarely ended with a glorious cavalry charge, except in a poet's imagination. The two major European wars, 1914–1918 and 1939–1945 were fought on land by armies, starting with horses but ending with motorized vehicles, often sinking in the mud. The first one ended in a surrender by the Germans when America entered the war and the German high command realized it couldn't win. The second one ended with another total German defeat, partly because the German side "ran out of gas" (actually oil).

The first War expanded beyond Serbia, where it was started by the assassination of the heir to the Emperor of Austria-Hungary. At the time Austria wanted to crush Serbia and Russia wanted to support Serbia. But Germany was allied to Austria and Russia was allied to France, which was allied to Britain. Germany wanted access to African colonies and Middle Eastern oil (via the Berlin to Bagdad railway) and the British didn't want them to have either. All of the leaders were "born to rule" and all of them thought their and rights and privileges were at risk and must be defended at all costs. Soldiers lives didn't count as costs.

John Kenneth Galbraith used several pages of his book on the Great Crash about the Great Depression to point out that the ranks of landed aristocratic decision-makers in Europe "born to rule" consisted of men who got positions and promotions because of birth, not competence (Galbraith 1954). Many of them were spectacularly incompetent. None was fired for incompetence. One of those emerged from deserved postwar anonymity to say that "*the next war will be won by a decisive cavalry charge*" (op cit p. 16).

The prewar "Great Powers" were no longer Great powers after the first world war, although Briseveral governments thought they were entitled to be great and wanted to be. The war of 1914–1918 ended three of the ancient Royal Houses of Central Europe. The Bourbons, the Romanovs and the Hapsburgs became extinct, not to mention the Ottoman Caliphate. Only the English Hanoverians survived, and they were strictly kept in a luxurious cocoon for ceremonial purposes. The British Navy ceased to rule the waves and the British Empire became a storybook memory of glory earned by heroes trained on the playing fields of Eton.

Positivism, born in the nineteenth century, glorified empirical science derived by reason and logic from sensory experience. Other ways of knowing, such as theology, metaphysics, intuition, or introspection were rejected or considered meaningless. Although the positivist approach has been a recurrent theme in the history of western thought since Bacon, Hume and Kant, modern positivism—first articulated in the early nineteenth century by Auguste Comte—began to seek scientific laws in logic, psychology, economics, historiography, and other fields of thought. This movement reached its maximum influence in the last years of the nineteenth century, just before WW I.

The new emperors of the world economy were American industrialists: Vanderbilt, Rockefeller, Edison, Westinghouse, Carnegie, Ford, Harriman and the super-banker J P Morgan. Texas was the gusher in the center of the new world of oil. After WW I Marxist ideas, feminism and prohibition were suddenly rampant, along with flying, baseball and quantum mechanics. The Gold standard was flaky. The war between Marxist socialism, being propagated by the Communist International (Comintern) headquartered in Moscow and Wall Street capitalism began in earnest. There were other underground phase changes.

As J. K. Galbraith said, World War II was just a continuation of World War I. The second war in Europe was primarily about the desire by Hitler's Nazi Germany for revenge for mistreatment by the Treaty of Versailles, and secondarily about acquiring land for settlement and access to Middle Eastern Oil, either via the Suez Canal or Azerbaijan. The second war expanded to Asia after the Japanese attack on Pearl Harbor. That, too, was also very much about oil. It was triggered by the 1937 cutoff of US exports of oil and steel to Japan from California (due to the Japanese invasion of Manchuria). The Japanese military regime hoped to replace California oil by oil from Indonesia.

OK, it was somewhat more complicated than that, but access to oil was centrally involved. What is true for sure is that all of the countries that started those two wars were losers. Both the German and Japanese governments ended WWII as war criminals. By 1945 the US and the USSR were winners, and luckily the US didn't engage in a vengeful looting spree in Europe or the Far East. There was a serious attempt after the war, initiated by Franklin Roosevelt and continued by Harry Truman, to create a stable international system, optimistically called the United Nations, without the weaknesses of the League of Nations. The existence of nuclear weapons undermined this effort.

The Stalinist leaders of the USSR, who wanted to keep Germany divided and to create a permanent security system for Russia (the Warsaw pact) has kept the UN from ever achieving its original objectives. The US created NATO as a counterweight to the Warsaw Pact, and became the global policeman, for a few decades, the "Cold War". But that role is no longer tenable or affordable. Some Russians are (in 2022) still trying to recreate the Warsaw pact, starting with an invasion of the Ukraine. It looks like a very bad mistake. The future state of the world depends on the US-China relationship.

After WW II oil was suddenly important. Nuclear power was even more important; it was the "elephant in the room". From 1946 until 1989 there were two "great powers, but one of them was "great" only by consent of the other. The centrally planned USSR had a great military machine and many ICBMs, based on a narrow centrally planned industrial base. But it did not have the underlying economic-industrial system to create or support the underlying and supporting technology. In 1989 the USSR collapsed and Russia reverted to its Czarist habit of top-down government supported by secret police. Since 1989 there has boon only one super-power, though the US financial and technological hegemony is now declining and China will soon be the second superpower (and maybe the first by mid-century.) Will Europe unify—more than federation—and become the third?

16.2 From Woodrow Wilson to Adolph Hitler

The concept of territorial sovereignty was set forth, in 1648, at the Treaties of Westphalia, which ended the Wars of religion and the "thirty years war" in

Europe. It was spread throughout the world by European powers, which were establishing colonies and spheres of influences over virtually every society. Territorial nationalism reached its peak in the late nineteenth century. The concept of a peaceful community of nations was proposed in 1795 by Immanuel Kant in *Perpetual Peace: A Philosophical Sketch*", which outlined the idea of a league of nations. The league was supposed to control conflict and promote peace between states. Kant wanted a peaceful world community, but not in a sense of a global government. His hope was that each sovereign country would declare itself a "free state" that respects its own citizens and foreign visitors as fellow rational beings, thus promoting peaceful society worldwide. He was a dreamer.

International co-operation to promote collective security originated in the Concert of Europe that developed after the Napoleonic Wars in the nineteenth century in an attempt to maintain the status quo between European states and so avoid war (see 4.6). International Law is a misnomer, since without enforcement there is no law. The phrase evolved through the colonial expansion of the European powers, in the eighteenth and nineteenth centuries. Rapid decolonization across the world in the 1960s and 1970s resulted in the creation of scores of newly independent states, mostly small. The varying political and economic interests and needs of these states, along with their diverse cultural backgrounds, forced the principles and practices of international law to take into account, and adapt to, new influences.

By 1910 international law had developed further, with the Hague Conventions of 1899 and 1907 governing rules of war and the peaceful settlement of international disputes, as well as first Geneva Conventions establishing laws dealing with humanitarian relief during wartime. In 1910 Theodore Roosevelt said, when he accepted his Nobel Peace Prize (for reconciliation of violent factions in the Philippines): "*it would be a masterstroke if those great powers honestly bent on peace would form a League of Peace.*" Maybe his successor, President Wilson, heard him say that.

At the start of the First World War, the first schemes for an international organization to prevent future wars emerged in Great Britain and the United States. A British political scientist, **Goldsworthy Lowes Dickinson** (1862–1932) drafted a scheme for a "League of Nations" in 1914. Together with Liberal politician (and former ambassador to the US) **James Bryce** (1838–1922) he played a leading role in the founding a group of internationalist pacifists known as the Bryce Group, later the League of Nations Union. The group gained some influence within the governing Liberal Party. In Dickinson's 1915 pamphlet "After the War" he wrote of his "League of Peace" as being essentially an organization for arbitration and conciliation. Dickinson argued that the secret diplomacy of the early twentieth century had brought about the war, and greater transparency would be beneficial to increase the "the impossibility of war" (his phrase). The 'Proposals' of the Bryce Group were circulated widely, both in England and the US. They had a significant influence on the nascent international movement.

In January 1915, American social worker and sociologist **Jane Addams** (1860–1935) was elected national chairman of the Woman's Peace Party. She was invited by European women peace activists to preside over the International Congress of Women in The Hague, Netherlands, hoping to end the war. Coordinated by Mia Boissevain, Aletta Jacobs and Rosa Manus, the Congress opened on 28 April 1915. It was attended by 1136 participants from neutral nations, and resulted in the establishment of an international organization of women's rights activists linked by opposition to the war.

At the Congress, there was a meeting of ten leaders, to discuss mediation. The delegates adopted a platform calling for creation of international bodies with administrative and legislative powers to develop a "permanent league of neutral nations" to work for peace and disarmament. Addams was elected president of the International Committee of Women for a Permanent Peace, established to continue the work of the Hague Congress, at a conference in 1919 in Zurich, Switzerland. The International Committee developed into the Women's International League for Peace and Freedom (WILPF). Addams continued as president, a position that entailed frequent travel to Europe and Asia (Fig. 16.1).

In 1915, a similar body to the Bryce group was set up in the United States led by former president William Howard Taft. It was called the "League to Enforce Peace". It advocated the use of arbitration in conflict resolution and the imposition of sanctions on aggressive countries. None of these early organizations envisioned a continuously functioning body. With the exception of the Fabian Society in England, they maintained a legalistic approach that would limit the international body to a "court of justice". The Fabians were the first to argue for a "Council" of states, necessarily the Great Powers, who would adjudicate world affairs, and for the creation of a permanent secretariat to enhance international co-operation across a range of activities.

In the course of the diplomatic efforts surrounding World War I, both sides had to clarify their long-term war aims. By 1916 in Britain, fighting on the side of the Allies, and in the neutral United States, long-range thinkers had begun to design a unified international organization to prevent future wars. When the new coalition government of David Lloyd George took power in Great Britain in December 1916, there was widespread discussion among

Fig. 16.1 International Congress of Women in 1915—Wikipedia. Left to right in the picture: 1. Lucy Thoumaian—Armenia, 2. Leopoldine Kulka?, 3. Laura Hughes—Canada, 4. Rosika Schwimmer—Hungary, 5. Anika Augspurg—Germany, 6. Jane Addams—USA, 7. Eugenie Hanner, 8. Aletta Jacobs—Netherlands, 9. Chrystal Macmillan—UK, 10. Rosa Genoni—Italy, 11. Anna Kleman—Sweden, 12. Thora Daugaard—Denmark, 13. Louise Keilhau—Norway

intellectuals and diplomats of the desirability of establishing such an organization. When Lloyd George was challenged by Wilson to state his position with an eye on the post-war situation, he endorsed such an organization. Wilson himself included, in his Fourteen Points, in January 1918 a "*league of nations to ensure peace and justice.*" British foreign secretary, Arthur Balfour, argued that, as a condition of durable peace, "*behind international law, and behind all treaty arrangements for preventing or limiting hostilities, some form of international sanction should be devised which would give pause to the hardiest aggressor.*"

On his December 1918 trip to Europe, Woodrow Wilson gave speeches that "*reaffirmed that the making of peace and the creation of a League of Nations must be accomplished as one single objective*". Wilson foolishly neglected to invite William Howard Taft, or any other Republican, to join U.S. delegation. Instead, he instructed his protégé, Edward M. House, to draft a US plan which reflected Wilson's own idealistic views (first articulated in the Fourteen Points of January 1918), as well as the work of the Phillimore Commission. The outcome of House's work and Wilson's own first draft proposed the termination of "unethical" state behavior, including forms of espionage and dishonesty. Methods of compulsion against recalcitrant states would include severe measures, such as "*blockading and closing the frontiers of that power to commerce or intercourse with any part of the world and to use any force that may be necessary ….*"

At the Paris Peace Conference in 1919, Wilson, Robert Cecil and Jan Smuts all put forward their draft proposals. Wilson's was based on his "14 points". Several of the young reformers, who were hoping for a restructuring of the old economic order, resigned from their delegations in disgust when they realized that the other leaders of the "allies" were narrowly focused on territorial adjustments and a desire to weaken and 'punish' Germany, as a nation. The new regime in Russia should have been represented in Versailles, but it was excluded.

After lengthy negotiations between the delegates, the Hurst–Miller draft was finally produced as a basis for the Covenant. After more negotiation and compromise, the delegates finally approved of the proposal to create the League of Nations (French: Société des Nations, German: Völkerbund) on 25 January 1919. The final Covenant of the League of Nations was drafted by a special commission, and the League was established by Part I of the Treaty of Versailles. On 28 June 1919, 44 states signed the Covenant, including 31 states which had taken part in the war on the side of the Triple Entente or joined it during the conflict.

French women's rights advocates invited international feminists to participate in a parallel conference to the Paris Conference in hopes that they could gain permission to participate in the official conference The Inter-Allied Women's Conference asked to be allowed to submit suggestions to the peace negotiations and commissions and were granted the right to sit on commissions dealing specifically with women and children. Though they asked for enfranchisement and full legal protection under the law equal with men, those requests were ignored. Women did win the right to serve in all capacities, including as staff or delegates, in the League of Nations organization. They also won a declaration that member nations should prevent trafficking of women and children and should equally support humane conditions for children, women and men laborer's.

At the Zürich Peace Conference held between 17 and 19 May 1919, the women of the WILPF condemned the terms of the Treaty of Versailles for both its punitive measures, as well as its failure to provide for condemnation of violence and exclusion of women from civil and political participation. Upon reading the Rules of Procedure for the League of Nations, Catherine Marshall, a British suffragist, observed that the guidelines (written by men) were completely undemocratic. They were modified based on her suggestions (Fig. 16.2).

Despite Wilson's personal efforts to establish and promote the League, for which he was awarded the Nobel Peace Prize in October 1919, the United States never joined. Senate Republicans led by Henry Cabot Lodge wanted a

Fig. 16.2 President Woodrow Wilson of the United States (1913), Frank Graham Cootes—Wikipedia

League with the reservation that only Congress could take the U.S. into war. Lodge gained a majority of Senators and Wilson refused to allow a compromise. The Senate voted on the ratification on March 19, 1920, and the 49–35 vote fell short of the needed 2/3 majority. The US never joined. The League held its first council meeting in Paris on 16 January 1920, six days after the Versailles Treaty and the Covenant of the League of Nations came into force. (It ceased operations in 1946).

The new international order in Europe after WW I was intended by the victors—apart from the US—to be the same as the old order, except for the exclusion of Germany and Austria (and Bolshevik Russia) and the expanded role of the state in economic affairs. The war had seen an unprecedented expansion in the role of the state, involving extensive control of production. In all the warring countries, except the US, the state had taken over, directly or indirectly, important sections of production and transport during the war. The 'progressives' argued—as Andrew Hamilton would have—that the modern state should retain control over certain basic industries, such as railroads and utilities, in the interests of the national welfare. This argument was lost: the industries taken over during the war were mostly returned to private hands in the years immediately following the Treaty.

The new industrial giant, the United States of America, was having a good time getting richer, during the "roaring twenties". Charles Lindbergh and Babe Ruth were the heroes of the decade. That changed in October 1929 when the New York stock market crashed. But the US government was still not interested in the problems of old Europe or East Asia. But the argument concerning the role of the Federal Government versus "states rights" and the role of the Federal Reserve Bank (FRB), continued. When the Great Depression hit bottom in 1932 it was argued by progressives like Keynes, that the state should be more active in providing social welfare provision for the poor, especially in the case of unemployment. Franklin Roosevelt's "New Deal" (1933–1936) was a serious attempt to do this, by federal legislation. Yet it was struck down in its entirety in 1937 by a conservative Supreme Court.

Above all, since 1914–1918 money has increasingly became both the measure and the driver of everything, To begin with, Russia, France and Italy all borrowed a lot of money from Great Britain (i.e. British banks) to finance their military activities. The British banks, in turn, borrowed $8.7 billion from the US, not from the US government (which was not in the lending business) but from New York-based private banks.

Moreover, thanks to a growing trade surplus, US gold reserves had been growing steadily from a very low level in 1900 through the war years (thanks to the profitable sale of munitions), and even faster in the post-war years as debtor countries transferred their gold to New York to pay for needed imports of food and other goods. N.B. most of those wartime debts were later converted into long-term Dawes and similar bonds sold to US savers and investors, and most of those bonds became worthless during the 1930s or during WW II.

In 1913 Britain had a money supply (currency in circulation and bank deposits) of $5 billion ($104 billion in $2011). This was backed by $800 million ($17 billion $2011) in gold, of which only $150 million ($3.1 billion $2011) was in the vaults of the British central bank (BoE). The rest was in the form of coins or bullion held by individual businesses or in other British banks. During the war the British money supply increased to $12 billion ($200 in $2011) whereas the gold supply did not change. Britain spent $5 billion ($85 billion $2011) on the war itself, largely by selling its overseas investments to private American investors. Domestic prices increased by a factor of two and a half. The problem for the BoE in the post-war era was what to do about the gold standard and the reserve status of the pound sterling (Ahamed 2009).

France spent $30 billion ($500 billion $2011) on fighting the war, of which only 5% was paid for directly by French taxes. The rest was borrowed. Half was covered by war bonds sold domestically and $10 billion ($170 billion 2011) came from loans by the US banks or British banks. The loans left an unpaid gap of $2.5 billion that was filled by "printing new money" i.e. creating government debt. As a result the currency in circulation in France tripled whereas the quantity of goods produced did not, and prices rose accordingly (Ahamed 2009).

At the beginning of the Great War a gold-backed Deutschmark was fixed at 4.1 Marks to the US dollar, but by the end of the war it was 8.91 marks per dollar. By the end of 1919 it was 47 marks per dollar and by November 1921 it was 300 marks per dollar. The "London ultimatum" of May 1921 insisted that the reparations be paid in gold or dollars at the rate of 2 billion gold marks per year, plus 26% of German exports. By 1921 Germany was collecting just 10 Marks in taxes for every 100 marks of expenditures, and had lost all but $120 million of its $1 billion pre-war gold reserves. The reparations to France and England (agreed under the Treaty of Versailles) accounted for a third of the German budget deficit during those two years.

The German hyper-inflation of 1922–1923 was only partly due to the Treaty of Versailles. Very little of the German reparations was actually paid. The inflation did not greatly hurt the owners of industry (and land) but it destroyed the thrifty German middle-class: teachers, civil servants, professionals and savers of all kinds were left with nothing. Anti-Semitism found fertile ground, because it was easy to blame the Jews for whatever went wrong in the world of finance. (Henry Ford was a leading anti-semite.) Socialists on the left and the right (Nazis) battled it out on the streets. There is no need to recapitulate here what followed the election of 1933 in Germany (and the rest of the world.)

What followed at the end of the second World War was the Bretton Woods Conference in 1944. The International Monetary Fund (IMF) was created at Bretton Woods. It was formed in 1944, primarily based on the ideas of Harry Dexter White and John Maynard Keynes. It came into formal existence in 1945 with 29 member countries and the goal of reconstructing the international monetary system. It now plays a central role in the management of balance of payments difficulties and international financial crises. Member countries contribute funds to a pool through a quota system from which countries experiencing balance of payments problems can borrow money. As of 2016, the fund had XDR 477 billion (about US$667 billion).

The IMF works, in various ways, to improve the economies of its member countries. The organization's objectives stated in the Articles of Agreement are: to promote international monetary co-operation, international trade, high employment, exchange-rate stability, sustainable economic growth, and making resources available to member countries in financial difficulty.

Keynes argued that the role of the central bank must be to reduce interest rates and encourage greater investment. Keynes specifically discussed underconsumption in the General Theory (Chap. 22, Sect. IV and Chap. 23, Sect. VII). Keynes did not view saving as an independent decision process, but rather as a diversion of income away from spending. While consumption of goods and services helps increase national aggregate income, saving is an element of income that has "leaked" out of the circular flow of income.

Prior to Keynes, a situation in which aggregate demand for goods and services did not meet supply was referred to by classical economists as a "glut". (There was disagreement among them as to whether a general glut was actually possible.) Keynes argued that when a glut occurred, it was the over-reaction of producers and the laying off of workers that led to the fall in demand. Keynesians therefore advocated an active stabilization policy to reduce the amplitude of the business cycle, which they ranked among the most serious of economic problems. Keynes argued that government spending can be used to increase aggregate demand, thus increasing economic activity, reducing unemployment and deflation. This seems obvious today, but it wasn't obvious to neoclassical theorists—advocates of thrift in the past.

The Liberal Party in the UK fought the 1929 General Election on a promise to "reduce levels of unemployment to normal within one year by utilising the stagnant labour force in vast schemes of national development". David Lloyd-George launched his campaign in March of that year with a policy document, "We can cure unemployment", which tentatively claimed that, "Public works would lead to a second round of spending as the workers spent their wages." Two months later Keynes and Hubert Henderson collaborated on a political pamphlet seeking to provide academically respectable economic arguments for Lloyd-George's policies. It was titled "Can Lloyd George do it?" and endorsed the claim that "greater trade activity would make for greater trade activity … with a cumulative effect".

This became the mechanism of the "ratio" published by Richard Kahn (1905–1989) in his 1931 paper "The relation of home investment to unemployment" (described by Alvin Hansen as "one of the great landmarks of economic analysis") (Kahn 1931 #8247). The "ratio" was soon rechristened the "multiplier" at Keynes's suggestion. The multiplier of Kahn's paper is based on a mechanism familiar nowadays from textbooks. Samuelson put it as follows: "Let's suppose that I hire unemployed resources to build a $1000 woodshed. My carpenters and lumber producers will get an extra $1000 of income …. If they all have a marginal propensity to consume of 2/3, they will now spend $666.67 on new consumption goods. The producers of these goods will now have extra incomes … they in turn will spend $444.44 … Thus an endless chain of secondary consumption via re-spending is set in motion by my primary investment of $1000" (Samuelson 1966 #4433).

Samuelson's treatment above closely follows Joan Robinson's account of 1937 and is the main channel by which the multiplier has influenced Keynesian theory (Robinson undated #4302). It differs significantly from Kahn's original paper and even more from Keynes's book.

Keynes saw his work as constituting a clear break with the Neoclassical orthodoxy—which he described as "classical economics": "I accuse the classical economic theory of being itself one of these pretty, polite techniques which tries to deal with the present by abstracting from the fact that we know very little about the future" (Keynes 1937, p. 215). Keynes specifically denied Say's identity—that savings equal investment—by insisting on the reality and importance of money hoarding (under the mattress) behavior, usually attributable to uncertainty about the future.

However, Keynes's revolutionary ideas were somewhat de-revolutionized by John Hicks (1904–1989) in a paper that claimed to reach a reconciliation between "Mr Keynes and the Classics". The trick was Hick's so called Investment-Savings Liquid Money IS-LM model, which is a mathematical version of the argument in Fig. 16.3 (Hicks 1937 #8251) p. 153.

Hicks defined saving with the formula $S = Y(1-t) - C$. That is, savings is a part of the income that is deducted from total consumption.

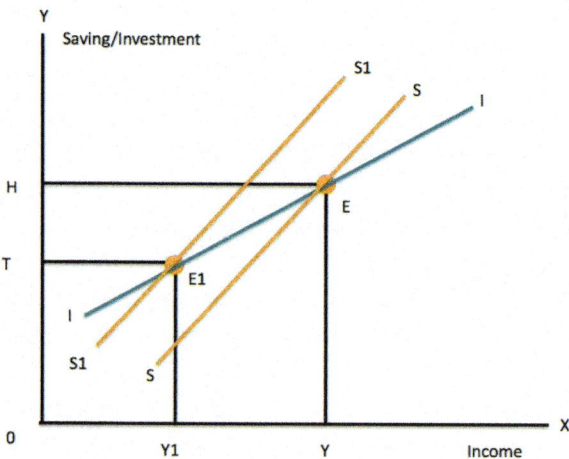

Fig. 16.3 Saving/investment versus income. https://cdn.corporatefinanceinstitute.com/assets/paradox-of-thrift1-1.jpg

Line 1 in the graph shows a hypothetical relationship between savings and personal income. Net savings occur when income is higher than E and net dis-savings occur when income is lower (e.g. for retired people). When people, on average, increase the savings rate from S to S1, the increase in savings available for investment (from T to H is compensated by a decline in current net income (from Y to Y1). If (and only if) the net savings is actually invested (i.e. spent on "bricks and mortar") the GDP remains the same. But if savings accumulate in an inactive bank account or is used to reduce debt, the GDP will decrease as saving increases.

The crucial point of this exercise is that human behavior called thrift, or "the propensity to hoard" that is widely regarded as admirable—"saving for a rainy day" or hiding gold under the mattress (as French peasants were once reputed to do)—is also a leak from the circular flow of money and consequently deflationary and anti-growth. Thrift is an economic headwind. This is one of the paradoxes of economics. It is also a key part of Keynes theory.

Though he presented his model as "a convenient synopsis of Keynesian theory", and it was accepted as such by the majority of economists, Hicks later admitted that it was a Neoclassical, "general equilibrium" model he had sketched out (Hicks 1981 #8252, p. 140). The gap between what Hicks claimed to be Keynesian economics, and the actual economics of Keynes, was not trivial. This can be seen by comparing Hicks's "suggested interpretation" of Keynes, and Keynes's own 24-page summary of his economics in "The General Theory of Employment" (Keynes 1936 [2007] #7572).

The key passage in Keynes's summary is the following: The theory can be summed up by saying that ... the level of output and employment as a whole depends on the amount of investment ... More comprehensively, aggregate output depends on the propensity to hoard, on the policy of the monetary authority, on ... But of these several factors it is those which determine the rate of investment which are most unreliable, since it is they which are influenced by our views of the future about which we know so little. This that I offer is, therefore, a theory of why output and employment are so liable to fluctuation" (Keynes 1937, p. 221). His point was that capital investments are bets on future demand, by investors, that is partly determined by those investments. But the Laissez Faire system (no government intervention) is not self-correcting, so recessions can become deep depressions.

The paradox of thrift was stated in 1892 by John M. Robertson in his The Fallacy of Saving, and in earlier forms by mercantilist economists since the sixteenth century, and similar sentiments date to antiquity. The Paradox of Thrift is the argument that increased savings in the short term can reduce savings, or rather the ability to save, in the long term. The Paradox of

Thrift arises out of the Keynesian notion of an economy driven by aggregate demand. The Paradox of Thrift, while logically reasoned, attracted numerous criticisms from neo-classical economists.

Intellectual precursors of Keynesian economics were influenced by consumption theories associated with John Law, Thomas Malthus, the Birmingham School of Thomas Attwood, as well as the American economists William Trufant Foster and Waddill Catchings, who were influential in the 1920s and 1930s. These men, like Keynes after them, worried about failure of aggregate demand to consume potential output, calling this "underconsumption" (focusing on the demand side), rather than "overproduction" (which would focus on the supply side), and advocating economic interventionism.

In 1936, Keynes wrote his controversial book called "The General Theory of the Economy" in which he declared that spending and investment in the economy were the keys to increasing economic growth. He believed that the level of output and employment did not rely on the capacity of produce, but rather on the decisions taken by individuals in society to spend and invest their money. (Investment, for him, intended to allow greater consumption in the future.) Keynes said that saving money reduces the amount of money that people spend and invest to meet future demand. When demand falls, investment also lags, reducing current demand. This increases unemployment, and further reduces demand. He called it the "Paradox of Thrift."

So "the Keynesian revolution" was a misnomer. It didn't happen. What did happen was that Keynes' successors have developed approaches to economics that are neither Keynesian nor Marshallian. The main examples are (Sraffa 1960; Goodwin 1967; Minsky 1982, 1986; Keen 1995, 2011}.

But a true revolution in mainstream economic thought, like the rejection of Ptolemy's earth-centric vision of the solar system and its total replacement by Copernicus's sun-centric vision, has not (yet) happened.

16.3 Unemployment and Financial Crises

During the Great Depression of the 1930s, Joseph Schumpeter took up the subject of cyclic crises and wrote *"Business Cycles: A Theoretical, Historical and Statistical Analysis of the Capitalist Process"* (Schumpeter 1939). Since Schumpeter's typology the main economic cycles are nowadays named after their first discoverers or proposers. They include:

- 3–5 year "inventory cycle", identified by Joseph Kitchin (1923);

- 7–11 year "fixed investment" cycle, identified by Clement Juglar (1862);
- 15–25 year infrastructure investment cycle, identified by Simon Kuznets (1930);
- 45–60 year long wave technological cycle of Nikolai Kondratieff.

These are the best-known, but a few others have been proposed, including a building cycle, suggested by Arthur Burns, and the theoretical Goodwin and Minsky cycles. Kitchin studied the existence of "Minor Cycles" with an average length of about $3^{1/3}$ years or 40 months for which he concluded that two or three 'minor cycles' fit within one Juglar (or Business) cycle. Schumpeter described the Great Depression as the simultaneous convergence of the Kitchen, Juglar and Kuznets cycles.

The inventory cycle is conventionally explained as a build-up of stocks in the inventory of retail shops, resulting in a downturn in orders to manufacturers, and a slowdown in production. When the inventory oversupply is used up, orders increase and production increases again. The GDP may not actually turn negative during the inventory disinvestment phase, but the rate of overall growth decreases. The period of the cycle is roughly the time it takes to increase and decrease production and/or the time it takes for consumers to reach the limits of their ability to buy.

The first conceptual breakthrough insight (apart from that of Marx) came from Juglar (1862), who shifted focus, no longer looking at the isolated problem of the individual crisis. He described business cycles as wave motions in which crises followed periods of unsustainable growth and over-speculation. Schumpeter contributed to the development of the cyclical theory by developing the asymmetric three-phase model of Juglar (1862) into a sinusoidal four-phase model consisting of prosperity, recession, depression and recovery (ibid, p. 167), of which the depression phase is not necessarily included in the cycle. The Schumpeterian wave is indicated in Fig. 16.4).

Certainly, the Juglar "cycle" of 7–11 years seems to be correlated closely with successive economic crises, albeit not quite waves. Simon

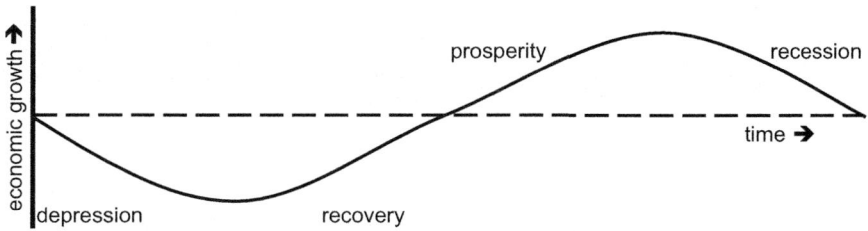

Fig. 16.4 The Schumpeterian wave. *Source* unknown

Kuznets (1930) investigated second-order secular wholesale price trends and concluded that they are related to demographic phenomena and immigration. He also claimed to find a relationship between his swings and income inequality, with inequality rising during booms and declining during recessions. His results were sharply criticized at the time, and seem less relevant today than they did in 1930. The subject became central to macroeconomics after the National Bureau of Economic Research (NBER) took it up in the 1940s. That research program culminated in the publication of the book "Measuring Business Cycles" by Arthur Burns and Wesley Mitchell (Burns and Mitchell 1946).

Figure 16.5 shows the Fed Funds rate (blue) against the intended version (black), from 1975 (post Nixon) to 2010, just after the Housing Bubble of 2008–2009. The Troubled Asset Relief Program (TARP) anks and brought interest rates below zero, where they remained for some time. The "recovery" that followed was driven by speculation in the stock market (led by Facebook, Amazon, Apple, Netflix and Google, known as FAANG) but left a large number of home-owners "under water" because their mortgages were suddenly larger than the revised lower value of their homes. TARP and the Fed saved the global economic system from collapse, just barely, but left a lot of middle class people in the dust. Of course, the inflation rate did fall to almost zero.

The possible existence of 'long cycles' in prices and economic activity about 50 years from peak to peak was noted more than a century ago by Jevons (1884). In fact Jevons cited even earlier articles. However the first author to subject the hypothesis of long cycles to systematic analysis was the Marxist Dutch economist Van Gelderen (1913).

The existence of long-term economic waves has been widely speculated after the 1925 publication of the Soviet economist Nikolai Kondratieff in the "*Voprosy konyunktury*", or "Long Economic Cycles". Kondratieff covered a period of 2½ waves of which the first two were 60 and 48 years. Based on this analysis he indicated an average length of about 50 to 55 years. Others have followed him in his research, notably Van Duijn (2007) and Korotayev et al. (2010). The table below is an overview of the various Kondratieff waves that have been identified since the beginning of the Industrial Revolution.

Van Gelderen proposed a causal hypothesis, even before the long waves were discovered. He suggested that a long period of rising prices (prosperity) is driven by the rapid growth of one or more 'leading sectors'. He also discussed and tried to explain other important features of the process, including periodic over- and under-investment of capital, periodic scarcity

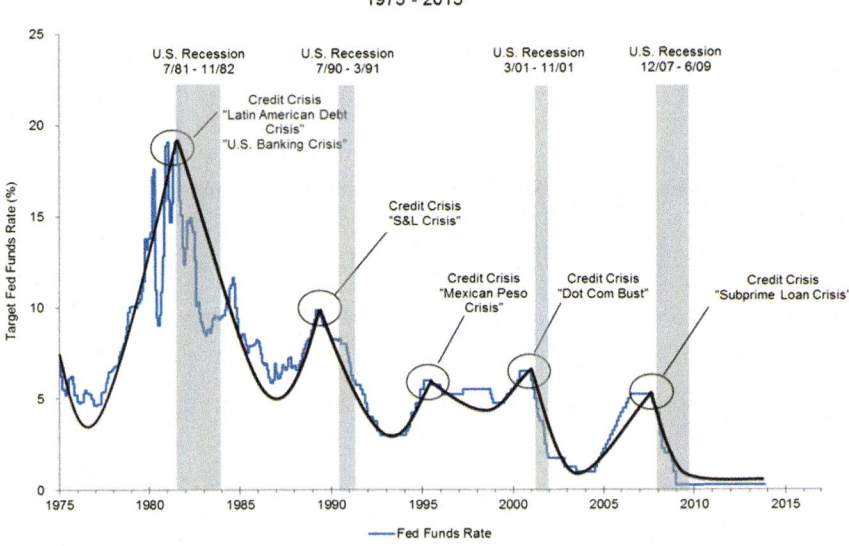

Fig. 16.5 The boom-bust cycles since 1975, from a Fed perspective. Real forecasts.com Federal Reserve. http://realforecasts.com/does-the-federal-reserve-really-create-the-boombust-cycle

and abundance of basic resources, credit expansion and contraction, and so on. Finance is obviously relevant.

Schumpeter's study of business cycles was, in many ways, an extension and update of Van Gelderen's ideas (Schumpeter 1939). He proposed that temporal clustering of a number of major technological innovations during periods of deflation and recession might account for the dramatic growth of the so-called "leading sectors" which seems to drive the inflationary half of the cycle. This idea was immediately and sharply challenged by Simon Kuznets, who doubted both the existence of Kondratieff cycles and the causal explanation suggested by Schumpeter (Kuznets 1940).

However, Kuznetz seems to have taken the idea rather more seriously in a later book (Kuznets 1953). The following graph (Fig. 16.5) depicts the Kondratieff cycle in historical context, extrapolated into the future. The red part of the curve, added by RUA, is obviously guesswork but has some basis in theory. The "third wave" (1876–1932) is far from obvious, though the fourth and fifth waves, ending in 2008, seem evident. A sixth wave starting in 2009 (in red) is pure conjecture (Table 16.1).

The subject of long waves has been revived since Schumpeter's work, especially by Rostow (1975, 1978), Mensch (1979), and Forrester (1985). For

Table 16.1 Historical overview of past Kondratieff waves

Kondratieff	1st wave	2nd wave	3rd wave	4th wave	5th wave
Depression	1764–1773[a]	1825–1836	1872–1883	1929–1937	1973–1980
Recovery	1773–1782[a]	1836–1845	1883–1892	1937–1948	1980–1992
Prosperity (War)	1782–1792 (1802–1815)	1845–1856	1892–1903 (1913–1920)	1948–1957	1992–2000
Recession	1815–1825	1866–1872	1920–1929	1966–1973	2009–2018[a]
Length	61 years	47 years	57 years	44 years	45 years
Excl. War	48 years	47 years	50 years	44 years	45 years

Source Van Dorsser (2015), originally based on Van Duijn (2007)
Note [a] Estimated on the basis of an average 9 year Juglar Cycle

more recent updates see Freeman (1996). Rostow's interest was primarily directed to the phenomenon of "take-off" leading to sustained long-term economic development. He viewed Van Gelderen's 'leading sectors' as not only the drivers of the long wave, but as the engine of long-term growth for the whole economy. Mensch attempted to explain the gaps between innovation clusters by invoking a theory of investment behavior. He postulated that during periods of general prosperity investors will shy away from risky long-term ventures (innovations) whereas during periods of stagnation or recession they may be more willing to invest in new ventures (Fig. 16.6).

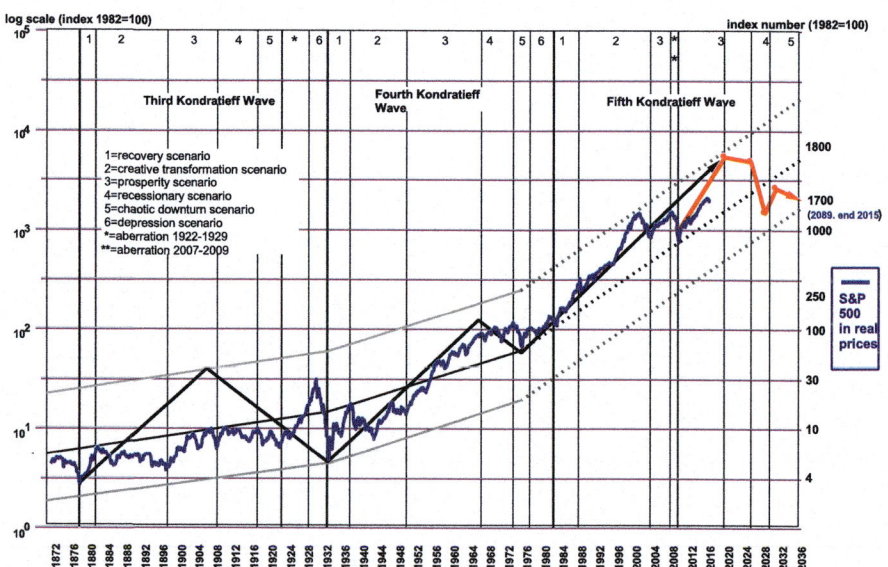

Fig. 16.6 Kondratieff chart expanded to 2035. http://beleggenopdegolven.blogspot.fr/2010/11/de-kondratieffgolf-volgens-ter-veer-en.html

At least one important variant of the Mensch thesis, associated primarily with David Freeman and his co-workers, has emerged from this debate (Dosi et al. 1988; Freeman 1996). It is that the rapid growth period of the long wave is not necessarily driven by innovations occurring in the immediately preceding "trough". There seem to be other cases where the rapid growth period was driven partly, or mainly, by the adaption/diffusion of important technologies that were tentatively introduced much earlier, but which needed a long gestation or were not yet "ripe" because of the lack of some enabling factor. For example, incandescent lamps using carbon or tungsten filaments depended on the availability of efficient vacuum pumps, applications of stainless steel and "super-alloys" required very high temperatures (from electric furnaces), and the basic oxygen steel process, as well as large rocket engines, needed pure oxygen from cryogenic air liquefaction.

This notion does not dispute the importance of the basic innovation (or the key facilitating inventions preceding it), but it does put major emphasis on the subsequent processes of development, improvement, application to new (and sometimes unexpected) purposes, and subsequent adoption. In all this there is a continuous and vital feedback between the innovator and the user, characterized by learning on both sides. The technology diffusion process, as this set of interactive phenomena is usually called, thus becomes quite central to any complete theory of long waves or of economic growth.

Important innovations don't come out of thin air. They take place when the underlying technical capabilities are present, financial support is available from government or entrepreneurs, and (usually) when there is a pressing social or economic problem to be solved. But when the conditions (including the last) are met, inventions sometimes occur simultaneously in different places. (The telephone, the carbon-filament light-bulb, the Hall-Heroult aluminum smelting process and the micro-processor "chip" are four examples of simultaneous invention in different places.

A quite different mechanism for cyclic boom-bust behavior has been suggested by **Hyman Minsky** (1919–1996). A "Minsky moment" is a sudden, major collapse of asset values which marks the end of the growth phase of a cycle in credit markets or business activity. The concept of a "Minsky cycle" is based on mass psychology. Minsky's most famous sentence was "*Stability—or tranquility—in a world with a cyclical past and capitalist financial institutions is destabilizing*" (Minsky 1978) p. 10.

Economic history, in Minsky's view, consists of a repetitive chain of "Minsky moments": Every period or productive activities or of stability encourages increased risk-taking, which leads to increasing the leveraged risk by investing borrowed money instead of cash. In an ideal world those investments would be for productive activities or "bricks and mortar". But in the real world many of those investments are speculative, based on expectations of a price increase for some asset. The debt-leveraged financing of speculative investments eventually exposes investors to a potential cash flow crisis, when the expected price rise doesn't happen. A crisis may begin with a short period of modestly declining asset prices, but that—in turn—triggers a wave of leveraged debt calls.

When risks are realized as losses market participants reverse course. They go into a risk-averse psychosis that triggers de-leveraging, restoring stability and setting up the next boom. The Minsky model presupposes irrational behavior both on the 'up-side' of each boom and on the down-side of each bust. It is exactly the same mechanism that operated in the great financial bubbles of the past, from the Mississippi Bubble, the South Sea Bubble, the railway bubble in England, the Florida real estate bubble leading up to the Stock Market Crash of 1929–30, the "Dot.Com Bubble" of 1999–01 and the sub-prime mortgage bond Housing Bubble of 2007–08.

Does Minsky's psychological explanation seem unrealistic to you? Curiously, it was dismissed outright by mainstream economists, notably ex-Chairman of the Federal Reserve, Bernanke (2000) p. 43. Bernanke considered himself an expert on the Great Depression. He wrote in his book "*Hyman Minsky and Charles Kindelberger have, in several places, argued for the inherent instability of the financial system, but in doing so have had to depart from the assumption of rational economic behavior.*" In other words, by allowing for the possibility of irrational behavior, Minsky (and Kindelberger) were not considered (by Bernanke) to be members of the Neoclassical Club. Things have hopefully changed since then.t

What I think we (with Steve Keen) can safely say is this: Minsky's model explains the mechanics of the bubble periodicity phenomenon, per se. What it does not explain is the why, when or the how of the transition from boom to bust. It is not predictive. We come back to this question later in this chapter (Fig. 16.7).

In this context, the investment-debt cycle has also been considered by **Richard Goodwin** (1913–1996). Goodwin's model exhibits a cyclic behavior of borrowing and repayment to banks for purposes of investment in capital stock and growth (but not speculation) (Goodwin 1967, 1987). At first, when debt is low, the growth is brisk. But as demand approaches capacity, costs increase (and wages rise) so profits decline. Meanwhile, there is an accompanying build-up of debt to the bank. This leads to an eventual collapse, as debt service consumes more and more of the economic surplus from the non-bank

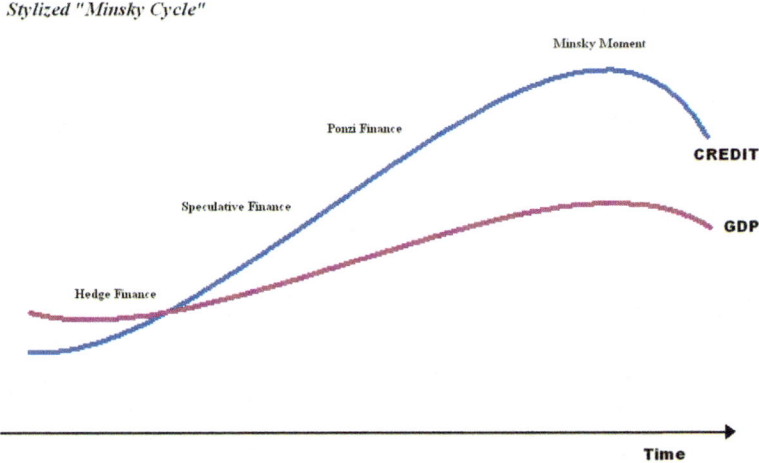

Fig. 16.7 The Minsky moment—Wikipedia

sectors. As in the case of Minsky's theory, the Goodwin theory cannot predict when the collapse will occur.

The collapse ends with a large debt write-off, like the Minsky model, and the cycle begins again. This usually accompanies a war, a major recession or the bursting of a large financial bubble (psychology through the back door). It is worthy of note that the Goodwin bubble mechanism works (theoretically) in a "normal" economy, meaning one driven only by the accumulation of capital stock per worker, without any irrationality or Schumpeterian "creative destruction". The Goodwin model does not explain real financial bubbles, but it has spawned more realistic models of technological substitution and diffusion, e.g. (Linstone 1976; Bianchi 1985; Ayres 1987; Vasko 1990).

A different perspective, as applied to the rise and fall of nations has been put forward by **Mancur Olson** (1932–1998) in two landmark books: "The Logic of Collective Action" (Olson 1965 [1971]) and "The Rise and Decline of Nations" (Olson 1982). Olson's thesis about nations is very similar to that of C.S. Hollings, as regards ecosystem cycles, except for changes in terminology. Starting after a disaster of some sort—e.g. a forest fire in the ecological case or a war or depression in the human case—the system recovers fast, at first, because most of the barriers that were present during the previous "climax" phase, have been eliminated. But as growth continues, more and more of those growth inhibitors also reappear.

In the case of the ecosystem, the growth inhibitors are the longer-lived but slower growing shrubs and deep-rooted trees that capture the most water and the most sunlight. In the case of a firm or a nation, the inhibitors are competitors, government regulations, and long-term investors, such as pension funds and insurance companies, favoring dividends and share "buybacks" rather than growth. In order to make rational decisions about policy, economists argue that there is a need to put a monetary cost (e.g. a Pigouvian tax) on exchanges causing environment damages.

It is not enough to say that a landscape or a coral reef is "priceless" in a world where funds for social purposes as well as environmental protection are limited. More specifically, it would be very helpful for governments to know the external costs of specific kinds of pollution, especially Greenhouse Gas (GHG) emissions. The obvious example is coal combustion, but petroleum, natural gas, animal husbandry and dairy products are also GHG emitters.

Mancur Olson's theory (summarized briefly above) amounts to a cyclic model of organizational and economic behavior, just as Holling's cyclic model explains patterns of ecological succession (Holling 1973). These models explain some otherwise puzzling phenomena. They also make the point that change in both of these domains is inherently a cyclic phenomenon. Change is never smooth, gradual or monotonic.

As time passes those organizations may combine to "lock in" a given development path and prevent or discourage departure from that path (innovation). The same happens in management. It is clear that no manager can deal personally with more than 6 or 7 immediate subordinates. For this reason a firm employing thousands of people is likely to have at least half a dozen hierarchical "levels" of management, and an army or a civil service may need ten or more. The more layers of management there are, the longer it takes to make (or approve) any decision.

Several philosophers have elaborated this pattern into theories of the rise and fall of civilizations. One of the first was **Nikolai Danilevski** (1822–1885), one of the promoters of "Pan Slavism". He was a creationist, who disagreed with Darwin and believed that language-cultural "types" are like species that cannot interbreed. Each civilization, in his view, has its own teleological "life cycle", starting with infancy, adolescence, maturity and decadence. In his view the Slavic culture was destined to overtake the "West". Was the current ruler of Russia (Putin) one of his students?

Oswald Spengler (1880–1936), German philosopher and author of *Der Untergang des Abendlandes* ("The Decline of the West"), got some of his ideas from Danilevski. Spengler, like Danilevski, regarded "civilizations" as species, with natural life-cycles. While Danilevski and Spengler are no longer taken seriously, they influenced later sociologists, including **Vilfredo Pareto** (1848–1923) and **Pitirim Sorokin** (1889–1968) (Pareto 1916) (Sorokin 1937 [1957)]. **Joseph Tainter** (b. 1949) has expressed a view with some cyclic aspects, focused on complexity, energy economics and diminishing marginal returns on investments (closer to the perspective of this book) (Tainter 1988).

16.4 Unemployment and Wages, Short Run Versus Long Run

Alban William Phillips (1914–1975) an economist at LSE, wrote a paper in 1958 titled *The Relation between Unemployment and the Rate of Change of Money Wage Rates in the United Kingdom, 1861–1957*. The paper describes an inverse relationship between money wage changes and unemployment in the British economy over the period. Similar patterns were found in other countries by Phillip's students.

In the years following Phillips' 1958 paper, many economists in the advanced industrial countries believed that his results showed that there was a permanently stable relationship between inflation and unemployment. One implication of this for government policy was that governments could control unemployment and inflation, using monetary policy and/or fiscal policy to stimulate the economy, raising GDP and lowering the unemployment rate. In short, the curve justified a Keynesian deficit policy.

In 1960 Paul Samuelson and Robert Solow took Phillips' work and postulated a single equation model to link inflation and unemployment: high inflation goes with low unemployment and vice versa. The Phillips curve predicted an inverse relationship between unemployment and inflation, implied that unemployment could be reduced by government stimulus with a calculable cost to inflation.

Critics today argue that this view is historically false, that neither economists nor governments took that view and that the 'Phillips curve myth' was an invention of the 1970s. Indeed, criticisms of Keynes's ideas had begun to gain acceptance by the early 1970s. It was possible to make a credible case that Keynesian models no longer reflected economic reality. Keynes himself included few formulas and no explicit mathematical models in his General Theory. For economists such as Hyman Minsky, Keynes's limited use of mathematics was partly the result of his skepticism about whether phenomena as inherently uncertain as economic activity could ever be adequately captured by mathematical models.

Since 1974, seven Nobel Prizes have been given to economists for work involving, or critical of some variation of the Phillips curve or its apparent implications. The authors receiving those prizes include Thomas Sargent, Christopher Sims, Edmund Phelps, Edward Prescott, Robert A. Mundell,

Robert E. Lucas, Milton Friedman, and F.A. Hayek. Some of this criticism is based on the United States' experience during the 1970s (during and after the Viet Nam war), which saw periods of high unemployment and high inflation at the same time (Fig. 16.8).

In the 1970s, many countries experienced high levels of both inflation and unemployment also known as stagflation. Theories based on the Phillips curve suggested that this could not happen, and the curve came under a concerted attack from a group of economists headed by Milton Friedman. In 1968, Milton Friedman published a paper arguing that the fixed relationship implied by the Philips curve did not exist. Friedman suggested that sustained Keynesian policies could lead to both unemployment and inflation rising at once—a phenomenon that soon became known as "stagflation". In the early 1970s stagflation appeared in both the US and Britain just as Friedman had predicted, with economic conditions deteriorating further after the 1973 oil crisis.

More recent research suggests that there is a moderate trade-off between low-levels of inflation and unemployment. George Akerlof, William Dickens, and George Perry, argued that if inflation is reduced from two to zero percent, unemployment will be permanently increased by 1.5%. This is because workers generally have a higher tolerance for real wage cuts than nominal ones. For example, a worker will more likely accept a wage increase of two percent when inflation is three percent, than a wage cut of one percent when the inflation rate is zero.

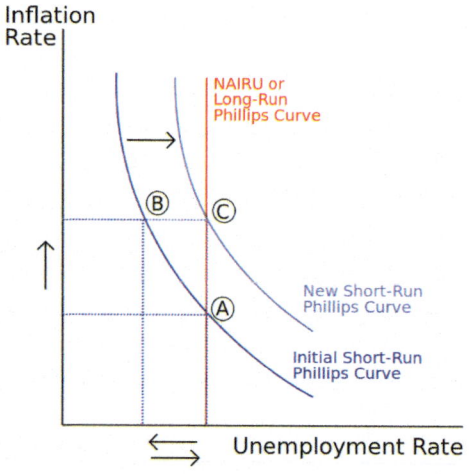

Fig. 16.8 Abstract Simple version of the Phillips curve. Wikipedia

Edmund Phelps and Milton Friedman argued that the "short-run Phillips curve" also called the "expectations-augmented Phillips curve" shifts up when inflationary expectations rise, In the long run, this implies that monetary policy cannot affect unemployment, which adjusts back to its "natural rate", also called the non-accelerating inflation rate of unemployment ("NAIRU") or "long-run Phillips curve". However, this long-run "neutrality" of monetary policy does allow for short run fluctuations and the ability of the monetary authority to temporarily decrease unemployment by increasing permanent inflation, and vice versa.

16.5 Money Creation and Monetary Policy

For most of human history money has been regarded as a "store of value" having intrinsic value in itself. The underlying value of the tokens coins or paper letters of credit or numbers on a ledger was supposed by some economists to be determined by its labor content, while others evoke the scarcity factor. "The Theory of Money and Credit" was a 1912 economics book written by **Ludwig von Mises** (1881–1973). In it Mises expounded his new theory of the origins of "commodity money" through his regression theorem, a statement backed by logical reasoning. Mises theory explains why money is demanded in its own right, not just as a simple "veil" as suggested by David Ricardo.

Mises insisted on the spontaneous and non-state origin of money as an evolutionary development from barter. He asserted (falsely), that demand for money as a commodity arose historically from a barter economy. He tried to re-integrated money in the marginalist theory by arguing that it is a product of labor and capital, like any other. He argued that all the several functions of money "are only particular aspects of its primary and unique function, that of a medium of exchange. He distinguished between money in the "strict sense" and in the "broad sense". He argued that an increase in the money supply does not only increase the price scale uniformly, but that it also introduces distortions. He argued that the classical law of supply and demand also applies to money, and confers on it a "price", which is its purchasing power. Therefore, he said, establishing an equation of money with value is impossible.

Von Mises still has a significant following. He is one of the foundational libertarians. But as regards the priority of barter, as the origin of money, he was factually wrong. Many anthropologists have searched, but none have found any evidence of the barter theory of money.

In older economics textbooks debt and credit are supposed to cancel out, since when credit is created (by banks or other lenders) it is accompanied by the creation of a corresponding debt by the borrower to the creditor. This borrowed money (debt) is automatically converted into bank deposits.(assets) prior to expenditure. Debt, in turn, is a liability to the borrower and an asset to the lender. However the correspondence of debt and credit is imperfect, because marketable assets can change quickly in value – up or down - and debts can be (and are) sometimes wiped out by defaults when borrowers cannot repay. (Consider the Greek, Argentine, Venezuelan and Zimbabwean national debts and many city and county debts, as well as the threatened default of the Chinese real estate giant EverGrande, with $305 billion in debt.)

With the existence of credit money, **Knut Wicksell** (1851–1926) argued, two interest rates prevail: the "natural" rate and the "money" rate. The natural rate is the rate of return on capital—or the real profit rate. It can be roughly considered to be equivalent to the marginal product of new capital investment. The money rate, in turn, is the central bank loan rate, a purely financial construction. Credit, meaning the ability to borrow, is perceived as the equivalent of "money in the bank". Banks provide credit by creating nominal deposits upon which borrowers can draw. Since deposits constitute part of real money balances, therefore the bank can, in essence, "create" money. This fact, while recently denied by Paul Krugman in a column (Krugman 2012), has recently been acknowledged openly by the Bank of England (Kumhof 2021; Jakab 2021). The essential point is that increasing credit is stimulative and decreasing it is.

For Wicksell, the endogenous creation of money, and how it leads to changes in the real market is fundamentally a breakdown of the classical dichotomy between the monetary sector and the real sectors. Money is not a "veil"; economic actors (agents) do react to monetary incentives. This is not due to some irrational "money illusion". However, for Wicksell, in the long run, the quantity theory still holds: money is still neutral in the long run.

The theory of money creation by banks is straightforward. The mechanism for money creation is "new" lending, by banks. This means lending money faster than the rate of debt repayment of prior loans. Loans create deposits in the banking system as a whole. (Say's law for money). Drawing down a bank loan (by a non-bank borrower) gets money moving and—because it must go somewhere—creates more cash or new deposits in other banks. On the other hand, repayment of a bank loan destroys credit and is deflationary.

Textbook economics still pretends that banks are mere "warehouses for money", i.e. that they lend only what others have deposited previously. But this is not the case, as Basil Moore and Alan Holmes pointed out years ago, based on empirical data (Keen 2001) p. 308. When a bank makes a loan, it also creates an asset for its balance sheet. There is no limit (except Basel rules on leverage) to stop it from doing this as often as it can find a likely-looking (barbered and shaved) customer willing to borrow now and repay later. That is what small local banks have always done with local customers. (Older readers may remember the 1946 movie "It's a wonderful life" with James Stewart.)

In most countries a solvent bank is not reserve-constrained or funding-constrained: it can always obtain reserves or funding either from the inter-bank market or from the central bank. Banks rationally pursue any profitable lending opportunities that they can identify up to the level consistent with their level of capital, treating reserve requirements and funding issues as matters to be addressed separately and later at an aggregate level.

The other common mechanism for money creation is by governments "printing" money. What that means is spending more than is received from tax revenues. i.e., allowing a current account deficit. This deficit has to be financed by increasing debt, by selling long-term treasury bonds to the public (or to other countries) or by allowing inflation to monetize the debt. In the first case active (liquid) money from the bond-buyer' account (his "wallet") is converted into passive money (bonds) and thus removed from circulation. This slows the economy and reduces inflationary pressures. Thus, surprisingly, deficits financed by bonds are actually means of inflation control. (This was not understood in the 1970s.) On the other hand, when the Fed buys bonds—of any kind—from the banks, the banks have more money to lend. This manoeuvre is called quantitative easing (QE). It is "stimulative" and may be inflationary in excess.

Commercial banks do need to have positive equity (financial reserves), in order to lend. In fact, the minimum ratio of equity to loan portfolio, for US banks is around 10% (slightly more for the largest banks). Deposits are not part of bank equity; they are the property, and part of the equity of the depositors. For the bank, a deposit is also a debt, and for a borrower, the debt is an asset of the lender (the bank). The central bank is an arm of the government, with certain mandates, one of which is to control inflation and others may (or may not) include reducing unemployment or preventing financial harm to foreign countries.

The Federal Reserve Bank in the US—and other central banks—have the legal authority to create money, not by actually "printing" banknotes (as members of the public seem to think), but by allowing banks to lend more (still subject to a minimum reserve requirement). The central bank itself may also lend money to the commercial banks, at an interest rate that it (i.e. its directors) decide. This "prime" interest rate determines the income of bondholders and the costs of debt service to borrowers. Finally, as mentioned already, the central bank can purchase debt instruments (bonds) from the banks, to relieve their equity constraints. This is called "quantitative easing" or QE.

Money supply consists of two components. The first component is "liquid" money that can be spent immediately. It consists of cash and checking deposits (M1), often linked directly to newly created credit. M2, is defined as M1 plus timed savings accounts, short-term time deposits, money market accounts, and mutual funds. All of these can be "cashed" within a few hours or days, if necessary. Zero Maturity Money (ZMM) is the equivalent of cash; it includes some, but not all, of M2. M3 (no longer publicized) consists of M2 plus long-term deposits like mortgages and bonds that can be sold but not exchanged for cash; they are not liquid. Figure 16.9 shows the growth of the key categories US money supply, since 1981, excluding M3. The illiquid component, labelled "Board of Governors Monetary Base (BOGUMBNS) is by far the largest.

Active liquid assets (ZMM)—and credit can be converted quickly into passive assets (i.e. invested in long-term assets or repayment of debt). In so doing, the active money-supply is reduced. However, the reverse is not true. Long-term deposits (e.g. mortgages, bonds) cannot be turned into cash automatically (i.e. sold overnight) partly because big transactions require buyers with a lot of liquidity to complete the transaction. Liquidity can be a problem

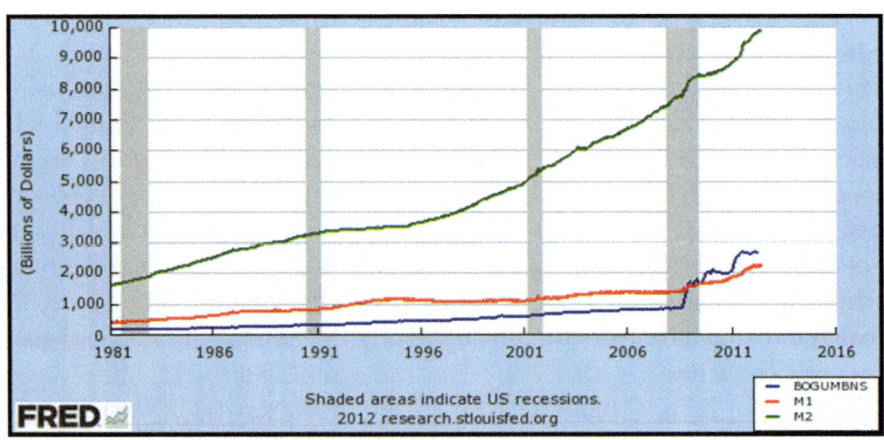

Fig. 16.9 Major categories of US Money supply—Wikipedia

for any enterprise with debts that need to be paid immediately, even though long term prospects may be excellent.

For example, in 1984 the Continental Illinois National Bank (CINB) was the seventh largest bank in the US. Penn Square Bank, a much smaller bank in Oklahoma, specialized in lending to oil and gas prospectors. In 1982 those prospectors were drilling too many "dry holes" and couldn't replay their loans. Penn Square Bank, in turn, owed a billion dollars to CINB, which it couldn't repay. Major institutional depositors in CNB got nervous and began to move their assets to other banks. Eventually the Federal Deposit Insurance Corp. (FDIC) had to step in. FDIC paid out $4.5 billion—many times more than the original loan to Penn Square—and CINB itself was swallowed up by Bank of America. All because of a few dry holes in Oklahoma.

Banks make a lot of their profits by foreclosing on the collateralized debts of borrowers e.g. homeowners or small businesses in trouble. But banks are also vulnerable. They depend on "borrowing short" (i.e. taking deposits) and "lending long" by exploiting the "fractional reserve" system. Banks need liquid funds sufficient to cover the normal needs of depositors. But it can happen that many depositors simultaneously decide to withdraw their funds. This can happen in response to unfavorable news, or just a rumor. This is why "runs on the bank" occur from time to time. Bubbles often end with such occurrences.

In fact the continuous decline in US inflation, since 1983, that has surprised and puzzled some economists is actually attributable, in part, to the increasing US budget and trade deficits. Those deficits increase US government debt. But, since the Federal Reserve Bank (FRB) controls interbank interest rates—the cost of debt service for the US government can be (has been) kept to a small fraction of the current budget. This "comfort zone" becomes smaller and tighter as market interest rates rise.

As the next graph (Fig. 16.10 shows, from 1998 to 2008 there was no obvious correlation between the annual inflation rate and the active money supply (M2). That changed dramatically in 2009, when the US money supply grew suddenly and dramatically, thanks to the $800 billion Troubled Assets Relief Program (TARP)—while the inflation rate fell drastically from 5% (peak) to −1% as the economy went into reverse. Evidently, as mentioned above, increasing government debt (up to a point) is stimulative. It is a "tailwind" for the economy, while debt repayment (deleveraging) is an economic "headwind".

In static Walrasian equilibrium money plays no role. In the real world it plays a very important role. Money supply needs to be defined. There are two

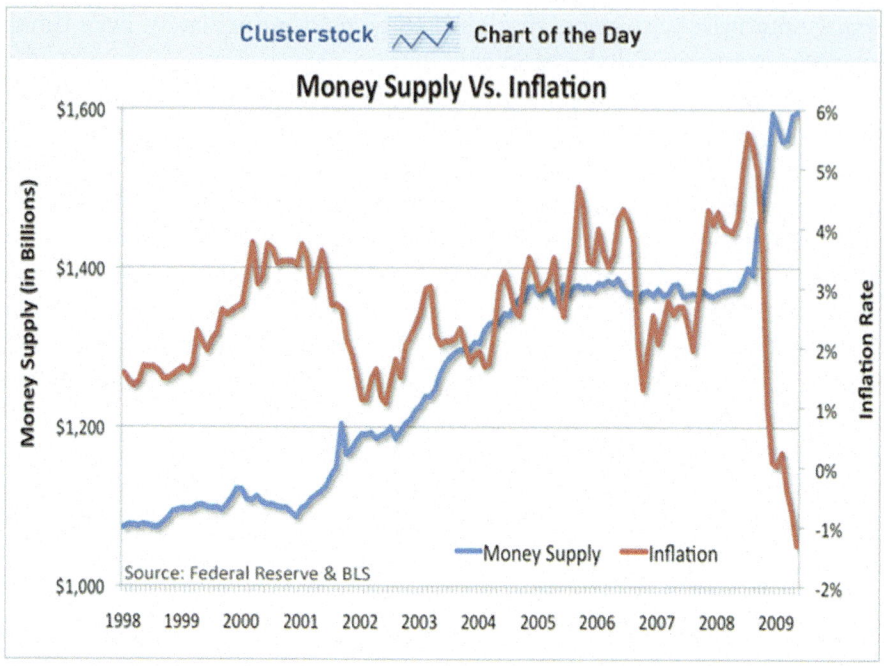

Fig. 16.10 Money supply versus Inflation in the US, 1998–2009—businessinsider.com (not found)???

components. The first category is "liquid" money that can be spent immediately. It consists of cash and checking deposits (M1), often linked directly to newly created credit. M2, is defined as M1 plus timed savings accounts, short-term time deposits, money market accounts, and mutual funds. All of these can be "cashed" within a few hours or days, if necessary. Zero Maturity Money (MZM) is the equivalent of cash, including some, but not all, of M2. M3 (no longer publicized) consists of M2 plus long-term deposits. Figure 16.13 shows the growth of the key categories US money supply, since 1981, excluding M3.

The key systematic issue is this: Active liquid assets (MZM)—and credit—can be converted into passive assets (i.e. invested or repayment of debt) in a very short time. In so doing, the active money-supply is reduced. However, the reverse is not true. Long-term deposits (e.g. mortgages, bonds) cannot be sold overnight, partly because big transactions require extensive "due diligence", which takes time, and unless there is a buyer, or a broker-bank, with enough cash reserves—liquidity—to complete the transaction.

Liquidity can be a problem for any firm—including banks—with debts that need to be paid immediately, even though long term prospects may be excellent. Banks make a lot of their profits by foreclosing on the collateralized debts of borrowers e.g. homeowners or small businesses in trouble. But banks are also vulnerable. They depend on "borrowing short (i.e. taking deposits) and lending long" by exploiting the "fractional reserve" system. Banks need liquid funds sufficient to cover normal the needs of depositors. But it can happen—and has happened—that many depositors simultaneously decide to withdraw funds. This can happen in response to unfavorable news, or just a rumor. This is why "runs on the bank" occur from time to time.

The other mechanism for money creation is by governments "printing" money, which actually means spending more than is received from tax revenues i.e., allowing a current account deficit. This deficit has to be financed by selling Treasury bonds to the public (or to other countries). In this case active (liquid) money from the bond-buyer' pockets is converted into passive money (bonds) and thus removed from circulation. This is deflationary: it slows the economy and reduces inflationary pressures. Thus, surprisingly, deficits are actually means of inflation control.

In older economics textbooks debt and credit cancel out, since when credit is created (by banks or other lenders) it is accompanied by the creation of a corresponding debt. This borrowed money (debt) is automatically converted into bank deposits (assets of the bank) prior to expenditure. Debt, in turn, is a liability to the borrower. However the correspondence is imperfect, because marketable assets can change quickly in value—up or down—and debts can be (and are) sometimes wiped out by defaults when borrowers cannot repay. (Consider the Greek, Argentine, Venezuelan and Zimbazian debts.)

When profits, or credit, are put to work by investment in "bricks and mortar", or in R&D for new products, the economy grows and jobs are created. That is desirable. When the credit is used for stock market speculation or as fuel for "activist investors" the economy does not grow. In fact, the activist investors of today are polite versions of the "corporate raiders" like H. Boone Pickens and KKR back in Michael Milken's heyday. They are speculators who seek to gain control over successful companies by "financial engineering", usually with borrowed money from the sale of high-yield "junk bonds". Once in control of a target firm, they convert long-term corporate assets into short term "savings" making balance sheet look better. They call themselves "turnaround specialists" and they are greatly admired on Wall Street.

None of the theoretical growth models of standard mainstream economics deals explicitly with the role of debt. Contrary to most mainstream economists, including Reinhart and Rogoff (Reinhart and Rogoff 2009, 2010), we agree with Keen that increasing government debt is inherently stimulative, while "deleveraging" (paying off debt) is intrinsically deflationary.

Paying off government debt is not stimulative because it does not put money back into the economy. It merely changes the Fed's balance sheet. However, paying off private debt is stimulative because the money can be "recycled" through the banking system.

A model capable of explaining economic growth (and de-growth) must reflect the various roles of money, both credit as an enabler ("tailwind") of growth and debt as a growth "headwind". Debt is a headwind partly for the obvious reason that interest payments constitute a cost of business and a drain on profits, resulting in less money for re-investment. On the other hand, debt is an asset of the lender. Indeed, that sort of asset can also be used as collateral for other loans. (This called "leverage").

The less obvious consequence of private debt, at the macro-level, is that the risk of failure (bankruptcy) increases with the magnitude of debt in relation to assets. Moreover business failures result in unexpected d costs to suppliers and customers. These "third party" effects (externalities) increase the need for— and the cost of—insurance and can trigger other failures. Consolidation by merger or acquisition is not only driven by economies of scale; it is partly driven by the assumption that large size offers protection against risk, and against being swallowed by an even larger shark or tiger.

To the lenders (banks or bond-holders), government debt within a country is theoretically a risk-free asset. That is why people buy government bonds under the delusion that governments will never go bankrupt. Within a country bonds issued by the government are as secure as the rule of law and the economic strength of the country and the government itself. The market rate of interest on government bonds is a measure of combined economic strength and political stability. Germany, Switzerland, Sweden, Norway, Japan and China are now "safe havens" that can sell bonds with low interest rates because they all have a favorable balance of trade and a recent history of political stability. The US is also a "safe haven" despite its negative trade balance and large budget deficits, because the US economy is very big and the US dollar is the world's reserve currency.

Government (sovereign) debt has been widely regarded as a safe asset, backed by the "faith and credit" of the nation as a whole. Debt service on government debt is normally covered by tax revenues paid partly by businesses and partly by households. Because of its presumed safety, sovereign debt instruments (bonds) can be used as collateral for other loans. Non-sovereign debt, in the form of bank loans to business, corporate bonds, commercial paper, mortgages etc. are also capital assets of banks, insurance companies and pension funds. These assets are also usable as collateral for loans, albeit at higher interest rates thanks to higher perceived risk. This makes it possible for borrowed money to be used as collateral for further borrowing, creating ever-growing leverage "pyramids" supported by relatively small fixed real assets. Those leverage pyramids—often involving real estate or oil prices have a tendency to magnify the economic damage caused by a failure at the bottom layer of the pyramid.

As an example of what could happen, the recent change in the government of Saudi Arabia, together with the proposed IPO of its nationalized oil company, Saudi Aramco, certainly reflects the cumulative effects of financial pressures on all the Middle Eastern governments. These pressures resulted from the sharp decline in global oil prices from above $100/bbl in the summer of 2014 to a low around $37/bbl in the following winter. By late 2018, oil prices recovered to about $60/bbl—partly due to voluntary production cuts, as well as an uptick in global economic recovery. Saudi Arabia hopes to beef up its declining financial reserves by selling a piece (perhaps 5%) of Saudi Aramco, which means selling part-ownership of its oil reserves for cash. Then came covid19 and the Russian invasion of Ukraine and all bets were off, for the moment.

The war in Ukraine is driving oil and natural gas prices up, because Western Europe—especially Germany is currently very dependent on oil and gas from Russia. The European Union wants to cut imports of those commodities to "punish" Russia for invading Ukraine. The price of oil and natural gas (especially LNG) rose sharply, on account of the sanctions, and currently (2022) remains high. This has caused a spike in inflation, which affects every consumer in Europe, but also in the rest of the OECD countries. Elections in Europe and the US are likely to be affected by inflation fears.

For example, mortgage rates for new houses are currently (2022) rising sharply, to levels not seen since the 1950s. That will adversely affect house construction, which will affect the demand for building materials and employment in those sectors. The demand for new cars, electric or not, will be adversely affected by fuel prices and by car loan rates, as well. High fuel prices will affect demand for air transport, and the tourism sector. All of this That will be reflected by an economic slowdown—a recession. This sequence of consequences is only one possibility.

The COVID pandemic had its own set of adverse consequences, as all of us are all aware. China has embarked on a series of major city shut-downs affecting industrial output and global supply chains. In the US and Europe, various public health measures have been adopted to keep hospitals from being overloaded, including restrictions on travel, on activities resulting in crowds, on restaurants, entertainment and sports. Schools in some countries were shut down. The net result was that many vulnerable people lost their jobs or had to work from home. To compensate for these losses, most countries have spent money far in excess of government revenues. Government deficits have resulted in large increases in government debt. How far can this strategy be continued?

More questions: Will the Russian invasion of Ukraine cause Europe to unify and adopt common policies? Or will it split the EU? Will some countries be forced into bankruptcy? Which ones?

Another sharp drop in petroleum prices would reduce the market value of oil reserves, everywhere, starting with Aramco. But Exxon, Chevron, BP, Shell and Total would also lose market value, while some of the US shale producers that have been hanging on, would finally fail. This set of events could—conceivably—be the trigger that converts market euphoria to pessimism and sets off the next financial crash, as margin-debts are suddenly called.

To prevent this, most countries now insure small bank deposits up to a certain level. However larger deposits, loan renewals and small businesses (such as farms), are at risk if the bank's capital is cut by external events. This happened in 2008, when the capital assets of many banks—and much of the collateral for corporate loans—included bundles of mortgage-based bonds (known as "collateralized debt obligations" or CDOs). Since the individual mortgages included within these CDOs were "invisible" to the buyers, nobody (not even the credit agencies) knew which ones were safe and which ones were in danger of default. When national default rates unexpectedly rose above the level that was assumed when those mortgage-based bonds were securitized, the CDOs all became non-marketable and illiquid overnight. This had nothing to do with the value of the mortgages themselves. It happened because it became clear to potential investors that the underlying assumption, upon which their "investment grade" AAA or AA ratings were based, was false.

In the fall of 2008, almost overnight (from one week to the next) banks—and their depositors—found that the banks' capital reserves (which are supposed to be liquid) were not liquid, and thus were much less capable of supporting lending than had been previously assumed. This initiated a ripple effect that nearly destroyed the global financial system. Banks stopped lending to each other, and to other clients. Insurance companies, notably American International Group (AIG), had insured a lot of the CDOs by selling derivatives (called "credit default swaps" or CDSs). Suddenly the CDS derivatives lost value and AIG suddenly owed vast sums of money they didn't have in reserve. House prices started dropping rapidly as demand for mortgage loans dried up. Construction stopped and construction workers were laid off. Bank shares plummeted in value, and one major bank (Lehman Brothers) collapsed. The consequence was a major recession that would have been much worse without the government bailouts the Troubled Asset Relief Program (TARP) that came to the rescue.

Figure 16.11 shows the close correlation between margin debt (money borrowed to purchase shares) and share values. Since 2009 the margin debt has increased faster than share values. This is bad news. The other message of that diagram is that most private borrowing is for speculation, not for investment in factories, new products or infrastructure.

Government debt (at all levels) is not collateralized by hard assets for most countries, except in a few cases of oil or mineral exporters. It is based on "faith and credit", which basically means reputation and trust. A hundred years ago, government debt was widely regarded as perfectly safe because lenders thought it was "inconceivable" that a government would not repay. After the Russian revolution, and the Bolshevik government's repudiation of Czarist debt in 1917 and the Nazi repudiation of the much reduced WW I German reparation debt agreed in Lausanne (1932), the inconceivable has become conceivable.

Repayment of government debt to lenders (bond-holders) in other countries is enforced mainly by the International Monetary Fund (IMF) or (in the

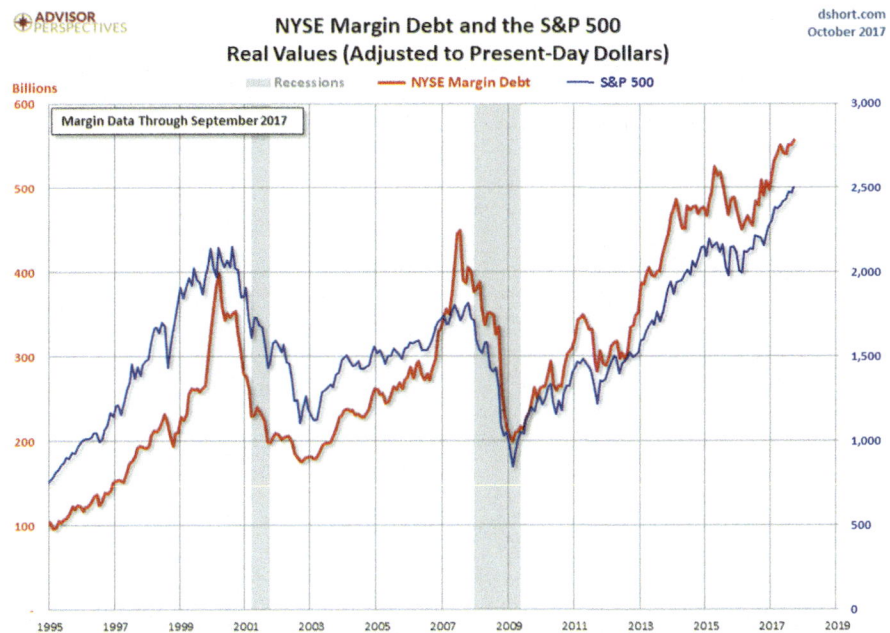

Fig. 16.11 Money supply M2 versus the stock market—investing.com (not found)???

case of Europe) by the terms of its membership in the European Union. In practice, a small weak political entity—a country, territory, state, or city—with excessive debt, can find itself effectively ruled by foreigners (in the case of a country, like Greece), or by bankruptcy courts, until the debt is either paid (e.g. by the sale of assets), re-structured (e.g. by extending the maturity date) or written off. In all cases the lenders defense against outright default is the threat that defaulters will be unable to obtain credit in the future. Nevertheless, lenders to countries, states, cities and public institutions can, and occasionally do, lose money when economic (or political) conditions change. Lenders to Argentina lost money recently. Lenders to Greece and Puerto Rico, and many US cities, will lose money.

Figure 16.12 shows US debt during most of our history. During most of our hi1919 and story private debt has increased, compared to government debt. The exceptions were 1860–65 (the Civil War), and the two world wars (1915–1919), and (1942-1946). Since WW II private debt has risen steadily except for two brief declines (1990–95) and (2008–2012). But government debt also rose sharply during each of the last two periods of private debt deleveraging. This behavior deserves further examination.

The global capitalist economy almost self-destructed in 2008 due to a housing bubble. Keynesian policy was resurrected at the very last moment (called "bailouts") but was applied only to the banks, AIG, GM and others "too big to fail". Russia, powered by oil and gas exports to Europe, annexed a

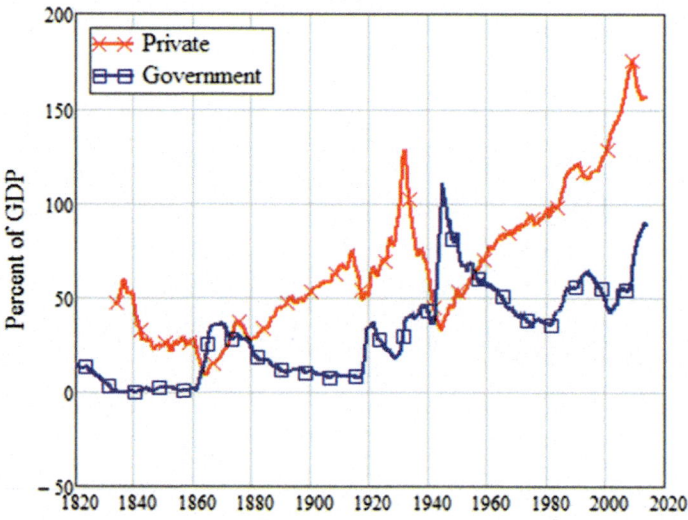

Fig. 16.12 Public versus private debt in the US since 1820—debtydeflation.com (not found)???

Fig. 16.13 Judy Garland as Dorothy Gale, with her dog Toto—Wikipedia

chunk of the Ukraine, in 2014 with scarcely a peep by the US or NATO. Putin's attempted takeover of the rest of Ukraine, starting in 2022, has displaced over 5 millions of people, killed tens of thousands of Ukrainians, as well as (as of 2022up to 20,000 Russian conscripts, destroyed much of the infrastructure of Ukraine, and yet stalled militarily. The outcome is uncertain as this is being written.

To finish this section (with a thud), the economy is a continuing sequence of investments—mostly speculative based on credit, that create new jobs and increased demand. But the credit has costs. Increasing private debt beyond a certain point is dangerous because the costs of debt service ("headwinds") can rise faster than the GDP. One reason is that much of the borrowed money is used for mergers and acquisitions, which moves asset ownership around among investors, but produces nothing new. The big fish keep getting bigger, at the expense of the minnows.

Some fraction of the newly created credit (40%?) is productive. But sooner or later, the cost of debt service in some part of the economy becomes greater than the resulting profits. At that point there will be a bankruptcy failure of some large over-indebted enterprise that grew too fast and made a bad bet. But that failure can cause other failures resulting in an avalanche of linked failures. Such avalanches have occurred a number of times in the past (Ayres 2020).

16.6 What Causes Recessions and Busts?

In the discussion of business cycle theories (this Chap. 18.3) we pointed out that there is still no accepted theoretical explanation for the "boom-bust" cycle in economic history. Basically, neoclassical theory—the Solow model explains growth but not the end of growth (decline). We also introduced the "Minsky moment" (Fig. 16.7) and the accompanying commentary by Steve Keen.

Please excuse a brief digression. In November 2008, just after the bankruptcy of Lehman Brothers on September 15 of that year, Queen Elizabeth of England was inaugurating a new £71 million campus addition for the prestigious London School of Economics (LSE). The Queen, who normally doesn't express opinions on economic or political matters, addressed one question to the hosts in the greeting party. She asked, as many others have: *"Why did nobody notice?"* referring to why the credit crunch of two months earlier had not been predicted—or anticipated—by any of the high-powered economists in that building.

Here we note a number of economists (and others) did notice. The movie "The Big Short", based on a book by Michael Lewis, was about some of them (Lewis 2010). In fact, during the year 2006–07 there were at least 12 forecasts of the sub-prime housing bubble of 2008, in the economics literature. They were identified later by Dirk Bezemer, an economist at the University of Groningen, in the Netherlands. But none of the forecasts were based on the standard neo-classical economic growth model relied upon by most people in the Queen's audience. Two of the forecasts were based on other mathematical models using stock-flow consistent modelling and empirical data (Keen 1995; Godley 2007). Robert Shiller, of Yale, also did forecast the coming collapse in his book "Irrational Exuberance" (Shiller 2006).

The Queen's question was specifically directed at the chairman of the welcoming committee, Professor Luis Garicano. Prof. Garicano responded with a blackboard lecture. In that lecture he said (according to the journalists who were listening): *"At every stage, someone was relying on somebody else; and everyone thought they were doing the right thing."* In short, nobody at LSE was guilty of any error or omission. What he neglected to say was that the economic growth models used and taught by LSE—and all its major teaching competitors is still based on a core equilibrium assumption (from Jevons, Menger, Walras and Marshall), that assumes growth is a rational process that occurs in or near a state of disequilibrium. That underlying assumption is demonstrably wrong.

The explanation of "busts" that best fits the facts is called the "Minsky cycle", mentioned earlier. That explanation was ignored, or rejected, by mainstream macro-economists because it introduced irrational behavior—mass psychology—that neoclassical mainstreamers considered inessential to the neoclassical theory. In this context, we note that the importance of psychology was emphasized long ago by Charles Mackay in his book "Extraordinary Popular Delusions and the Madness of Crowds" (Mackay 1841 [1996]). For a modern example, consider "Panic: The story of modern financial insanity" (Lewis 2008).The whole point was that the "bubbles" of economic history were frequently, if not usually, based on irrational behavior by crowds. Macroeconomics is not derivable from microeconomic foundations because humans are social animals: like birds—humans tend to form flocks and follow the leader. There is nothing in microeconomic textbook theory to explain this phenomenon.

But, since Daniel Kahneman received the Nobel Prize for Economics, in 2002, for his earlier work with Amos Tversky on "prospect theory", psychology is now a respectable part of theoretical economics, so the neglect of Minsky has since fallen by the wayside. At this point in time, the "Minsky moment" is the best theory we have to explain recessions, although it has not yet been statistically tested against evidence of panic buying or selling of shares, for instance. Moreover, the Minsky theory cannot be used for prediction: It does not explain the timing of the crash, the point where the boom ends and the bust begins. We point out, later, that the trigger events come in all sizes and shapes. The unifying factor is that they are mostly caused by rational actors making bad financial bets, based on inadequate knowledge, in the absence of regulation.

Another bit of economic mythology has also fallen by the wayside, but only very recently. In fact, most economic textbooks have not yet realized this change. The standard idea about banks is that they are "warehouses" for the storage of savings deposited by a person or institution. The truth is otherwise: banks actually create money by creating credit (making loans), and they can do that freely subject only to the overall capital reserve requirement. The reserve requirement is the capital/loan ratio which, in turn, is fixed periodically by the Basel Committee on Banking Supervision. The Basel Committee consists of 46 central banks, of which the US Federal Reserve, the bank of England, the European Central Bank (ECB), the central banks of Japan and China and a few others are the dominant ones. The Basel Committee is the primary global standard-setter for the prudential regulation of banks and the only international forum for cooperation on banking supervisory matters.

This truth—that banks are money factories, not warehouses has finally been acknowledged openly by the Bank of England (Jakab 2021). Actually Basil Moore and Alan Holmes pointed this out, years ago, based on empirical data (Keen 2001) p 308. When a bank makes a loan, it also creates an asset for its balance sheet. There is no limit to credit creation (except "Basel rules" on leverage) to stop it from doing this as often as it can find a customer willing to borrow now and repay later. The main mechanism for money creation is "new" lending, by banks. This means lending money faster than the rate of debt repayment of prior loans.

As noted, banks do need to have positive equity (financial reserves), in order to lend. In fact, the minimum ratio of equity to loan portfolio, for US banks is around 10% (slightly more for the largest banks). Deposits are not part of bank equity; they are the property, and part of the equity of the depositors. For the bank, a deposit is also a debt, and for a borrower, the debt is an asset of the lender (the bank). The central bank is an arm of the government, with certain mandates, depending on the country. One of them is to control inflation and others may (or may not) include reducing unemployment and/or causing financial harm to foreign countries.

The US Federal Reserve Bank—and other central banks—have the legal authority to create money, not by actually "printing" it (as members of the public seem to think), but by allowing banks to lend more by reducing the reserve requirement). The central bank may also lend money to the commercial banks, at an interest rate that its directors decide. This "prime" interest rate determines the income of bond-holders and the costs of debt service to borrowers (e.g. mortgage rates). Finally, the central bank can purchase debt instruments (bonds) from the banks, to relieve their equity constraints. This is called "quantitative easing" or QE. Such a purchase is a purely digital operation on the Fed's "balance sheet". No currency is involved.

A third bit of mythology that has bit the metaphorical dust is the idea, energetically espoused by Robert Lucas, at Chicago, that macroeconomic models need to be based on microeconomic foundations (Lucas 1976). By "foundations", Lucas meant the basic assumptions mentioned previously as the "Solow Trinity"—i.e. that all decisions about transactions are made by utility-maximizing consumers or profit-maximizing firms. The idea that macroeconomics should be derived from microeconomics meant that supply and demand curves in the market must be based on individual consumer or firm behavior, leading to the assumption of a "representative consumer".

Almost 60 years ago—before Robert Lucas—it was proved mathematically that representative consumers can't exist (Gorman 1953). Lucas didn't read Gorman's paper, or didn't believe it. But the fact remains that Gorman was correct and Lucas was wrong. Steve Keen explains it thus "*The individual demand curve is derived by assuming that relative prices can change without affecting the consumer's income. This assumption can't be made when you consider all of society—which you must do when aggregating individual demand to derive a market demand curve—because changing relative prices will change relative incomes as well*" (Keen 2017) p. 27. Because income affects preferences, changes in income affect demand, and the demand curve can have any shape at all. For an example, see (Keen 2011) pp. 51–53. Ironically, Lucas was awarded a Nobel Prize for his work on "rational expectations", which was based on his mistaken ideas about deriving macroeconomics from micro-foundations.

Lucas' mistake, at a deeper level, was that he didn't understand physics. The idea that macroeconomic behavior (of markets) can be based on microeconomic behavior of individual consumers is quite a bit like saying that the behavior of water must be based on the behavior of water molecules. After all, the individual molecules are identical with each other (unlike real consumers) except for their velocities and directions. Is that enough to predict the boiling point, the freezing point and the shapes of snowflakes? Obviously not. One would also have to know the properties of the individual water molecules themselves and how they interact with each other at close range (so-called van der Waals forces), and a lot more.

The point is that groups of people are not collections of identical carbon copies. The only way to learn about the behavior of societies, and firms, is by observation of many different groups and markets to identify common factors (variables) by which they can be differentiated. Luckily, there are some variables that can be used—as distributions—for model-purposes. Age, gender, family size, education level, income, and health are among them. The practical consequence of Robert Lucas' erroneous attempt to derive macroeconomic models from those supposed microeconomic foundations were that the dynamic stochastic general equilibrium (DSGE) models in use by treasuries and central banks around the world were useless. They gave wrong and unbelievable results e.g. (Romer 2016; Kocherlakota 2016). In fact, the DSGE models at the OECD predicted that the year 2008 was going to be a "banner year".

There is an important kind of balance (or imbalance) in the economic system, namely the balance between credit and debt. In principle, credit and debt are balanced, because every increase in credit provided by lenders (banks) is accompanied by an increase of debt. Interest payments on debt are incomes for creditors. However, this theoretical balance is only enforceable when debt is fully secured by other assets, such as land, and not always then). Unsecured debt is inherently risky, although a great deal of such debt (in the form of credit cards and student loans) has been issued on the basis of statistical evidence that borrowers will usually repay, if they can, to protect their credit ratings.

But there is a variety of rational loss mechanisms that can make debt unpayable and—if the corresponding asset is being used as collateral for other loans, whole financial structures based on leverage can also collapse. This can happen at the individual, corporate, municipal or national level, as we see currently in the case of Greece (Varoufakis 2016, 2017). Similarly, financial derivatives are inherently risky, depending on the reality of the underlying asset. Financial assets based on rumors, fantasies or lies can also disappear in a moment, as has happened in numerous "bubbles" since the Dutch tulip bubble.

One common feature of the "loss trigger" mechanism is the repeated use of borrowed money—often as "junk bonds" issued by Drexel—to take control of a larger entity. The next step is financial engineering that makes the "balance sheet" look better and drives the share price of the target firm higher, followed by the use of its shares as collateral to borrow still more money (more "junk bonds"), to take control of a still larger enterprise and force it to do something the raider wants. This scheme, later called "drilling for oil on Wall Street", enabled a Texas oil-man named Boone Pickens, starting in 1982 with tiny Mesa Petroleum, to take over much larger Hugoton Production co. Skipping the details, Pickens made subsequent raids on Phillips Petroleum, Unocal and Cities Service. In 1985 Pickens attacked Gulf Oil Co., one of the original "six sisters". He forced Gulf to sell itself to Chevron for $13.2 billion, of which Pickens personally walked away with $400 million. This scoop did not cause a financial crash, but similar games have done so in the past.

One example will suffice to make the point. In 1907 United Cooper Co. was fighting in a lawsuit against Anaconda Copper for ownership of s small lot on the top of the hill where Anaconda was mining. The basis of the lawsuit was a theory that the underground recourse was legally owned by whoever owned the land at the "apex". United had won twice in lower courts and forced anaconda to stop operations, resulting in a lot of unemployment. The owners of United Copper used their shares (worth $39) as collateral to borrow money from the Heinze Bank of Butte, Montana to buy more shares, hoping to drive up the price to squeeze out the "shorts" (investors who had borrowed United Copper shares and sold them, hoping the price would go down. The "short squeeze didn't work. The price of United shares rose to $60, but then fell suddenly to $10. The Heinze brothers and their bank were ruined.

But that wasn't the end of it, because the Heinze's broker was also ruined. Other firms using United Copper shares as collateral for loans were ruined. The third largest bank in New York, Knickerbocker Bank and Trust Co. failed when borrowers couldn't repay. All the banks then demanded instant repayment of loans based on shares as collateral. The resulting panic of 1907 ruined many corporate borrower who had nothing to do with copper. One of them was George Westinghouse, who had used his personal shares to borrow money for corporate operating purposes. (General Electric had sold shares to reduce debt, the previous year, and so avoided the panic). The Westinghouse Electric Corporation was bankrupted. It recovered under new management, but there is no Westinghouse fortune. The financial games that fail don't always cause crashes but virtually financial crash in history was triggered by some variant of this story, a financial game played for big rewards using borrowed money, that went wrong.

Economic theory must, therefore, take account of money and the behavior of real financial institutions and the related phenomenon of "leverage", meaning the use of derivative assets purchased with borrowed money as collateral for further loans. Financiers have been very clever in devising ways to do this without any visible indication of the extent of the leverage and the corresponding risk. (For a lot more detail on the mechanisms and the financial history see RUA's two earlier books "The Bubble Economy" (Ayres 2014) and "On Capitalism and Inequality" (Ayres 2020).

16.7 The Other Side of Capitalism

There are two sides to every coin and every dispute. In this context, the main feature (and arguably, the crucial virtue) of theoretical capitalism, as understood by academic economists, is that it engages selfish (amoral) motives in competitive activities that may yield indirect benefits to society as a whole (Adam Smith's "invisible hand"). For Adam Smith, who was a Deist—the invisible hand was literally divine intervention. Today that view is obsolete. But the supposed societal benefits of the "invisible hand"—mainly trade—have always been secondary, at best. Gordon Gekko, the central character in writer Thomas Wolfe's novel "The Bonfire of the vanities"—made into the movie "Wall Street"—put it simply and memorably: "*Greed works; Greed is Good*".

Most economic theorists since Adam Smith have insisted that self-interest (greed) is the dominant driver in every part of society, allowing no role for cooperation, still less altruism. In effect, some libertarians, like **Ayn Rand**

(1905–1982) denied that "society" has any existence, as an entity in itself (other thanas as a framework for markets). They doubt that true altruism actually exists in the "real" world. (They argue that actions that appear to be altruistic are just another form of selfishness. In their view, Buddha, Jesus Christ, St. Francis of Assisi and Mother Theresa were either masochists, or they were accumulating "brownie points" for their expected post-mortem sojourns in paradise.)

Frederick Soddy (1877–1956) was an English chemist and physicist who worked in Montreal with Ernest Rutherford, studying the radioactive properties of uranium, thorium and radium. The result of their collaboration is the theory of atomic decay: they suggest that each radioactive atom breaks up forming another element and emitting an intra-atomic particle. Soddy called this phenomenon transmutation. Soddy and Rutherford proposed the existence of two radioactive series, one starting with uranium and the second starting from thorium, both ending with lead. They were among the first to calculate the energy released by radioactive transmutation.

By 1913, fifteen years after the discovery of radioactivity, chemists had discovered more than forty new "elements" in thorium and uranium ores. This was many more than Mendeleev's table could accommodate. To interpret these observed "facts", Soddy proposed the theory of isotopes: isotopes occupy the same box in the periodic table, have the same chemical properties, but differ in their atomic weights and their radioactive lifetimes. Soddy shared the 1921 Nobel Prize in Chemistry.

Frederick Soddy wrote four books on economics, all ignored or dismissed by the mainstream Professoriat, who dismissed him as a crank. They were "Science and Life" (Soddy 1920); "Cartesian Economics" (Soddy 1922), "Wealth, Virtual Wealth and Debt" (Soddy 1933) and "The Role of Money" (1935). Soddy campaigned for a radical restructuring of global monetary relationships, offering a physics perspective on economics rooted in the laws of thermodynamics. Many of his later proposals—"*to abandon the gold standard, let international exchange rates float, use federal surpluses and deficits as macroeconomic policy tools that could counter cyclical trends, and establish bureaus of economic statistics (including a consumer price index) in order to facilitate this effort*"—were far ahead of his time, though now conventional practice. Only his critique of fractional-reserve banking still "*remains outside the bounds of conventional wisdom*" according to a reviewer, although a recent paper by the IMF may have shifted those boundaries.

Soddy wrote, long before Michael Hudson (this Chapter), that financial debts grows exponentially at compound interest but that the real economy is based on exhaustible stocks of fossil fuels. Exergy obtained from the fossil fuels cannot be used again, as the second law of thermodynamics states. This criticism of neoclassical economic growth is echoed by his intellectual heirs in the now emergent field of ecological economics. Soddy's work has been reconsidered post mortem by Herman Daly (1980). **Michael Hudson** (b. 1939) is an American economist, Wall Street analyst, political consultant, commentator, journalist and gadfly. He identifies himself as a classical economist and as a Marxist despite his disagreement with most Marxists. His interpretation of Marx is unique. He has devoted his career to the study of debt, both domestic debt (loans, mortgages, interest payments), and external debt. He consistently argues that loans and exponentially growing debts skim profits from the real economy (as interest payments and fees to "usurers and rentiers") leaving borrowers short of income to buy goods and services. Hudson's bugaboos are American economic imperialism and debt deflation.

In 1968, Hudson joined the accounting firm Arthur Andersen. There he conducted a detailed analysis of fund flows for all areas of US production from 1950 through 1968 (Hudson 1970). He discovered that the United States trade deficit was limited to the military sphere: "*My charts revealed that the U.S. payments deficit was entirely military in character throughout the 1960s. The private sector—foreign trade and investment—was exactly in balance, year after year, and "foreign aid" actually produced a dollar surplus (as it was required to do under U.S. law).*" However, the accounting system used in the US after WW II mixed the trade balances of individuals, corporations and government entities into a single balance that concealed the true source of budget deficits. Hudson proposed dividing US balance of payments figures into governmental and private sectors. This has not been done.

In 1972, Michael Hudson published a book entitled "Super Imperialism", which traced the history of American financial imperialism after the end of World War I (Hudson 1968). In Hudson's interpretation, US policy was aimed at "colonializing" other states, making them into client book states by dollar diplomacy. Continuing the position outlined in "A Financial Payments-Flow Analysis of U.S. International Transactions, 1960–1968." Hudson stressed the aid systems, World Bank and IMF formed after the end of World War II. In his view, all American foreign politics (including tied aid and debts) were aimed at restraining the self-sufficient economic development of Third World countries in economic sectors where the United States was afraid of emerging competition. At the same time, the US imposed so-called free trade policies on developing countries, a policy which was the reverse of the protectionist one the US used in the early nineteenth century to create the American System of Manufacturing.

In 1971, after Nixon cancelled the right to redeem gold for dollars, the US forced foreign central banks to buy US treasury bonds. This income was used to finance the US federal deficit and large, overseas military expenditures. In exchange for providing a net surplus of assets, commodities, debt financing, goods and services, foreign countries were forced to hold an equal amount of US treasuries. This kept US interest rates low, which also drove down the dollar's foreign exchange rate, making US exports more competitive overseas. Hudson argues that "keyboard credit" and treasury outflows to repay indebted foreign treasuries with devalued dollars in exchange for foreign resources, is akin to military conquest. He believes that the surplus balance of payments countries (like Germany and France) should have been entitled to stable exchange rates and the right to expect repayment, in full, of their loans even as industry shifts from the United States to creditor nations.

Michael Hudson argues that the parasitic costs of a real economy, instead of being deducted from profits, as in standard accounting methodology, are presented as a contribution by the finance sector to the gross domestic product (GDP). Rather than extracting taxes from the rentiers to reduce the cost of labor and assets and use the tax revenue to improve infrastructure to increase production efficiency, Michael Hudson says that the US tax system, with bank bailouts and quantitative easing, punished US labor and industry for the benefit of the finance sector. According to Hudson, the neoliberal Washington consensus means that "*everyone is worth what they get*" so there is no "unearned increment" to be taxed.

Hudson stresses that the global success of neoliberal Dollar Diplomacy and financialization is closely connected with its educational support in all big universities. He cites the story of Chile. One of the first acts of the Chicago Boys in Chile after the military junta overthrew the Allende government in 1973 was to close down every economics department in the nation outside of the Catholic University, a University of Chicago monetarist stronghold. The junta then closed down every social science department and fired, exiled or murdered critics of its ideology in the terrorist Project Condor program waged throughout Latin America and even in the United States itself.

What the Chicago Boys recognized is that free market ideology requires totalitarian control of the school and university system, totalitarian control of the press and control of the police where intellectual resistance survives against the idea that economic planning should become much more centralized, but moved out of the hands of government into those of the bankers and other financial institutions, stating: "*Free market ideology ends up as political Doublethink in countering any freedom of thought. Its remarkable success in the United States and elsewhere thus has been achieved largely by excluding the history of classical, conservative economic thought from the early 1800s, which culminated in many ways with Marx. These have been expunged from conventional economics curriculum"*.

Hudson identifies himself as a Marxist economist, but his interpretation of Karl Marx is different from most other Marxists. Whilst other Marxists emphasize the contradiction of wage labor and capital as the core issue of today's capitalist world, Hudson rejects this idea. Hudson argues for enhanced consumer protection, state support of infrastructure projects, and taxation of rentier sectors of the economy rather than taxation of workers incomes.

Hudson sides with those who understand Marx as wishing to eliminate all forms of feudalistic rent seeking. If encouraged, these can only lead to a new feudalism and economic serfdom for the 99%. The original meaning of a "free market" as discussed by classical political economists was a market free from all forms of rent. The gist of classical political economy was to distinguish earned-production from unearned-non-productive economic activity. The "free market" in its original 1800s definition was "free from non-productive rents". The current Wall Street version of "free market" means reducing all regulation and taxation to permit asset stripping both domestically and foreign. Here it seems Hudson and Hayek are on the same page by some twist in the fabric of the universe.

Hudson argues that Marx was too optimistic. History did not go in the direction of Capitalism evolving into Socialism–at least not yet. Since the 1930s today's modern capitalism is dominated by non-productive rentier classes. In classical economics, which includes Marx, the proletariat as a class is better off paying as few rents as possible. This is because wages can be lower if workers have less overhead. This lowers the price of goods, making them more competitive on the international market. This is also the logic of making healthcare a public commons run by the government. This enables wages to be lower for workers.

Non-productive rents, tactics and strategies are making all countries, the US included, less self-sufficient. This connects back with the idea of a debt jubilee; and, with taxing non-productive activity, not workers and manufacturing.

Michael Hudson was strongly influenced by Henry George and is a supporter of the Georgist reform of taxing 100% of the rental value of land. In "A Philosophy for a Fair Society" Hudson claims that Marxism has failed, welfare capitalism is crippled and argues that Georgist tax policy as necessary for rebuilding the community. Michael Hudson argues that debt which can't be repaid won't be repaid. It is a possible consequence of the increase in US and other national debts that has accompanied the COVID 19 pandemic.

A Debt Jubilee in the Jewish tradition was said to occur roughly every 50 years. It was a time for total forgiveness of debt and the freeing of slaves. Pope Boniface VIII proclaimed the first Christian Jubilee in 1300 AD. Is such a thing conceivable under current circumstances?

At the same time, Hudson is a critic of the Georgist political movement, historically blaming Henry George for not cooperating with socialists and thereby ultimately failing to implement his crucial policy change. He considers the American Georgist movement too libertarian, right-wing and unambitious. He was part of a group that attempted to convince the Russian Duma in 1996 to adopting Georgist policy. He is frequently featured in Georgist media. However, interviewed by *The Grayzone* in October 2021, Hudson said: "*I loathe Henry George, … Henry George did not have a theory of value and price, and without that you don't have a concept of economic rent.*"

16.8 The End of the Gold Standard, Hayek and the Washington Consensus

In 1895 the US Government suffered a gold shortage resulting from legislation that allowed politically influential silver miners to exchange silver for gold at a fixed ratio. The mining interests did what the (new) law allowed them to do, trading silver for gold and nearly exhausting the Treasury's modest gold supply. Since the US dollar at the time—was based on the gold standard there was a financial crisis. The banker's banker, JP Morgan, came to the rescue. He organized a group of bankers (including the Rothschilds) to sell gold to the government in exchange for a 30 year bond.

This saved the Treasury but hurt the agrarian wing of the Democratic Party and became a political hotcake. In the election of 1896 William Jennings Bryan campaigned against a "cross of gold"—meaning that banks were not lending to farmers because of lack of gold (reserves)—but he lost the election. The episode inspired a famous children's story called "The Wizard of Oz". It was about Dorothy Gale, a girl from Kansas, who was carried (by a tornado) with her dog Toto to "Munchkin-land" where she followed a yellow brick road to meet with the scary Wizard. This was made into a movie that is still the most watched movie of all time, starring Judy Garland. Who was the model for that wizard?

In an allegory the Yellow Brick Road represents the gold standard, and the Silver Shoes represent the sixteen-to-one silver to gold ratio (dancing down the road) or the pro-silver movement. The City of Oz earns its name from the abbreviation of ounces "oz" in which gold and silver are measured.

Dorothy—naïve, young and simple—represents the American people. She is Everyman, led astray and seeking the way back home. But, by not following the yellow brick road, she goes to Emerald City, a fraudulent world built on greenback paper money, (currency that cannot be exchanged for gold or silver). When Dorothy is taken to the Emerald Palace before her audience with the Wizard she is led through seven passages and up three flights of stairs, a subtle reference to the Coinage Act of 1873 which caused a lot of trouble. The Scarecrow was a representation of American farmers and their troubles in the late nineteenth century. The Tin Man representing the industrial workers, especially steel workers. The Cowardly Lion was a metaphor for William Jennings Bryan.

In the real world, J.P. Morgan and Wall Street bankers donated heavily to Republican William McKinley, who was elected in 1896 and re-elected in 1900. Morgan was the Wizard, as you already guessed (Fig. 16.13).

President Roosevelt nationalized monetary gold in 1933. Starting in the 1959–1969 a "gold exchange standard" for nations was established by the agreements established after WW II at Bretton Woods, a spa in New Hampshire. Under this system, many countries fixed their exchange rates relative to the U.S. dollar and central banks could exchange dollar holdings into gold at the official exchange rate of $35 per ounce (later raised in steps); this option was not available to firms or individuals. All currencies pegged to the dollar thereby had a fixed value in terms of gold, but paper money was no longer redeemable in gold.

The fiscal strain of expenditures for the Vietnam War and persistent US balance of payments deficits, induced President Charles de Gaulle's France to exchanged France's dollar reserves for gold at the official exchange rate. Switzerland and Germany followed. This led President Richard Nixon to end international convertibility of the U.S. dollar to gold on August 15, 1971 (the "Nixon Shock").

This suspension of convertibility was meant to be a temporary measure, pending a revaluation of the dollar, keeping the price of gold fixed. But, no official revaluation or redemption occurred. The dollar subsequently floated. In December 1971, the "Smithsonian Agreement" was reached. In October 1976, the government officially changed the definition of the dollar; references to gold were removed from the legal statutes. From this point, the international monetary system was disconnected from gold, becoming pure fiat money. The "super-imperialist" exchange rate shenanigans that Michael Hudson complains about began at that time.

Most nations today are members of the World Trade Organization (WTO) and multilateral trade agreements, dating back to 1947. Free trade, of a sort, was exemplified by Great Britain, which reduced regulations and duties on imports (the end of the corn laws) from the 1850s to the 1920s. That was all about keeping the British pound strong and using it to acquire resources from colonies and less developed countries. An alternative approach, after WW II, was to create "free trade" zones between groups of developed countries. Examples included the European Economic Area and Mercosur. This creates a protectionist barrier between that free trade area and the rest of the world. Most governments still impose some protectionist policies to support local employment. Governments may also limit exports of natural resources. Other barriers to trade include import quotas, taxes and regulatory legislation.

In government, free trade is associated with political parties that claim to hold economic liberal positions, while economic nationalist and left-wing political parties generally support protectionism, the opposite of free trade. Historically, openness to free trade substantially increased from 1815 to the outbreak of World War I. Trade openness increased again during the 1920s, but collapsed (in particular in Europe and North America) during the Great Depression. Trade openness increased substantially again from the 1950s onwards (albeit with a slowdown during the 1973 oil crisis).

There is a broad consensus among economists that protectionism has a negative effect on economic growth and economic welfare while free trade and the reduction of trade barriers has a positive effect on economic growth and economic stability. However, in the short run, liberalization of trade can cause significant and unequally distributed losses and the economic dislocation of workers in import-competing sectors.

Friedrich August von Hayek (1899–1992), was an Austrian economist, legal theorist and philosopher who is best known for his defense of "classical liberalism", whatever that is. Hayek shared the 1974 Nobel Memorial Prize in Economic Sciences with Gunnar Myrdal for their work on money and economic fluctuations, and the interdependence of economic, social and institutional phenomena. His account of how changing prices communicate information that helps individuals coordinate their plans is widely regarded as an important achievement in economics, justifying his Nobel.

Hayek served as a young soldier in World War I during his teenage years. He said that this experience in the war, and his desire to help avoid the mistakes that had led to the war, drew him into economics. At the University of Vienna, he studied economics, eventually receiving his doctoral degrees in law in 1921 and in political science in 1923. During the inter-war period he worked in Austria, Great Britain, the United States, and Germany. He became a British subject in 1938. He wrote his famous book "The Road to Serfdom" in 1941–42 during WW II. That book has sold 2.25 million copies (as of 2020). If you haven't read it, it is about how government regulation, and taxation to pay for it, tends to get more and more onerous once it gets started.

Hayek's comparison between medieval and modern serfdom (4 days work per week for the state in 1950 vs 3 days back in 1500 AD) was arguably valid for some in post-war Britain, where income taxes on salary could approach 90% in the 1950s. But it is nowhere near true for twenty-first century America, where taxes of all kinds, federal, state and local, add up to 30% of total income (only 34% for the top 20% of US earners). Even the citizens of highly taxed European welfare states pay only around 40% of total income in taxes, while getting superb municipal services, public transport, beautiful parks, excellent health care and retirement benefits. The real problem in Europe is that government debt and inflation appear to be getting out of control.

The book's message was the intellectual basis of Thatcherism and Reaganomics ("government is not the solution, it is the problem"). According to the book, a medieval serf worked 3 days for his lord. But Hayek asserted that "*if you aggregate all the taxes you pay, not just income taxes, you work 4 days for the state.*" His book went on to assert (without evidence) that "personal freedom" is worth far more than welfare benefits provided by the state. Hayek's philosophy is fundamentally libertarian, spiced with fears of what can happen when central government gets too much power, as illustrated by a few actual cases.

The underlying issues are still important book today because now economists and politicians are debating how to solve the high unemployment and long-term disequilibrium in the financial markets. Government monetary and fiscal policy seem ineffective.

The answer in Hayek's book was simple: less government. He argued that If politicians try to influence the economy, it will result in a loss of freedom and prosperity for both the poor and the rich. The Government bureaucracy gains power like the feudal lord once did. Once this system is in place, the process is almost irreversible. It comes in increments so you do not notice it. Why is Hayek he frequently cited as the counterpart of Keynes? The short answer—doubtless much too short—is that Hayek argued very effectively that central planning is dangerous because it leads inevitably to tyranny (one man rule). There were, and still are, enough examples to make this prospect frightening. Hence, for Hayek, the only acceptable form of government is as little government as possible.

In 1947 Hayek co-founded the Mt Pelerin Society, an international organization composed of economists, philosophers, historians, intellectuals and business leaders. Its other co-founders included Frank Knight, Karl Popper, Ludwig von Mises, George Stigler and Milton Friedman. The society advocates freedom of expression, free market economic policies and the political values of an open society. The members see it as an effort to interpret in modern terms the fundamental principles of economic society as expressed by classical Western economists, political scientists and philosophers (free speech, free trade, free enterprise). Further, the society seeks to discover ways in which free enterprise can replace many functions currently provided by government entities.

He is widely considered a leader of the Austrian School of Economics, although in recent years he has been more closely associated with the Chicago School, despite not being an admirer of Milton Friedman. (Friedman was an admirer of Hayek).

There is a popular story, perhaps a little too good to be actually true, that as Leader of the Opposition in 1978 (?) Margaret Thatcher once cut short a presentation by a leftish member of the Conservative Research Department by fetching out a copy of Hayek's "The Constitution of Liberty" from her bag and slamming it down on the table, declaring "this is what we believe". It was also what soon-to-be president of the US, Ronald Reagan, believed.

The "Washington Consensus" was a set of ten economic policy prescriptions that were supposed to constitute the "standard" reform package promoted for crisis-wracked developing countries by Washington, D.C.-based institutions such as the International Monetary Fund (IMF), World Bank and United States Department of the Treasury. The list was compiled by John Williamson of the Peterson Institute for International Economics in 1989. The list was: (1) Fiscal policy discipline, with avoidance of large fiscal deficits relative to GDP; (2) Redirection of public spending away from subsidies ("especially indiscriminate subsidies") toward broad-based provision of key pro-growth, pro-poor services like primary education, primary health care and infrastructure investment; (3) Tax reform, broadening the tax base and adopting moderate marginal tax rates; (4) Interest rates that are market determined and positive (but moderate) in real terms; (5) Competitive exchange rates; (6) Trade liberalization: liberalization of imports, with particular emphasis on elimination of quantitative restrictions (licensing, etc.); any trade protection to be provided by low and relatively uniform tariffs; (7) Liberalization of inward foreign direct investment; (8) Privatization of state enterprises; (9) Deregulation: abolition of regulations that impede market entry or restrict competition, except for those justified on safety, environmental and consumer protection grounds, and prudential oversight of financial institutions; (10) Legal security for property rights.

As a point of historical accuracy, Williamson has partly credited the Peruvian neoliberal economist Hernando de Soto for the prescriptions, saying his work was *"the outcome of the worldwide intellectual trends to which Latin America contributed ... The Washington Consensus is not interchangeable with the term "neoliberalism"*, More specifically, Williamson noted that only the first three of his ten prescriptions are uncontroversial in the economic community, while the other seven are more or less controversial. He points out that one of the least controversial prescriptions, the redirection of spending to infrastructure, health care, and education, has often been neglected by neoliberals, in practice. He also points out that, while the prescriptions were focused on reducing certain functions of government (e.g., as an owner of productive enterprises) they would—if implemented—also strengthen government's ability to undertake other actions such as supporting education and health.

Williamson regretted the use of "Washington" in the Washington Consensus, as it incorrectly suggested that development policies stemmed from Washington and were externally imposed on others. Williamson said in 2002, *"The phrase "Washington Consensus" is a damaged brand name... Audiences the world over seem to believe that this signifies a set of neoliberal policies that have been imposed on hapless countries by the Washington-based international financial institutions and have led them to crisis and misery. There are people who cannot utter the term without foaming at the mouth. My own view is of course quite different. The basic ideas that I attempted to summarize in the Washington Consensus have continued to gain wider acceptance over the past decade, to the point where Lula has had to endorse most of them in order to be electable. For the most part they are motherhood and apple pie, which is why they commanded a consensus."*

In spite of Williamson's reservations, the term "Washington Consensus" has been used as a label to describe the general shift towards free market policies that followed the decline of Keynesianism in the 1970s and the election of Ronald Reagan in 1980. Recent commentators have suggested that the Consensus in its broader sense survived until the time of the 2008 global financial crisis. Following the strong intervention undertaken by governments in response to market failures, a number of journalists, politicians and senior officials from Washington-based global institutions began saying that the "Washington Consensus" was dead. There were no mourners. After the G-20 Seoul Development Consensus, in 1910, the *Financial Times* editorialized that *"Its pragmatic and pluralistic view of development is appealing enough. But the document will do little more than drive another nail into the coffin of a long-deceased Washington consensus."*

The global financial crisis of 2007–08 led to public skepticism about the free market consensus even from some on the economic right. In March 2008, Martin Wolf, chief economics commentator at the *Financial Times*, announced the death of the dream of global free-market capitalism. In the same month macroeconomist James K. Galbraith used the 25th Annual Milton Friedman Distinguished Lecture to launch a sweeping attack against monetarist economics and argued that Keynesian economics were far more relevant for tackling the emerging crises. Economist Robert J. Shiller had begun advocating robust government intervention to tackle the financial crises, specifically citing Keynes. Nobel laureate Paul Krugman also actively argued the case for vigorous Keynesian intervention in the economy in his columns for *The New York Times*. Other prominent economic commentators who have argued for Keynesian government intervention to mitigate the financial crisis include George Akerlof, J. Bradford DeLong, Robert Reich, and Joseph Stiglitz. Newspapers and other media have also cited work relating to Keynes by Hyman Minsky, Robert Skidelsky, Donald Markwell and Axel Leijonhufvud.

A series of major financial bailouts were pursued during the financial crisis, starting on 7 September 2008 with the announcement that the U.S. Government was to nationalize the two government-sponsored enterprises which oversaw most of the U.S. subprime mortgage market—Fannie Mae and Freddie Mac. In October, Alistair Darling, the British Chancellor of the Exchequer, referred to Keynes as he announced plans for substantial fiscal stimulus to head off the worst effects of recession, in accordance with Keynesian economic thought. Similar policies have been adopted by other governments worldwide.

This was a stark contrast to the action imposed on Indonesia during the Asian financial crisis of 1997. In that crisis Indonesia was forced by the IMF to close 16 banks at the same time, prompting a bank run. Much of the post-crisis discussion reflected Keynes's advocacy of international coordination of fiscal or monetary stimulus, and of international economic institutions such as the IMF and the World Bank, that (many had argued) should be (and should have been already) reformed as a "new Bretton Woods" before the crises broke out. The IMF and United Nations economists advocated a coordinated international approach to fiscal stimulus. Donald Markwell argued that in the absence of such an international approach, there would be a risk of worsening international relations and possibly even world war arising from economic factors similar to those present during the depression of the 1930s.

By the end of December 2008, the *Financial Times* reported that "*the sudden resurgence of Keynesian policy is a stunning reversal of the orthodoxy of the past several decades.*" In December 2008, Paul Krugman released his updated book *The Return of Depression Economics and the Crisis of 2008*, (originally published in 1999) arguing that economic conditions similar to those that existed during the Great Depression, earlier in the twentieth century, had returned, making Keynesian policy prescriptions more relevant than ever. In February 2009 Robert J. Shiller and George Akerlof published *Animal Spirits*, a book where they argue the current US stimulus package is too small as it does not take into account Keynes's insight on the importance of confidence and expectations in determining the future behavior of businesspeople and other economic agents.

In the March 2009 speech entitled *Reform the International Monetary System*, Zhou Xiaochuan, the governor of the People's Bank of China, came out in favor of Keynes's idea of a centrally managed global reserve currency. Zhou argued that it was unfortunate that part of the reason for the Bretton Woods system breaking down was the failure to adopt Keynes's "bancor". Zhou proposed a gradual move towards increased use of IMF special drawing rights (SDRs). Although Zhou's ideas had not been broadly accepted, leaders meeting in April at the 2009 G-20 London summit agreed to allow $250 billion of special drawing rights to be created by the IMF, to be distributed globally. Stimulus plans were credited for contributing to a better than expected economic outlook by both the OECD and the IMF, in reports published in June and July 2009. Both organizations warned global leaders that recovery was likely to be slow, so counter recessionary measures ought not be rolled back too early.

While the need for stimulus measures was broadly accepted among policy makers, there was much debate over how to fund the spending. Some leaders and institutions, such as Angela Merkel and the European Central Bank, expressed concern over the potential impact on inflation, national debt and the risk that a too large stimulus will create an unsustainable recovery.

Among professional economists the revival of Keynesian economics has been even more divisive. Although many economists, such as George Akerlof, Paul Krugman, Robert Shiller and Joseph Stiglitz, supported Keynesian stimulus, others in Chicago did not believe higher government spending would help the United States economy recover from the Great Recession. Robert Lucas, questioned the theoretical basis for stimulus packages. Others, like Robert Barro and Gary Becker, said that empirical evidence for beneficial effects from Keynesian stimulus "does not exist". However, there is a growing academic literature that shows that fiscal expansion helps an economy grow in the near term, and that certain types of fiscal stimulus are particularly effective.

In 2003, in his Presidential Address to the American Economic Association, Robert Lucas began with the words "*My thesis in this lecture is that macro-economics …has succeeded. Its central problem of Depression prevention has been solved, for all practical purposes and has been solved for many decades.*" Lucas's first generation followers in the late '70's and early '80's built Real Business Cycle (RBC) Models that assumed all markets worked perfectly. Those models led to very unrealistic implications about unemployment.

There was a split in the ranks. But the progressive camp allowed for some market imperfections. This led to the development of "New Keynesian" or "Dynamic Stochastic General Equilibrium (DSGE) Models. By 2007 these DSGE models were widely used by national Treasuries and Central Banks. New Keynesians believed that the system in place was working. They coined the term "Great Moderation" to describe the falling peaks in unemployment and inflation. Ben Bernanke (Chairman of the Federal Reserve Bank from 2006 to 2014) may have coined the phrase. He said in a 2004 panel discussion at the FRB, St. Louis on monetary policy since 1979: "*The sources of the Great Moderation re is evidence for the view that improved control of inflation has contributed in important measure to this welcome change in the economy.*"

The Great Moderation from the mid-1980s to 2007 was a welcome period of relative calm after the volatility of the Great Inflation. Under the chairmanships of Volcker (ending in 1987), Greenspan (1987–2006) and Bernanke (starting in 2006), inflation was low and relatively stable, while the period contained the longest economic expansion since World War II. Looking back, economists may differ on what roles were played by the different factors in contributing to the Great Moderation, but they agreed that better monetary policy was part of the story.

But three years later, in 2007–8 the global financial system nearly fell apart. The academic world is still struggling with the implications of the housing crisis, as it is now labelled. The COVID 19 pandemic has exposed a number of deep-seated economic problems, including greater inequality, social??, skyrocketing debt and all of the financialization problems identified by Michael Hudson and others. Above all, our society faces a looming climate crisis for which our institutions are utterly unprepared. Where next? (Fig. 16.14)

16.9 SVM, Buybacks and Inequality

Inspired by Schumpeter, the work of Mensch et al., among others, argued that weak consumer demand, governed by the business cycle, enables increased

Fig. 16.14 Alan Greenspan; Paul A. Volcker; Ben S. Bernanke 2014—Wikimedia

levels of industrial R&D resulting in more product innovation (Mensch 1979, 1988). There is some evidence for this behavior in the past. But in recent decades it appears that the classical R&D investment mechanism in corporations has been short-circuited. When revenues and profits declined because of economic slowdowns, it seems that profits are less and less retained and diverted to R&D or other long term objectives, as Mensch suggested. Instead they are now mostly returned to shareholders, via buybacks. Most economists seem to think that this is perfectly rational behavior, allowing the "free (financial) market" to re-allocate capital into the most profitable opportunities. Maybe this is true if financial sector profits are counted, but for "brick and mortar" sectors that produce goods and non-financial services, the evidence is murky.

As Adam Smith pointed out long ago: "*The directors of such [joint-stock] companies, however, being the managers rather of other people's money than of their own, it cannot well be expected, that they should watch over it with the same anxious vigilance with which the partners in a private co-partner frequently watch over their own. Like the stewards of a rich man, they are apt to consider attention to small matters as not for their master's honor, and very easily give themselves a dispensation from having it. Negligence and profusion, therefore, must always prevail, more or less, in the management of the affairs of such a company...*" (Smith 1776 [2007]). It was first expressed as an assertion that "the only business of business is business", by Milton Friedman (Friedman 1970).

The "principal-agent" theory of business economics was initiated by business school professors Michael C. Jensen and William H. Meckling (Jensen 1976). Their article, later reprinted and elaborated in several books, rapidly gained traction in the executive suites of the business world. It integrates elements from the theory of agency, the theory of property rights and the theory of finance to develop a comprehensive theory of the firm. Jensen and Meckling defined the concept of agency costs and showed its relationship to the 'separation and control' issue due to the existence of debt and outside equity). It provided a new definition of the firm, and showed how debt and equity claims differentiate owners interests from managers. The new managerial mantra is "shareholder value maximization (SVM), where shareholder value is measured by stock price. This is not the place to discuss the details (Chapter 18.7).

When companies first make an initial public offering (IPO), stock is sold to the broad public on one of the main stock markets. In principle, the sale of the stock can be used to raise money to finance further growth. More typically, the secondary reason for the IPO is to give the early investors in the company—venture capitalists, early employees, and founders—the opportunity to "cash out", i.e. be repaid, in part, for their risky investments. A stock buyback is basically a secondary offering in reverse—instead of selling new shares of stock to the public to put more cash on the corporate balance sheet, a cash-rich company expends some of its own funds on *buying* shares of stock from the public.

What does this mean for the economy as a whole? From 2008 to 2017, 466 of the S&P 500 companies distributed $4 trillion to shareholders as buybacks, along with $3.1 trillion as dividends (Lazonick 2014). The 10 biggest share buybacks during 2003–2012 added up to $859 million.[1] The average CEO pay for those firms was $168 million, while the next 4 highest paid executives got $77 million each. The CEO pay was 58% based on stock performance (options and awards) while the other top executive pay was 56% based on stock prices. Incredibly, *all but three of those companies spent more than their net income on buybacks.* Hewlett-Packard (177%) was the highest on that list, followed by Pfizer (146%), Microsoft (125%), Cisco Systems (121%), Procter and Gamble (116%), IBM (111%) and Intel (109%). The lowest of the ten was Walmart (73%).

---

[1] The "top 10" in order were Exxon-Mobil, Microsoft, IBM, Cisco-Systems, Procter & Gamble, Hewlett-Packard. Walmart, Intel, Pfizer and GE.

But, looking at the US as a whole, as in Fig. 16.15, there is a periodic variation in the fraction of GDP devoted to investment, ranging between 8 and 11% p.a. with peaks in 1983 (Reagan), 2002 (the dot-com bubble) and 2007 (the housing bubble) followed by declines. The average stays around 9% p.a. Buybacks, on the other hand, have been wildly erratic and not closely correlated with investment behavior. This conclusion, namely that buybacks have not significantly affected aggregate investgment or R&D spending has been confirmed by statistical analysis, both for the US and internationally (Gruber 2017; Fried 2018). The arguments are not worth presenting here. Those studies do not shed any light on the consequences for income distribution, debt accumulation or corporate growth strategy.

Along the same lines, the $1.5 trillion Republican Tax Cuts and Jobs Act of 2017 slashed the corporate tax rate to 21% from 35%, reduced the rate on corporate income brought back to the United States from abroad to between 8 and 15.5% instead of 35%, and exempted American companies' foreign income from US tax. Since the tax bill, companies have been doing a lot of buybacks. Share buybacks in 2018 averaged $4.8 billion per day, double the pace from the same period in 2017.

Goldman Sachs estimated that after the 2017 tax cuts S&P 500 firms would return $1.2 trillion to shareholders via buybacks and dividends in

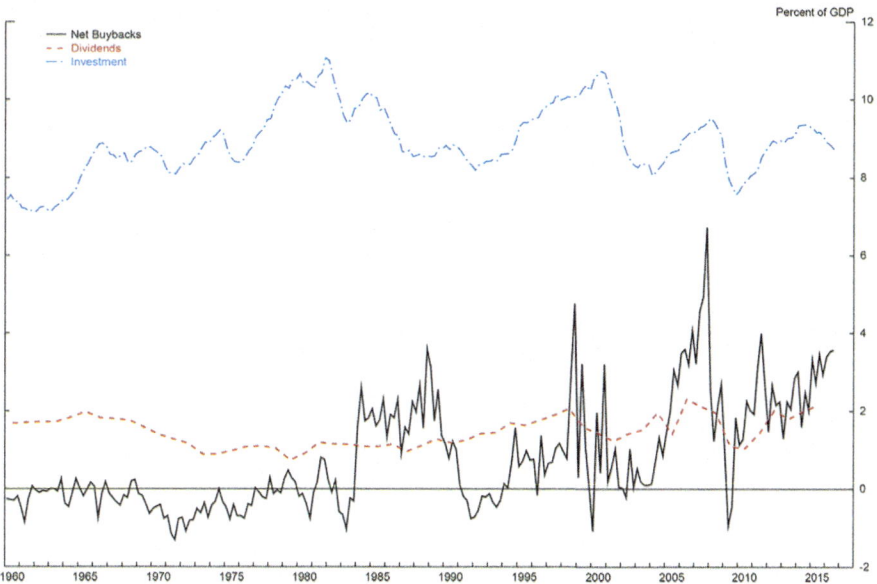

Fig. 16.15 Investment and buybacks as fraction of GDP 1960–2015. https://www.federalreserve.gov/econres/notes/ifdp-notes/corporate-buybacks-and-capital-investment-an-international-perspective-20170411.htm

2018, increasing share buybacks by 23% to $650 billion. A Bloomberg analysis found that about 60% of tax cut gains would go to shareholders, compared to 15% to employees. A Morgan Stanley survey found that 43% of tax cut savings would go to stock buybacks and dividends, while 13% will go to pay raises, bonuses, and employee benefits. Just Capital's analysis of 121 Russell 1000 companies found that 57% of tax savings would go to shareholders, compared to 20% directed to job creation and capital investment and 6% to workers. By one tally, the tax cut scoreboard stands as follows: Workers $6 billion; Share buybacks $171 billion.

There is another kind of evidence against buybacks. In the next few lines, you will see the results of unpublished research on this topic at INSEAD, conducted by me, jointly with my colleague, Michael Olenick (Ayres 2017). We compiled a list of all corporate buybacks between January 1, 2000 and Dec. 31 2016, by US firms trading on the three major exchanges, with market cap of $100 million or more at the latter date. This yielded 5448 share-purchase transactions by 1015 US companies. For each business we computed its total expenditure on buybacks, during that period, adjusted for inflation. We also compiled the data on current market value for each company, as compared to its market value 5 years earlier. We then computed, for each company, the ratio of inflation-adjusted buybacks to current market cap as a percentage. That is, if a business had a market cap of $100 M and repurchased $50 M of shares that business would have a ratio of 50%. We then rank-ordered them and plotted these percentages against the 5-year growth percentage.

The results of our research are shown graphically in Fig. 16.16. The vertical axis is growth; the horizontal axis is the ratio of buybacks to market value at the end of 2016. The trend is clear. The more a company spent on buybacks, the less it grew, in market value, over a five year time-scale. Companies that have spent a large fraction of their current market cap on buybacks are virtually guaranteed to decline in the coming years. The 535 firms that repurchased less than 5% of their market value as of Dec. 31 2016 saw their market value increase an average of 247.8% over the prior five years. The 64 firms that repurchased 100% or more of their final market capitalization experienced a 21.7% decline in value over the same timeframe. Note that the curve must continue further and lower beyond the 100% point, although we didn't bother to plot it.

As mentioned, market cap growth in this chart is based on the five years 2012–2016. Five years was used as a benchmark because recent data is more reliable and many firms actually disappeared during the "crash years" making interpretation of the results much more difficult. The strength of

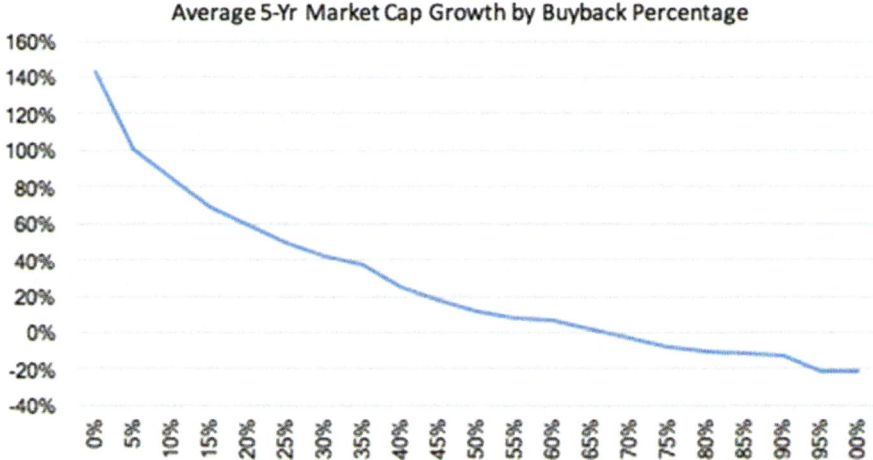

Fig. 16.16 How share buybacks affect company growth or decline. https://ruayres.wordpress.com/2017/07/11/secular-stagnation-or-corporate-suicide/

this correlation relationship can be tested statistically, and it is obviously (by the eyeball test) extremely strong. For statistics mavens, the chi value is 0.02544, which means the chances of non-correlation are negligible. In other words, there is a strong causal relationship between buybacks and corporate growth rates. Indeed, the graph suggests that companies that engage in excessive buybacks—beyond 50% or so of market cap—will almost certainly lag behind the S&P in growth. Firms where buybacks exceed 65% of market cap are likely to experience zero net growth, over five years, and beyond that point absolute declines can be expected. Large wealth management funds and pension funds should be using this information in making long-term investment decisions.

Admittedly, the direction of causation is ambiguous. Proponents will say that the declining firms are doing the rational thing, by returning capital to their shareholders, who can presumably invest more productively elsewhere. But, given the case histories of IBM, Xerox and H-P we are skeptical. Those firms had wonderful investment opportunities—in some cases based on their own research—that they threw away by "investing" surplus cash in their own shares, rather than in the future.

What does all this mean for the economy? For one thing, it means that firms that have "invested" in buybacks (to support the price of the stock and to keep the senior executives happy) *have actually wasted money that should probably have been invested in the business, especially in R&D*. It is also clear that buybacks make inequality worse, thus reducing opportunity. Barely half of Americans own stocks at all. What's more, the richest 10 percent of Americans own 80% of all traded shares. The bottom 80% of earners own just 8 percent of shares.

William Lazonick recently told a CNN Money audience: "*Buybacks have been a prime mode of both concentrating income among the richest households and eroding middle-class employment opportunities.*" Congress is taking notice: the Reward Work Act introduced by Senator Tammy Baldwin in March would ban stock buybacks done as open market repurchases. (It would still allow buybacks done through tender offers, which are used for different purposes.) The chances of passage seem minimal as long as the Republicans hold the Senate.

Coincidence or not, the compensation of the top executives has increased much faster than the compensation of lower level employees in public companies since the 1980s (Ayres 2020). But since 1980 the incomes of the top 10% have doubled and the income of the top 1% has tripled. Another sign of increasing inequality is that the chances of escaping from that bottom pool have declined. In the year 1970 most children grew up to earn more than their parents. In 1990 the odds of moving up from the bottom income quintile (0–20%) to the middle income quintile (40–60%) in ten years were 23%. By 2011 they were down to 14%. This is a sharp decline in "upward mobility" which was once the great attraction of the Statue of Liberty.

16.10 Positive Returns: Short Term Versus Long Term

Neoclassical economic theory does not distinguish very well between the short term and the long term. The "short term" in this context is the time-period during which external factors affecting a decision can be assumed to be fixed and unchanging. This time may be as little as a few minutes or hours in the case of decisions regarding the buying or selling of goods that cannot be stored (notably electricity) or perishable consumables (e.g. food). It may be months, years or decades where the transaction involves land, real-estate, heavy machinery or financial securities with long maturities.

It is intuitively clear that a sequence of short-term income or wealth maximizing decisions does not necessarily lead to an optimal long-term result. (It not infrequently leads to disaster, in the field of international relations.) This is a consequence of the non-linear dynamics of the system. The empirical evidence for the difference between short-term and long-term optima is massive. Recognition of, and allowance for, non-linear dynamics is an aspect of rationality. It is irrational to ignore non-linear dynamics. Yet mainstream economic theory has little to say on the subject. In fact, many orthodox economists still insist on 'declining returns' as a fundamental axiom of utility theory (since Jevons and Menger), and that 'positive returns' is either impossible or very exceptional.

Conventional economic theory is largely built around the axiom of declining marginal returns to scale of consumption of goods and services. Indications of approaching market saturation for many products, from shoes to cars to i-Phones, can be seen in the industrialized countries today (c. 2020). There is a negative feedback due to increasing product lifespan and (in some cases) increasing renovation and remanufacturing. This suggests that the economic system is approaching a steady state of maximum consumption. That state looks like an equilibrium where economic growth would cease without the constant introduction of new products or services to stimulate demand.

Diminishing returns to scale, as applied to agricultural land, in particular, was the basis for Malthus' concerns about over-population (Malthus 1798 [1946]). Malthusian concerns lie behind much of the argument in "Limits to Growth" (Meadows et al. 1972). In this context, see also (Freeman 1976), and (Goodwin 1978). The Malthusian argument, based on declining returns, also underlies subsequent responses by the mainstream (Solow 1973, 1974; Stiglitz 1974; Nordhaus 1992).

The common assumption of declining (or zero) returns-to-scale, as an axiom for the real economy, is mathematically convenient (it is the so-called "Euler condition", since the eighteenth century). But it is both incorrect and unnecessary. It is factually wrong and inapplicable to "network" service industries (like the telephone system), and most information-based "platform" services (e.g. Google, Twitter, Facebook) that demonstrably exhibit *increasing* returns to scale.

Brian Arthur (b. 1945) has shown that economic growth (as well as the other economic phenomena) can be explained by invoking positive feedbacks, including increasing returns to scale, but also increasing returns to learning and to experience (Arthur 1994). For example, the "experience curve" is a particularly important component of increasing productivity as a function of scale (Young 1928; Verdoorn 1949, 1951). For more technical discussions see (Mattsson and Wene 1996; Wene 2000). In fact, much, if not most of the US economic growth in recent years has resulted from the growth of Tech firms that have exploited increasing returns from networking.

The simple explanation for positive returns in network sectors is that the larger the network the greater the number of people connected to each node, resulting in increased value to each customer. This phenomenon, in more general terms, is also responsible for population clustering (the existence of cities), the success of department stores, browsers, search engines and a variety of other economically important activities. All of those phenomena are impossible to explain in terms of economic theories based on constant or decreasing returns to scale.

Change in any dynamical system is likely to involve feedbacks, either positive of negative. The re-investment of profits is a positive feedback. The buildup of debt from borrowing money is a negative feedback. Positive feedbacks tend to act as accelerators, while negative feedbacks tend to act as brakes.

The dynamical equations for an economy that is not in equilibrium are non-linear. For non-linear systems it is well-known that there can be multiple alternative equilibria (Poincaré 1885; Thom 1989; Gottinger 2017). As the rate of change increases the system can reach a so-called '*bifurcation point*'. At such a point the system then chooses one path, for short-term reasons, e.g. (David 1985, 1988). There is no guarantee that the path adopted at a bifurcation point leads to a feasible long-term solution. On the contrary, the path selected is almost invariably sub-optimal and often leads to a dead-end. It is tempting to assume that the greater the range of choice among multiple equilibria the better the outcome in terms of wealth creation. This is also not true.

Perhaps the most obvious example of inferior outcomes is the phenomenon of "lock-in/lock-out" where choice among technologies or competitors or business models becomes effectively irreversible once initial advantages (e.g. learning or experience) kick in (Arrow 1962; Ayres and Martinás 1992; Wene 2000). A simple example of "lock-in" is the fact that the Anglo-Saxon countries have been unable to adopt the metric system of measurement, despite its demonstrated superiority. The more important example, today, is the fact that the whole US—and global industrial system is "locked in" to dependence on a road-based transport system requiring private automobiles (and trucks) using liquid hydrocarbon fuels. The "lock-in" of uranium-based nuclear power technology (and the "lock-out" of a potentially much superior thorium-based technology) is another example (Cowan 1989; Hargraves and Moir 2010). Other examples of "lock-in" have been noted (Arthur 1983; Liebowitz and Margolis 1995).

The "lock-in" phenomenon is also applicable to political choices as well as technological ones. For an economy the result may be catastrophic if there is no scope for remedial action. (Often, the approaching catastrophe is invisible until it is almost too late). The electoral system in the US, which gives excessive power to small states and rural constituencies, is one example of political "lock-in". The UN Security Council, that gives vetoes to five countries (including China and Russia), is another example. The political structure giving important decision-making authority on fiscal policy and taxes to poorly educated representatives elected for only two years is another example. (Arguably, decision-making authority in certain fields—such as finance and medicine—should be based on educational credentials). There are more dangerous examples, including the dynamics of arms races and the fact that it is much easier to start a war than to end it. Alliances are dangerous because small provocations can result in disastrous outcomes (as happened during the lead-up to WW I). The German decision embark on unrestricted submarine warfare in 1917 order to win the war quickly had the opposite outcome. Sometimes short-term competitive dynamics between nations, or firms, leads to a *cul-de-sac* with "lose-lose" outcomes.

There is another interesting example of "lock in", namely the existence of democratic governments. It is possible to see democracy as an unstable state between autocracy (police state) on one side and anarchy on the other. Democracies have difficulty in defending themselves against determined dictatorships, as we see today in Afghanistan, Mianmar, Belarus, and the Ukraine. Democracies are slow to make decisions because many interests have to be consulted. They may be defeated in war, but they tend to bounce back. There must be some kind of "attractor" that makes democracies increasingly stable, over time, while autocracies ("might makes right") are inherently unstable unless there is a strong tradition of divine selection, and inheritance from father to son. A few republics. Including Athens, Greek city-states, Rome and Venice, had long lives. They usually collapse when the founding conqueror or dictator dies or is assassinated.

We think evolutionary game theory (EGT) might be the right tool for understanding the dynamics in more detail. Robert H. Axelrod (b. 1943) is one of the leaders in this area of research. He is best-known for the "tribute model" and subsequent work. His major publications are *The Evolution of Cooperation, Basic Books, (1984); The Complexity of Cooperation: Agent-Based Models of Competition and Collaboration, (1997) and The Evolution of Cooperation (1997)* and Axelrod, *Harnessing Complexity with Michael D. Cohen (2001).*

The work over the past decade of the economist Daron Acemoglu and political scientist James Robinson is probably most relevant. Acemoglu and Robinson build game theoretic models of competition between elites and between elites and regular citizens, and ask under what conditions does democracy form? Their "Why Nations Fail" is the popular version of a more technical book with the explicit models, and argues that dictatorship and democracy are simply two competing forms of governance. (The so-called "Glorious Revolution" in England of 1688 is their nominal foil, when Parliament takes over form the monarchy.) Their analysis is static. The first book, *Economic Origins of Dictatorship and Democracy*, proposed a theory of the emerge and stability of democracy and dictatorship (Acemoglu 2005). Their second book *Why Nations Fail: The Origins of Power, Prosperity, and Poverty* (translated into 41 languages since its publication in 2012) proposed a theory of why some countries have flourished economically while others have fallen into poverty (Acemoglu 2012). Their most recent book, *The Narrow Corridor: States, Society and the Fate of Liberty*, examines the incessant and inevitable struggle between states and society and theorizes that the actual path to democracy is bounded by autocracy on one side and anarchy on the other, with democracy being hard to achieve in practice (Acemoglu 2019).

17

The Future of Economics and the Economics of the Future

17.1 The Population Problem

Let's start with the good news. As we all know (rightly or wrongly) the discovery of America put off the evil day predicted by Malthus, back in 1798, when population growth would lead to famine and starvation. Malthusianism became popular again in environmentalist circles in the 1960's when Paul Ehrlich wrote a best-seller "The Population Bomb" (Ehrlich 1968). "Famine 1975! America's Decision: Who Will Survive?" was a 1967 best-seller by William and Paul Paddock. They described a rapidly growing population of the world, and the impossibility of feeding the entire global population within the short-term future. They believed that widespread famine would be the inevitable result. There were other pessimistic books by Lester Brown, Paul Ehrlich and Herman Daly (Brown 1963; Ehrlich 1970, 1973; Daly 1973).

Seen in the 1960s, the population growth trend, which had been rising explosively, showed no sign of reversing. Ehrlich, Brown and others predicted global famine, global pandemics, and resource wars, resulting from unchecked growth (Fig. 17.1). Sixty years later, in 2020, demographers predict that global population will peak at around 10 billion, plus or minus a billion. The peak will occur either late in the twenty-first century or early in the twenty-second century. (N.B. even in the 1960s the decline in birthrates was very clear). The annual population growth rate peaked at 2.1% p.a. in 1968. By 2019 it was down to 1.08% p.a. By 2100 the projected global birth rate will be about 0.1% p.a. This is based on existing trends, not requiring new technology or government policy on family size (as in China).

The primary cause of the rapid global population growth in the nineteenth and twentieth centuries was declining death rates. The slowdown was caused by declining birth rates. Death rates have been declining since the middle ages, but the decline accelerated dramatically in the late nineteenth century due to public health measures, especially vaccination against smallpox (1797), which is estimated to have killed 300 million people in the twentieth century alone. In 1885 Louis Pasteur developed a vaccine treatment of rabies. Since then vaccines have been developed to protect against whooping cough (1914), diphtheria (1926), tetanus (1938), influenza (1945) and mumps (1948). Vaccines against polio (1955), measles (1963), rubella (1969) and other viruses were added to the list over the decades that followed, and worldwide vaccination rates shot up dramatically thanks to successful global health campaigns. The world was announced smallpox-free in 1980, the first of many big vaccine success stories. There was still a long way to go with other infectious diseases. The covid-19 virus that became a pandemic of 2020–2022 was only the latest.

Other antibiotics appeared on the scene, as by-products of German developments in the synthetic dye industry. So-called "sulfa drugs" were

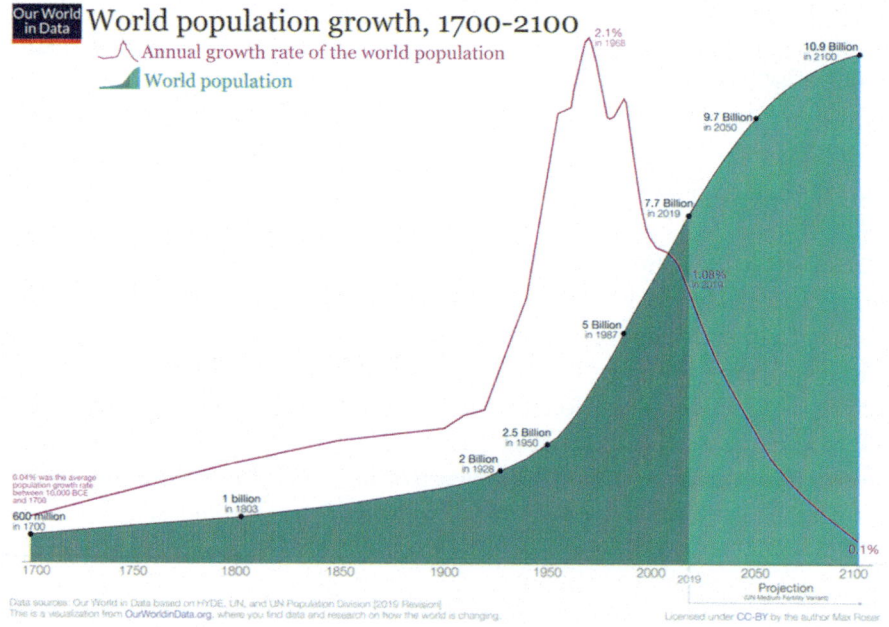

Fig. 17.1 Global population from 1700 to 2050—Wikipedia

introduced in 1932 as anti-bacterial agents by Gerhard Domagk, at Bayer, starting with one called sulfamidochrysoidine (marketed as Prontosil). He received a Nobel Prize in 1939. Penicillin (discovered by Alexander Fleming in 1928, became medically available for the first time in 1942). These drugs and their cousins, reduced the mortality of war—not to mention traffic accidents—enormously. The spectacular declines in death rates seems to have slowed down by 1980 and practically ended by the year 2000 (Fig. 17.2). This slowed the rate of population increase.

Yet birth-rates have declined even faster than death rates, contrary to the fears of Malthus and his followers in the 1960s. Population experts now predict a peak, without any regulatory action by governments (as in China). The number of children per woman has actually declined below the replacement rate—resulting in a negative population rate—in a number of industrialized European countries, as well as Russia and Japan. The US population continues to grow only because of immigration from Latin America.

The reasons for the decline in birth rates are several. Women's education is generally regarded is the most important. There is a strong negative correlation between female education (years of schooling) and children per woman, The availability of birth control technology—especially the invention of "the pill" (since 1960)—is the other important factor. Urbanization is a third factor. Rural families employ children for a variety of useful tasks on a farm. On farms children are an economic asset. In cities, especially now (2020) that education of children is mandatory, children are an expensive luxury. When Ehrlich et al. wrote, there were 2.6 or 2.7 billion people on

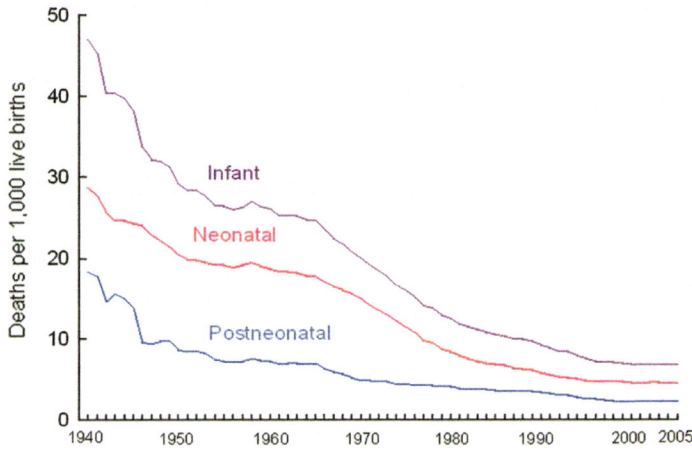

Fig. 17.2 Deaths per 1000 live births 1940–2005—Wikipedia

this planet, two thirds of them in rural areas. In 1987 the global population reached 5 billion, half of them in cities. In 2020 the global population is 7.7 billion, and most of the additional population lives in urban agglomerations. By 2050 the urban fraction will be at least two thirds or higher.

17.2 The Problem of Resource Exhaustion

The source of virtually all useful energy (exergy) currently available to humans in the twenty-second century is (and will be) nuclear fusion in the center of our sun. That process drives all photosynthesis and all hydrological processes, including wind and ocean currents. (A tiny amount will come from nuclear fission or geothermal heat.) You may ask: what has this to do with economics? The point is simple: We humans now see the end of the energy "supply chain". We encounter the supply chain as food to eat, as heat for cooking our food (much of which would be inedible without cooking), as warmth in a cold winter night, as light for reading, as motive power for machines that enhance our muscles and make us stronger, quicker and tireless, and as input components for chemical processes that create new materials not found in nature, including drugs, dyes, plastics and explosives.

The intermediates of the supply chain are familiar. They include natural materials (stone, clay, sand, wood, wool, fibers), that can be used, after a little processing (by human labor) to make things. They also include fossil fuels (coal, petroleum and natural gas) that can be used, after some processing, for heating a room, cooking, smelting a metal ore, and for engines that drive vehicles. The other, most important, intermediate is electricity that energizes a host of devices, ranging from motors that drive other devices, to toasters, hearing aids, flashlights, TVs and PCs.

The fossil fuels were created by geological processes from photosynthesis hundreds of millions of years ago. Stone, clay and sand are geological leftovers from the creation of the Earth. They are not scarce. Natural materials, including food, are also based on photosynthesis. Finally, electricity can be generated directly from sunlight by photo-voltaic devices, or indirectly by exploiting the hydrological cycle using turbo-machines from flowing water, blowing wind, or by steam from the combustion of fossil fuels. And, yes, electricity can be generated by nuclear heat, either from magma below the earth's crust, or by controlled fission of heavy radioactive metals (uranium, thorium) left over from the creation of the Earth itself. In short, all of the important intermediates, today, are derived from sunlight, past or present. A brief lesson in cosmology makes this clearer.

What powers the sun? According to current cosmological theory, the beginning of the universe, known as the "Big Bang" (BB) occurred 16.87 billion years ago. Skipping over never-seen sub-nuclear objects like "quarks", and "neutrinos", cosmologists suppose that, a short time after that event (BB) there were only three kinds of elementary particles, all in a super-heated plasma state: *electrons* (with a negative electric charge), *protons* (with a positive charge) and *neutrons* (with no electric charge). Apparently the negative and positive charges balance exactly because the universe as a whole is apparently electrically neutral.

The neutral "couple" of one proton and one electron is called a Hydrogen atom. When the plasma had cooled sufficiently—370,000 years after the BB—hydrogen atoms were formed as the electrons and protons combined. One could say that they were "married". The marriage yielded hydrogen atoms and photons (electromagnetic radiation), that are pure energy. We see that radiation (extremely "red-shifted") as background radiation, from all directions, at a temperature of 2.74 °K. (This was discovered by Penzias and Wilson at Bell Telephone Laboratories in 1964). It is regarded as strong evidence that the Big Bang (BB) actually occurred 13.787 billion years ago. The argument is too complicated to explain here.

When the positively charged nucleus of a hydrogen atom (a proton) encounters a free neutron, the free protons and neutrons are attracted to each other, by short-range nuclear forces. They can decide to live together as a heavy hydrogen (deuterium) nucleus, consisting of 1 proton and 1 neutron, emitting an anti-electron plus an electron neutrino and 2 photons. (The anti-electron annihilates a passing electron, producing another high energy photon.) This marriage is called "fusion". With an electron to balance the charge, it yields an atom of "heavy hydrogen".

Two heavy hydrogen nuclei can combine, yielding a Helium 3 nucleus plus another proton plus another photon. Two of those Helium 3 nuclei can combine to form a Helium 4 nucleus plus 2 protons (hydrogen nuclei) and another photon. Altogether it takes 9 fusions to produce a single Helium 4 nucleus, *yielding 15 photons along the way.* Those photons are oscillating electromagnetic fields acting like particles, but are pure energy, with no mass. The mass of the universe—consisting of all the shining stars—370,000 years after the Big Bang (BB), when it became visible, was about 75% hydrogen and 25% helium, with no other elements yet in existence.

Helium atoms can also meet and combine spontaneously with Hydrogen, Deuterium, He 3 or He 4 with or without free neutrons to make heavier isotopes, like boron and beryllium and neon, and more photons. Those heavier atoms can also combine by fusion to make still heavier atoms, like nitrogen and oxygen, and still more photons, and so on. In other words, the mass of the universe keeps decreasing gradually, as the fusion process continues in stars. Each of these fusion reactions releases some energy (exergy) to the environment in the form of a "photon" of electromagnetic radiation with a unique frequency characteristic of that reaction. This is the meta-process that made all the 26 elements with atomic weights up to and including iron. It also makes the stars shine and creates solar radiation (we see it as visible light) covering the whole range of frequencies.

Since the BB the mass of Hydrogen and Helium in the universe has declined by 2% and the mass of the 24 elements between helium and iron has risen to 2% of the total. (The heavier atoms, from cobalt to uranium, were all made in exploding stars called supernovae, long before our sun was formed. The total mass of the atoms heavier than iron is infinitesimal, as a percentage, however important for technology. That 2% of the mass of the universe has combined and recombined and created complexity: scores of simple chemical compounds, tens of thousands—maybe millions—of species of organic molecules and many millions of species of living organisms, on Earth, not to mention super-organisms, like corporations or universities, or the economy. Our planet Earth consists almost entirely of atoms from that 2% fraction. All living organisms and almost everything we humans have produced is made from hydrogen plus those heavier atoms. That mass is pure energy (exergy).

The solar furnace that drives photosynthesis and the hydrological cycle will run out of hydrogen fuel one, or several, billion years in the future (Morris 1980). This will be followed by the "red giant" phase, as the sun starts burning its accumulated helium "ash"—and swallows up the inner planets—followed by the "white dwarf" stage when the helium is also used up creating carbon, oxygen and iron. When fusion gradually slows down to a stop, billions of years from now, the sun will become a "black dwarf", according to current cosmological theory. But for the present, and the foreseeable future, what matters is that there is plenty of useful energy available for foreseeable human purposes, and that will be true for a very long time to come.

From those chemical elements a number of very stable inorganic chemical "building blocks" have self-created, either in interstellar space, or on Earth. They include H_2O, H_2S, HNO_3, CH_4, CO_2, SO_2, SiO_2, PO_4, $NaCL$, KCl, $CaCl_2$ simple amines, etc. It is from these (plus hydrogen) that the nuclide bases—adenine, thymine, cytosine, guanine and uracil—are constructed. From the nuclide bases, in turn, DNA and proteins are constructed.

The primary sources of useful energy (exergy) available to us humans on Earth are carbohydrates from photosynthesis (including fossil fuels), the hydrological cycle (wind, and flowing water), and nuclear heat from radioactive decay in the Earth's core. All of these are elements of "natural capital". The fossil fuels are stores of chemical exergy from photosynthesis that occurred in the distant geological past. This reservoir is gradually being exhausted, although there is still enough left, as some witty journalist has noted, "to fry us all". The same is true of the Earth's geological reservoir of radio-nuclides, and its store of useful chemical combinations, such as metallic sulfides. Minerals and ores are valued because they are anomalous concentrations of useful elements. But the elements, themselves, do not disappear.

It is also evident that both biological and mineral resources are finite, not infinite. Gold, silver, copper and tin are quite scarce in the Earth's crust. But in the 1960s, environmental economists realized that finite resources, like topsoil, forests and fresh water are also essential for the health of the ecosystem, within which the economic system is embedded (Boulding 1966). Others included Howard Odum (Odum 1973), Herman Daly (Daly 1973, 1977), Robert Costanza (Costanza 1980, 1982) and Cutler Cleveland (Cleveland 1984). It follows that the economic system cannot exist in the absence of material (and energy) flows from (and back to) the environment.

An influential distraction came in 1921 from the respected Rumanian economist, Nicolas Georgescu-Roegen (G-R), whose "magnum opus" was a book published by Harvard University Press in 1921, entitled "Entropy and the Economic Process" (Georgescu-Roegen 1921). Georgescu-Roegen's book argued (echoing Soddy (Soddy 1920)) that economic activity can be seen as a linear process in which valuable (low entropy) natural resources are extracted from the Earth, and converted irreversibly into less valuable—if not harmful—high entropy wastes that are eventually dissipated or discarded and returned to the environment.

This entropic process gradually eliminates all physical gradients in gases, or liquids subject to energetic activity of any kind. Hence, all concentrations of mineral resources that were created by geological processes in the past are gradually being converted into to a homogeneous, gradient-free—hence useless—material (ash, GHGs). This process of homogenization is a consequence of the second law of thermodynamics, known as the "entropy law".

Georgescu-Roegen pointed out that recycling can never be absolutely perfect (also true) and therefore that all high quality mineral concentrations (useful ores of copper and other metals) are being irreversibly exhausted, which is also true. He implied that this is happening in a time scale of centuries or even decades, which is not true. He mistakenly thought that solar and wind energy could not substitute for energy from combustion of hydrocarbons.

That was a crucial error. He was far too skeptical about the potential for solar power, wind power and other renewables in the short term. G-R is widely considered by ecologists to be the father of "degrowth", even though his analysis was seriously faultyWhat he did do was to get the economists to pay attention.

G-R pointed out, correctly, that recycling has limits and the "circular economy" (not yet named) is not feasible. He claimed, incorrectly, that there is a "4th Law" applicable separately to matter, even though this is denied by physicists (Ayres 1999). He was also too skeptical about the potential for solar power, wind power and other renewables in the short term. G-R is widely considered by ecologists like to be the father of "degrowth", even though his analysis was seriously faulty. The possibility of imminent hydrocarbon (petroleum) exhaustion was revived and written about ("peak oil") extensively in the late 1990 s (Campbell 1998; Laherrere 2014). But the subject has become less interesting, since the best strategy to oppose climate change is "decarbonization", meaning that use of fossil fuels must end soon to keep the Earth from over-heating.

Geological processes in the magma will continue to recycle sediments in the ocean as long as the molten core of the earth is heated by radioactive decay. Micro-organisms extract phosphorus from the ocean water and incorporate it DNA, and in shells, bones and teeth of marine animals. Phosphorus is concentrated by the food chain. Such recycling processes—and life itself, which quite good at recycling—will continue as long as the sun shines. It is a fact, much bemoaned by environmentalists, that remanufacturing and recycling of the metals and plastics in most finished industrial products is currently impractical and uneconomic. This is because existing industrial processes are still able to extract and use high quality raw materials from the Earth's crust instead of re-use, renovating, remanufacturing or recycling. This will continue as long as obtaining chemical energy (exergy) by combustion of fossil fuels is much too cheap to justify conservation.

Thus the use of energy taxes to reduce the consumption of fossil fuels will have an automatic benefit in terms of recycling scarce metals. We will continue to use mineral ores from mines, despite declining ore quality, as long as cheap fossil fuels are available to smelt them. Electrolytic smelting is already happening. But there will come a time (and a price)—possibly sooner than most politicians believe—when process wastes and discarded devices—especially small appliances and electronic devices—will become the new "ores".

It may happen sooner than you think. There are policy options that could make it happen much sooner.

Even now, the rate of dissipation of some geologically scarce metals (such as gold and platinum) is nearly zero. Most of the gold ever mined now resides in bank vaults, jewelry shops or on Indian women's arms (as dowries). This low dissipation will be true for other scarce metals, such as neodymium or indium or rhodium, if they become sufficiently valuable. What this means is that *Homo Sapiens* needs to apply economic principles (prices), to conserve scarce resources, as Allen Kneese pointed out many years ago (Kneese 1977). But except for phosphorus, *H. Sapiens* is not in immediate danger of "running out" of scarce metals. The case of phosphorus is special, and needs special attention, but not in this book (Fig. 17.3).

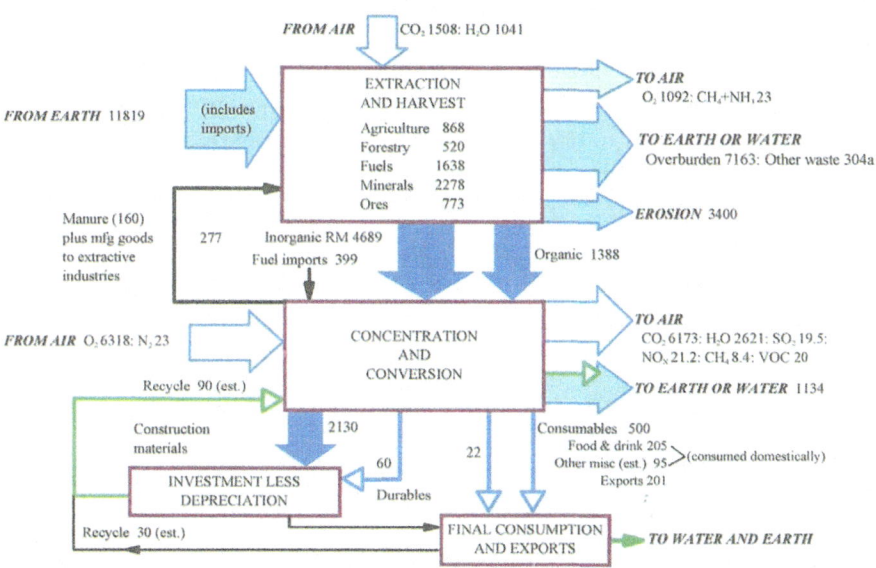

Fig. 17.3 US economic system as a whole from a mass flow perspective (1993 in MMT)—RUA own work

17.3 Pollution as an Inevitable By-Product of Extraction and Industrial Production

Pollution was not a new problem in the 1960s. Allen Kneese quoted in his book from a royal document in the middle ages about the state of the Thames, near the Sea Coal Lane, where the butchers plied their craft and cast the refuse (blood and guts) into the river *"abominable and most filthy stinks proceed"* ... resulting in *"sickness and many other evils"* (Kneese 1977). Pollution, in short. The problem is remembered most wittily, perhaps, in the ditty by Samuel Taylor Coleridge, who visited Cologne in 1798: *"The River Rhine, it is well known, Doth wash the City of Cologne: But, pray, dear God, what power divine will henceforth wash the River Rhine?"*.

As it happens, the River Rhine has been significantly cleaned up since 1798, although there are problems from time to time. (My Chair, at INSEAD, was created by Sandoz Corp.as the result of an industrial accident in which mercury was accidently dumped into the Rhine, motivating the polluter to improve its image.) Luckily there were no deaths.

It has also recently become clearer that economic growth is driven not only by production and trade, but also partly by economic surplus based on the extraction of high quality raw materials (gifts of nature)—especially fossil fuels and phosphates—from the environment and conversion of those raw materials into useful products and services. Thus, human welfare is partially dependent both on the "consumption" of finished products from those raw materials and on the disposal of process wastes, some of which are harmful or toxic. Clearly, an adequate economic theory must reflect this physical reality.

But even in the earliest period of industrialization some process wastes, apart from metabolic wastes, including but not limited to smoke, turned out to be toxic and dangerous. Thus, human welfare is partially dependent both on the "consumption" of finished products from those raw materials and, on the disposal of process wastes, some of which are quite harmful. Clearly, an adequate economic theory must reflect this aspect of physical reality.

An acute methylmercury poisoning tragedy occurred in Minamata, Japan following release of methylmercury into Minamata Bay and its. It was caused by the release of methylmercury in the industrial wastewater from a chemical factory owned by the Chisso Corporation. Emissions continued from 1932 to 1968. A second outbreak of Minamata disease occurred in Niigata Prefecture in 1965. The original Minamata disease and Niigata Minamata disease are considered two of the Four Big Pollution Diseases of Japan. As of March 2001, 2265 victims had been officially recognized as having Minamata disease (1784 of whom had died) and over 10, had received financial compensation from Chisso. By 2004, Chisso had paid US$86 million in compensation, and in the same year was ordered to clean up its contamination. On March 29, 2010, a settlement was reached to compensate as-yet uncertified victims.

Certain chemical processes involving mercury (as a catalyst) have been eliminated. The process for manufacturing vinyl chloride (for PVC) using a mercury compound as a catalyst was one of them. The chemical industry made this change in response to the Minimata cases.

Another undesired consequence of economic progress, as industrialization, was exemplified in a landmark 1962 book "Silent Spring" by biologist **Rachel Carson** (1907–1964). It attacked the widespread use of toxic chlorinated pesticides, notably DDT (Carson 1962). Birds depend a lot on eating insects, but the DDT killed birds by making their eggshells too fragile to hatch (hence the silence in spring). This book was alone among the important environmental best-sellers of that era; it led to the banning of DDT (at least in parts of the Western world) and major shifts later in agricultural practice.

Another milestone was the 1968 article by Garrett Hardin that popularized the term "tragedy of the commons" (Hardin 1968). That article—based on game theory—made the uncomfortable argument that "common property" ("first come, first served") resources tend to be over-used (abused). The problem is that because every potential user has an interest in exploiting it before others do. This is an argument for private, rather than communal, ownership of some natural resources.

Air pollution (smog) became seen as a killer, for the first time, in the 1930 Meuse Valley Fog that killed 60 people (and made thousands sick). The 1952 London Great Smog that lasted nearly a week killed about 12,000 people (based on comparative death rates). The China air pollution event of 2013 covered 1/3 of China in a brown cloud and affected 800,000 people. Nobody knows how many of those people died, but the number must have been significant. These disasters were regarded as "acts of God", nobody's fault.

But those acts of god were getting more frequent and worse. A few heterodox economists at RFF recognized smog events (and other such disasters) as externalities, meaning unintended consequences for "third parties" of economic transactions between buyers and sellers of products or services. Economists in the 1960s began to realize that externalities are not necessarily small and unimportant.

A new environmental threat appeared in the late 1960s. It was the stratospheric ozone depletion of about 4% per year, first observed by NASA scientists and publicized by UK futurist and environmentalist James Lovelock (known for his Gaia hypothesis) that states living organisms interact with their inorganic surroundings on Earth as a self-regulating system that helps maintain the conditions for life on Earth. The ozone (technically O_3) is created in the stratosphere by absorbing solar radiation flux and is broken up by chlorine or bromine atoms, and then released by chemical reactions in the stratosphere. This was important because the ozone in the stratosphere is largely responsible for protecting terrestrial plants and animals from harmful ultraviolet (UV) radiation from the sun. UV is known to cause cancer and several other health problems of humans. A related phenomenon is the "ozone hole" which occurs in Spring over Antarctica and part of the southern hemisphere. It was becoming larger and expanding northward, every year (Fig. 17.4).

The technical details of how this happens do not matter here. The important point is that a few years later, Sherwood Rowland and Mario Molina proposed another ozone depletion mechanism. Their theory was that ozone depletion was due to the increasing concentration of certain fluorocarbons—especially one, known as FC-12—in the atmosphere. This was an industrial bombshell, because FC-12 was mass produced by Dupont, Union Carbide and German companies like BASF and Bayer. It was used primarily as refrigerant in refrigerators and air conditioners, and as "propellant" for spray paints, air fresheners, shaving cream and all kinds of other products.

Industry representatives strongly disputing the Rowland–Molina hypothesis. A National Academy of Sciences (NAS) Committee was created to investigate substitution possibilities. The NAS committee reported in 1976,

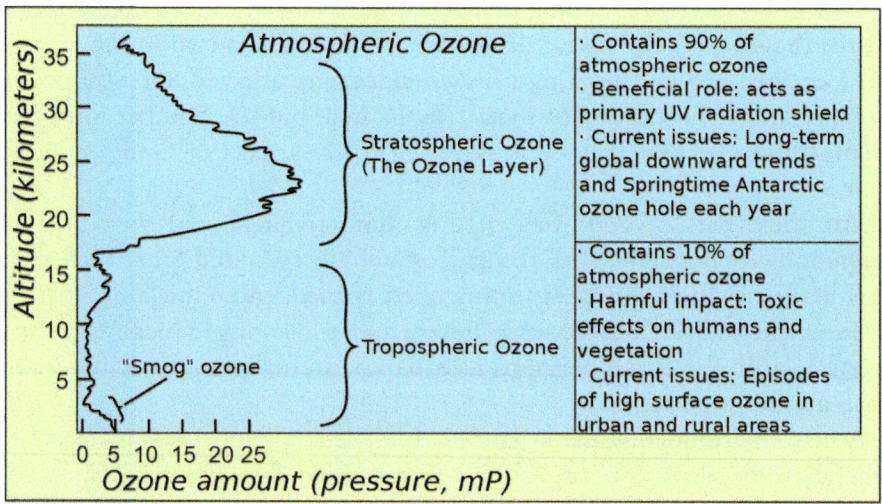

Fig. 17.4 The distribution of atmospheric ozone in partial pressure as a function of altitude. Rastrized and improved by RedAndr—Wikipedia

resulting in the Kyoto Protocol that helped initiate the UN's International Panel on Climate Change (IPCC) and its periodic climate reports. The Montréal Protocol (1987) initiated action. That action effectively reversed the ozone depletion trend. It arguably is the first major success of the environmentalist movement. Rowland and Molina shared the 1995 with Paul Crutzen, who had earlier shown that nitric oxide (NO) and nitrogen dioxide (NO_2) react catalytically with ozone, accelerating its reduction. The 1995 Nobel Prize in Chemistry recognized the three scientists for their work in atmospheric chemistry, particularly concerning the formation and decomposition of ozone.

In summary, the use of fluorocarbons as propellants in spray cans and as refrigerants, has caused an "ozone hole" in the stratosphere. That phenomenon sharply increased the level of dangerous ultra-violet (UV) radiation on the ground, especially in the arctic and Antarctic regions. Fluorocarbons have had to be been sharply restricted for this reason. Oil spills, like the recent one in the Gulf of Mexico, are becoming more dangerous.

The additive, tetra-ethyl lead (TEL) was invented by scientists working for GM back in the 1920s to enabled gasoline engines to stop "knocking" (pre-ignition) by enabling the engine to operate at much higher compression ratios (and increased both power output and fuel efficiency). TEL is an organo-lead compound with the formula $Pb(C_2H_5)_4$. It is a fuel additive, first being mixed with gasoline. It was patented in the 1920s and marketed as an octane rating booster that allowed engine compression to be raised substantially. This in turn increased vehicle performance and fuel economy.

Concerns were later raised over the toxic effects of lead, especially on children. Lead and lead oxides also poison catalytic converters and are a major cause of spark plug fouling. From the 1970s many countries began phasing out and eventually banning TEL in automotive fuel. In 2011, a study backed by the United Nations estimated that the removal of TEL had resulted in $2.4 trillion in annual benefits, and 1.2 million fewer premature deaths. As of 2021 sales of automobiles capable of using leaded gasoline were banned in every country around the world, according to the UN Environment programme (UNEP) (Fig. 17.5).

Some externalities, such as COVID 19 involve very serious health damages to millions of people. Others cause degradation of the natural environment (Kneese 1977). Rachel Carson's "Silent Spring" told the story of how pesticides used by farmers to kill destructive insects and increase food output, also killed off the birds that ate the insect eggs and grubs (by making their egg-shells too thin to survive).

Fig. 17.5 No explanation needed—Photo credit: Godfrey Kneller; Wikimedia Commons

17.4 Energy Economics: The Price of Energy

Economics is often succinctly defined as being concerned with the efficient allocation of resources. Energy is a resource. So-called second law energy efficiency is a measure of the potential for efficiency improvement as a means of energy conservation one illustration was a demonstration of the huge inefficiencies involved in automobile transport. The efficiency of automobiles was estimated to be around 10% (at the time) but only around 1% in terms of transporting passengers, when considering that the goal of personal transportation is move people (Ayres 1975, 1976, 1977). A greater recognition of this fact in resource economics might have led societies to be less enthusiastically embracing oil as a driver of economic growth, something that has been countered only recently.

In the same vein, we considered the efficiency of the energy and material use in the production of semiconductor devices (Williams 2003). We showed that the energy inefficiency of the "chip" manufacturing process, at the time, was great enough to endanger the digital transition to a "greener" economy, rather than facilitate it. The relevance of this work extends to data centres and blockchains. Laitner recently calculated that 86% of the primary energy used in the United States can be regarded as inefficiency lossest and avoidable (Laitner 2013). See also (Ayres, 2003, 2004, 2005, 2009).

This work found that exergy efficiency is really the driver of long-term US economic growth. Moreover, exergy efficiency improvements explained the part of growth that previously was assigned to black-box "technological progress" The meaning of this result is that without accounting for exergy/energy one obtains a grossly incomplete picture of economic production and growth.

The global environment is, to a large extent, composed of four interacting global "nutrient cycles": carbon–oxygen, nitrogen, sulfur and phosphorus. See Appendix A. All of them are maintained by continuous dissipation of exergy from external sources. Being physically active, they are far from general thermodynamic equilibrium (where nothing changes). All of them evolved naturally, although the phosphorus cycle operates—as far as we know—only on geological time scales. Human industrial activity is not only capable of disrupting those cycles, but is doing so on an increasing scale. Geological scarcity is becoming a factor in the case of phosphorus.

17.5 The Avalanche Model

In this section, we (RUA and KM) offer a generic "avalanche theory" of that is applicable to a wide range of historical examples that differ from business cycles in being non-financial. The avalanche model is driven by the difference between short-term and long-term consequences of decisions. The avalanche model can be regarded as a generalization of the static Walras-Marshall-Solow paradigm of economic growth. That paradigm postulates growth-in-equilibrium, driven by rational actions of self-interested agents of the sub-species *Homo economicus*. (The three core assumptions, self-interest, rationality and equilibrium, are known as "Solow's Trinity" or just ST). The paradigm also postulates what Kenneth Boulding has called a "cowboy economy", i.e. an economy with no resource limits to growth (Boulding 1966).

Our generalization of the ST paradigm eliminates several other unnecessary assumptions in it. In an earlier book we introduced a modified "*Homo economicus+*" whose decision rule is simply myopic: "avoid avoidable loss" (AAL). In this rule gains and losses are subjective for each agent, not objectively measurable (Ayres 2006) p. 124 *et seq*. Application of the AAL rule means that every voluntary exchange transaction leaves both parties "better off" in their own (subjective) terms.

The AAL rule does not assume, as the ST paradigm does, that each party seeks to maximize its utility in monetary terms—like counting poker chips. Maximization in a contest means "I win, you lose" or "winner takes all". That condition makes cooperation or compromise between the players impossible. However, in contrast to the ST model, where everything is measured in terms of money, the avalanche model allows each agent to have different desires and motives.

It also does not presuppose that the economic system is in equilibrium. We have shown that the AAL rule guarantees that, in the absence of externalities and losses resulting from "acts of God" (accidents, natural disasters) *societal wealth will increase automatically as a consequence of voluntary exchange transactions*. In other words, if an exchange occurs it must have been profitable for both traders. This is a modern restatement of the Smith-Ricardo explanation of the wealth of nations due to trade. It qualitatively explains the "boom" part of "boom-bust".

N.B. our avalanche paradigm—hereafter we call it the ST + paradigm—is valid far away from economic equilibrium, as conventionally defined in terms of the intersection of static supply and demand curves. Thence it is essentially dynamic, not static. The static Solow paradigm derives an "equation of motion" by postulating a "production function" of time $F\{K(t), L(t)\}$ with a conventionally defined mathematical form that can be mathematically maximized (by equating the time derivative to zero). This procedure describes an economy with continuously growing maximum output. But it does not explain the down-turns in real economic behavior.

Our dis-equilibrium theory (S+) eliminates that assumption. We postulate, instead, a function of time $Z(t)$, that can be interpreted, roughly, as subjective wealth for an individual or "societal wealth" for a country. The $Z(t)$ function for a 'player' does not necessarily increase monotonically over time. This is because the AAL rule (being myopic) allows for exchange transactions that make both parties feel better off in the short term, but that neglect external effects, such as long-term stress buildups that result in periodic losses at longer intervals (such as the increasing weight of the snow accumulating on the slope).

We suggest that the $Z(t)$ functions for a nation or another large aggregate, may be inferred quantitatively from observed behavior (Ayres 2006). Conflicts between nations may be represented by changes in national Z functions. It is conceivable that both nations can "win", in such a conflict, because national wealth means different things to each of them. On the other hand, both parties can also lose—an outcome seen too often in the past.

Hence the generic explanation of downturns in wealth (busts) is that decisions (trades) that leave both parties of every transaction momentarily better off are normal. Encounters in the real world are not accidental. They normally take place in a structured environment—a "market". Markets existing in the real world are not creations of the Gods. They are complex evolutionary entities, that involve interactions with clients (the traders) and "guardians", who enforce the rules and protect the traders. So, interactions between the clients and the structure are normal. Accompanied by externalities (third party effects) that can—and do—create problems for the whole society. Some of these externalities are unavoidable. For example, nearly all economic transactions in the real world are associated directly or indirectly with the extraction of natural resources from the environment, their processing and conversion into material goods, final consumption and ultimate disposal as wastes.

One externality is the fact that extraction process is inevitably accompanied by some degree of exhaustion of those non-renewable natural resources. Georgescu-Roegen and Herman Daly saw that as a consequence of the entropy law (Georgescu-Roegen 1971; Daly 1973, 1980, 1985). On the other hand, it appears that, up to now, technological progress in exploration, extraction and processing of mineral ores have more than compensated for the entropic reduction in ore grades, at least for industrial metals like copper and nickel, resulting in long-term declines in commodity prices, rather than the increases one would expect if scarcity were perceived in the market-place a near-term problem (Barnett 1963; Potter 1968; Smith 1979; Simpson 2005).

The raw materials extracted from the environment are transformed into other commodities and products. They are eventually returned to the environment, in different forms, but the mass-energy never disappears. This is a consequence of one of the most fundamental laws of nature, known as the first law of thermodynamics, viz. conservation of mass-energy. It follows that all material extraction, conversion (and consumption) processes in the economic system generate wastes and pollutants (Ayres and Kneese 1969).

These pollutants may harm people directly or indirectly (by affecting other organisms) The point is that the damages affect people who were not parties to the original exchange transactions (mining, processing, etc.) hence they are externalities by definition In fact, the existence of such externalities is a direct consequence of the laws of thermodynamics. Moreover, virtually all economic actions—from haircuts to construction are driven by material changes and energy flows. While many social services, like education and entertainment, are not directly accompanied by the processing or destruction of material goods, physical changes are nevertheless taking place in the background. So, we can say that economic "busts" typically result from an accumulation of externality-based stresses triggered by the preceding "boom", just as the avalanche results from the buildup of snow on a mountain slope.

As noted previously, the AAL rule leaves both parties of any transaction "better off" in subjective terms (otherwise the exchange would not take place) The magnitude of that subjective gain can be interpreted as the "driving force" of the transaction. Since the transaction is uni-directional (hence irreversible) it also reflects the irreversible increase of entropy, which is equivalent to the second law of thermodynamics.

This "driving force" can be monetized in many cases, in terms of profits. Moreover, the larger the economic gain, whether monetized or not, the greater the "strength" of the transaction, and the greater the physical flows indirectly associated with it. The strength of such flows can also be interpreted as measures of the economic transactional gains. They can also be interpreted as measures of the associated entropy increase or exergy dissipation.

As noted, externalities are third party effects resulting indirectly from economic transactions. They do not occur in a "perfect" classical market economy consisting of binary transactions involving abstract goods and services without physical causes or consequences. Strangely, the possibility of market imperfections resulting in third-party consequences did not occur to economic theorists, at all, until the twentieth century, in a book on welfare economics (Pigou 1920). In that book, the only examples given were relatively minor deviations from the perfect market operation, e.g. pollination services by bees from a neighboring bee-keeper, or smoke damage from a neighboring fire. It was assumed that compensation for any damage could always be negotiated between the parties (Coase 1960).

The possibility of large-scale environmental or societal harm resulting from large numbers of micro-economic transactions, accompanied by seemingly small externalities, did not appear until forty years after Pigou's book. The most dramatic—and effective—example was probably Rachel Carson's book "Silent Spring", about the adverse environmental consequences (to birds) of large-scale agricultural use of DDT (Carson 1962). DDT is now banned in many countries because of its effects on the egg-shells of insectivorous birds that feed on insects that ingest pesticides from crop-plants sprayed with DDT. Other examples of macro-stress buildup due to indirect micro-transactions include soil erosion due to monoculture, or pollution of the urban water supply.

Economic stress can also have non-physical causes. It can be due to growing private debt due to excessive financial leverage driving the "boom" phase of the business- cycle. It could occur to excessively loose, or excessively "tight" monetary policy. Or the stress might result from increasing socio-economic inequality associated with mergers, takeovers and "financial engineering" (Stiglitz 2012).

We suggest that the common feature in stress build-up is a series of short-term transactions by individuals or companies that neglect longer-term consequences. This happens because short-term decisions in business or commerce are normally based on short-term gains subject to the "Avoid Avoidable Loss" (AAL) rule. By contrast, the Solow paradigm postulates that self-interested economic agents carry out Arrow-Debreu type utility maximization calculations, despite the fact that such calculations are impossible, in practice, due to computational limits and lack of data about the future (Simon 1955, 1959).

The difference between short and long-term utility maximization causes an increasing deviation from the optimal long-term survival (wealth-increasing) strategy as time passes. This deviation from the optimal path—or, in some cases, from the survival path—frequently leads to a build-up of some form of financial stress, such as unpaid environmental damage-prevention costs, or inadequate insurance or other protection costs, noted above. The greater the stress, the higher the probability and/or magnitude of a crash and the greater the wealth destruction when the crash—the avalanche—finally occurs.

But, first things first: how should coupling (and de-coupling) be measured? The simplest procedure is to lump very heterogeneous materials into a single category (resources), which are then measured only in mass terms e.g. (Hagedorn 1992; Adriaanse 1997; Fischer-Kowalski 2011).

But, while large scale mass-flows like floods or erosion often cause environmental harm, the potential for environmental harm, in principle, is by no means proportional to mass. What we seek, really, is a measure of the potential for reducing value or causing harm, which might be termed (for lack of a better word) "eco-toxicity". In an ideal University-of-Chicago world of efficient markets where all transactions are binary and there are no third-, party effects (externalities), the aggregate wealth changes from exchange transactions will be uni-directional (up) and irreversible (Ayres and Martinás 2006). In other words, in such a world every enterprise gets richer automatically, just by making things, providing services and trading them. The rate of enterprise wealth increase can be accelerated, of course, by saving, specialization and capital investment. Schumpeterian innovation (creative destruction) amplifies the growth rate.

In the real world there are negative third-party consequences of all, or nearly all, kinds of transactions, apart from unavoidable losses from "acts of God" or natural disasters. The latter—such as covid-19—can (and do) occur at random times. Negative outcomes can also be consequences of long-term macro-economic mechanisms that are unexpected or invisible to agents making short-term micro-economic decisions. Evidently the mechanisms by which unavoidable losses, such as financial "crashes" can occur, also become crucial aspects of a realistic theory of economic growth.

The "short term" in this context needs clarification. For us it is the time-period during which external factors affecting the decision can be assumed to be fixing and unchanging. This time may be a little as a few minutes or hours in the case of decisions regarding the buying or selling of goods that cannot be stored (notably electricity) or perishable consumables (e.g. food). It may be months or years where the transaction involves education, new product testing, agriculture, or real-estate development.

Borrowing money for consumption purposes using credit cards, or taking on a mortgage to buy a house, are simple examples of short-term behavior that can result in long-term losses for consumers. However, as already mentioned, we do not think that the AAL rule is applicable to ordinary people in their every-day activities. Short term credit-enables individual consumers, households, firms, communities and nations to consume goods by spending money not yet earned. This is harmless, even beneficial, if the extra spending induces consumption or investment resulting in economic growth. But it is not harmless if the extra spending causes monetary inflation or unpayable debt.

When an individual's credit-card spending exceeds her income for a while, the outcome may be socially beneficial: a term of higher education may be financed, or a viable new business may get started. Borrowing may finance a period of recovery from an illness. A resulting debt default may be painful for one individual, or a business, but it normally does not affect many others. And, temporary over-drafts need not be harmful to the economy as a whole—provided they are limited in magnitude and scope. Credit-card issuers allow for some defaults. Small defaults are not "infectious".

But borrowing can be addictive, both for individuals and for countries; and—like addiction to alcohol or opiates—it can also be lethal. When aggregate expenditure exceeds aggregate profits or revenues for an extended period, the ripple effects grow larger and extend further. At some point, the ripple may become 'auto-catalytic' where one bad business decision results in failures of multiple suppliers, or lenders or clients. Thus a local bank failure or corporate failure can trigger a series of other failures (domino effect) as when a bush fire creates a local "tornado" that ignites fires in neighboring areas or where an avalanche triggers other avalanches.

One of the most dangerous (and surprisingly frequent) non-physical examples is a "run on the bank". This happens when too many of the depositors in a bank or investment fund try to get their money out, all at once. That is often caused by a story—true or false does not matter—that the bank, or fund, is in trouble. This kind of bank failure can trigger others because the banks all borrow and lend to each other. The collapse can get out of control unless there is a central bank, or a government "lender of last resort", to step in and provide a believable guarantee to the depositors. This specific scenario has happened many times in economic history e.g. (Graeber 2011).

Arguably, one of the principal risks for a modern nation is excessive private debt, especially where collateral for loans is based on assets created by borrowing, such as "margin debt" (Keen 2017). Again, if the debt is localized and not too great, no further damage may result. But if the debt of some large industrial or financial enterprise has been collateralized by other financial assets purchased with borrowed money, the consequences of a default may be magnified further, depending on the degree of "leverage" employed. This also has happened repeatedly in the past.

As in the case of snow buildup on the mountain slope, when the overall debt level is low, the risk to the whole financial system arising from a single default is not serious. In fact, debt is an essential financial tool for financing investment and economic growth. The cost of increasing debt, when the debt is low, can be overcome by income growth. But as overall debt grows, the growth rate tends to slow down as the costs of servicing that debt rises. The end result is a recession.

In the case of nations, the cost of debt service rises, not only when the absolute debt (per capita) increases but when the interest rate on it, controlled by the central bank, rises due to worries about the inflationary potential of the debt. This is a "double whammy" for the economy. If a significant part of the national debt is owed in foreign currencies—as is true for many developing countries—the situation is even worse: it is a "triple whammy." Then that sovereign debt can rapidly become literally unpayable (as is the case now for Greece, Argentina, Venezuela, and Zimbabwe). When that happens, the international lenders are also in trouble. When (if) the lenders-of –last-resort stop lending, the world economy collapses (Keen 2017).

17.6 The Sources of Value

Philip Mirowski identifies three distinct groups (1) Those who associated energy with value (2) Those who tried to quantize the theory and apply it and (3) Nicolas Georgescu-Roegen (Mirowski 1988). In the first category he places Patrick Geddes, George Helm, Wilhelm Ostwald, Sergei Podolinski, and Ernest Solvay. Sergei Andreević Podolinsky (1850, 1891) was a Ukrainian socialist, physician, and an early pioneer of ecological economics. He set out to reconcile socialist thought with the second law of thermodynamics by synthesising the approaches of Karl Marx, Charles Darwin and Sadi Carnot.

In his essay "*Socialism and the Unity of Physical Forces*" (1880), Podolinsky theorized a labor theory of value based on embodied energy. He was the first to introduce the concept of energy return on energy input EROEI, now a commonplace efficiency measure. (Of course, the Marxists didn't like it.)

Alfred Lotka, the father of mathematical biology, saw energy as the "fundamental underlying principle of economics" (Lotka 1922). **Frederick Taylor**, known as the founder of scientific management, tried to determine the parameters of a "full day's work". Perhaps the most persistent of them was **Frederick Soddy**, who "*wanted to obtain a physical conception of wealth that would obey the physical laws of conservation*". Soddy had a simple energy theory of value He argued that economists often confuse monetary (financial) capital with real physical capital and that maximizing short term exchange value is not the same as maximizing long-term value. He showed that monetary divergences violated physical principles (Soddy 1933).

More recently, the ecologists Howard and Elizabeth Odum tried to popularize and energy theory of value, triggered by the Petroleum Crisis of the 1970s (Odum 1973, 1976). They used energy flows to analyze the combined systems of human industry and nature. Odum is credited for emphasizing the fact that every energy flow in the economy is matched by a money flow in the reverse direction and every money flow is matched by an energy flow. (I thought I had discovered that phenomenon). Howard Odum is well known for his inventive terminology (for red that) instance "emergy")???.

Mirowski's third group consists of one man, **Nicolas Georgescu-Roegen**, who saw the relationship between scarcity, depletion and entropy and became famous for it (Georgescu-Roegen 1971). Mirowski credits G-R with four main points, one of which is scientifically erroneous and the others are irrelevant today. G-R claimed a "fourth Law" of Thermodynamics, also scientifically incorrect. For a negative review see (Ayres 1997).

Before moving on, it should be pointed out that the crucial distinction between available energy (exergy) and unavailable energy (anergy) was only realized in the 1970s. Before that, Myron Tribus, et al.

We conclude with an obscure unpublished paper by Edwin T. Jaynes, a pioneer of information theory and the man most responsible for introducing time, as a variable, in Gibbs' static formalism of thermodynamics. The following paragraphs are from "The Economic—Thermodynamic Analogy" (Jaynes 1991).

On this analogy, the failure of Keynesian and Monetarist mechanisms to account for recent economic behavior would be attributed, at least in part, to their failure to recognize the entropy factors that must ultimately control economic change and equilibrium, just as they do in thermodynamics.

That is, it may be that a macroeconomic system does not move in response to (or at least not solely in response to) the "forces" that are supposed to exist in current theories; it may simply move in the direction of increasing entropy as constrained by the conservation laws imposed by Nature and Government just as a thermodynamic system makes its approach to equilibrium in the direction of increasing entropy as constrained by the conservation of mass, energy, etc.

In physics, the thermodynamic entropy of a macro-state (denoted by specifying pressure, volume, energy, etc.) is essentially the logarithm of the number of microstates (quantum states) consistent with it; i.e., the number of ways the macro-state can be realized.

Likewise, the "economic entropy" S to which we refer is a function

$$S(X; Y; Z) = \log W(X; Y; Z)$$

of whatever macroeconomic variables (X; Y; Z) our theory recognizes. Here W is the multiplicity factor of the macroeconomic state (number of different microeconomic ways in which it can be realized). In a probabilistic model of the economy, we ought to include in the probability of any macroeconomic state an entropy factor (exp(S)) to take this multiplicity into account. This is one of the factors, possibly the only variable factor, in the prior probability of that state. If we failed to do this in statistical mechanics—particularly in chemical thermodynamics—we would get grossly, qualitatively wrong predictions. The same may be true in macroeconomics.

Of course, merely to conjecture this does not prove that entropy is the crucial missing factor; it may be that some other unrecognized factor is even more important. But entropy is at least a promising candidate, because it is clearly relevant, and it is not now being taken into account (we might add that "entropy" is completely non-ideological, having nothing to do with any social philosophy; and so the idea ought to be equally acceptable to all).

The physical analogy can help us much more than this. At what velocity does the economic system drift up the entropy hill? How widely will it fluctuate about the deterministic path? The answers were first seen intuitively in early work of Einstein, Fokker–Planck, and Onsager. Today they are all subsumed in the general formalism of Predictive Statistical Mechanics (Jaynes 1980, 1985), in which the equilibrium maximum entropy variational principle of Gibbs is generalized to time-varying phenomena.

What that theory suggests is the following: Even though a neighboring macroeconomic state of higher entropy is available, the system does not necessarily move to it. A pile of sand does not necessarily level itself unless there is an earthquake to shake it up a little. The economic system might just stagnate where it is, unless it is shaken up by what an Englishman might call a "dither" of some sort.

Of course, stagnation is not necessarily bad in itself; stagnation at a point where everybody is happy might even be perceived as the goal of economics. But in the past, stagnation seems to have occurred at points where almost everybody was unhappy, and wanted a change (as political slogans of the genre: "Let's get the country moving again!" testify).

On this analogy, the failure of Keynesian and Monetarist mechanisms to account for recent economic behavior would be attributed, at least in part, to their failure to recognize the entropy factors that must ultimately control economic change and equilibrium, just as they do in thermodynamics.

That is, it may be that a macroeconomic system does not move in response to (or at least not solely in response to) the "forces" that are supposed to exist in current theories; it may simply move in the direction of increasing entropy as constrained by the conservation laws imposed by Nature and Government, just as a thermodynamic system makes its approach to equilibrium in the direction of increasing entropy as constrained by the conservation of mass, energy, etc. (Jaynes 1991).

17.7 The Circular Economy?

Sustainable development has its roots in ideas developed in Europe during the seventeenth and eighteenth centuries about sustainable forest management, in response to the depletion of timber resources. In his essay "Sylva" (1662), John Evelyn argued, "Sowing and planting of trees had to be regarded as a national duty of every landowner, in order to stop the destructive overexploitation of natural resources."

In 1713 Hans Carl von Carlowitz, working for the Elector Frederick Augustus I of Saxony published Sylvicultura economics, a 400-page work on forestry. Building upon the ideas of Evelyn and French minister Jean-Baptiste Colbert, von Carlowitz was the first to develop the concept of forest management for "sustained yield". His work influenced others, including Alexander von Humboldt and Georg Ludwig Hartig, eventually leading to the development of the science of forestry. This, in turn, influenced people like Gifford Pinchot, the first head of the US Forest Service, whose approach to forest management focused on wise use of resources, developed further in the 1960s by Resources for the Future, Inc. (RFF).

The World Wildlife Fund (WWF) was founded on April 29, 1961 by British biologists Julian Huxley, Peter Markham Scott, Guy Mountfort and

Edward Max Nicholson. WWF was the acronym for world wildlife fund when the organization was founded. In 1986, it was renamed the World Wide Fund for Nature. Now simply WWF. This private foundation, supported by 5 million members, aims to protect and nature in general. Currently it is active in 100 countries offering 12,000 nature protection programs. Financially, it had a budget of €447 million in 2008, 56% of which was provided by individual members, and the rest by governments, endowments, and commercial activities. Its objective is to: *"Stop environmental degradation in the world and build a future where human beings can live in harmony with nature: preserving the biodiversity of the globe, ensuring the sustainable use of renewable natural resources; encouraging measures to reduce pollution and overconsumption"*. Today there are quite a few other voluntary non-profit organizations devoted to environmental causes, ranging from activist groups like Greenpeace, to Natural Resource Defense Council (NRDC) and the Sierra Club.

In the 1960s, much of the environmental literature available (for example, authors such as Paul Ehrlich and the Paddock Brothers) projected an apocalyptic future, whereas the message of The Survival Equation was one of hope. Its view was that while it is certainly true that forces and pressures to destroy the planet's life support systems do exist, so does the knowledge to reorient the behavior of economies and prevent this from happening. The course and the book itself, had a considerable influence on the field of resource management and the environment. In fact, "The Earth in Balance: Ecology and the Human Spirit", written by a student of the course, Al Gore, pays extensive homage to this course.

In 1983, Ashok Khosla, one of the early champions of WWF and later a director of the UN's environment program (UNEP) initiated another approach to conservation. He created Development Alternatives (DA), made possible by a $100,000 project grant from UNEP. Ashok's idea was to create an organization that would make good businesses, providing employment, by delivering environmentally sound development. Recognizing that 70% of the people of India live in villages, he felt that the bulk of the actions of industry and civil society must be aimed at their needs. As a result, it combined the objectives of a civil society organization with the profit-orientation (and management discipline) of a private sector business, even though DA itself is a not-for-profit entity. This created a niche in the Indian economy for a whole new breed of organization, which can meet social objectives in a scalable and sustainable manner.

Such organizations are now known as the Social Enterprises. The technologies underlying those enterprises need to be more human in scale, less wasteful in resources, and directly responsive to the basic needs of people. In a developing country, such as India, where economic and social disparities in society are large, the poor may overutilize and destroy renewable resources out of the exigencies of immediate survival and need. On the other hand, the rich tend to overutilize and destroy other kinds of resources, especially non-renewable resources, often out of greed. Thus, only by increasing social equity, and eradicating poverty, can humankind make an impact on environmental conservation and reduce the threats to the resource base.

Another sustainability milestone was "Limits to Growth" by the MIT group, inspired by Jay Forrester, for the Club of Rome (Meadows 1972). Describing the desirable "state of global equilibrium", the authors wrote: "*We are searching for a model output that represents a world system that is sustainable without sudden and uncontrolled collapse and capable of satisfying the basic material requirements of all of its people.*" It was a best-seller, from which nobody received any royalties. Five million copies of "Limits" were sold in 15 languages.

Following the Club of Rome report, the MIT group prepared ten days of hearings on "Growth and Its Implication for the Future" for the US Congress. Those were the first hearings ever held on sustainable development as such. William Flynn Martin, David Dodson Gray, and Elizabeth Gray prepared the hearings under the Chairmanship of Congressman John Dingell.

The publication of "Limits to Growth" sparked a fierce global debate among neoclassical economists (William Nordhaus, Robert Solow, and Joseph Stiglitz) and ecologists like C.S. Holling, Howard Odum, Robert Costanza and students of Nicolas Georgescu-Roegen. The controversy led to no changes in government policy. The same can be said of the two subsequent Reports to the Club of Rome, in 1974 and 1976, which were also studiously ignored by the economics profession.

The year 1972 also saw the publication of another influential book, "A Blueprint for Survival". It started as a special edition of "The Ecologist" (magazine) in January 1972 and later in book form that sold over 750,000 copies (Goldsmith 1972). The Blueprint's influence was due to having been signed by over thirty of the leading natural scientists of the day, including Sir Julian Huxley, Sir Frank Fraser Darling, Sir Peter Medawar, E. J. Mishan and Sir Peter Scott. But it was written by Edward Goldsmith and Robert Allen (with contributions from John Davoll and Sam Lawrence of the Conservation Society, and Michael Allaby). The signatories argued for a radically restructured society as the only way to prevent "*the breakdown of society and the irreversible disruption of the life-support systems on this planet*". The Blueprint recommended small, decentralized and largely de-industrialized communities, modelled on idealized tribal societies. It provided no plausible policy recommendation for achieving such an outcome.

The disconnect between excessive private use of common property resources (like forests, fisheries or grazing land) and harm to the public welfare, was generalized in Kenneth Arrow's "impossibility theorem" and work on "social cost" and "public choice" in the 1950s and 60s (Arrow 1951; Scitovsky 1954; Coase 1960; Davis and Whinston 1962; Buchanan and Tullock 1962). An underlying theme of several of those papers was that negative incentives resulting from competition and congestion are increasingly dominant in high density urban society as compared to the importance of cooperation among neighbors in a low-density "Jeffersonian" society advocated by the signatories of "Blueprint for Survival" mentioned earlier. Coase and Scitovsky were especially relaxed about pollution problems like "smoke nuisance", for instance, on the grounds that such problems are rare to begin with or (Coase) they can be resolved easily by means of government regulation or tort law (civil lawsuits).

The culmination of this publishing activity was another ambitious Report, called "Global 2000 Report to the President". This one was initiated by U.S. President Jimmy Carter in 1977, and supervised by his Council on Environmental Quality under James Gustave Speth (Speth 1980). It was an attempt to bring together under one umbrella (so to speak) all of the trends regarding resource needs and resource availability that might confront a future President in the year 2000.

The libertarian-leaning anti-doomsters attacked the Global 2000 report, led by Julian Simon, of the Cato Institute and supported by Herman Kahn of the Hudson Institute. Both of them were strong believers in the nuclear dream (cheap nuclear power) Appendix D. Both argued that there would never be any shortages of anything, because human ingenuity would always come to the rescue as "long as the sun shines" (Simon 1977, 1981, 1984). Simon and Kahn have been called "Cornucopians' (by the "Doomsters") for obvious reasons. But the nuclear dream has faded—if not died—thanks to Chernobyl and Fukushima, since those days.

However, while the fear of unlimited exponential growth is no longer justified, the next question is more technical: can Earth support that (peak) level of population sustainably, without irreversible, and possibly lethal, environmental consequences for our species? Resource exhaustion, rising sea levels, reduced bio-diversity and new diseases resulting from climate change are among the threats. We suggest that the possibility of "new diseases" deserves more attention than it has received.

It has been suggested plausibly that the black plague, that killed up to 60% of the population in Europe in the fourteenth century was triggered by climate changes in Africa resulting from a very large volcanic explosion in the seventh century (Keys 1999). David Keys has made a very strong case that the arrival of the plague can be traced back to a series of migrations and other events beginning with a massive volcanic eruption in Indonesia—of which surprisingly little is known—that actually occurred 800 years earlier, in or about the year 535 CE.

The first consequence of that huge volcanic explosion was a stratospheric cloud causing darkness and cold that lasted for several years. David Keys goes on to argue that the following century was truly the "dark ages" of which we know so little. Occurring, as it did, during the last years of the (western) Roman Empire, when the central government in Rome was falling apart, it is not altogether surprising that there was nobody like Pliny the Elder (who documented the eruption of Vesuvius in the year 79 CE) to tell the tale. According to Keys, the climate changes resulting from the event in 535 CE may suffice to explain the gradual migration of the virus (actually its carriers) out of Africa, in stages. The climatic consequences of the eruption may have triggered regional famines, and triggered ecological changes in Africa that led to a series of terrible epidemics. The Black Plague (1348–50 CE) arrived in Europe, carried by fleas and rats, on ships from Africa, by way of Constantinople. The Hundred Years War (based to the English claim to the French throne began the same year.

Equally ominous are the social pathologies like radical Muslim Jihadism, resulting indirectly from over-crowding and resource scarcity. Turkish dams blocking the headwaters of the Tigris and Euphrates resulted in a permanent reduction in the level of ground water in central Syria and Iraq. That led to the migration, in a few years, of several million people from unsustainable rural agricultural communities into the cities, where there were no jobs or housing, or health services, for them. Al Qaeda and ISIS were predictable consequences. The comparable radical Islamic movements in Uganda, South Sudan, Egypt, Ethiopia and the Horn of Africa can all be similarly traced, at least partly, to diversions of the head-waters of the Nile River and its tributaries and the gradual desertification of the Sahel. Again, climate change is partly responsible for the radicalization of religion, compounded by short-sighted political decisions.

Can the wealthy democratic countries of the world close their borders by technological or any other means if (when) the numbers of desperate refugees from Africa, south Asia or Central America multiply again by a factor of ten? Would closed borders suffice to save the West, still less save the planet? Vladimir Putin is betting on autocracy. This question is still unanswered.

"Neo-Malthusianism" is a branch of ecological economics, based on the premise that planet Earth is overpopulated. Of course, it is a finite system and its natural resources are limited. The Earth system can only rely on its internal dynamics, plus exergy from solar radiation to ensure its survival. Therefore, for internal dynamics to ensure the sustainability of the system, they must be based on the consumption and regeneration of resources between the emission and absorption of pollution. These equilibrium points define the "carrier capacity" of the Earth or the maximum pressures that the planet can withstand while ensuring its sustainability.

In the public debate about the limited nature of available resources, Malthusianism concerns about scarcity are contradicted by pro-nuclear Cornucopianism, especially promoted by Ayn Rand (Rand 1957, 1967; Simon 1977, 1980, 1981). Both the expression 'neo-Malthusians' and that of 'Cornucopians' are negative and are mainly used by their detractors to discredit opponents. The majority of Neo-Malthusian authors subscribe rather to a "green" environmentalist perspective and Cornucopian authors to the laissez faire—or libertarian—perspective (Chap. 17).

"Planetary boundaries" is a concept involving Earth system processes for which clear limits have been or can be defined. The concept was proposed in 2009 by a group of Earth system and environmental scientists, led by Johan Rockström from the Stockholm Resilience Centre and Will Steffen from the Australian National University. The scheme was to delineate the "safe operating space" for sustainable development in the form of guidelines for governments, civil organizations and the private sector.

The boundaries are not absolute; however, in their words "*transgressing one or more planetary boundaries may be deleterious or even catastrophic due to the risk of crossing thresholds that will trigger non-linear, abrupt environmental change within continental-scale to planetary-scale systems.*" The Earth system process boundaries mark the safe zone for the planet to the extent that they are not crossed. As of 2009, two boundaries had already been crossed. By 2020 two more had been crossed or were about to be crossed, while others are in imminent danger of being crossed (Fig. 17.6).

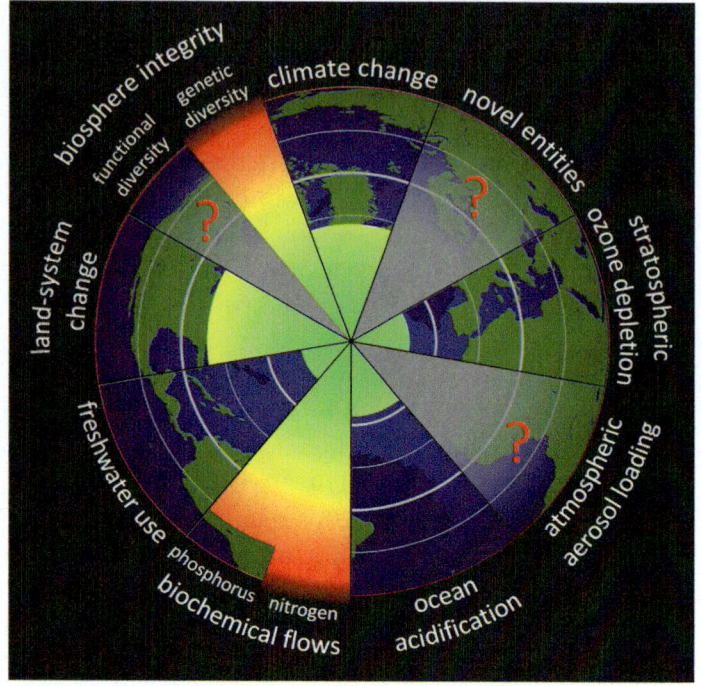

Fig. 17.6 A visualization of planetary boundaries—Wikipedia

Appendix A: Bio-Geochemical Cycles*

It is convenient for purposes of exposition to deal with the nutrient cycles in functional terms, as illustrated by Fig. A.1. There are two kinds of cycles, briefly characterized as "short" (biological) and "long" (geological) (Schlesinger 1991). The carbon-oxygen cycle is a combination of the two types.

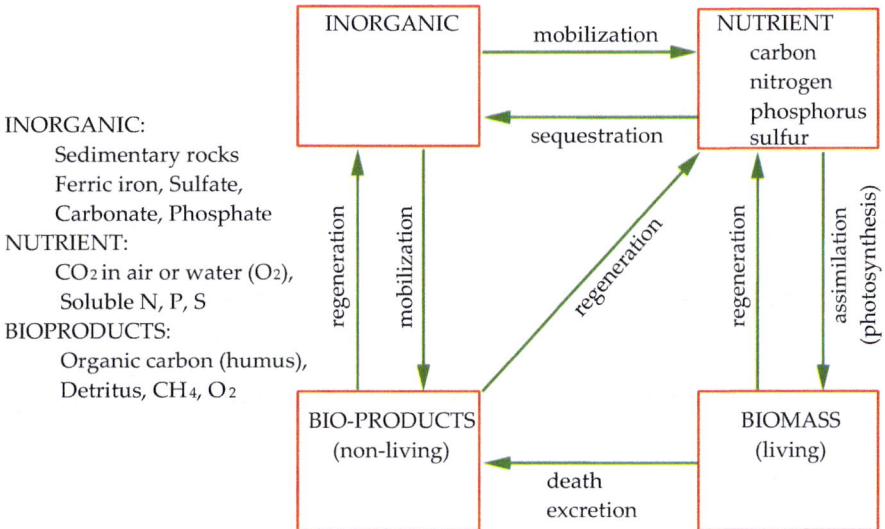

Fig. A.1 4-box scheme for bio-geochemical cycles—RUA own work

© The Editor(s) (if applicable) and The Author(s), under exclusive license to Springer Nature Switzerland AG 2023
R. U. Ayres, *The History and Future of Economics*,
https://doi.org/10.1007/978-3-031-26208-1

The cycles differ markedly in terms of the physical and chemical form of the major inorganic reservoir, and the mechanisms for transfer from one reservoir to another. When an element passes from the bio-unavailable inorganic reservoir to the bio-available reservoir it is said to be *mobilized*. In the case of nitrogen, mobilization essentially consists of splitting the di-nitrogen N_2 molecule, which is quite stable. When a nutrient moves in the reverse direction it is *sequestrated*. (In the case of carbon, the term is also used in connection with the accumulation of carbon or carbon dioxide in a reservoir from which CO_2 cannot reach the atmosphere). A nutrient can pass from an organic reservoir (e.g. dead plant material) to an inorganic reservoir by *decomposition* or (in the case of nitrogen) bacterial *denitrification*.

Apart from reservoirs, it is important to identify carriers. For carbon there are two main gaseous carriers: carbon dioxide (CO_2) and methane (CH_4). The water soluble form of carbon is bicarbonate (HCO_3^-), which is also a carrier. For nitrogen the main gaseous carriers are nitrogen oxides (NO_X) and ammonia (NH_3); most ammonium compounds and nitrates are soluble in water, but the main aqueous form is nitrate (NO_3^-). In the case of sulfur, the inorganic gaseous media are hydrogen sulfide (H_2S), carbonyl sulfide (COS), carbon disulfide (CS_2) and dimethyl-sulfide (DMS = $(CH_3)_2S$) and sulfur dioxide (SO_2); the main aqueous form is sulfate ($SO_4^=$), but DMS is also quite soluble in water. The only phosphorus carriers are phosphate ions $PO_4^=$. The aqueous form is phosphoric acid (H_3PO_4).

The second much faster sub-cycle is an exchange between the bio-available nutrient reservoir and living organisms themselves (which constitute a secondary reservoir of the nutrient). The reverse transfer, by decomposition or mineralization, has already been mentioned. In the case of carbon the conversion of CO_2 to its primary biological form (ribose, a kind of sugar) is accomplished by photosynthetic organisms, from algae to trees. Most of the other transfers in this sub-cycle are carried out by specialized bacteria or by enzymes within cells. For instance, nitrogen in living (or dead) organisms is normally in the amine group ($-NH_2$). A few free-living bacteria—notably *Rhizobium*—and some anaerobic cyanobacteria and yeasts have the ability to split the di-nitrogen molecule and *fix* nitrogen in a bio-available form.

It is tempting to compare the preindustrial nutrient "cycles" (C, N, S) with the current fluxes, on the assumption that these three cycles were, or very near, a steady-state in preindustrial times. Steady-state, in this context, means that each of the major reservoirs remains essentially constant or fluctuates within narrow limits. Inputs and outputs of each species to each reservoir must exactly balance (on average) any chemical transformations from one species to another in a steady-state condition. Even by this straightforward test, as will be seen, none of the nutrient cycles is in steady-state now. However, it seems that the nutrient cycles are seldom in balance for long, if ever, thanks to climate change, great extinctions, and geological processes such as continental drift, uplifts, episodic vulcanism and ice ages that occur over geological time scales. Thus, it can be quite misleading to compare the current state of imbalance with a hypothetical balance condition.

A.1. The Carbon–Oxygen Cycle

Biogeochemical cycles are interlinked at different levels, from the molecular to the global scale. These natural cycles interact in a variety of ways through feedbacks. Photosynthesis and the hydrological cycle are the most obvious. Other feedbacks include water vapor and cloud formation, oceanic acidification, vulcanism, carbon dioxide and NOx fertilization, and more {den Elzen, 1995}.

The main carbon–oxygen cycle (sometimes called the fast oxygen cycle) reflects the interaction between the biosphere and the atmosphere. Atmospheric CO_2 is biologically transformed by photosynthesis into sugars and cellulose. Oxygen is produced by photosynthesis, by producing carbohydrate monomers from carbon dioxide and water, via the endothermic reaction:

$$nCO_2 + nH_2O \rightarrow (CH_2O)_n + nO_2$$

where a photon provides the activating exergy. The reverse flow is due to respiration of living organisms and decay of dead organisms. The exothermic reaction equation is

$$(CH_2O)_n + nO_2 \rightarrow nCO_2 + nH_2O$$

with heat given off in the process. The biological function of respiration is to provide exergy for other cellular functions by "burning" glucose more efficiently than the primitive cells, depending on fermentation, could do. The atmosphere is the only reservoir of molecular oxygen. It contains about 1.2×10^6 gigatons (GT) of oxygen (Jacob 2002). A molecule of oxygen produced by photosynthesis "lives" in the atmosphere about 5000 years (on average) before being re-converted to carbon-dioxide.

The "fast" carbon reservoirs are the atmosphere itself, plus the biosphere and the soil and oceans. The atmosphere contains 790 GT of carbon as CO_2 while another 700 GT of organic carbon is embodied in the biosphere and about 3000 GT of organic carbon is embodied in dead plants, soil humus and organic detritus in the oceans.

Aerobic respiration is the reverse of carbon fixation. On a longer time scale, CO_2 fertilization of terrestrial vegetation is a factor (along with temperature) tending to maintain atmospheric CO_2 at a constant level. Rising atmospheric carbon dioxide directly enhances the rate of photosynthesis, other factors being equal. It also causes climate warming, and increased rainfall, both of which further enhance the rate of plant growth, subject to the availability of other nutrients, water, etc.

However, the organic carbon cycle cannot be understood in terms of the biochemistry of photosynthesis alone. Nor is all sedimentary carbon in the form of carbonates. There is a significant reservoir of reduced organic carbon (kerogen), buried in sediments, some of which has been aggregated by geological processes and transformed by heat or biological activity to form coal, petroleum and natural gas. Of course, it is the geologically concentrated sedimentary hydrocarbons that constitute our fossil fuel resources and which are currently being reconverted to CO_2 by combustion.

Methane (CH_4) has its own sub-cycle. In any anaerobic environment—including the guts of cellulose-ingesting animals such as ungulates and termites—organic carbon is broken down by bacteria. In sediments, these anaerobic bacteria produce "swamp gas" (while the organic nitrogen and sulfur are reduced to ammonia and hydrogen sulfide). In the stomachs and intestines of grazing animals such as cattle and sheep, or termites, the methane is eliminated by belching or with solid excreta. As noted previously, the existence of free oxygen in the atmosphere is due to the fact that so much organic carbon has been sequestered over eons by burial in silt. Nevertheless, at least half of all buried organic carbon is recycled to the atmosphere by anaerobic methanation. The methane in the atmosphere is gradually oxidized, via many steps, to CO_2. Methane is not recycled biologically, as such. However at present methane is being emitted to the atmosphere faster than it is being removed.

There is a "slow" carbon–oxygen cycle involving mineral (silicate) weathering. The major inorganic reservoir of carbon is sedimentary carbonate rocks, such as limestone or calcite ($CaCO_3$) and dolomite ($CaMg(CO_3)_2$). This reservoir contains more than 10^5 times more carbon than the atmosphere and the biosphere together. These reservoirs participate in a "slow" (inorganic) cycle, in which, carbon dioxide from the atmosphere is taken up by the weathering of silicate rocks, driven by the hydrological cycle.

The calcium and carbonate part of the marine system can be summarized as:

$$Ca(OH)_2 + H_2CO_3 \rightarrow CaCO_3 + 2H_2O$$

In due course the organic precipitates and shells drift down to the ocean floor as sediments. Sediments contain around 10^7 Pg of organic C which is gradually compressed eventually being converted by heat and pressure into shale, limestone, chalk and quartz. The sum of the two reactions together is

$$CaSiO_3 + CO_2 \rightarrow CaCO_3 + SiO_2$$

The observed rate of oceanic calcium carbonate deposition would use up all the carbon dioxide in the oceans in about 400,000 years. If that happens, the Earth may experience another "snowball Earth" period, similar to the one that seems to have occurred several times in the past.

However, just as volcanos eject hot lava and gases onto the surface from under the Earth's crust, there are subduction zones (mostly under the oceans) that carry sediments back into the reducing magmatic layer. There is another chemical reaction that occurs at the high pressures and temperatures of that region. This reaction reverses the weathering reaction and reconverts sedimentary calcium and/or magnesium carbonate rocks (mixed with quartz) into calcium or magnesium silicate, releasing gaseous CO_2 that is vented through volcanic eruptions or hot springs. Weathering rates are relatively easier to measure (Holland 1978) (Berner, Lasaga, and Garrels 1983) compared to outgassing rates (Berner 1990) (Gerlach 1991) (Kasting and G. Walker 1992). But insofar as the data is available, the two rates (CO_2 uptake and emission) appear to agree within a factor of two (Kasting and G. Walker 1992). The fact that agreement is not closer is an indication of the fact that much remains to be learned about the details of these (and most other) bio-geo-chemical processes e.g. (Smil 2001).

In principle, there is a somewhat crude geological mechanism that would tend to keep the silicate weathering rate roughly equal to the volcanic outgassing rate, over very long time periods. A buildup of CO_2 in the atmosphere would lead to greenhouse warming. This increases the rate of evaporation (and precipitation) of water, thus accelerating the weathering process, which removes CO_2 from the atmosphere. The silicate weathering rate is directly dependent on climate conditions, including the precipitation rate and the surface exposure. This would eventually halt the temperature rise. If the atmospheric CO_2 level rises, due to abnormal volcanic activity, there will be an increase in the rate of weathering and CO_2 uptake. Conversely, if the CO_2 level is dropping, so will the temperature and the weathering rate.

The carbon cycle as a whole is summarized in Figs. 19.6 and 19.7. The carbon cycle is not now in balance. Whether it was truly balanced in preindustrial times is debatable: However, a preindustrial carbon cycle has been postulated, where the atmospheric reservoir contained 615 Pg, the terrestrial biosphere contained 730 Pg and the surface ocean biota contained 840 Pg with annual photosynthesis of 60 Pg on land and 60 Pg in the surface of the oceans, balanced by equal reverse flows from respiration and decay (Jacob 2002). In any case, the carbon dioxide level of the atmosphere has been rising sharply for over a century, from a hypothesized pre-industrial 615–790 Pg in the late 1990s. The current level (c. 2015) is several percentage points higher and rising every year (Figs. A.2 and A.3).

The Jacob model of the preindustrial carbon "balance" is, by no means, established fact. Smil reports that estimates of the carbon content of late twentieth century terrestrial biomass range between 420 and 840 Pg (as compared to 730 Pg in Jacob's model), whereas a group of Russian biologists have estimated that terrestrial biomass amounted to 1100 Pg 5000 years ago, before human deforestation began (Smil 2001) p. 81. Jacob's implication that the "preindustrial" carbon cycle as of (say) 200 years ago was a steady-state is misleading.

In fact, deforestation and land clearing for agriculture in North America peaked during the nineteenth century. (As it happens, there has been some reforestation in North America during the twentieth century, partly due to agricultural mechanization—no more need to feed horses—and partly due

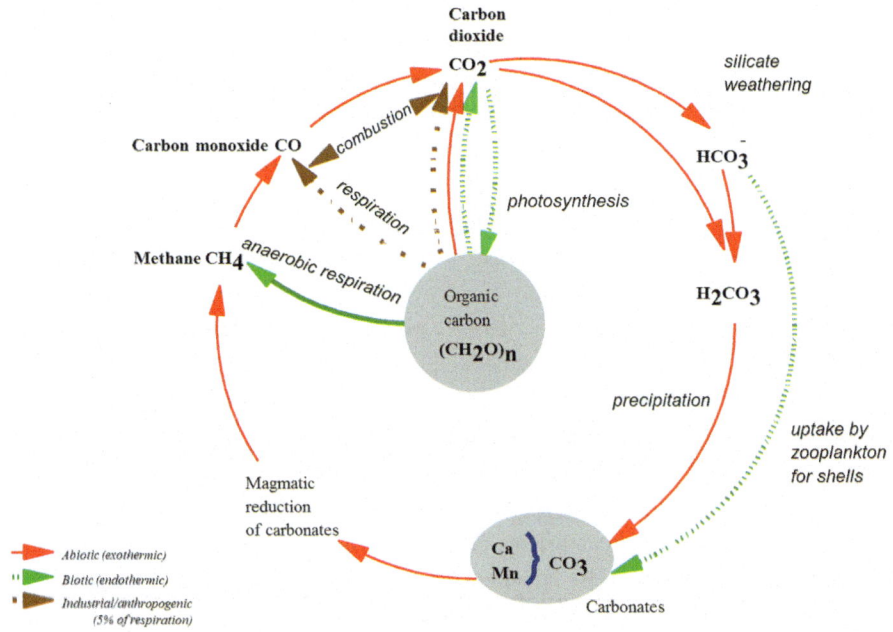

Fig. A.2 Carbon cycle; chemical transformations—??? (not found)

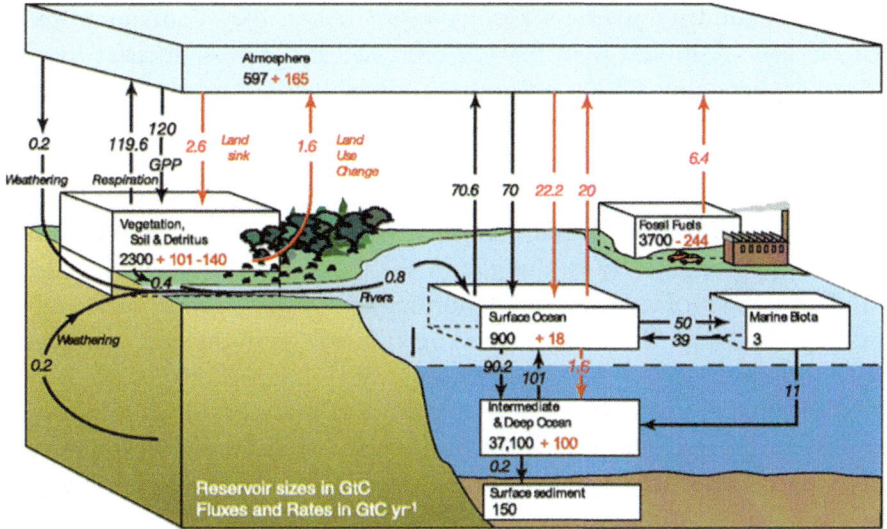

Source: IPCC https://www.ipcc.ch/publications_and_data/ar4/wg1/en/fig/figure-7-3-1.png

Fig. A.3 The carbon cycle in the 1990s. https://www.researchgate.net/profile/Gavin-Cawley/publication/263946928/figure/fig1/AS:296577282396162@1447720943003/The-global-carbon-cycle-for-the-1990s-showing-the-main-annual-fluxes-in-GtC-yr-1.png

to CO_2 and NOx fertilization—the fact that plants grow faster as the carbon dioxide and nitrogen oxides levels in the atmosphere increases.)

Anthropogenic extraction and combustion of carbonaceous fuels, together with deforestation to clear land for agriculture, have contributed significantly to altering the atmospheric CO_2 balance. About 5% of total CO_2 emissions from the land to the atmosphere are anthropogenic (Bolin, Doeoes, and Jaeger 1986). The CO_2 concentration is now 400 ppm (2013), 60% above the preindustrial level (estimated to be 280 ppm). The rate of increase in recent years has been about 0.4% per year, although it fluctuates. According to ice-core (and other) data, during the quaternary glaciation 2 million years ago, the atmospheric concentration of carbon dioxide was as low as 180 ppm, while during the Carboniferous era 300 million years ago, it was as high as 7000 ppm.

As of 1990 approximately 5.4 Pg/year of carbon was being converted to CO_2 by combustion processes and transferred from underground reservoirs of reduced carbon to the atmosphere. A further 1.6 Pg/year was attributed to tropical deforestation, for a total of 7 Pg/year (Stern, Young, and Druckman 1992). Roughly half of this excess anthropogenic flux, or 3.5 Pg/year, was known to be accumulating in the atmosphere. At first glance, it would appear that the remainder must be accumulating either in the oceans or in terrestrial biomass. A molecule of oxygen produced by photosynthesis "lives" in the atmosphere about 5000 years (on average) before being re-converted to carbon-dioxide.

Although it was assumed for a while that the ocean must be the ultimate sink; e.g. (Peng et al. 1983), there is increasing evidence that the known atmosphere–ocean transfer mechanisms cannot account for all the carbon disappearance (Tans, Fung, and Takahashi 1990) (Schlesinger 1991) (Sundquist 1993). However, simulation models of the carbon cycle, working both "forward" and "backward, have contributed significantly to clarification of the situation.

To summarize, it appears that the most plausible way to balance the fast carbon budget, within historical emissions and parametric uncertainty ranges, is to introduce a terrestrial biospheric "sink" for CO_2—mostly in the northern hemisphere—partially attributable to reforestation thanks to a combination of carbon and nitrogen fertilization (Houghton, Callander, and Varney 1992).

There is physical evidence to support the hypothesis of enhanced plant growth in the northern hemisphere as a sink for atmospheric CO_2. Notwithstanding increased timber and wood-pulp harvesting, the forest biomass of the north temperate zones, North America and northern Europe—and perhaps Russia—is actually *increasing* (Kauppi, Mielikainen, and Kuusula 1992) (Sedjo 1992). This finding was confirmed by the 1994 IPCC *Scientific Assessment* (Schimel et al. 1994). Quantitative estimates now appear to confirm the sufficiency of the N-fertilization hypothesis (Galloway et al. 1995) (den Elzen, Bensen, and Rotmans 1995).

A "box model" of the carbon cycle, combining both the chemical and biological branches, has been able to match the history of atmospheric CO_2 concentration since 1850 remarkably well, both before and after 1950. See (Valero Capilla and Valero Delgado 2015) Fig. 10.1. (Tomizuka 2009) (Valero, Valero, and Gomez 2011).

A.2. The Nitrogen, Sulfur and Phosphorus Cycles

Nitrogen compounds are extremely soluble. In general, vegetation can utilize either soluble nitrates or ammonium compounds, but not elemental nitrogen. Thus, all life depends on nitrogen "fixation". Some of the fixation is attributable to lightning (which induces oxidation) and some by diazotrophic bacteria having a nitro-genase enzyme. The enzyme combines atmospheric nitrogen (N_2) with hydrogen to form ammonium ions. Some symbiotic bacteria then convert the ammonium into amino acids used by plants. Other bacteria convert ammonium into other nitrogen compounds such as nitrites and nitrates. Nitrites are toxic to plants but with oxidation they become nitrates, which are also toxic.

The nitrates are incorporated in a number of important biological chemical and processes, where the oxygen is stripped off and combined with carbon forming carbon dioxide, while the NH_2 ions are embodied in amino acids that combine to form proteins. By the same token, the nitrogen cycle (Figs. A.4 and A.5) depends intimately on other denitrifying bacteria that convert the organic nitrogen compounds in dead organisms back into molecular nitrogen (Figs. A.4 and A.5).

Because nitrogen was (and is) a limiting factor in many agricultural regions, it has been relatively easy to increase biomass output by supplementing natural sources of available nitrogen by the addition of synthetic sources. Smil points out that the amount of reactive nitrogen added to soils now roughly equals the amount fixed by legumes and other nitrogen fixing organisms (Smil 2004). But the chain of transformations resulting in protein for human food is inefficient. One unfortunate consequence is that a lot of soluble nitrogen is lost to groundwater and runoff. For this reason the imbalances in the nitrogen cycle may prove to be extraordinarily difficult to correct (or compensate for) by deliberate human action.

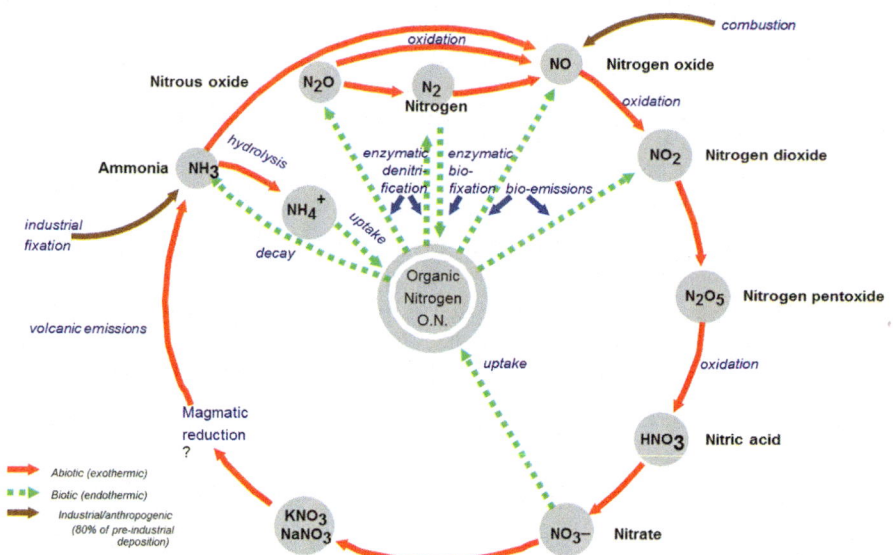

Fig. A.4 Nitrogen cycle: chemical transformations—(not found)???

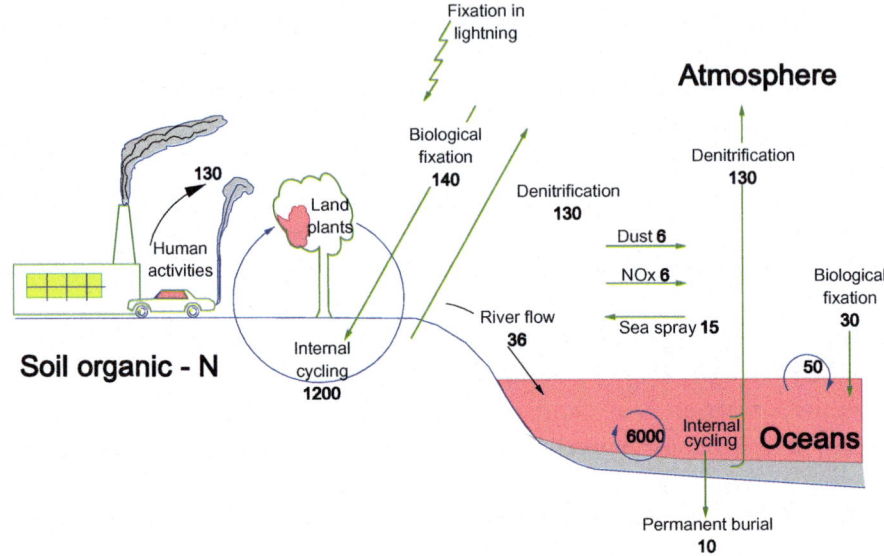

Fig. A.5 1990s nitrogen cycle; intermediate flux 10^{12} g N. https://link.springer.com/chapter/10.1007/978-3-319-30545-5_6

Nitrogen fluxes to the atmosphere (the major reservoir of inorganic nitrogen) are of two kinds. Bacterial de-nitrification from the decay of organic materials, and de-nitrification of nitrate fertilizers return nitrogen to the atmosphere as inert N_2 or N_2O. This loss must be compensated by N-fixation. On the other hand, ammonia volatilization from the soil, combustion of organic materials (generating NO_X) and bio-emissions from marine organisms are recycled as "odd" nitrogen. Fluxes from the atmosphere to the land and ocean surface include deposition of nitrate (NO_3) ions (from "acid rain") and ammonium (NH_4) ions. Fluxes to the biosphere include uptake of soluble nitrates and ammonium compounds, recycling of organic detritus (e.g. manure), and bio-fixation by microorganisms. None of these fluxes, except the application of synthetic fertilizers, is well quantified.

Synthetic fertilizers from industrial nitrogen fixation (mainly as ammonia, NH_3) became important only in the twentieth century. Current global annual ammonia-based fertilizer production is 160 million metric tons, or 130 Tg/year of fixed N Of the 160 Tg of ammonia produced worldwide each year, 16 Tg or so is used to manufacture other industrial chemicals, notably explosives, pesticides, plastics (nylon) etc. The rest is made into fertilizer chemicals, starting with urea. These products eventually become wastes and are disposed of, either in landfills or via waterways. All of this nitrogen eventually finds its way back into the global cycle. China is now the world's biggest producer and consumer, having reached that pinnacle by 1995, from a fairly low level in just 40 years, starting in 1960. China now applies fertilizer at the rate of 190 kg N/ha, compared to just 60 kg N/ha for the US. The most intensively fertilized areas receive more than 300 kg-N/ha, enabling a hectare of land to feed 30 people on a vegetarian diet or 20 people on a high protein diet. This has enabled China to feed itself.

The only global reservoir of nitrogen is the atmosphere, which is 78% elemental nitrogen gas N_2. The total stock of molecular nitrogen (di-nitrogen) in the atmosphere is estimated to be 3.8 billion Tg. Di-nitrogen (N_2) and nitrous oxide (N_2O) are not biologically available, because of the tremendous amount of exergy needed to break the triple bond holding the two N atoms together (about double the exergy required to break the oxygen (O_2) bond. There are only four sources of biologically available ("odd") nitrogen compounds. These are (1) biological fixation, (2) atmospheric electrical discharges (lightning), (3) high temperature combustion and (4) industrial processes for producing synthetic ammonia.

Only a few very specialized bacteria and actinomycetes (yeasts) can utilize (i.e., "fix") elemental di-nitrogen. There are some 25 genera of free-living or symbiotic bacteria. The most important is *Rhizobium*, which attaches itself to the roots of legumes, such as alfalfa. In addition, there are 60 genera of anaerobic cyanobacteria, such as *anabaena* (leftovers from the early evolutionary history of Earth), and 15 genera of actinomycetes (most prominently, *Frankia*). The range of estimates for biofixation, in the literature, is from 100 to 170 Tg/year on land and from 10 to 110 Tg/year in the oceans. Overall, biological N-fixation, from all sources, may be as little as 110 Tg/year and as much as 280 Tg/year. The most recent estimates are 140 Tg fixed by terrestrial vegetation, plus 30 Tg from marine phytoplankton (Smil 2001).

The rate of natural atmospheric nitrogen fixation as NOX by electrical discharges is even less accurately known than the bio-fixation rate. Estimates vary from 1.2 to 220 Tg/year, although the latter figure now looks much too high. The most plausible estimate is 20–30 Tg/year (Smil 2001) p. 172. Nitrogen oxides (NOX) are also produced by high temperature combustion processes. Anthropogenic activities, mostly automobiles and trucks and electric power generating plants, currently generate around 40 Tg/year of NOX. There is a further contribution (estimated to be around 12 Tg/year from natural forest fires. Finally, of the order 5 Tg/year of ammonia (NH3) is also discharges by volcanoes and fumaroles, on average, although this flux can vary a lot from year to year.

Evidently, known anthropogenic inputs of fixed nitrogen from industrial processes are already comparable in quantity to (and may even be significantly larger than) estimated natural fixation rates. Assuming the nitrogen cycle to have been balanced in pre-industrial times (possibly unjustified) it would follow that inputs and outputs to some reservoirs are now out of balance by a large factor. Of course, it would be very difficult to detect any changes in total atmospheric nitrogen content (i.e. pressure) over any short period of time. However, it is known that nitrous oxide (N_2O) has increased in recent years, from approximately 300 ppb in 1978 (Weiss 1981) and—extrapolating from a graph—probably close to 330 ppb today (Smil 2001) p. 135.

Management of soil fertility has been the preoccupation of farmers for thousands of years. Egyptians, Romans, Babylonians, and early Germans are recorded as using minerals and or manure to enhance the productivity of their farms. The modern science of plant nutrition started in the nineteenth century with the work of German chemist Justus von Liebig, among others.

The Birkeland–Eyde process was one of the competing industrial processes in the beginning of nitrogen based fertilizer production. https://en.wikipedia.org/wiki/Fertilizer-cite_note-6 This process was used to fix atmospheric nitrogen (N_2) into nitric acid (HNO_3), one of several chemical processes generally referred to as nitrogen fixation. The resultant nitric acid was then used as a source of nitrate (NO_3). A factory based on the process was built in Rjukan and Notodden in Norway, combined with the building of large hydroelectric power facilities.

The 1910s and 1920s witnessed the rise of the Haber process and the Ostwald process. The Haber process produces ammonia (NH_3) from methane (CH_4) gas and molecular nitrogen (N_2). The ammonia from the Haber process is then converted into nitric acid (HNO_3) in the Ostwald process. The development of synthetic fertilizer has significantly supported global population growth—Vaclav Smil has {Smil, 2000 #6616}estimated that almost half the people on the Earth are currently fed as a result of synthetic nitrogen fertilizer use.

The use of commercial fertilizers has increased steadily in the last 50 years, rising almost 20-fold to the current rate of 100 million tonnes of nitrogen per year. {Smil, 2004}. Without commercial fertilizers it is estimated that about one-third of the food produced now could not be produced. The use of phosphate fertilizers has also increased from 9 million tonnes per year in 1960 to 40 million tonnes per year in 2000. A maize crop yielding 6–9 tonnes of grain per hectare (2.5 acres) requires 31–50 kg (68–110 lb.) of phosphate fertilizer to be applied; soybean crops require about half, as 20–25 kg per hectare. Yara International (Norway) is the world's largest producer of nitrogen-based fertilizers.

Controlled-nitrogen-release technologies based on polymers derived from combining urea and formaldehyde were first produced in 1936 and commercialized in 1955. The early product had 60% of the total nitrogen cold-water-insoluble, and the unreacted (quick-release) less than 15%. Methylene ureas were commercialized in the 1960s and 1970s, having 25% and 60% of the nitrogen as cold-water-insoluble, and unreacted urea nitrogen in the range of 15–30%. In the 1960s, the Tennessee Valley Authority National Fertilizer Development Center began developing sulfur-coated urea; sulfur was used as the principal coating material because of its low cost and its value as a secondary nutrient.

N_2O is a co-product (with N_2) of natural de-nitrification by anaerobic bacteria and other microorganisms. Aggregated data on the N_2O/N_2 ratio is scarce. Data for fertilized land implies that the ratio of N_2 to N_2O production on land is probably in the range 10–20, with a most likely value of about 16:1 (Council for Agricultural Science and Technology 1976). If so, N_2O is about 1/16 of the total terrestrial de-nitrification flux. There is no *a priori* reason to assume this ratio should not hold true for marine conditions or pre-industrial times, although it might actually vary quite a bit. It would follow from this assumption that the current apparent N_2O flux of 13 Tg/year should be accompanied by a corresponding N_2 flux of about $16 \times 13 = 208$ Tg/year. (This compares with $2 \times 130 = 260$ Tg/year in Fig. 19.8). Obviously the numbers are quite uncertain).

Nitrous oxide is not oxidized in the troposphere. In the stratosphere it is photolyzed yielding N_2 and O, or it is oxidized by ozone to NO_X. In fact, oxidation of nitrous oxide is the major source of stratospheric NO_X. The disappearance rate (of N_2O) by these two mechanisms in combination is estimated to be 10 Tg/year (Weiss 1981) (Liu and Cicerone 1984) (McElroy and Wofsy 1986). This process has aroused great interest in recent years because of the discovery by Crutzen and others that this set of processes governs the stratospheric ozone level, at least in the absence of chlorine compounds (which also catalytically destroy ozone) (Crutzen 1970) (Crutzen 1974).

It now appears that de-nitrification of nitrate fertilizers now accounts for 0.7 Tg/year of N_2O emissions. According to one source, approximately 0.3% of fertilizer nitrogen is converted to N_2O (Galbally 1985). A calculation by Crutzen sets the figure at 0.4%, which would correspond to N_2O emissions of 0.35 Tg/year at current fertilizer production levels.[2] An industrial source of

---

[2] Denitrification bacteria reduce nitrates (NO_3) to obtain oxygen for metabolic purposes. They do not metabolize ammonia. Thus the denitrification flux from fertilizers depends somewhat on the chemical form in which it is applied. The N_2O/N_2 proportion depends on local factors, such as carbon content of the soil, acidity and dissolved oxygen. It must be acknowledged that the combined

N_2O is the production of adipic acid, an intermediate in nylon manufacture (Thiemens and Trogler 1991). This source could theoretically account for as much as 0.4 Tg/year or 10% of the annual increase, in the absence of any emissions controls. However, the actual contribution from this source is probably much less. One other possible source of N_2O is explosives. Virtually all explosives are manufactured from nitrogenated compounds (such as nitrocellulose, ammonium nitrate, trinitroglycerin, and various amines). According to simulation calculations, up to 9% of the nitrogen in explosives may end up as nitrous oxide.

De-nitrification is the complementary process to nitrogen fixation (as utilized by plants). Hence, the terrestrial contribution to de-nitrification must have increased in rough proportion to overall terrestrial and atmospheric nitrogen fixation. On this basis, preindustrial natural fixation (approx. 140 Tg/year) has been roughly doubled by anthropogenic contributions. In other words, human activity has doubled the amount of biologically available (reactive) nitrogen being produced each year.

It is tempting to assume that global de-nitrification should increase proportionally, along with the percentage increase in nitrous oxide (N_2O) emissions, since preindustrial times. This argument is not affected by uncertainties in the $N_2 : N_2O$ ratio. On this basis, it would follow that the overall rate of de-nitrification—including N_2O emissions—could have increased by over 50% in little more than a century. At first sight this hypothesis seems plausible. Unquestionably, global agricultural activity has increased sharply over the past two centuries, both in scope and intensity. The nitrate content of riverine runoff from land to oceans has increased sharply. At the same time, the organic (humus) content of most agricultural soils has declined. This would seem to be consistent with the notion of accelerated de-nitrification. However, while de-nitrification has also increased, it does not keep pace with nitrogen fixation.

The alternative is that reactive nitrogen is now accumulating. For one thing, global nitrogen fertilization (from acid rain and ammonium sulfate deposition) has increased the reservoir of nitrogen in biomes like grasslands and forests that are not cultivated. This explanation would be qualitatively consistent with the observations of increased forest biomass in the northern hemisphere mentioned previously: e.g. (Kauppi, Mielikainen, and Kuusula 1992) (Sedjo 1992). This explanation simultaneously provides a possible explanation of the "missing carbon" problem mentioned above.

---

uncertainties are quite large. Thus, for instance, a recent US study sets the N_2O emissions from fertilizer at 1.5 Tg/year, as compared to only 1 Tg/year from fossil fuel combustion. Other estimates in the literature range from 0.01 to 2.2 Tg/year (Watson et al. 1992).

Anthropogenic nitrogen fixation from all sources—especially fertilizer use and fossil fuel combustion—is certainly increasing quite rapidly. One predictable consequence of nitrogen fertilization will be a buildup of toxic and carcinogenic nitrates and nitrites in ground waters. This is already occurring in many agricultural areas and offshore. Increased forest and pasture growth rates is another likely consequence already mentioned. But along with the gross fertilization effect, there is a tendency to reduced bio-diversity. Regions where nitrogen availability has been the limiting factor for biological productivity are likely to shrink, or even disappear, to be replaced by regions where other plant nutrients are the limiting factor. This shift could lead to major and unexpected changes in species composition for both plants and animals.

The modern atmosphere reflects evolutionary changes in the *nitrogen cycle*. Early proto-cells probably obtained their nitrogen (an essential component of all amino acids and proteins) from dissolved ammonium (NH_4) ions or an iron-ammonium complex. However, as the soluble iron in the oceans was oxidized and atmospheric oxygen began to accumulate, free ammonia was more and more rapidly oxidized. One group of oxidation reactions yields oxides of nitrogen (NO_x), most of which eventually dissolve in water and form nitrous and nitric acids. These, in turn, can be metabolized by microorganisms to form nitrites and nitrates.

However other reaction paths for the direct oxidation of ammonia can lead back to molecular nitrogen (N_2) and water vapor. Molecular nitrogen is extremely stable and quite unreactive—hence unavailable to plants—except when endothermic oxidation reactions are caused by lightning. Consequently the atmosphere is a nitrogen "sink". In other words, the ultra-stable molecular nitrogen keeps accumulating. So-called "denitrifying" (more accurately, ammonia metabolizing) bacteria descended from these organisms still abound in the soil (where they are not in contact with oxygen) and play a major role in closing the nitrogen cycle.

However before moving on, we need to point out that natural processes (lightning, decay organisms, and nitrifying bacteria) are not sufficient to provide all the nitrogen needed by the global human population (over 7 billion) that exists today. A few years ago, Vaclav Smil wrote "Depending on the diet we would be willing to accept, our numbers would have to shrink by two to three billion in a world devoid of synthetic nitrogenous fertilizers. This dependence will only increase in the future" (Smil 1997) (Smil 2000). Human numbers when he wrote were about 6 billion, which implies that synthetic ammonia already accounts for up to half of all the soil nitrogen needed to support the human population. It happens that nitrogen synthesis is also extremely energy intensive. Synthetic ammonia production consumes, on average, 40 GJ per metric ton. Urea, the most common and transportable form of nitrogen fertilizer, requires an additional 25 GJ/t. Global production of synthetic ammonia, mostly for agriculture, is now over 100 million tonnes.

The global sulfur cycle resembles the nitrogen cycle thermodynamically, insofar as reduced forms of sulfur (S, H_2S) are gradually oxidized by atmospheric oxygen, ending in sulfur oxides (SO_2, SO_3) and finally sulfuric acid (H_2SO_4). See Fig. 19.10. Sulfate ions (SO_4^-) are eventually deposited on land or in the oceans in wet or dry form (e.g. as ammonium sulfate). The reverse part of the cycle, which converts sulfur back to reduced states of higher thermodynamic potential, is accomplished either by biological activity or by high temperature magmatic reactions in the Earth's mantle (Fig. A.6).

Various estimates of sulfur fluxes are available in the literature. Roughly, the pre-industrial inputs to the land surface must have been about 26 Tg/year, as compared to 84 Tg/year from atmospheric deposition (c. 1980) and a further 28 Tg/year as fertilizer. In short, the sulfur flux to land has more than quadrupled since the beginning of industrialization. It is likely that river runoff has doubled, e.g. from 72 Tg/year preindustrial to more than 213 Tg/year currently. It is clear that the global sulfur cycle is now extremely unbalanced.

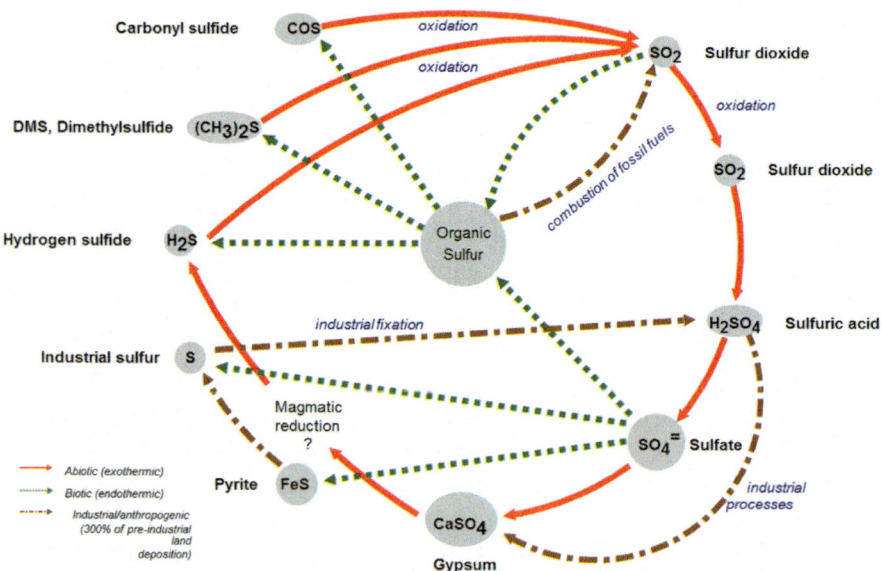

Fig. A.6 Sulfur cycle; chemical transformations (not found)???

Inputs to oceans appear to exceed deposition to the ocean bottom by as much as 100 Tg/year (Schlesinger 1991). It must be acknowledged that there is no known or obvious reason to worry unduly about this aspect of the anthropogenic perturbation of the sulfur cycle per se, based on current knowledge of downstream effects, except for one problem. Clearly, however, the oxidation of large amounts of reduced sulfur will continue to acidify the soils and the ocean. Deposition of sulfur oxides—sulfite/sulfate (SO_3/SO_4)—and nitrate (NO_3) onto the land or water surface does fertilize biomass growth, but it is also "acid rain". This causes measurable changes in the pH of rainwater, and fresh water lakes and streams. Acidification of the oceans is slower, but probably more dangerous in the long run. Ocean pH is currently much higher than it was in the early history of our planet (Fig. A.7).

Atmospheric haze, consisting mostly of sulfate aerosols in the micron size range, has increased by orders of magnitude over some land areas (China comes to mind). Sulfate haze is due to SO_2 emissions from the combustion of fossil fuels. This was a topic of major concern in the US during the 1980s, due to the association of sulfate particulates with acidification. However, it is not clear whether sulfate haze has increased significantly over the oceans, partly because it is unclear whether oceanic sulfates are attributable to terrestrial industry or marine biology.

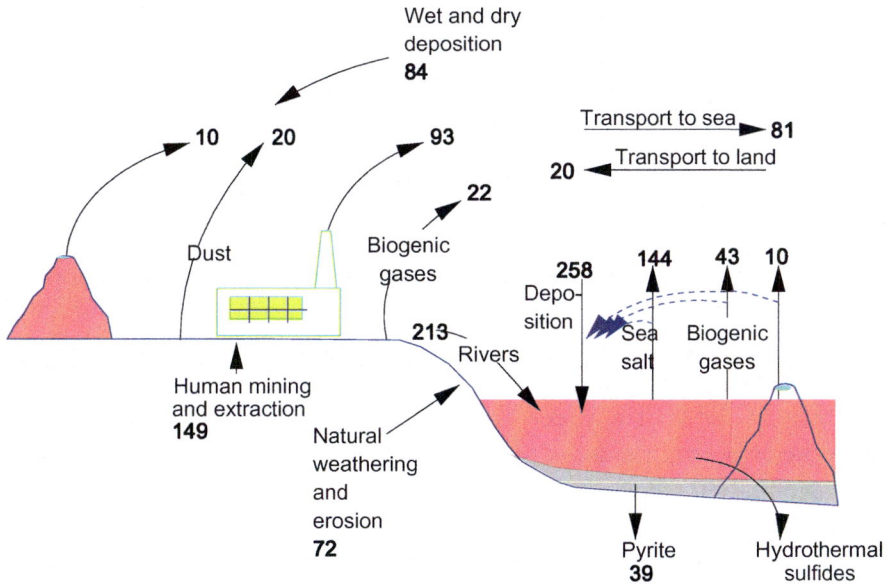

Fig. A.7 1990s sulfur cycle; intermediate fluxes 10^{12} g S. https://link.springer.com/chapter/10.1007/978-3-319-30545-5_6

There is some evidence that marine phytoplankton emit dimethyl-sulfide (DMS), which subsequently oxidizes to sulfate aerosols. The haze has a net cooling effect. The sulfate haze phenomenon is apparently sufficient to measurably increase the Earth's albedo (i.e. it's reflectivity to visible radiation) and, possibly, compensate partially for greenhouse warming in recent decades (Wigley 1989) (Taylor and Penner 1994). It is now incorporated in GCMs, where it largely accounts for the fact that climate warming has not occurred as rapidly as the earlier models predicted. On the other hand, sulfate haze is proportional to the current rate of sulfate emissions, whereas the greenhouse phenomenon is a function of the atmospheric concentration, or total buildup, of greenhouse gases. Thus, the greenhouse warming and sulfate cooling cannot continue to cancel each other indefinitely.

A.3. Recycling of Scarce Metals and Phosphorus

Unlike the nutrient elements, C,N,S) there is no obvious mechanism for recycling metals in nature, except in the life cycle of stars and planets.

But speaking of geologically scarce elements, there is one case that may be special. This one is special because there is no possible substitute and because exhaustion known resources in the foreseeable future is a distinct possibility. That element is phosphorus. Of course there are quite a few phosphorus minerals in the Earth's crust, but only two are conceivable worth mining. They are phosphate rock (phosphorite) constitutes 0.279% of the earth's crust, followed by fluorapatite (0.0403% of the crust). The next most common after that (Francolite) constitutes only 0.00435% of the crust. (How these numbers are determined so precisely is a long story, too long to tell here).

Despite its geological scarcity, phosphorus is essential for all kinds of life. It is required for the nucleic acids in RNA and DNA, in adenosine diphosphate and triphosphate (ADP, ATP) the universal energy carrier in all living cells in every species. It is also used in the teeth and bones of vertebrates and in some lipids. Without phosphorus there can be no life. That is why there is no substitute for it. It is concentrated in the food chain: the higher on the ladder the organism, the more phosphorus it needs. Protozoans at the bottom of the chain are 0.6% P_2O_5 (dry weight) but human bodies are 2% P_2O_5.

Phosphate rock is the only practical mineral source of phosphate fertilizer for terrestrial agriculture. According to the US Geological Survey, almost all (95%) of the phosphorus in the Earth's crust is now embodied in the two minerals, of which 87% is sedimentary and of biological origin (Krauss, Saam, and Schmidt 1984). Most of the phosphorus in the world is now tightly combined with calcium. There are no known biological processes, analogous to photosynthesis, that break that tight chemical bond. What this implies is that the phosphorus in the Earth's crust is gradually becoming insoluble by being attached to calcium, from which no known biological process is able to separate it. (In the subsurface magma, the bond is broken by heat; in the fertilizer industry, the phosphate rock is digested by reaction with concentrated sulfuric acid).

According to one calculation, phosphate (P_2O_5) now constitutes about 0.045% of the mass of river flows, but less than 0.005% of mass of the oceans. This is noteworthy because the concentration of other dissolved salts (mainly sodium, potassium and magnesium chlorides) in the oceans is much higher than the concentration of those salts in the rivers. (Thus, chlorides are accumulating in the oceans and are not utilized extensively in biomass nor are they transferred back to the land by natural processes.) Yet, the concentration of phosphate in the oceans is much lower than the concentration in rivers: phosphate accounts for less than 0.005% of the ocean mass and 0.18% of the mass of dissolved salts in the ocean. The numbers are important.

Since most of the phosphorus in the Earth's crust is in solution or is embodied in that mineral, it follows that it—like the oxygen in the atmosphere—must be of biological origin. If that logic holds water (so to speak) it suggests that the biomass of the Earth is actually phosphorus limited. Conceivably there may be significant recycling within the deep oceans, but we haven't found it.

John Bennet Lawes, an English entrepreneur, began to experiment on the effects of various manures on plants growing in pots in 1837, and a year or two later the experiments were extended to crops in the field. One immediate consequence was that in 1842 he patented a manure formed by treating phosphates with sulfuric acid, and thus was the first to create the artificial manure industry. In the succeeding year he enlisted the services of Joseph Henry Gilbert, with whom he carried on for more than half a century on experiments in raising crops at the Institute of Arable Crops Research.

Needless to say, anthropogenic activity, notably phosphate fertilizers, has enormously increased the rate of terrestrial phosphate mobilization as well as the rate of phosphate loss, via erosion and runoff, to the oceans. While known reserves of mineable phosphate rock appear adequate for the next few centuries, phosphate loss will eventually be a limiting factor for terrestrial agriculture. Since there are no mineral substitutes, the only possibility in the long run must be some combination of changing diet, significantly enhanced recycling from agricultural wastes and/or fewer humans.

Whereas other important organic compounds are recycled naturally from the oceans to land in reduced gaseous forms (methane, ammonia, hydrogen sulfide) phosphorus is not naturally recycled from sea to land as a gas. Even if the calcium phosphate bond is broken by unknown bacteria in the very deep sea—which is conceivable—there is no phosphorus in the atmosphere and no gaseous form of phosphorus that could facilitate transfer from marine to terrestrial reservoirs. Phosphine gas (H_3P) is the only chemical possibility, but it oxidizes much too rapidly in the oxygen atmosphere (not to mention being extremely toxic).

Consequently, the phosphorus cycle is only "closed" (incompletely) by means of geological processes, plus small reverse flows from the oceans to the land as excreta from seabirds (guano) and anadromous fish, like salmon, that return to their spawning place and are consumed en route by terrestrial predators like bears. Given the depletion of ocean fisheries, the re-fertilization of land by means of guano droppings by sea-birds, is already far too slow to compensate for the loss of terrestrial phosphorus to the oceans. It follows that one of the most important future technologies to be developed must be closed cycle agriculture, like "vertical farms" in which the phosphorus is never released back to the environment.

RFF has pioneered in the economics of biological resources, from fisheries, to forests, to topsoil and bio-diversity. It was at RFF that the idea of the natural environment as a resource emerged. That idea was encapsulated by Kenneth Boulding's article "The Economics of the coming Spaceship Earth", in which he contrasted the economy of a space-ship to the "cowboy economy, a place where there are no limits on resource availability {Boulding, 1966}. Kenneth Boulding and other environmental economists realized that finite resources, like topsoil, forests and fresh water are also essential for the health of the ecosystem, within which the economic system is embedded. It follows that the economic system cannot exist in the absence of material (and energy) flows from (and back to) the environment. Those flows are driven by exergy dissipation.

Of course, opposition to the neo-Malthusianism of the 1960s—often scathing—followed as night follows day. The opposition among economists, mainly libertarian, was led by **Julian Simon** (of the Cato Institute) and a group known (not to themselves) as "Cornucopians" because of their faith in (nuclear) technology as the answer to every problem {Simon, 1977, 1980}. That faith has been severely shaken since the Chernobyl (1986), Three-Mile Island (1979) and Fukushima Daichi (2011) accidents. There have been many other less well-known nuclear accidents, around the world, viz. Kyshtym, Russia (1957); Simi Valley, USA (1957); Vaud, Switzerland (1969); Fukui Prefecture, Japan (2004); and Marcoule, France (2011). You can find others in Wikipedia.

Appendix B: Climate Change: The Externality that Makes Everything Else Irrelevant

B.1. The Climate Is Warming

Climate change is the "elephant in the room" today. Fossil fuels have provided cheap energy that has financed industrialization, and rapid economic growth, for many generations of humans {Jones, 2019 #8603}. But the buildup of combustion products (e.g. carbon dioxide, methane and nitrogen oxides) in the atmosphere causes adverse climate change (warming and increased storminess) ecological changes on Earth, such as reduced bio-diversity, and sea-level rise, in the long run. We now realize that sea level rise will literally flood a large part of the most productive croplands on Earth, not to mention destroying the water supply, or even drowning, coastal cities and islands. The only open question is: how soon?

The first law of thermodynamics (conservation of energy), says that energy inflows from the sun to the Earth in the form of short-wave (SW) light must always be balanced by energy outflows in the form of low temperature (infrared) heat or long-wave (LW) light. Otherwise, the Earth must warm up or cool down, as already explained in other publications e.g. {Ayres, 2016} Chap. 6. The possibility of climate change was suggested in 1896, by Swedish physicist Svante Arrhenius. Normally the energy (exergy) imbalances are small and responses to change are correspondingly slow. But recently the imbalance has increased in a short period, of time (geologically speaking) and the global climate is now changing faster in response.

Since Arrhenius, it is now accepted that the global energy balance is strongly affected by the chemical composition of the atmosphere, especially the so-called "greenhouse gases" (carbon dioxide, oxides of nitrogen and methane). While energy is conserved, exergy—the fraction capable of doing work—is not conserved. There are exergy gains or losses in natural systems, many of which are cyclic, with daily, lunar monthly, annual or millennium periodicity. The ice ages were periodic, due to very long cycles in the orbit of the Earth around the sun (Milankovitch 1941 [1998]) (Hays, Imbrie, and Shackleton 1976) (Muller and MacDonald 1997). Hence climatic comparisons between the present and earlier times need to take account of the orbital cycles.

As of 1995, the principal greenhouse gases (GHGs) were carbon dioxide (50%), methane (18%, CFCs and other halocarbons (about 25%) and nitrous oxide (6%). The all have industrial sources, including fossil fuel combustion, biomass burning, agriculture (fertilizers) and other industrial activities. It is now recognized that aerosols in the stratosphere—mainly ammonium sulfates and droplets of sulfuric acid—are affect cloud formation and condensation, as well as the albedo of the Earth. As we know from historical cases, aerosols have a cooling effect on the Earth that can be quite severe, as in the "year without a summer" in 1815, due to the eruption of Tomboro in Indonesia. Similarly, CFC's are the main cause of Stratospheric ozone depletion.

The oceans are by far the main storage system for heat in the short to medium term. They can absorb or emit heat much faster than solid rock, and far more (by a factor of 1000) than the atmosphere. The thermal conductivity of the Earth's solid crust is very low and vertical convection in the crust is almost zero (except during volcanic eruptions). The mass of the atmosphere is less than that of the top 50 m of the oceans. Hence the tropical oceans store heat in summer that is released during the winter, as the warm currents, like the Gulf Stream, flow toward the Poles.

Until the 1950s it was assumed that essentially all of the excess solar heat due to atmospheric greenhouse gas (GHG) buildup would be permanently absorbed by the oceans. However, **Roger Revelle** (1909—1991) Director of the Scripps Oceanographic Institute, began to doubt this assumption. He initiated research on thermal uptake by the ocean, both by absorption at the surface, and via convection into the deep oceans. The first step was to determine what happens to excess atmospheric carbon dioxide. The research at Scripps concluded that about 50% of any *excess* carbon dioxide in the atmosphere is absorbed in the oceans, 25% is taken up by photosynthetic organisms (biomass) and 25% remains in the atmosphere (Revelle and Suess, 1957). Equilibration among these reservoirs is very slow.

Since 2001 the Argo project, part of the Global Ocean Observing System (GOOS), in the Global Ocean Data Assimilation Experiment (GODAE), has distributed over 3800 expendable bathythermographs (XBTs) around the globe to observe temperature, salinity, currents, and, recently, bio-optical properties in the Earth's oceans. The real-time data it provides is used in climate and oceanographic research. A special research interest is to quantify the ocean heat content (OHC).

The Argo floats are deployed worldwide (Fig. B.1) Each float weighs 20–30 kg. In most cases probes drift at a depth of 1000 m (the so-called parking depth) and, every 10 days, by changing their buoyancy, dive to a depth of 2000 m and then move to the sea-surface, measuring conductivity and temperature profiles as well as pressure. Each one takes three measurements per month and transmits the data via satellite to the GODAE server in Monterey Cal. From these data, salinity and density can be calculated. Seawater density is important in determining large-scale motions in the ocean. Average current velocities at 1000 m are directly measured by the distance and direction a float drifts while parked at that depth.

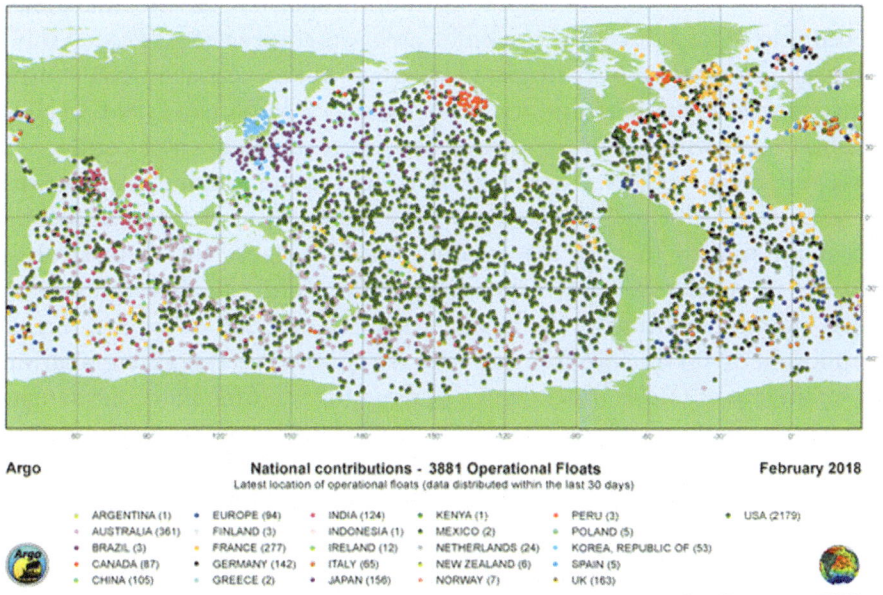

Fig. B.1 The distribution of active floats in the Argo array, color coded by country that owns the float, as of February 2018—Wikipedia

It now seems likely that the rate of heat exchange in the deep oceans (not measured by Argo), depends on the thermo-haline ("conveyor belt") circulation of ocean currents. It is probably much lower than heat exchange on the surface because mixing induced by storms is less important. The rates of mixing vs. conduction and convection are still not well-known. (The residence time of a water molecule in the oceans is estimated to be 3200 years.) As of 2015, it appears that 90% of the excess solar heat warms the oceans, and only 10% warms the land surface. The heat taken up by the oceans causes thermal expansion, which is one of the two main causes of sea-level rise (the other being glacial melting). It accounts for about 3 cm per decade.

Hydrological processes do not only "consume" exergy; they are driven by exergy dissipation. Heat storage, and heat release, processes are quite slow. Glaciation is an example of both; freezing water releases heat, while melting absorbs heat. Photosynthesis also accumulates and stores some exergy in the form of carbo-hydrates, thus changing the environment, and the climate, both in the short and long term. The accumulation of methane as clathrates in under-sea sediments is another case in point. These storage capabilities allow potentially significant imbalances between incoming solar and outgoing thermal radiation.

Human survival on Earth depends on the answer to a scientific question: How sensitive is the global climate is to anthropogenic activities, especially the burning of fossil fuels and the build-up of other greenhouse gases (GHGs) in the atmosphere? In other words: How much will the average global temperature of Earth, in equilibrium, rise in response to a doubling of the CO_2 level? And how soon will it happen? The answer is called *climate sensitivity*.

Radiative forcing is the term for driving climate change due to GHG increases above the prehistoric level. It is expressed as the additional solar heat input needed to raise the equilibrium temperature of Earth by 1° C. This can be determined from the *radiance* (formerly called "brightness") of the IR radiation emitted by the Earth, which is a function of temperature and of atmospheric GHG composition. This is expressed in energy units of watts per square meter (W/m^2) per degree of temperature difference. Here I quote from an earlier publication: "*It turns out that doubling the CO_2 concentration from 140 to 280 ppm would have the same warming effect as increasing the radiation impinging on the Earth from the sun by* 3.7 W/m^2. *This doubling, in turn, would raise the temperature of the Earth's surface by approximately* 1 °C *(Ad Hoc Study Group on Carbon Dioxide and Climate 1979)*" {Ayres, 2016} p. 170.

The above number 3.7 watts/m^2 per °C. is called—for technical reasons—the *radiation damping coefficient*, for the Earth. It is also a constant for the Earth, independent of GHG levels, at least within wide limits. It also happens, rather conveniently, that the "radiative forcing" effect of GHGs is proportional to the logarithm of the atmospheric CO_2-equivalent GHG concentration. In principle the answer might depend on boundary conditions, such as the starting (reference) CO_2 level or on the starting (reference) temperature. Luckily it appears that the climate sensitivity does not depend on either of those boundary conditions; evidently it is (almost) a constant of nature, for the Earth.

Unfortunately, scientists have not yet been able to determine the Earth's climate sensitivity—however constant—with great accuracy due to feedback effects. A little arithmetic, tells us that increasing the GHG (CO_2 equivalent) concentration from 180 ppm, in the glacial maximum period, to 280 ppm in the pre-industrial period would be the equivalent of increasing the solar power at the top of the atmosphere by about $180/280 \times 3.7 = 2.37$ watts/m^2 (Previdi et al. 2013). That, in turn, would have raised the Earth's temperature by about 0.64° C. But the global average temperature actually increased by around 5° C. during that period. So, by this "top down" argument, there seems to be an amplification factor of $5/(0.64) = 7.8$. to account for. If such an amplification factor is still applicable today, global warming may be much greater than currently anticipated.

The most dangerous externality of all is probably the increasing concentration of so-called "greenhouse gases" (carbon dioxide, methane and nitrous oxide) in the atmosphere. The GHG build-up is mostly due to the combustion of fossil fuels, plus a significant contribution of methane from cattle, sheep and other grazing animals. It has the potential for changing the Earth's climate in ways that will harm people in large parts of the world. Extended droughts in some areas (e.g. the Sahel), floods from melting mountain glaciers, rising sea-levels, and powerful storms hitting coastlines in unexpected places, are happening. These will be followed by massive population shifts, of which we have seen only the first hint of what is coming.

Figure 19.15 shows emissions and concentrations of carbon dioxide in the earth's atmosphere since the beginning of the Industrial Revolution (Climate.gov). It is also a direct consequence of a technological choice, namely to burn fossil fuels for heat and power. The relationship between the two lines in the chart reflects the fact that emissions of carbon dioxide, the most important greenhouse gas (GHG), stay in the atmosphere for a long time—300 to 1000 years (NASA) (Fig. B.2).

Prior to 1900, anthropogenic GHG emissions were so low as to be undetectable against the background of natural processes. They were absorbed

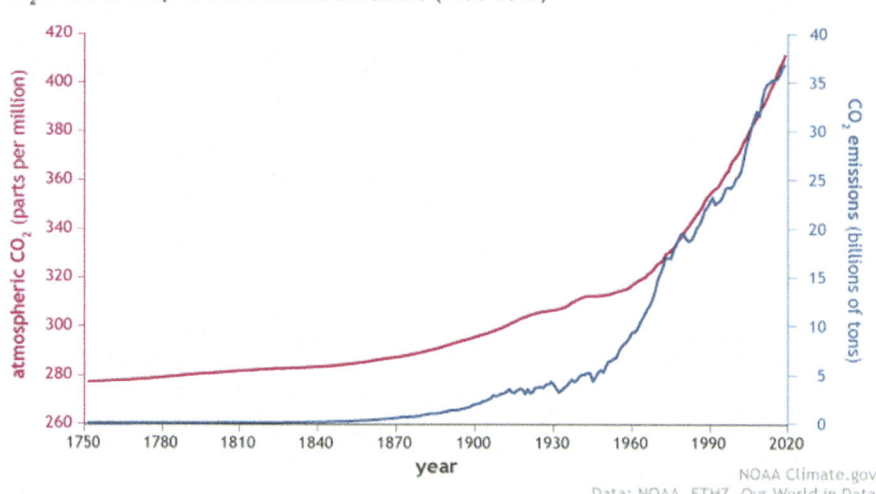

Fig. B.2 CO₂ in the atmosphere and annual emissions—https://www.researchgate.net/figure/CO2-in-the-atmosphere-and-annual-emissions-1750-2019_

by natural sinks and did not cause any cumulative rise in GHG concentrations in the atmosphere. After 1900 the rate of GHG emissions from fossil fuel combustion exceeded the absorptive capacity of natural sinks and atmospheric concentrations increased, but until the 1970s there was no evidence of significant climate warming. (In fact there were climatologists who worried about climate cooling).

Hans Suess and Roger Revelle co-authored a 1957 article using carbon-14 isotope levels to assess the rate at which carbon dioxide from fuel combustion since the industrial revolution had accumulated in the atmosphere {Revelle, 1957}. They concluded that most of it had been absorbed by the Earth's oceans. This was contrary to the assumption made by early geoscientists (Chamberlin, Arrhenius and Callendar) that it would accumulate in the upper atmosphere and increase the average temperature near the Earth's surface by the "greenhouse effect". Up to that date, there had been almost no sign of the greenhouse effect causing the anticipated warming. But the Suess–Revelle article suggested that increasing human gas emissions might change this. They said that "human beings are now carrying out a large scale geophysical experiment of a kind that could not have happened in the past nor be reproduced in the future".

Revelle told journalists about the issues and testified to Congress that "*The Earth itself is a space ship*" (phrase borrowed from Ken Boulding) and that it is endangered by future rising seas and desertification. A November 1957 report in The Hammond Times described his research as suggesting that "*a large scale global warming, with radical climate changes may result*". This was the first use of the term global warming. While other articles in the same journal discussed carbon-dioxide levels, the Suess–Revelle article was the only one to call attention to the fact that it might cause global warming over time.

Revelle and Suess described the "buffer factor" (now the "Revelle factor"), which is a barrier to atmospheric carbon dioxide being absorbed by the ocean surface layer, due to bicarbonate chemistry. In water, carbon dioxide gas (carbonic acid) can ionize into any of three components, viz., carbonate ions, bicarbonate ions, or "protonated" carbonic acid. The combination of these chemical dissociation constants factors into a kind of back-pressure that limits how fast the carbon dioxide enter the ocean surface. This article was one of the earliest examples of "integrated assessment".

In the November 1982 Scientific American Letters to the Editors, Revelle stated: "*We must conclude that until a warming trend that exceeds the noise level of natural climatic fluctuations becomes clearly evident, there will be considerable uncertainty and a diversity of opinions about the amplitude of the climatic effects of increased atmospheric* CO_2. *If the modelers are correct, such a signal should be detectable within the next* 10 *or* 15 *years.*" He was correct.

In 2015, COP 21 concluded with a non-binding agreement of 196 countries to cut emissions in the coming decade, so as to prevent the global temperature from rising above 2 °C, which is considered (by the scientists) to be a critical tipping point, beyond which continued increase will become uncontrollable. (The tipping point has since been lowered from 2° to 1.5°.) The perceived importance of climate change had prompted public demonstrations in over a hundred countries in 2015. Every country in the UN agreed to take voluntary steps to reduce GHG emissions, to keep the global temperature rise below the limit of 2 °C. This agreement was praised as a major turning point in human history.

Six years later it is clear that many of the promises of COP 21 in 2015 were not kept. Global GHG emissions continue to rise, albeit slight less rapidly than before. A notable absence, up to now, has been public education in climate and environmental science. That absence is especially troublesome at the top levels of business and politics. A campaign of disinformation over many years, led by Exxon, promoted by energy (i.e. fossil fuel) interests has allowed busy senior executives—who don't have scientific backgrounds and don't have time to dig deep into unfamiliar subjects—to believe (until very recently) that climate change is just a "theory", not yet proven.

This reflects a deliberate strategy to undermine science itself, by pretending that science is something like court-room law, insofar as it must "prove" its conclusions beyond any possible doubt. If absolute proof of a scientific conclusion—for example, that climate change is anthropogenic—is impossible, the people behind this strategy argued that (as in a law court) "not guilty beyond doubt" is effectively "proof of innocence". On the contrary, the business of science is not to prove theories (very difficult), but to disprove false ones (much easier). As to climate change, science has now effectively disproved all of the alternative hypotheses s offered by "skeptics" to the proposition stated above, namely that climate change is caused mainly by human actions.

The Intergovernmental Panel on Climate Change (IPCC) is an intergovernmental body of the United Nations was established in 1988 by the World Meteorological Organization (WMO) and the United Nations Environment Programme (UNEP). It was later endorsed by United Nations General Assembly. The IPCC is comprised of 195 member states, with headquarters in Switzerland. The first chairman was Rajendra Pachauri.

The IPCC does not conduct original research nor monitor climate change, but rather undertakes a periodic, systematic review of all relevant published literature. Thousands of scientists and other experts volunteer to review the data and compile key findings into "Assessment Reports" for policymakers and the general public, along with numerous special-purpose documents. The sixth of those Assessment Reports was published in 2022.

A total of 234 scientists from 66 countries contributed to this report. The report's authors reviewed over 14,000 scientific papers to produce a 3949 page document. The latter was then circulated and approved by 195 governments. According to the report of the physical scientists working group, it is only possible to avoid warming of 1.5 °C or 2 °C if massive and immediate cuts in greenhouse gas emissions are made. In a front page story, The Guardian described the report as "its starkest warning yet" of "major inevitable and irreversible climate changes".

The specific threats due to projected climate change include sea level rise (which threatens several island countries, such as the Maldives, with drowning), extended droughts (as currently happening in several parts of the world, including in the, forest fires (as in California now) increased storm violence, shifting growing seasons for plants, and increased probability of epidemic diseases. Secondary consequences of these will include massive migrations.

The carbon-dioxide concentration in the atmosphere is increasing. See Figs. B.3 and B.4. The first figure shows the actual emissions of carbon dioxide (based on fuel use data) during the twentieth century. The increase has accelerated after World War II, mainly because of industrialization of developing countries, increased consumption of electricity, and increased use of private cars and substitution of automotive (and air) transportation for rail-based transport.

Figure B.5, shows the actual CO_2 measurements, taken from an observatory on Mauna Loa in Hawaii. The question until recently was whether atmospheric CO_2 accumulation is—or is not—the driver of global warming and climate change. The evidence strongly supports the anthropogenic thesis. The question now is what can be done to reverse the trend, and whether it will be done.

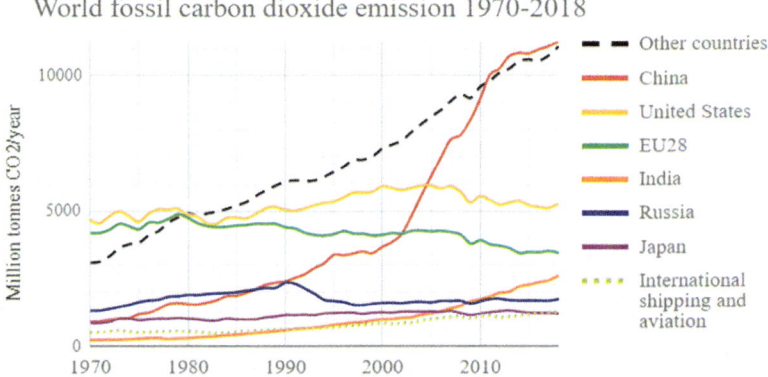

Fig. B.3 World fossil carbon dioxide emissions 1970 to 2018—Wikipedia. *Data source* EDGAR—Emissions database for Global Atmospheric Research., September 2019. CC BY-SA 4.0

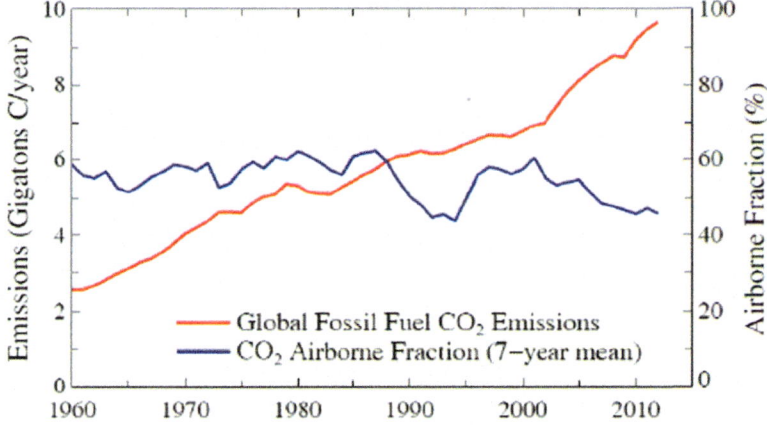

Fig. B.4 Carbon dioxide emissions from fossil fuels during the twentieth century—researchgate.net

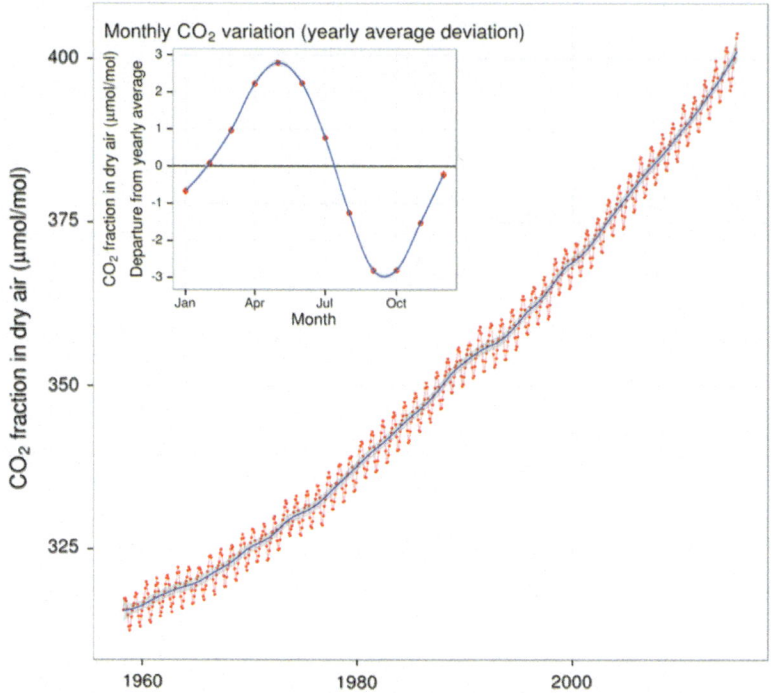

Fig. B.5 Monthly CO_2 concentrations on Mauna Loa (NOAA)—Wikimedia

And yet the skeptics still argue that carbon dioxide is the "food" for all plants. Plants capture and "fix" that carbon to create the carbohydrate based food for all animals. That natural process, which produces oxygen as a by-product, is called photosynthesis. Without photosynthesis we (and all the other animals) would starve. (I, n fact, we could never have involved in the first place.) Carbon-dioxide is the basis of the Earth's food chain. It is also the source of all the carbon embodied in the fossil fuels our industrial economy depends on.

Moreover, photosynthesis is also the source of the oxygen in the air. We humans (and almost all animals) require oxygen to metabolize our food, and without oxygen we would suffocate. In fact, carbon dioxide is a fertilizer: as the concentration of CO_2 in the atmosphere increases, the rate of production of carbon-fixation in organic matter also increases. This "fertilization effect" is exploited commercially in Dutch (and other) greenhouses. It is said that photosynthesis—hence crop production—could increase by up to 15% in a more carbon-intensive world.

Meanwhile, six years have passed since COP 21, with virtually no action by the business leaders and politicians who have the power to act but only if they act in concert. China, India and much of the world still invest heavily in coal for electric power generation. Carbon taxes that would raise the consumer price of gasoline or diesel fuel remain largely at the talking stage. Serious investment in measures to improve building insulation remains a distant prospect. The only good news is the continued decline in the cost of renewables, especially PV and wind power.

One immediate effect of excess heat is an acceleration of the hydrological cycle plus increased photosynthesis and biomass accumulation (partly from CO_2 fertilization), resulting more evapotranspiration, and more water vapor in the atmosphere. Water vapor is the most potent of all the greenhouse gases (GHGs). The increased storm frequency and destructiveness that we observe is a direct consequence of increasing evaporation and atmospheric humidity.

A second fairly immediate effect of climate warming is to melt some of the winter snow-cover from the Arctic and Antarctic, thus decreasing the reflectivity (albedo) of the Earth and increasing heat absorption of the oceans (Budyko 1969). Warming of the atmosphere will accelerate the melting of mountain glaciers and further increase the evaporation of water from the warmer oceans.

A third consequence is that, as the ocean warms up, it expands. This thermal expansion causes sea level rise. Moreover, the warmer ocean keeps less carbon dioxide in solution, thus keeping more of the excess CO_2 in the atmosphere. This so-called "carbon-cycle feedback" has different consequences in different General Circulation Models (GCMs), ranging from 0.1 to 1.5 °C (Previdi et al. 2013). This is still a contentious issue. Currently it is estimated that 57% of new CO_2 emissions are dissolved in the oceans, but that number can be wrong.

A fourth possible effect, not easily quantifiable or predictable, might be to alter the "conveyor belt" of surface and deep ocean currents. For example, this might cause the warm, salty Gulf Stream to abort its northward passage on the surface, and sink prematurely. This could be due to cooling and dilution by melting Greenland ice, plus increased salinity due to salt release from the melting of Arctic sea ice. Increased salinity makes the water denser and causes it to sink sooner than it otherwise would (Wadhams et al. 2003). This may have happened in the past, during the rapid melting of the Wisconsin glacier. Was this the cause of the "little ice age"? If something like this to happen again, northern Europe could be cooled as a direct consequence of general global warming! Some think it is already happening.

A fifth possible effect of atmospheric warming would be to thaw some of the Siberian "permafrost" area, both above ground and under the Arctic ocean. Climate warming is happening much faster in the polar regions, than the tropics. All the General Circulation Models (GCMs) show this effect. The rapid thinning of the ice and likely disappearance (in summer) of the ice in the Arctic Ocean, is already happening.

The fact that the poles are getting warmer faster than the tropics means that the north–south temperature gradient is getting smaller and less sharp. That, in turn, is pushing the northern jet stream northward (on average) at the rate of 2 km per year. This would permit both aerobic and anaerobic micro-organism activity under the soil surface to accelerate, releasing both carbon dioxide and methane into the atmosphere. The undersea "cousin" of permafrost on land, methane clathrate, could also start to thaw, releasing methane into the ocean and thence into the atmosphere, resulting in positive feedback.

It seems likely that the rate of heat exchange in the deep oceans (not measured by ARGO), depends on the thermo-haline ("conveyor belt") circulation, mentioned above. It is probably much lower than heat exchange on the surface, since mixing induced by storms is less important. The rates of mixing vs. conduction and convection are still not well-known. (The residence time of a water molecule in the oceans is estimated to be 3200 years.) It looks like 90% of the excess heat warms the oceans, and only 10% warms the land surface. The heat taken up by the oceans causes thermal expansion of the water. Thermal expansion is one of the three possible causes of global mean sea-level (GMSL) rise. It amounts to about 1.7 mm/year since 1901 and about 3.2 mm per year since 1993 (Church and White 2011). The heating of the oceans is evidently accelerating.

The other two causes of sea-level rise are glacial ice melting and vertical land motion (VLM). Vertical motion results from the removal of the weight of glacial ice in certain terrestrial areas that were once ice-covered, such as Northern Canada and Scandinavia. The VLM adjustment is fairly localized. In fact it is negative (the sea floor is actually sinking, not rising, on average) because the land areas formerly covered by ice are now "springing back" as the weight of ice was removed. The liquid magma under the Earth's crust gradually rearranges itself as the ocean gets heavier and the land gets lighter.

In recent years it appears that about two thirds of the GMSL rise—roughly 1.6 mm/year—is due to the melting of glacier ice (mainly Greenland and Antarctica). The quantitative change in ocean mass from glacier ice melting—as opposed to increased volume due to thermal expansion—is now being measured directly, not just estimated from indirect evidence.

The threat of sea-level rise is evident from Fig. B.6, which shows that it is accelerating:

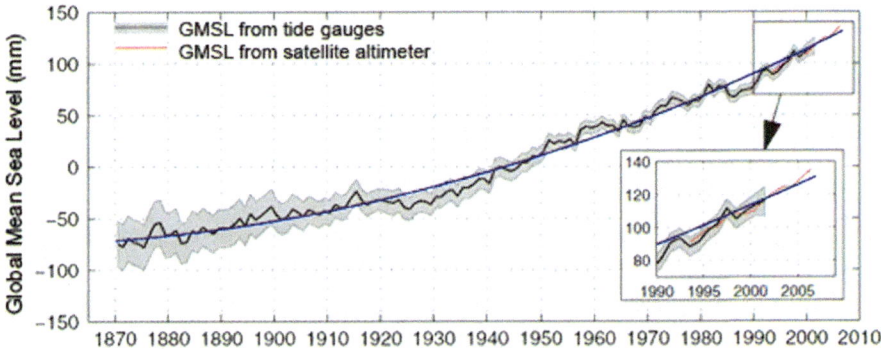

Fig. B.6 Sea level rise as measured from tidal gauges and satellites, since 1870—https://skepticalscience.com/Sea-level-rise-the-broader-picture.html

The consequences of global climate change range from increased frequency of storms and floods, increased frequency of drought and sea level rise (Fig. B.7). The latter is arguably the most serious, since many of the world's largest cities are near sea-level and a disproportionate share of the world's agricultural output is from low-lying lands like Bangla Desh and the Nile Delta. Even a relatively modest rise in sea-levels could have catastrophic effects from major storms, compared to which the damage to New York City due to Hurricane Sandy in 2012 would seem negligible.

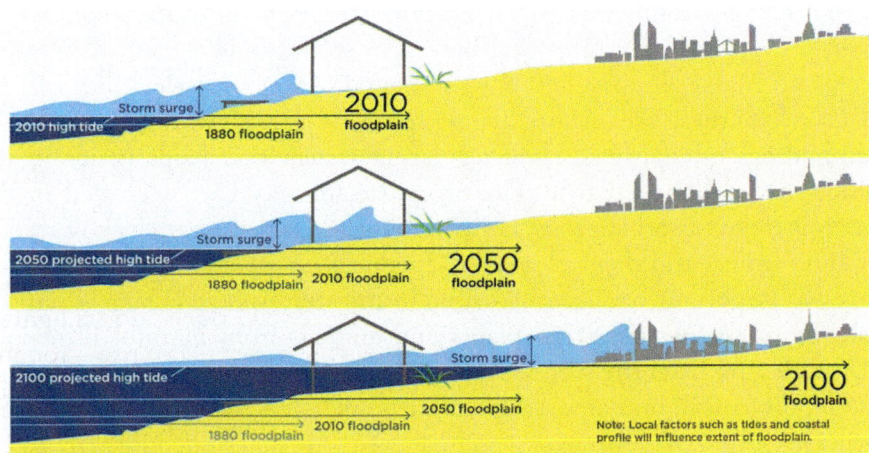

Fig. B.7 How even a small sea-level rise will threaten coastal areas. http://www.change-climate.com/Sea_Rising_Levels_Rise.htm

The consequences of climate change are already global in scope. The most serious of those consequences is probably sea-level rise, which is already under way, and which—if it continues—will literally drown many island countries and much of the low-lying land where food crops (especially rice) are grown now and where the world's most important cities are located. Some countries will do what the Dutch have done: build protective dykes (at enormous cost). This may save important world cities like London, Tokyo, Shanghai, Lagos, Hong Kong, Bombay, Madras, Bangkok, Buenos Aires, Rio de Janeiro, Havana, Barcelona, Naples and Marseilles. But Bangla Desh? The Philippines? Indonesia? Myanmar? Maybe the Persian Gulf can be enclosed. Maybe the Baltic can be enclosed. Maybe the whole Mediterranean can be enclosed. But what about the South China Sea? What about the island republics?

B.2. The Ozone Hole

As mentioned elsewhere, the ozone layer in the stratosphere protects us (and all terrestrial species) from the harmful effects of ultra-violet (UV) radiation. Ozone (O_3) is a reactive form of oxygen that is created in the stratosphere by that same UV radiation from the sun. The ozone layer exists because of the oxygen in the atmosphere, which exists because of photosynthesis. Clearly, atmospheric carbon dioxide CO_2 plays an essential role in the natural world. We could not live without it. The problem arises from having too much.

The new environmental threat was the stratospheric ozone depletion of about 4% per year, first observed by NASA scientists in the late 1960s and publicized by UK futurist and environmentalist James Lovelock (known for his Gaia hypothesis) that states living organisms interact with their inorganic surroundings on Earth as a self-regulating system that helps maintain the conditions for life on Earth. The ozone (technically O_3) is created in the stratosphere by absorbing solar radiation flux and is broken up by chlorine or bromine atoms, and then released by chemical reactions in the stratosphere. This was important because the ozone in the stratosphere is largely responsible for protecting terrestrial plants and animals from harmful ultraviolet (UV) radiation from the sun. UV is known to cause cancer and several other health problems of humans. A related phenomenon is the "ozone hole" which occurs in Spring over Antarctica and part of the southern hemisphere. It was becoming larger and expanding northward, every year (Fig. B.8).

The technical details of how this happens do not matter here. The important point is that a few years later, Sherwood Rowland and Mario Molina proposed another ozone depletion mechanism. Their theory was that ozone

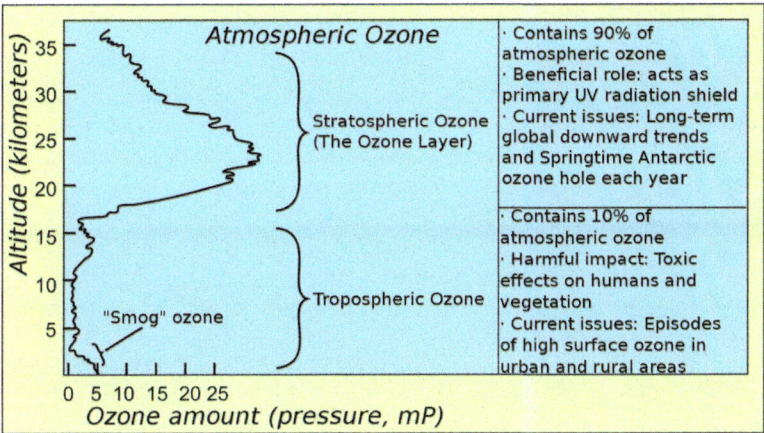

Fig. B.8 The distribution of atmospheric ozone in partial pressure as a function of altitude. Rasterized and improved by RedAndr—Wikipedia

depletion was due to the increasing concentration of certain fluorocarbons—especially one, known as FC-12—in the atmosphere. This was an industrial bombshell, because FC-12 was mass produced by Dupont, Union Carbide and German companies like BASF and Bayer. It was used primarily as refrigerant in refrigerators and air conditioners, and as "propellant" for spray paints, air fresheners, shaving cream and all kinds of other products.

Industry representatives strongly disputing the Rowland–Molina hypothesis. A National Academy of Sciences (NAS) Committee was created to investigate substitution possibilities. The NAS committee reported in 1976, resulting in the Kyoto Protocol that helped initiate the UN's International Panel on Climate Change (IPCC) and its periodic climate reports. The Montréal Protocol (1987) initiated action. That action effectively reversed the ozone depletion trend. It arguably is the first major success of the environmentalist movement. Rowland and Molina shared the 1995 with Paul Crutzen, who had earlier shown that nitric oxide (NO) and nitrogen dioxide (NO_2) react catalytically with ozone, accelerating its reduction. The 1995 Nobel Prize in Chemistry recognized the three scientists for their work in atmospheric chemistry, particularly concerning the formation and decomposition of ozone."

Appendix C: The Rise and Fall of the Nuclear Dream

Nuclear fission, as a process, was postulated independently by several physicists in the 1930s, including Chadwick, Joliot-Curie and Fermi. This discovery was a shock, because many of the scientific authorities of the day, including J.B.S Haldane and Ernest Rutherford, were convinced that it was impossible. The fission of the element uranium was discovered in 1938 by Lise Meitner, Otto Hahn and Fritz Strassman. Enrico Fermi discovered how to induce fission by neutron bombardment. Leo Szilard recognized the possibility that nuclear fission could be used to create a nuclear chain reaction that could be used as a weapon of mass destruction. In August 1939, Leo Szilard and Albert Einstein sent the "Einstein–Szilárd letter" to President Roosevelt, warning of the possibility of a German project to develop nuclear weapons based on that discovery. Roosevelt feared the consequences of allowing Germany to have sole possession of the technology, so he authorized preliminary research into nuclear weapons.

Nuclear technology was developed, for military purposes, in the United States during the years 1942–45. The first use of nuclear weapons by the US, in 1945, was approved by President Truman, on the grounds that Japanese defense of Saipan, Iwo Jima and Okinawa was so fierce that a land invasion of Japan would have cost hundreds of thousands—perhaps millions of lives, on both sides. After the second atomic bomb (Nagasaki) Japan surrendered, thanks to intervention by the emperor.

Fig. D.1 Estimated global nuclear warhead inventories 2021—https://pl-pl.facebook.com/fascientists/

The U.S. attacks on Hiroshima and Nagasaki in Japan in 1945 were also the beginning of a strong public anti-nuclear movement. Peace movements emerged in Japan and in 1954 they converged to form a unified "Japanese Council Against Atomic and Hydrogen Bombs". Japanese opposition to the Pacific nuclear weapons tests was widespread, and "an estimated 35 million signatures were collected on petitions calling for bans on nuclear weapons". However, as the Cold War escalated, gaining increasing international and national attention, military power and national security became paramount. Scientists who were actively against military use of nuclear power were discredited.

During the following years, the focus on weapons technology continued and intensified. Thermonuclear (hydrogen) bombs were developed by a group of scientists, led by Edward Teller. Klaus Fuchs, a physicists, who was also a communist spy, provided the key information to help the competitive weapons program in the USSR. By 1950 (when Fuchs confessed) the USSR had virtually caught up to the US in nuclear weapons, and delivery systems. Both sides were testing their weapons, sometimes underground, but also on Pacific islands or in remote deserts. A nuclear arms race was under way.

The nuclear arms race continues. This is not the place to provide details, but the diagram (Fig. D.1) indicates the present state of affairs.

The prototype nuclear power reactor was developed, during the period 1942–45, by a group led by Enrico Fermi, under the west stands of the football stadium at the University of Chicago. That demonstrated the feasibility of controlled nuclear fission, how to control it and how to capture the fission by-products (including plutonium) and the energy released. That was enough to build the nuclear weapons that were used against Japan in 1945.

The first practical applications of nuclear energy to produce power for non-explosive purposes (i.e. to drive a steam turbine) was led by Admiral Hyman Rickover. The turbines were used to power US submarines, to allow longer voyages without the need to refuel. The first full-scale electric power reactor was built by Westinghouse Inc. at Shippingport, Pennsalvania, in 1957. In a power reactor the chain reaction is kept under control by the use of materials that absorb most of the neutrons, allowing just enough to keep the reaction going. Obviously, this is fairly tricky; accidents happen when something goes wrong with the controls. Still, the benefits seemed very great and well worth the cost and effort needed to develop the technology. Westinghouse Corp. and General Electric Co. became major suppliers of nuclear power generating equipment for utilities. For a few years, there was a lot of euphoria about nuclear power.

On Dec. 8 1953, U.S. President Dwight D. Eisenhower delivered a speech to the UN General Assembly, entitled "Atoms for Peace". The United States then launched an "Atoms for Peace" program that supplied equipment and information to schools, hospitals, and research institutions within the U.S. and throughout the world. The first nuclear reactors in Israel and were built under the program by US manufacturers.

In 1954, Lewis Strauss, then chairman of the United States Atomic Energy Commission, made a speech to the National Association of Science Writers. He, said: "*Controlling a reaction is tricky, but it is not too much to expect that our children will enjoy in their homes electrical energy too cheap to meter, will know of great periodic regional famines in the world only as matters of history, will travel effortlessly over the seas and under them and through the air with a minimum of danger and at great speeds, and will experience a lifespan far longer than ours, as disease yields and man comes to understand what causes him to age.*" Needless to say, those optimistic words, and especially the phrase "too cheap to meter" created a brief bubble.

As mentioned, controlling a nuclear reactor can be tricky. There have been three major accidents around the world and a number of lesser ones. The first was at three-mile Island near Harrisburg Pennsylvania in 1979, caused by an open valve that allowed coolant to escape, resulting in a partial melt-down of the reactor core, but no deaths and not much effluent escape.

The second accident (1986) was at a power reactor at Chernobyl in the Ukraine, where a shut-down experiment at night went wrong. What followed was a steam explosion in the core, and a fire that burned for 9 days. That resulted in a major escape of radioactivity and 30 direct deaths plus 16 or so likely deaths from thyroid cancer. The third accident, at Fukushima in Japan (2011), was caused by a tsunami that disabled the emergency generators. That resulted in insufficient cooling which led to partial melt-downs in 3 reactors, necessitating in widespread evacuation. These were only the worst. According to Wikipedia, over 24 other nuclear accidents occurred between 1957 and 2011, with losses costing more than $100 million (2006 dollars).

Since Fukushima, it is fair to say that "conventional" (uranium-based) nuclear power is in a decline, notwithstanding many projects in China and the Hinkley Point project in England. A French designed plant in Finland is years behind schedule and billions of dollars of cost over-runs. A few years ago Westinghouse Electric Co. bid on major contracts based on a new construction technology. This new technology depended on prefabrication of major components by distant factories. That ran into regulatory and design problems, as well as management problems, causing huge cost overruns and major delays. The company had to abandon the projects (still half built) and seek bankruptcy protection. Toshiba, it's Japanese parent company, is now in danger of collapse itself.

The problem of nuclear waste and dismantling and safe disposal of materials from end-of-life nuclear power plants remains unsolved. And the growing stockpile of plutonium that can be made into bombs also remains a continuing threat. Moreover, the costs of uranium-based nuclear power plants have not been declining over time. On the contrary, they have been rising as safety requirements keep being tightened. Indeed, the costs of wind and solar power are already competitive with nuclear power in some locations. The only strong argument for conventional nuclear power is that it provides a 24/7 h. base-load capability that is not coal-based.

Stafford Warren (1896–1981) was an American physician and radiologist who was a pioneer in the field of nuclear medicine and best known for his invention of the mammogram. Warren was commissioned as a colonel in the United States Army Medical Corps in 1943 and appointed Chief of the Medical Section of the Manhattan Engineering District. He was responsible for the health and safety of the thousands of personnel involved in the Manhattan Project. He was present at the Trinity nuclear test in Alamogordo, New Mexico where he was responsible for the safety aspects of the detonation of the world's first nuclear weapon. He led a survey team from the Manhattan Project to assess the effects of the atomic bombings of Hiroshima and Nagasaki.

Although the subject was controversial, Stafford Warren talked about the dangers of nuclear fallout from weapons testing from about 1947 onwards.

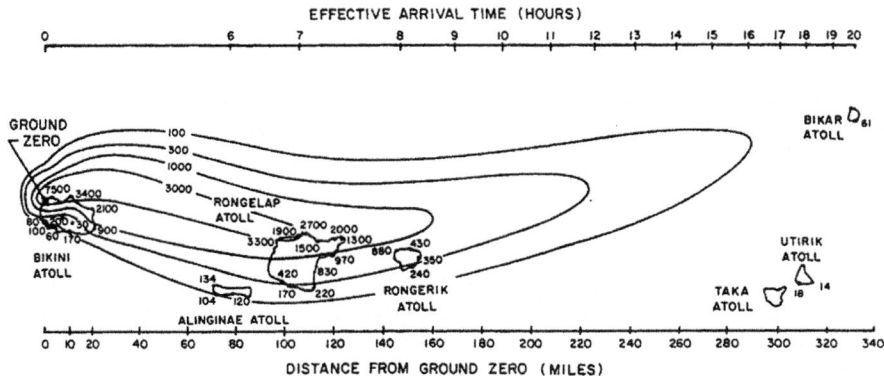

Fig. D.2 Castle Bravo fallout plume—Wikimedia

Eisenhower succeeded Truman as President in 1952. There was already public support for a test ban, to stop the arms race. During the next two presidential elections, 1952 and 1956, Eisenhower defeated challenger Adlai Stevenson, who ran in large part on support for a test ban. The ban-the-bomb movement gained in strength after a test explosion called Castle bravo, on Bikini Atoll in 1954. The explosion spread radioactive fallout up to 240 miles from the site (Fig. D.2). After the Castle Bravo test in 1954, Stafford Warren's views were taken more seriously by Eisenhower.

Eisenhower, as president, first explicitly expressed interest in a comprehensive test ban that year, arguing before the National Security Council, "We could put (the Russians) on the spot if we accepted a moratorium … Everybody seems to think that we're skunks, saber-rattlers and warmongers. We ought not miss any chance to make clear our peaceful objectives."

In 1954, just weeks after the Castle Bravo test, Indian prime minister Jawaharlal Nehru made the first call for a "standstill agreement" on nuclear testing. He saw a testing moratorium as a stepping stone to more comprehensive arms control agreements. In the same year, the British Labor Party, then led by Clement Attlee, called on the UN to ban testing of thermonuclear weapons. The new Soviet leader, Nikita Khrushchev first proposed talks on the subject in February 1955.

On 10 May 1955, the Soviet Union proposed a test ban before the UN Disarmament Commission's "Committee of Five" (Britain, Canada, France, the Soviet Union, and the US). This proposal, which closely reflected a prior Anglo-French proposal, was initially part of a comprehensive disarmament proposal meant to reduce conventional arms levels and eliminate nuclear weapons.

Despite the closeness of the Soviet proposal to earlier Western proposals, the US suddenly reversed its position and rejected the Soviet offer "in the absence of more general control agreements," including limits on the production of fissionable material and protections against a surprise nuclear strike. Harold Stassen, Eisenhower's special assistant for disarmament, argued that the US should prioritize a test ban as a first step towards comprehensive arms control, conditional on the Soviet Union accepting on-site inspections, over full disarmament. Stassen's suggestion was dismissed by others in the administration over fears that the Soviet Union would be able to conduct secret tests. On the advice of Dulles, Atomic Energy Commission (AEC) chairman Lewis Strauss, and Secretary of Defense Charles E. Wilson, Eisenhower rejected the idea of considering a test ban outside general disarmament efforts. This argument continued for the next seven years. The US kept insisting on stopping underground as well as atmospheric tests, and on-site verification, and the Russians kept refusing that condition.

Prior to Eisenhower's UN speech, the information and expertise needed for atomic development were kept secret, under Quebec Agreement (of the Allies) in 1943, intended as defense against other countries (notably the USSR and its allies) which were developing and using the same weaponry. There were no safety protocols and no standards developed. Eisenhower's speech was an important moment in political history as it brought the atomic issue—which had been kept quiet for "national security"—into the public eye, asking the world to support his solution. Eisenhower was determined to solve "the fearful atomic dilemma" by finding some way by which "*the miraculous inventiveness of man would not be dedicated to his death, but consecrated to his life.*"

Unfortunately, Eisenhower was not completely effective in his repurposing; Eisenhower himself approved the National Security Council (NSC) document which stated that only a massive atomic weapon base would deter violence from the Soviet Union. "Atoms for Peace" created the ideological background for the creation of the International Atomic Energy Agency (IAEA) and the Treaty on the Non-Proliferation of Nuclear Weapons. It also gave political cover for the U.S. nuclear weapons build-up, and the backdrop to the Cold War arms race. During Eisenhower's time in office the nuclear holdings of the US rose from 1005 to 20,000 weapons. Under programs related to "Atoms for Peace," the U.S. exported over 25 tons of highly enriched uranium (HEU) to 30 countries, mostly to fuel research reactors, and is now regarded as a proliferation and terrorism risk. Under a similar program, the Soviet Union (now Russia and some neighboring countries) exported over 11 tons of HEU.

Appendix C: The Rise and Fall of the Nuclear Dream

In 1959 Fidel Castro led a band of communist revolutionaries from the mountains of Cuba to defeat the US supported regime of Fulgencio Battista. (Many Cubans moved to Miami and plotted to defeat Castro with CIA help). In 1960 Russia agreed to supply Cuba with oil. The US-owned refineries refused to process the oil. Russia then agreed to supply refined oil products to Castro's Cuba. This decision committed Russia to defending Cuba against US aggression, as exemplified later by the disastrous "Bay of Pigs" and other CIA operations to support Cuban exiles.

When John F. Kennedy ran for president in 1960, one of his key election issues was an alleged "missile gap" with the Soviets leading. Actually, the US at that time led the Soviets by a wide margin that would only increase. In 1961, the Soviets had only four intercontinental ballistic missiles (R-7 Semyorka). By October 1962, they may have had a few dozen, with some intelligence estimates as high as 75.

The US, on the other hand, had 170 ICBMs and was quickly building more. It also had eight George Washington- and Ethan Allen-class ballistic missile submarines, with the capability to launch 16 Polaris missiles, with a range of 2500 nautical miles (4600 km). Khrushchev increased the perception of a missile gap when he loudly boasted to the world that the Soviets were building missiles "like sausages" but Soviet missiles' numbers and capabilities were nowhere close to his assertions. The Soviet Union had medium-range ballistic missiles in quantity, about 700 of them, but they were very unreliable and inaccurate. The US had a considerable advantage in total number of nuclear warheads (27,000 against 3600) and in the technology required for their accurate delivery. The US also led in missile defensive capabilities, naval and air power; but the Soviets had a 2–1 advantage in conventional ground forces in Europe, especially in field guns and tanks.

The Kennedy administration was embarrassed by the failed Bay of Pigs Invasion in April 1961, by a CIA-trained force of Cuban exiles. Afterward, former President Dwight Eisenhower told Kennedy that "the failure of the Bay of Pigs will embolden the Soviets to do something that they would otherwise not do." The half-hearted invasion left Soviet premier Nikita Khrushchev and his advisers with the impression that Kennedy was indecisive and, as one Soviet adviser wrote, "too young, intellectual, not prepared well for decision making in crisis situations… too intelligent and too weak". US covert operations against Cuba continued in 1961 with the unsuccessful Operation Mongoose.

Khrushchev's impression of Kennedy's weakness was confirmed by his response during the Berlin Crisis of 1961, particularly to the building of the Berlin Wall. Speaking to Soviet officials in the aftermath of the crisis,

Khrushchev asserted, "I know for certain that Kennedy doesn't have a strong background, nor, generally speaking, does he have the courage to stand up to a serious challenge." He also told his son Sergei that on Cuba, Kennedy "would make a fuss, make more of a fuss, and then agree".

In response to the failed Bay of Pigs Invasion of 1961 and the presence of American Jupiter ballistic missiles in Italy and Turkey, Nikita Khrushchev agreed to Fidel Castro's request to place nuclear missiles on the island to deter a future invasion. A formal agreement was reached during a secret meeting between Khrushchev and Fidel Castro in July 1962, and construction of a number of missile launch facilities started later that summer.

By May 1962 Khrushchev and Castro agreed to place strategic nuclear missiles secretly in Cuba. Like Castro, Khrushchev felt that a US invasion of Cuba was imminent and that to lose Cuba would do great harm to the communists, especially in Latin America. He said he wanted to "confront the Americans". In May 1962, Soviet Premier Nikita Khrushchev was persuaded by the idea of countering the US's growing lead in developing and deploying strategic missiles by placing Soviet intermediate-range nuclear missiles in Cuba, despite the misgivings of the Soviet Ambassador in Havana, Alexandr Ivanovich Alexeyev, who argued that Castro would not accept the deployment of the missiles.

Khrushchev faced a strategic situation in which the US was perceived to have a "splendid first strike capability" that put the Soviet Union at a huge disadvantage. In 1962, the Soviets had only 20 ICBMs capable of delivering nuclear warheads to the US from inside the Soviet Union. Therefore, Soviet nuclear capability in 1962 placed less emphasis on ICBMs than on medium and intermediate-range ballistic missiles (MRBMs and IRBMs).

A second reason that Soviet missiles were deployed to Cuba was because Khrushchev wanted to bring West Berlin, controlled by the American, British and French within Communist East Germany, into the Soviet orbit. The East Germans and Soviets considered western control over a portion of Berlin a grave threat to East Germany. Khrushchev made West Berlin the central battlefield of the Cold War. Khrushchev believed that if the US did nothing over the missile deployments in Cuba, he could muscle the West out of Berlin using missiles in Cuba as a deterrent to western countermeasures in Berlin. Thirdly, missiles in Cuba would neutralize the threat of US invasion and keep the country in the Socialist Bloc.

On September 11, the Soviet Union publicly warned that a US attack on Cuba or on Soviet ships that were carrying supplies to the island would mean war. The Soviets continued the Maskirovka program to conceal their actions in Cuba. They repeatedly denied that the weapons being brought into Cuba were offensive in nature. On September 7, Soviet Ambassador to the United States Anatoly Dobrynin assured United States Ambassador to the United Nations, Adlai Stevenson, that the Soviet Union was supplying only defensive weapons to Cuba. The events of the next two months are described in detail in many publications. They can be summarized in a few words. The two superpowers came very close to nuclear war. Somebody had to back off, and it was Khruschev. The Russian missiles were sent back to Russia, a number of US missiles were removed from Turkey a few months later and the US did not invade Cuba.

The fact that the superpowers came so close to the edge of nuclear war and avoided it by a hair, prompted both Kennedy and Khrushchev to seek accelerated rapprochement. After years of dormant or lethargic negotiations, American and British negotiators subsequently forged a strong working relationship and with Soviet negotiators found common ground on test restrictions later in 1963. After years of pursuing a comprehensive ban, Khrushchev was convinced to accept a partial ban, partly due to the efforts of Soviet nuclear scientists, including Kurchatov, Sakharov, and Yulii Khariton, who argued that atmospheric testing had severe consequences for human health. A partial test ban treaty was signed a year later, in October 1963.

The agreement was initialed on 25 July 1963, just 10 days after negotiations commenced. The following day, Kennedy delivered a 26-min televised address on the agreement, declaring that since the invention of nuclear weapons, "all mankind has been struggling to escape from the darkening prospect of mass destruction on earth ... Yesterday a shaft of light cut into the darkness." Kennedy expressed hope that the test ban would be the first step towards broader rapprochement, limit nuclear fallout, restrict nuclear proliferation, and slow the arms race in such a way that fortifies US security. Kennedy concluded his address in reference to a Chinese proverb that he had used with Khrushchev in Vienna two years prior. "'A journey of a thousand miles must begin with a single step,'" Kennedy said. "And if that journey is a thousand miles, or even more, let history record that we, in this land, at this time, took the first step."

In a speech in Moscow following the agreement, Khrushchev declared that the treaty would not end the arms race and by itself could not "avert the danger of war," and reiterated his proposal of a NATO-Warsaw Pact non-aggression accord. For Khrushchev, the test ban negotiations had long been a means of improving the Soviet Union's global image and reducing strain in relations with the West. There are also some indications that military experts within the Soviet Union saw a test ban as a way to restrict US development of tactical nuclear weapons, which could have increased US willingness to deploy small nuclear weapons on battlefields while circumventing the Soviet nuclear deterrent. Concern that a comprehensive ban would retard modernization of the Soviet arsenal may have pushed Khrushchev towards a partial ban.

Although that provided a level of control over nuclear research, it also led to nuclear weapons development in other countries. During that time both government and private industry were developing the first commercial nuclear power plants; government research into applications of nuclear power research was continuing; and the environmental effects of radiation were being investigated.

Appendix D: Capsule History

Here is our capsule history of economic thought. It can be summarized in eight periods characterized by underlying assumptions about the place of humans in the world.

From Pre-history to 1453: the crusades, the fall of Constantinople and the end of Byzantium. It was the age of absolute autocracy and divine right to rule, justified (by Thomas Hobbes) as the only alternative to "war of all against all". The age of exploration began. Wealth was land or gold.

From 1453 to 1550: Predestination and the Protestant Ethic; the rise of capitalism. Making money is doing the "Work of God", and poverty as a sign of immorality. Creation of money, trade, banks and credit. Wealth was land, not money.

From 1550 to 1650: the end of geocentrism; astronomy and physics; coal and steam; the rise of Europe based on guns and sea-power, the economics of colonialism; the wars of religion, the French physiocrats. Adam Smith and the "hidden hand" Labor and capital as factors of production.

From 1789 to 1870: Industrial Revolution (coal, steam power, railroads, steel); Marxism; Darwinism; voting rights; the laws of thermodynamics; biological evolution, the marginalists.

From 1870 to 1918. Technology creates more wealth (electric power, telegraph and telephone, petroleum, internal combustion engines, automobiles and aircraft); the invention of social democracy in Germany; the peak, and fall of European empires; women's suffrage; relativity, atomic physics; the end of vitalism; energetics, theory of evolution.

From 1918 to 1945. The rise of fascism and Hitler; the failure of the League of Nations; Gandhi vs Britain; Keynesianism; quantum mechanics; mass communications and soft power (radio and movies); radar and aircraft carriers overcome battleships; the collapse of the gold standard.

From 1945 to 1990. Nuclear weapons, the dream of nuclear power too cheap to monitor. Electronic computers; TV; The Cold War, the World Bank, UNO and the IMF; decolonialization, Pakistan, Israel; the rise of China; NATO; US financial hegemony; increasing inequality; worries about population growth.

From 1990 to 2020. Age of Wall Street; Financial services as the major source of wealth creation; money from money; growth of inequality; climate change is on the radar; parliamentary democracy is challenged by new autocracy in Russia, China, Brazil, Turkey.

The manufacturer's authorised representative in the EU is Springer Nature Customer Service Centre GmbH, Europaplatz 3, 69115 Heidelberg, Germany. If you have any concerns regarding our products, please contact ProductSafety@springernature.com

Printed and bound by CPI Group (UK) Ltd, Croydon, CR0 4YY
25/03/2026
02078169-0008